An anthology of
women's travel writing

MANCHESTER
UNIVERSITY PRESS

Exploring Travel

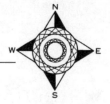

Series editors   Sara Mills and Jill LeBihan

Exploring Travel is a publishing initiative which makes accessible travel writing which may be out of print or difficult to obtain. Travel literature currently has enormous popular appeal, and there is widespread academic interest from a number of fields, including anthropology, colonial and post-colonial discourse theory, literary theory, history, geography and women's studies.

The series has two main aims. The first is to make available a number of key, edited texts, which will be invaluable to both the academic and general reader. The texts will be edited by scholars from a range of disciplines, and a full introduction to each edition will aim to set it within its socio-cultural context, and explain its literary and historical importance. The second aim of the series is to make available monographs and collections of critical essays on the analysis of travel writing. In this way, the *Exploring Travel* series aims to broaden perspectives on travel writing and the theoretical models used for its analysis.

Already published:

An anthology of women's travel writing

edited with notes and an introduction
by Shirley Foster and Sara Mills

Manchester University Press
Manchester and New York

distributed exclusively in the USA by Palgrave

Introduction and editorial matter copyright © Shirley Foster and Sara Mills 2002

The right of Shirley Foster and Sara Mills to be identified as the editors of this work has been asserted by them in accordance with the Copyright, Designs and Patents Act 1988.

Published by Manchester University Press
Oxford Road, Manchester M13 9NR, UK
and Room 400, 175 Fifth Avenue, New York, NY 10010, USA
www.manchesteruniversitypress.co.uk

Distributed exclusively in the USA by
Palgrave, 175 Fifth Avenue, New York, NY 10010, USA

Distributed exclusively in Canada by UBC Press
University of British Columbia, 2029 West Mall, Vancouver, BC, Canada V6T 1Z2

British Library Cataloguing-in-Publication Data
A catalogue record for this book is available from the British Library

Library of Congress Cataloging-in-Publication Data applied for

ISBN 0 7190 5017 0 *hardback*
      0 7190 5018 9 *paperback*

First published 2002

10 09 08 07 06 05 04 03 02   10 9 8 7 6 5 4 3 2 1

Typeset in Adobe Garamond 10 on 12pt
by SNP Best-set Typesetter Ltd., Hong Kong
Printed in Great Britain
by Bell & Bain Ltd, Glasgow

Contents

Contents

Acknowledgements

We would like to thank the following people for their help in the production of this anthology: Tony Brown for reading and commenting on drafts of the introduction; the Corvey Archive at Sheffield Hallam University for allowing us to use material from the collection; the librarian and bibliographer at the Portico Library, Manchester, for all their help with finding material and encouragement of the project. Matthew Frost and Lauren McAllister of Manchester University Press have been very supportive in the process of writing this book.

We would like to acknowledge John Murray (Publishers) Ltd for permission to quote extracts from *Baghdad Sketches* by Freya Stark and *Full Tilt* by Dervla Murphy, and Macmillan Publishers Ltd. for permission to quote extracts from *Tracks* by R. Davidson. Extracts from *Terra Incognita—Travels in Antartica* by Sara Wheeler, published by Jonathan Cape are reprinted by permission of The Random House Group Ltd.

Every effort has been made to obtain permission to reproduce copyright material in this book. If any proper acknowledgement has not been made, copyright-holders are invited to contact the publisher.

Introduction

In this anthology, we have included a selection of writing by women travellers from a range of different contexts, because we would like to present a more varied view of women as travellers. Previous anthologies have focused on the exceptional among women travellers, foregrounding only the more unusual, "eccentric", or adventurous accounts and omitting those texts which may seem more problematic: for example, those texts which seem to display a conventional "femininity" are often not considered, nor are those texts which are problematic because, rather than challenging racist or colonialist ideologies they appear to support them, or they do not proffer a simple, clear-cut position on racism (Morris, 1994). We offer instead in this anthology a more comprehensive picture of the genre, certainly including the writing of notable "eccentric" and proto-feminist figures, but also placing alongside them examples of more orthodox, albeit no less interesting, travellers.

All selections from texts for an anthology are necessarily partial and reflect ideological and political beliefs and represent a perhaps implicit argument about the subject matter. We would like to make our angle on women's travel writing explicit. We have included fairly lengthy extracts from a variety of women writers from different periods, travelling to different places, together with contextual material about them to provide the gendered discursive significance of the writings in terms of place, class, race and period, aiming to give a sense of what it means to travel as a woman of a particular race and class and what factors weigh on the codification of that material when women write about these experiences. In this way, we hope to be able to demonstrate the contextually and historically specific nature of gender conditions without losing a sense of the bigger picture of the importance of gender as a factor which consistently makes a difference (although not always in the same way). This reflects our belief in the difficulty of making global statements about the nature of women's travel writing. Gender interacts with other variables, such as race, age, class and financial position, education, political ideals and historical period, and it is the differences caused by these interactions of variables which make gender differ from context to context. Thus, a major factor in our selection of texts has been to demonstrate this diversity—the different ways that women travellers have managed to travel and have written about their travels for a reading public.

We have selected extracts of varying lengths from women's travel writing written in the period from the beginning of the eighteenth century to the end of the twentieth century. In this way, the selections reflect changes in women's writing before and during colonial involvement, as well as in a period of fast-developing feminist consciousness. In addition to texts written about travels to colonised countries, and to those which have experienced some form of imperial relation, there are extracts about travel to non-colonised areas; since much of the theoretical work about women's travel writing focuses on accounts of travel to colonised countries, we wished to broaden this to include narratives about Europe and America, among others. We have chosen texts from a wide range of writers, making it possible to examine shifts in the class status of women travel writers during our selected period. The broad range of our selections enables coverage of less well-known writers, such as Mary Anne Barker and Margaret Fountaine, along with their more famous counterparts, such as Mary Kingsley, Lady Mary Wortley Montagu, May French-Sheldon, and Isabella Bird. Where possible, texts have been chosen which are currently in print and therefore available for readers to follow up and read in their entirety. We have generally selected extracts from complete published works and have not drawn on manuscript diaries or letters. We have, however, included a certain number of extracts from texts which are not in print, in order to foreground the importance of publishing influence in determining textual accessibility and also to help redefine the parameters of women's travel writing. We have also included several extracts from texts from the Corvey archive of travel writing.[1]

We have included extracts from writing by women who conformed to the nineteenth-century lady traveller stereotype, that is, a woman who shocked her contemporaries by venturing into previously "unexplored" territory, or who travelled unchaperoned, or who put herself in dangerous and potentially life-threatening situations. However, we have also included extracts from those women for whom, as missionaries, settlers, or pioneers, travel was a form of predetermined or "professional" activity, alongside extracts from those women who travelled from choice, either as explorers or on already established tourist routes, as a form of leisure activity. The eccentric woman traveller must thus be seen as only one of a range of different roles which women travellers could and did adopt in very specific contexts, rather than as the dominant image. We would argue that this particular image of the woman traveller developed largely within the colonial context, and that it was by no means a universal stereotype of representation either for the woman herself or her critics. It is therefore important to stress that in different contexts and in different periods, there are other discursive frameworks within which the woman traveller can situate herself. For example, the emphasis on morality and propriety contingent upon "being a lady", so influential in mid-Victorian Britain, necessitated a similar insistence on socially acceptable gendered behaviour even for the most adventurous and apparently iconoclastic female travellers. Conversely, in both earlier and later periods, such essentialist restrictiveness was far less in evidence: neither the eighteenth-century nor the twentieth-century traveller had to represent herself so carefully in accordance with the age's strictures on femininity. Likewise, as mobility became a marker of social progression towards the end of the nineteenth century, it was no longer necessary to foreground the exceptionality of women who ventured beyond the normal parameters of womanly undertaking.

However, that is not to say that we are not aware of the force of the stereotypical figure of the eccentric and adventurous women traveller, even in the present day. This figure defined the parameters within which women have travelled and represented themselves travelling, and it remains a role-model for many women to aspire to. It is certainly a standard against which many women travellers measure themselves and it has set the discursive boundaries for women writing about their travels.

Each of the following sections of travel writing by women is prefaced by an introduction which focuses on specific issues in relation to gender and travel writing, such as the way that women travellers represent other women, the way they situate themselves spatially and so on. However, in this general introduction we would like now to consider some of the wider theoretical questions.

Difference of women travel writers

For many critics, it is self-evident that Western women travellers write in a qualitatively different way from men: various recent anthologies of exclusively women travel writers (e.g. Birkett and Wheeler, 1998; Morris, 1994; Robinson, 1995; Schriber, 1995), while usefully calling attention to hitherto little-known texts, simply assume that women's travel writing is different from men's writing and do not therefore address the pitfalls of such an essentialist position.

We would take issue with this contention, particularly in the light of theoretical work in feminist theory as a whole and in feminist linguistics where the notion of difference has been particularly interrogated (Bergvall, Bing and Freed, 1996; Butler, 1990). These feminist theorists argue that it is extremely difficult to make generalisations about the nature or behaviour, or even the oppression, of women. Working-class white women may have more in common with working-class white men in certain circumstances than they do with middle- or upper-class white women and they may feel politically more aligned with males than they do with other females in particular contexts. These feminist critics argue for a more complex model of gender and the way it interacts with other factors, rather than the simplistic model by which gender is perceived as merely another building block, added on to other blocks to form one's identity (McClintock, 1995; Skeggs, 1997). In particular contexts, gender may be the most salient variable, where, for example, a woman may feel that she is being discriminated against, or where a woman may feel solidarity with another woman from a different class or race, because of perceived similarities of gender. However, there are other contexts where gender is overridden by other factors, for example, where perceived racial or class antagonism prevents women from viewing others as similar to themselves: middle-class white British women's treatment of female servants in the nineteenth century being a case in point. This more complex view of gender makes generalisations about women as a whole more fraught and involves a tendency to mitigate those generalising statements. On the other hand, it helps us to recognise that in a colonialist context, for example, there are various positions of enunciation which women may occupy, in which gender is not the sole defining factor.

3

With these considerations in mind, questions like "How is women's travel writing different from men's?" are in danger of forcing all data into one or other of the gendered categories (such as language, subject-matter or narrational position), ignoring all material which cannot be fitted into these categories. For the feminist critics mentioned above, it is important to formulate more complex models of gender difference, in order to move away from a simple polarisation of gender difference, towards a multi-layered analysis where gender is sometimes the most salient feature in the production of a text and, at other times, is mediated through other factors. Tim Youngs (1997) makes a similar point in an article on the problems of focusing on the difference of women's travel writing in a colonial context, arguing that we should therefore focus on differences which are manifested textually and which we can demonstrate are different for men and women because of gender difference, rather than some other factor. Like many feminist critics, he cautions against the assumption that all Western women in this context necessarily oppose colonial rule, and suggests indeed that they should be seen as perhaps more ideologically dangerous in their apparent sympathy for women in colonised countries, since this sympathy is more difficult to counter (Chaudhuri and Strobel, 1992). Perhaps we should go further than Youngs, stressing that it is difficult to generalise about women's travel writing in the way that earlier critics have, because it is clear that openly racist statements occur alongside seemingly sympathetic statements; furthermore, such statements within texts serve different purposes according to the different socio-political environments within which they are produced, reviewed and read. Similarly, as we show in other introductory sections, the language of aesthetics used to describe both picturesque or romantic scenery and the "noble savagery" of indigenous peoples is common to both male and female texts. The difference between men's and women's travel writing here does not lie in the constituents of the texts, but rather in the way that communities of readers evaluate and interpret those texts according to their social and historical positioning.

We would argue that a more productive way of analysing this is to assert that Western women travellers have always been subject to a range of constraints which are different from those affecting the behaviour and writing of men, whilst at the same time partaking in some of the same ones, but on different terms. This mediated relationship to discursive constraints can result in different types of writing or different emphases in writing. Sometimes it results in women producing very similar writing to men, but which is then judged to be different by critics and the reading public who, as we have shown, may read from an essentialist viewpoint.

Not all women travel in the same way nor do they write in the same way, but there are similarities which can be noticed amongst their work, just as there are some similarities within men's writing as a whole. Youngs analyses the way that the female narrator in a travel text negotiates a relation to commodities as a way of trying to locate a gender difference more materially, arguing that women's different relation to material objects produces a consistent textual difference. We would argue that the difference of gender itself will differ according to the context of its production and reception.

We would also argue that it is necessary to focus on women's travel writing within this more complex definition of gender difference simply because of the way that texts have been categorised in the past. While, as has already been mentioned, the last decade has seen a marked expansion of interest in the phenomenon of the woman travel writer, this interest is still comparatively new; apart from a few notable exceptions (such as W.H. Adams's highly patronising study, *Celebrated Women Travellers of the Nineteenth Century*, published in 1882—so popular that it reached a seventh edition by 1896), travel writing as a genre has been perceived as prototypically masculine. Men's writing is often considered to be the standard here; it is significant that many surveys of travel literature have been written which contain reference to few or no women travel writers (Batten, 1978; Buzard, 1993; Fussell, 1980; Youngs, 1994), or which treat women's writing as a necessarily different and implicitly subordinate sub-genre (Pratt, 1992). Ideally, perhaps, we would like to see anthologies of travel writing and critical essays on travel writing which do not make any essentialist assumptions, which refer equally to men's and women's work and also which are aware of the extent to which men's as well as women's writing is gendered within its specific context. We still believe, however, that there is a place for an anthology devoted solely to women's writing, partly to indicate the range of texts waiting to be made available to a contemporary readership, and partly to suggest the diversity of discursive influences which gender has on female-authored representations of the foreign.

Discursive constraints

One of the central questions which this anthology seeks to address is the relationship of women's writing to discursive constraints. By discursive constraints, we mean the range of "rules" and systems of representation and meaning within which writers negotiate in order to write what they wish (Foucault, 1972; Mills, 1997). In describing travel writing, there is often an assumption that writers simply express themselves, or describe what they have seen. However, it is our contention that writing is produced in interaction with discursive constraints. Discourses are structuring frameworks which determine that certain elements are perceived as noteworthy and that they are classified in certain ways. Thus, even the way that one perceives a landscape, despite the fact that it feels as if it is a simple unmediated process of looking, is already mediated through discourses of aesthetics and imperialism which will determine that certain tracts of land are designated as landscape rather than others, and that the viewer experiences certain emotions in relation to particular geomorphological features.

As we have suggested, women are not excluded from certain high status, male-generated discourse, such as the discourses of imperialism and aesthetics, since many of their writings are formed in relation to these structuring frameworks (Bohls, 1995). We therefore set out to explore the way in which women's travel writing negotiates with various discourses. We investigate if their writing manifests the same type of "Othering" which has been described extensively in post-colonial discourse theory

(McClintock, 1995; Mills, 1991; Pratt, 1992; Said, [1978] 1991; 1993). We also examine the way that women's travel writing engages with other high status discourses, particularly in relation to the production of knowledge and the description of emotion. But we first consider the viability of drawing on discourse theory in this area.[2]

Within post-colonial theory, most theorists have either aligned themselves with psychoanalytically informed models of discourse theory (Bhabha, 1994; Young, 1993; Hulme, 1986) or they have attempted to synthesise one of these models with more materialist concerns in order to try to make these models more politically sensitive and more cognisant of the specificity of the historical context of the travel writing (McClintock, 1995). We are drawing on a modified form of discourse theory, since it is clear that it is possible to map out feminist analytical concerns without compromising our concerns with materialist specificity (Mills, 1997). Youngs has argued that discourse theory is itself problematic for this type of study, precisely because it may lend itself to an ahistorical analysis (Youngs, 1997). But we would argue, as Lewis has done (Lewis, 1996), that feminist discourse theory can at least defamiliarise for us the notion of gendered subjectivity, allowing us to describe the parameters of effects of gender differentiation on women and men without lapsing into essentialism, that is, the assumption that men and women are in some ways always different (Youngs, 1997). This allows us to describe the force of linguistic constraints on writing, without necessarily subscribing to the more ahistorical readings of Foucauldian discourse theory. One of the key problems with drawing on discourse theory to analyse women's travel writing is obviously that of agency: that is, how it is possible to act in relation to discursive structures or represent oneself as acting. If, as Foucault argues, resistance is simply an effect of power, then it is difficult to analyse the different political positions which are taken up in relation to imperialism and other oppressive systems. Not all of the women who wrote travel narratives were racists, nor were they racist in all circumstances, nor was the form and content of their racism the same in all narratives. But some of them were clearly prejudiced, and some of them used their seeming sympathy for indigenous women to further their own position of superiority and their own political agendas in obtaining the franchise in Britain (Chaudhuri and Strobel, 1992; see Lewis, 1996). We feel that it is necessary to move away from disembodied models of analysis, but also from models of complicity whereby whatever women writers in the nineteenth century wrote they are to blame, as Youngs seems to suggest (Youngs, 1997). In a sense, middle-class white British women are very easy to attack and to blame: if they write in a racist way about the inhabitants of the countries through which they travelled, they can be criticised; if they demonstrate sympathy for these inhabitants, it can be argued that they are making political arguments on behalf of indigenous women only in order to consolidate their own political position within the colonial context or in Britain. By campaigning for the rights of others, they allocated for themselves a powerful moral position which allowed them to intervene in debates about imperial policy. Thus, rather than simply trying to judge middle class British women, we feel it is necessary to take a more dispassionate view of them and their writings. This is not an attempt either to erase their racism or to minimise the very real efforts that some of them made to understand other nations; it is instead an attempt to move away from a position of interpretation where we as critics are forced to take up a judgmental position in relation to these women and their work.

It can be argued that in the post-colonial context of the later twentieth century this racist position is either absent or obliterated by notions of "political correctness". That is to say, we would not expect more recent women travellers to be so influenced by the discursive structures of colonialism, nor indeed constrained by them. Nevertheless, if we need to acknowledge the racism, subtextual or overt, of nineteenth-century writers, we also need to recognise that even the voices of an apparently liberal age may reveal colonialist oppositional paradigms—them/us, inferior/superior, and so on—in their writings. Here, too, discourse theory can be a helpful tool of analysis.

One of the most pervasive models of a modified form of discourse theory is Edward Said's *Orientalism* (Said, [1978] 1991). His well-known discussion of Orientalist discourse centres on the idea of the Other, "a collective notion identifying 'us' Europeans as against all 'those' non-Europeans . . . the idea of European identity as a superior one in comparison with all the non-European people and cultures" (Said, [1978] 1991). The traveller/observer accesses the alien or unfamiliar through various strategies contingent upon an imperialist position of Western supremacy, defining the foreign in terms of opposition (which often means negation or abstraction). Said's theories are dependent on two assumptions: first, that the sense of self against which the Other is positioned embodies the age's cultural hegemony, thus representing the dominant voice; and second, that the "self" here exists as a trope of positive function and value against which an alternative "not-self" can be measured. As many feminist critics (Lewis, 1996; McClintock, 1995) have pointed out, however, these theories construct the position of enunciation in colonialist or Orientalist discourse as essentially male. Said's argument also fails to deal with the question of whether or not Othering will occur in non-imperial contexts, and, if it does, how it will manifest itself.[3] Said's use of an essentially masculine linguistic register to describe the West's relationship to the East—"a certain *will* or *intention* to understand, in some cases to control, manipulate, even to incorporate, what is a manifestly different . . . world" (Said, [1978] 1991: 12; his emphasis)—excludes the possibility of a more feminine-oriented engagement with the foreign Other.[4] Furthermore, Said argues that the Orient has a principally feminine cultural resonance, centring on the notion of a sexuality which is both desired and feared by men; Gustave Flaubert's representation of his Egyptian courtesan becomes a model here—the male voice "possessing" the woman who cannot represent herself (Said, [1978] 1991).

On both counts, then, Said's theory becomes more questionable when the observer/writer is female: although women could and did speak with an imperialist voice, their relationship to colonialism as a whole was more problematic than for men. British women tended to develop a very different form of national subject position within the colonial context. As Jenny Sharpe has shown, British women were often used as foils in larger political struggles and were often represented and treated as if in need of protection, in order to portray non-European males as barbarous. This had a profound effect on British women's relation to imperialism, the form their interventions in political debates could take and the type of national subject position available to them (Sharpe, 1993). This is not to say that they did not take part in political activity within imperialism, but as Jayawardena has shown, the form of that campaigning differed markedly from men's activities (Jayawardena, 1995).

Furthermore, women's sense of self, on which the Orientalist oppositional discourse depends, was more likely to be negative than positive, as they themselves were defined according to a dualism which placed them in secondary or complementary roles. The extracts we have included suggest the extent and manner of women's engagement with the discourse of Othering, and the possibility of their speaking with an alternative voice free from or subversive of the dominant (male) discourse so as to produce a gaze on the Oriental Other which was both less monolithic and less reductive than Said's formulation suggests (Lewis, 1996).

Feminine conduct

Western women travelling in other countries were very aware of the way that they were often taken to be representative of Britain, especially within the colonial context. But even outside of colonised countries, British women often manifested a great concern in their texts about the necessity of dressing and behaving "correctly" and being judged to be doing so. This is partly as a result of the seemingly "unfeminine" nature of the published accounts of their travels, and also because the very activity of travelling seemed unfeminine and compromising to the ideal of female respectability. A certain amount of textual exposition is therefore often devoted to establishing the femininity of the narrator. For example, Mary Kingsley, in *Travels in West Africa*, frequently comments on the difficulty of maintaining clean and proper blouses and of keeping her hairpins in order (Kingsley, [1897] 1982). Other writers draw on even more extreme strategies; for example May French-Sheldon in *From Sultan to Sultan* describes herself trekking through the African jungle wearing a rhinestone ballgown with a pennant stating "Noli Me Tangere" (Do not touch me).[5]

Gender awareness was heightened by the advice given to women travellers in manuals as well as being expressed in the narratives themselves. Both manuals and travel texts focus on the particularities of travel for women, including physical problems to be overcome, reminding readers that writer and audience (potential future travellers?) share common concerns. In her *Hints to Lady Travellers*, Lillias Campbell Davidson highlights gender specificity in relation to the mechanics of travel. Not only does she discuss the practicalities of luggage and necessities for bodily comfort, but she emphasises that all her recommended items are in accordance with the respectability and modesty pertaining to the high ideal of womanhood (Davidson, 1889): dress must meet the requirements of both the pragmatics of physical movement and the canons of femininity; accompanying property will replicate the domestic sphere (hot water bottles, sewing kits), thus reinforcing the traveller's sense of domestic familiarity while abroad. These constant reminders of bodily needs are replicated in the texts themselves, in which problems relating to physicality are frequently stressed—how to walk in soaking wet skirts, or how best to keep cool in high temperatures, for instance. This awareness in itself triggers off a response to the female Other, in which questions of femaleness and its modes of negotiating an often hostile external environment become of paramount importance.

Emphasis on the special conditions attaching to the female body features in the texts in descriptions of physical conditions encountered and managed by the travellers. Although the more intimate details are omitted (how, for example did they cope with menstruation?), there is usually some reference to the difficulties faced by a woman travelling in an essentially male world.[6] Anna Jameson, on her canoe trip to Indian settlements in Upper Canada in the 1830s, explains that only the tact of the twenty-one men accompanying her in erecting her tent at some distance from the others allowed her to wash in private (Jameson, [1838] 1990). Others explain their strategies for dealing with the limitations imposed by their sex in the matter of dress. Isabelle Eberhardt sought to escape these limitations altogether by travelling disguised as a man; less radical solutions were to adapt the indigenous female costume (as riding dress, for example) to permit greater freedom of movement. At the same time, in most cases, travellers were anxious not to be seen as betraying the principle of female modesty, which, as Davidson herself suggests, was often the best weapon against offensive male behaviour and molestation. Kingsley's famous defence of "the blessings of a good thick skirt" (Kingsley, [1897] 1982: 270) is one example. Another is Bird's angry response to the *Times* reviewer of her *A Lady's Life in the Rocky Mountains* (1879) who remarked that she had "donned masculine habiliments for her greater convenience": not only did she write to her publisher, Murray, that her dress was that Hawaiian riding costume always worn by ladies, but she insisted that later editions of her work contain an explanatory note to this effect, plus a sketch which would confirm the femininity of her garb (Barr, 1985: 184–185).

Textual negotiations

Travel is a negotiable arena of activity in which mobility is defined by gender, race and class parameters as well as by topography. As the advice manuals and the travellers' own accounts indicate, this could be more problematic for women than for men simply because their departure from the interiority of the domestic sphere involved greater justification and management, both ideologically and practically. It is partly because such questions of gender were thus foregrounded for them that the travellers focus on similar areas in the foreign environment—how women dress, their family and societal roles, the degree of personal freedom available to them, and so on. In reflecting on the domestic habits of the female Other, they were, too, enabled to take a revisionary look at their own position, although this did not necessarily produce a radical subversion of the colonialist, white supremacist stance into which they may have been locked. The accounts themselves show the complexity of the narrative position which is produced: the narrating "I", both authorised by her "proper" knowledge of the material she is presenting and self-marginalised by speaking from the locus allotted to her, is able to offer new interpretations of femaleness in a context which involves self-evaluation as well as sympathetic observation.

The narrator's femininity, however, had to be guaranteed in order for her work to be appropriately authenticated in gender terms. Indeed, most women travel writers themselves were acutely aware of the textual constraints imposed on them by gender appropriateness. Many of their narratives are prefaced by apologia, protesting their inability to treat matters other than the social (or even trivial), in comparison with the political and scientific orientation of male texts. While this can be seen as a common strategy of female self-devaluation (Foster, 1990), it may also be viewed as a subversive masking gesture. So Fanny Trollope's prefatory disclaimer that she "leaves to abler pens the more ambitious task of commenting on the democratic form of the American government" in favour of treating "the principles, tastes, and manners, of its domestic life" (Trollope, [1832] 1984: xxxiii) deliberately blocks out those parts of her book in which she does in fact comment on the politics of American democracy; and Mary Kingsley's apologies for "giving so much detail on matters that really only affect myself" (Kingsley, [1897] 1982: 9) conceal the propagandist elements on which much of her text is based.

If statements such as these, combined with a concentration on domestic aspects of foreign life, are a means of avoiding accusations of entering the public space of male textuality, they also suggest how apparent adherence to accepted notions of literary "femininity" could be a source of empowerment. Many women travellers realised that they gained a voice precisely because they were able to treat areas usually ignored by men, so their seeming complicity with hegemonic structures was in fact a challenge to the stereotyping set up by those structures. By foregrounding gender-specific concerns, they could subvert the familiar hero/adventure/action paradigm of male travel narratives and generate and control their own discourse, as we argue in the later introductory section on Women and Adventure. Throughout female travel writing of the nineteenth century there is an assumption that, as the sole sources of certain kinds of information, women can overthrow the public/private, initiating/receptive binaries and speak with an authorising voice. In 1845, Elizabeth Rigby, writer and traveller, claims that the domesticity which is the supreme characteristic of English womanhood not only makes women good travellers (punctual, practical, brave and independent) but also equips them for sharp observation and attention to subjects that might otherwise pass disregarded (Rigby, 1845: 98–137). Furthermore, she argues that women's naturally superior knowledge of human nature and domestic affairs brings to travel writing its greatest interest; for her, the female vision, inherently different from the male one, is in fact that which best suits the genre. Eight years earlier, Harriet Martineau stressed that the kinds of experience accessible only to women are needed to complete knowledge of the foreign: "I am sure, I have seen much more of domestic life than could possibly have been exhibited to any gentleman travelling through the country [North America]. The nursery, the boudoir, the kitchen, are all excellent schools in which to learn the morals and manners of a people" (Martineau, 1837, I: xiv).

The domestic is of course also an area in which the female viewer can establish a common ground with her (female) readership without relinquishing her subject position in the narrative: while the woman travel writer is speaking from within the margins of the appropriately feminine, she is at the same time the "I" who is authorised by her peculiar knowledge of the material she is presenting and which she can share with her readers. Making claims that a female-gendered position of enunciation is dependent on perceived differences of subject matter and approach, however, may take us into those very areas of misleading essentialism referred to earlier in our discussion of the "difference" of women's travel writing. It is certainly true that women travellers often focus on domestic detail such as clothes and food; they show interest in family structures and treatment of children; they sometimes demonstrate empathy with their own sex and place themselves adjacent to, rather than in opposition to their objects of observation. But we also need to be aware that nineteenth-century critical opinion created a set of criteria for "appropriately" feminine writing, which included emotional and moral directives about "feeling" and "women's sensibility" as well as confining women's writing within certain prescribed areas. Representation which might be considered typically female, then, may be the result of strategic policy—especially if the writers wanted to get published—rather than a specifically gendered orientation. "Womanly" subject matter must not be used as proof of gender specificity nor must it be seen as solely biologically derived.

Thus, to conclude, we are asserting that women's travel writing is very varied, both partaking in high status, masculine discourses of aesthetics, imperialism and informative authority when those served women's overall aims, and drawing on more feminine discourses of care for others, domesticity and impressionistic response when those also served a purpose.[7] Because these different discursive frameworks were more or less salient within different contexts and even at different moments of the production of the text, these texts which we have included in the anthology can be seen as sites for women's difficult but productive negotiations with writing and travelling as women.

Notes

1 The Corvey Travel Archive is a collection of travel texts on microfiche which is housed at Sheffield Hallam University. Access to this archive can be obtained by contacting Dr Emma Clery, School of Cultural Studies, Sheffield Hallam University, Collegiate Crescent, Sheffield S10 2BP.

2 We consider these themes and issues in more detail in subsequent introductory sections.

3 This is clearly an issue within the texts which we have selected, since imperialism and discourses of imperialism cannot be said to only have an effect within clearly colonial and imperial contexts. Very often tropes and style of writing developed to describe specifically colonial relations are made use of in non-imperial contexts as tools of description, simply because they are available and familiar to writers and their audiences (Mills, 1995).

4 Terms such as "will, intention, control" and "manipulate" imply a kind of masculine, militaristic aggression. This statement also precludes seeing West/East relationships in any other terms than the desire to dominate—there is no notion of reciprocity or negotiation here (which might be considered to be more feminine).

5 See the new edition of this work by May French-Sheldon, especially the introduction by Tracey Jean Boisseau (2000), where she argues that Sheldon constructed a role for herself consisting of elements of straightforwardly masculine heroic acts which were then tempered by these seemingly excessively feminine markers to offset the danger of the appropriation of masculinity.

6 Menstruation is an issue which current travel writers have begun to address; for example, see Robyn Davidson's *Tracks*, her account of crossing the Australian desert, an extract from which is included in this anthology.

7 This may suggest a more agented process that we mean to imply; it is often simply the discourses which are available, familiar and not coded as "off-limits" which are negotiated with by writers.

1

Women writing about women

Western women, from the eighteenth century to the present day, have tended to write extensively about indigenous women in their travel writings. They have focused on the difference of "native" women, particularly when cultural customs relating to women have placed those women in a seemingly subordinate or more disadvantaged position to Western women. As we mentioned in the general Introduction, particularly in the nineteenth century, many of the accounts of "other" women's lives seem more to constitute the construction of a superior position for Western women, since, in the process of describing indigenous women's disadvantages and restrictions, Western women are presented implicitly and sometimes explicitly as being relatively free from restriction. At the same time, however, certainly in the late nineteenth century this critique of the oppression suffered by indigenous women also forms part of the critique of Western patriarchal oppression which was being formulated by Western feminists, particularly around questions of suffrage, but also around campaigns for legal rights in relation to property and marriage (Burton, 1992; Ware, 1992). For example, visitors to Middle Eastern harems note that, despite the apparently constrained, even enslaved, condition of harem women, they could in fact inherit and keep their property, a right not granted Englishwomen until the Married Women's Property Act of 1870 (Melman, 1995). Thus, this critique of indigenous women's oppression in the nineteenth century cannot simply be judged as either "colonial" or "sympathetic". Indeed, because of Western women's marginal status in relation to institutional imperialism, their statements with regard to indigenous women are often equivocal and cannot be taken as necessarily authoritative. In addition, because of their own agency within a colonialist framework and because of their ability to travel relatively freely, neither is it possible to see their statements on these women as simply empathetic and asserting "sisterhood".

We have already suggested that, without establishing an essentialist position, it is valid to claim that areas of traditionally female activity are frequent topics of observation in women's travel texts. Travellers' commentary in these areas well illustrates the ambiguous nature of this discourse. Thus, on the one hand, critique of such areas and the ways in which women engage in them, in both colonial and non-colonial contexts, can function as a validation of the commentator's own life-style or value-system. Conversely, detailed and appreciative concentration on domestic customs very different from those familiar to the observer may express challenge to Western cultural hegemonies. Clearly, commentary on the domestic is not necessarily to be taken as overtly political: that is to say, these women are not making direct comparisons, with the intent of deconstructing their own cultural traditions. But their seemingly natural concern with alternative female life-styles at least offers the possibility of questioning Western conventions and may provoke recognition that other patterns of female behaviour offer more freedom or opportunities than Western women enjoy.

The harem and the Western woman writer

The visit to the harem, which many Western female travellers to the Middle East, from the early eighteenth to the mid-nineteenth centuries, managed to accomplish, is a very particular aspect of British women's encounter with the foreign and cannot therefore be taken as paradigmatic of travelling as a whole. But precisely because of its particularity, it foregrounds many of the issues and questions raised in any examination of the female response to the Other, in social, sexual and cultural terms. Indeed, the experience, inscribed in the Western cultural consciousness through its representation, may also structure the way in which twentieth-century women see and depict indigenous women.

The cult of the harem is central to the fantasies which structure Orientalist discourse: in male-generated myth it is forbidden territory, a segregated space barred to Western men and males outside the family, charged with erotic significance about which knowledge can only be voyeuristically obtained. By the nineteenth century this mythology was well established, despite the fact that, firstly, the harem was merely the women's quarters where for much of the time nothing more exciting than eating and gossiping occured; and secondly, the harem (like the zenana) was restricted to certain elite groups in Moslem and Hindu societies and, despite popular assumption, was not widespread throughout the Middle East and India. This cultural arena became a trope for the Orient itself, an analogy for the desired unknown; at the same time, this trope was frequently employed as a means of discussing the condition of women in Europe. For British women, of course, it was not forbidden territory. They were able to gain access, and indeed a visit to a harem had become a regular part of the female tourist itinerary by the late 1840s and constituted a flourishing commercial venture by the 1870s, as is attested by Annie Jane Harvey's guide of 1871. *Turkish Harems and Circassian Homes* (Lewis, 1996; Melman, 1995). It could therefore reasonably be claimed that the only authoritative representations of the harem are made by women—and indeed that these representations subvert long-cherished male versions, in that they are authenticated by experience, however limited, pre-conceptualised and controlled that experience may have been. It can also be argued that Western women's representations of the harem were textually driven by the desire to challenge those of male travellers, and that the foregrounding of and approach to certain aspects of harem life create a separate and distinctive female discourse of the harem.

As Reina Lewis reminds us, British female accounts of the harem in the nineteenth century had a range of representational options, contingent upon various factors (Lewis, 1996). The woman's gaze, for example, is both female (where gender operates not only discursively but also enables access to the harem) and Western (the observer is still spectator within a "them/us" paradigm). Furthermore, it is essentially bourgeois, socially and politically; nineteenth-century female travellers were largely middle class, embodying contemporary assumptions about family, labour relations and female occupations, as well as some kind of awareness of gender and racial oppression. Their writings, therefore, reflect both colonialist and anti-colonialist positions. While the ideologies which underpin many of their representational strategies are essentially Eurocentric, some of their responses seem genuine attempts to see the Other as parallel, not antithetical, to the observing self. British women's voices here could both contest and support an Orientalist discourse.

The kind of female experience in the harem which travellers encountered and represented could seem a mirror image—albeit distorted—of Western middle-class feminine culture. Indeed, Inderpal Grewal has argued that the harem and the bourgeois hearth or home can be seen as mutually constitutive (Grewal, 1996). For this reason, perhaps, domestic details, such as dress, furnishings, female activities, food, and mother/child relationships are particularly noted; the female body is also the object of attention. More generally, the harem invited commentary of a more socio-political nature, not only as a mythologised institution but also as an analogue for concerns about individual freedom and gender roles. The harem—as literally a place where women live and converse—was thus an ambivalent space, whose dualities (liberty/imprisonment; exoticism/tyranny; activity/idleness) had an especial resonance for British female visitors. At the same time, their own ambiguous position as marginalised Other yet also privileged agent produces a response which is both hegemonically transgressive and representative of their own value systems.

The response of European women visitors to the Middle Eastern female appearance is paradigmatic of their approach to the harem as a whole, stimulating thinking about the observers' own culture as well as that of the Oriental Other. Richness and elegance are described, often in great detail. In a familiar strategy of colonialist discourse, difference is subsumed by a kind of aestheticising vision which, as in the case of other indigenous peoples, transforms the objects of gaze into Western cultural icons (comparisons are made with Roman empresses or Greek statues, for example). On the other hand, where external appearances cannot satisfactorily be referenced within a familiar cultural frame the response is more critical. Harriet Martineau, for instance, is quizzical about an Egyptian lady's black net headdress "bunched out curiously behind" (Martineau, 1848, II: 150), and the Eastern habit of pulling the eyebrows and painting lines or patches on the face is frequently dismissed as "ugly". Costume which seems both physically restrictive and aesthetically unpleasing is disparaged, and terms such as "vulgar and ugly", "hideous" and "frightful" come into play. In such cases, the gendered positioning of the observer enables cultural legitimisation. Thus mockery of seemingly odd cosmetics re-inforces the cultural mythology of the English rose (unpainted) female complexion, as well as confirming assumptions about the unhealthiness of Eastern skin; and fatness becomes a signifier of unfeminine indulgence of appetite and bad diet, as well as of indolence and lack of purposeful activity, in marked contrast to the Western middle-class codes of female abstinence and useful occupation. The physical characteristics which elicit the greatest admiration are those which most approximate to European standards (for example the light colouring of the Circassian slaves in Turkish harems) while less familiar features (such as the darker skin and non-European facial structures of the Nubian slaves) are frequently imaged as grotesque and hideous.

A closer move towards cultural reciprocity between women than this commentary would suggest is to be found in the practice of exchanging dress. Many British women travellers in the nineteenth century comment on the way in which harem women are fascinated by the strange garments of their European visitors, just as they themselves foreground the peculiarities of Oriental costume. Moreover, not only did they sometimes undress in order to satisfy the curiosity of the harem inhabitants, but they often actually replaced their own clothes with those of their hostesses. The earliest and most notable example of this is Lady Mary Wortley Montagu, who, on her visit to Turkey in 1717–18 (Montagu, [1718] 1993) had herself painted in her Eastern outfit, and later travellers similarly attempted to re-fashion themselves. For the Hon. Mrs William Grey, who visited the Middle East in the late 1860s in the suite of the Prince and Princess of Wales, cross-dressing was part of the adventure of harem-visiting; in Cairo the Viceroy's wives dressed her and the Princess of Wales in an ethnic outfit, including painted eyebrows and veils, with which the two Englishwomen hoped to astonish all their menfolk (Grey, 1869). Emilia Hornby, who submitted to the insistence that she dress in the vast selection of finery produced for her, notes how much she enjoyed the "masquerade" in which she was able to be Other, without relinquishing entirely her own sense of identity: "You would certainly never have known me in the gorgeousness of Eastern array, which however they pronounced became me very well", she remarks (Hornby, 1863: 326).

Such an exchange places the observer in the position of the observed: thus the particularities of Western costume such as dresses which fasten at the back, or layers of ruffled petticoats, may, seen through Eastern eyes, effect cultural revaluation. The adoption of Oriental costume also challenges the usual implications of disguise here; whereas both in artistic fantasy and in actuality (as is illustrated by Emmeline Lott's account of an Italian nobleman who managed to get into a Turkish harem disguised as a woman (Lott, 1865)), men used female costume as a means of entering the forbidden territory, women who dressed themselves in female Oriental clothes were engaging to some degree in a process of cultural reciprocity which temporarily reversed or at least challenged the stability of the subject/object positionality.

Sexuality—a taboo subject for middle-class Western women, especially in the nineteenth century—was potentially the most disturbing aspect of the harem to female observers, both fascinating and shocking. In contrast to Mary Kingsley's bold and extensive discussion of polygamy in Africa at the end of the century (Kingsley, [1897] 1982), the subject of Middle Eastern polygamy was only obliquely and gingerly touched on, from a social as well as a moral perspective. The actual confrontation with the female body, naked or semi-naked, and in this context apparently signifying female sexuality, caused most unease. While few women travellers actually visited a bath, the female body as revealed in Oriental slave dancing and in Indian "nautsch" dancing, indigenous entertainment often offered to visitors, precipitated a re-consideration of Western ideologies of feminine delicacy and purity. Such an overt flaunting of physical selfhood disturbed as much as pleased most observers, who, like Harriet Martineau, term it "disgusting" (Martineau, 1848, II: 165) or, like Mrs Grey, refer only obliquely to what made them so uneasy:

> ... some movements were graceful enough. Others, on the contrary, were simply frightful. For instance, they had a way of moving and shaking their heads and other parts of their bodies all separately, as if no one part belonged to the other parts, which was quite monstrous. (Grey, 1869: 28–29)

17

In complete contrast is the response of Lady Mary Wortley Montagu, who not only, unusually, actually visited a bath, but expresses unhesitating admiration for the beauty of the naked women (Montagu, [1718] 1993). Montagu, of course, is writing in the second decade of the eighteenth century, in an age before constraining notions of female modesty, decency and sexual propriety had become part of the cultural hegemony; furthermore, she recognises that what to Western observers may seem a constraining female life-style could in fact be a source of sexual liberation for women. Such unrestrained appreciation of the naked female form is not found again until the 1870s, in the writings of Lucie Duff Gordon, one of the most open-minded of later nineteenth-century travellers to Egypt. Gordon writes admiringly to her correspondent (interestingly, her husband) about the physical beauties of a "splendid negro girl" (Gordon, [1902] 1983) she has seen; like Montagu, she seems able to isolate the indigenous female body as an object of purely aesthetic appeal.

It was clearly difficult for nineteenth-century Western female observers to accommodate to the "difference" presented by the harem. One discursive strategy they employed was to render Oriental women as childish and petty-minded, beings of a lower mental amd moral stature who could be "othered" both pityingly and critically. More significantly, the critique of the harem as a shameful and tragic institution politicises it in Western feminist terms. As the introduction to this section suggests, the apparent sympathy with those whom Martineau calls "the most injured human beings I have ever seen" (Martineau, 1848, II: 167) must be viewed in the context of a growing critique at home of a less obvious, but no less constricting, patriarchal oppression.

A political voice forged in relations with other women?

As we argued in the opening comments to this section, Western women in the nineteenth century often carved out a voice for themselves through their campaigning, as they saw it, on behalf of indigenous women (Burton, 1992; Grewal, 1996; Jayawardena, 1995; Ware, 1992). They regarded themselves as campaigning against antiquated and oppressive indigenous customs, and they sometimes worked alongside indigenous women in these campaigns. Many nineteenth-century travel texts include discussions of the position of women in the country visited, and evaluation of that position in relation to the situation of women—usually middle class—within Britain is obviously of great importance to many of the authors considered here. There is no position which Western women can adopt easily in relation to this material, as is shown by critical evaluations of their writings in which they have been attacked for being colonialist or praised for being anti-colonialist (Midgley, 1998). It is clear that a certain, albeit covert, political consciousness motivated many of the women who travelled in the eighteenth and nineteenth centuries and that this political consciousness took many forms. Sometimes it was the very reason for travel or was the means whereby they were enabled to break conventions, and travel unaccompanied. Sometimes it manifested itself in the form of philanthropy (a common vehicle for political and religious sentiments for middle-class British women within

Britain) where difficult conditions were often alleviated by the charitable actions of those who, because of their gender, were themselves prevented from taking waged work (Longden, forthcoming).

Travel to the United States in the nineteenth century was frequently touched— if not directly inspired—by awareness of the wrongs done to both Native American Indians and Black people by a rapacious and ruthless developing nation. Such wrongs, as many of the women travellers point out, were especially ironic in view of the fact that the principle of democracy was supposedly the foundation stone of this new nation. Despite the discursive restraints upon women writers, which, as has already been mentioned, discouraged them from entering into the realms of the political, expressions of sympathy for oppressed indigenous peoples could be considered compatible with a "natural" female response, from the heart rather than from the head. In particular, when such sympathy was directed towards members of their own sex, it could be taken as an appropriate assertion of "sisterhood". Indeed it was often considered encumbent upon women to take up a position of empathy: New World visitors such as Frances Wright and Mary Duncan declared themselves especially horrified when "illiberal" statements concerning Black people were made by women, European as well as American (Wright, [1821] 1963: 41; Duncan, 1852: 235), and Frances Kemble saw anti-slavery bias as a requirement of gender and nationality—"I am an Englishwoman, in whom the absence of such a prejudice would be disgraceful" (Kemble, [1863] 1961: 11)

Protest about the Native American Indian situation tends to be formulated as conventional expressions of outrage at the United States Government, often aroused when travellers visited the Bureau of Indian affairs in Washington. With the exception of Anna Jameson, most travellers saw few Native Americans and then at a distance, encouraging only generalised statements of pity at their degraded state (often co-existent, as will be seen, with iconic representations of the Noble Savage). Jameson, however, because of the closer contact she experienced when she visited an American Indian settlement in Upper Canada in 1837, and because she was able to learn much more from her friendship with the Schoolcrafts (Henry Schoolcraft was the Indian government agent there), takes up a much more specifically defensive position on behalf of the indigenous population. Questioning assumptions that Western notions of "civilisation" are universal and applicable to all cultures and races, she claims that in many ways Native American values are superior to those of whites. Here, she uses colonialist arguments in reverse: though some Native customs may seem barbarous and savage, such as retaliatory attacks on pioneer American women and children, they are at least no worse than what is done by supposedly civilised and Christian nations; furthermore, although she asserts that only civilisation will be able to ameliorate woman's condition, she admits that "if our advantages of intellect and refinement are not to lead on to further moral superiority, I prefer the Indians on the score of consistency; they are what they profess to be, and we are *not* what we profess to be" (Jameson, [1838] 1990: 460). She also points out that while most travellers regard Native American women as victimised, degraded, and oppressed by men, their condition is consistent with the society in which they live

19

and is not subject to the gross discrepancy between ideology and actuality which exists in Western society. Jameson's observation has here engendered a re-visioning of her own culture.

In the nineteenth century, there was much more widespread indignation about the treatment of Black people in the United States. Slavery was a more obviously political arena with an inbuilt discursive framework; it was in fact especially difficult for white women to speak in favour of the institution, since, in so doing, they would have risked undermining their hegemonic status as the source of humanitarian and maternal values. Those who took a conservative or colonialist approach did so with caution or apology: Frances Trollope found it necessary to append a long note countering her initial impression of a slave State, in which "I was immediately comfortable, and at my ease" (Trollope, [1832] 1984: 154); and Matilda Houston admitted that the gap between theory and experience when actual conditions were observed led her to modify her initial antipathy towards the ownership of slaves (Houston, 1850, II: 161).

A particularly notable instance of a female pro-slavery position is that of Amelia Murray, a visitor to the States in the 1850s. Murray takes on a patriarchal, colonialist voice in supporting the masters rather than the slaves (the former are the unwilling agents of a system which has been forced on them, she claims), and she uses the example of history (the decline towards barbarism in the post-slavery West Indies) to show that abolitionists are "hot-headed zealots", well-intentioned but ignorant. She also implements the argument of racial essentialism to prove that Black people are inferior beings: "I now see the great error we have committed is in assuming that the African race is equal in capability with the European; and that under similar circumstances it is capable of equal moral and intellectual culture" (Murray, [1856] 1969: 219). While such a discourse can be seen as uncompromisingly frank, it shows that racist colonialist discourse is not restricted to males.

Objections to slavery often went hand-in-hand with overt commitment to women's liberation movements. This connection was made by committed feminist travellers such as Frances Wright ([1821] 1963), Marianne Finch ([1853] 1969) and Barbara Bodichon (1972) who directly linked abolition and Anglo-American women's rights, often using the discourse of slavery to forward their radical arguments on behalf of white women (a tactic also used by American feminists such as Lucretia Mott and Margaret Fuller). In such cases, outrage on behalf of oppressed Black people (particularly women) could be an expression of gender affiliation but also a more political strategy of subversion in which racial injustice became the signifier of Western patriarchal tyranny in general.

Nineteenth-century women's accounts of slavery tended to centre on two main experiences—a visit to a plantation and attendance at a slave auction—and in each case an implicitly gendered language, foregrounding feeling and suffering, is used to reinforce the underlying political impulse. Harriet Martineau, for instance, who went to America as an established abolitionist specifically concerned with investigating the treatment of Black people, moves out of her customary factual and analytical lexis into a more directly emotional register when she describes a woman being sold with her children at a Charleston slave-market (Martineau, 1838, I: 236). Most notable in this regard is Fanny Kemble's representation of slavery, in which she focusses particularly on the plight of women and their sufferings as exploited labourers and mothers. The emotionalism of her account is reinforced by her figuring of herself as a helpless observer, doubly trapped (as a foreigner and as the voiceless yet apparently complicit wife of the unyielding plantation owner) in systems which she is powerless to change. This textual self-dramatisation is particularly significant in that Kemble deliberately used her book as political weaponry: originally written as a series of observations made in 1838 while she was visiting her husband's Southern plantations, the *Journal of a Residence on a Georgia Plantation* was withheld from publication for reasons of personal diplomacy until 1863, when Kemble decided that, in view of the British Government's inclination to support the Confederate South, the true iniquities of slavery must be revealed (Kemble, [1863] 1961).

Underlying such textual representation may be a political impulse of protest against all female abuse. At the same time, observation of slavery in action could encourage a degree of self-assessment: the middle-class, privileged spectator could be led to turn her gaze upon her own position in the face of a womanhood which seemed such a grotesque contrast to her own and yet which reminded her of her own disadvantaged state.

One of the kinds of travel most likely to be politicised in representation—because proselytising in purpose—is that with a religious orientation. Like imperialist colonisers, missionaries seek to impose their own values on native peoples, hence they apprehend difference largely as ideologically distinctive. In this case, of course, the distinctiveness is perceived as transformable, while the observer's own position remains essentially fixed. Thus missionary texts tend to foreground their conversion programme: in their writings about Tibet, for instance, both Annie Taylor (Carey, 1902) and Susie Rijnhart (Rijnhart, 1901) continually remind us that they are there in order to enlighten the native peoples. Yet conviction of the rightness of Western Christian beliefs may co-exist with appreciation of areas of indigenous culture which do not challenge these beliefs.

This is most notably demonstrated in Mildred Cable and Francesca French's account of the fifteen years they (with Francesca's sister, Evangeline) spent in the Gobi Desert, carrying the Gospel beyond the westernmost station of the China Inland Mission, between 1926 and 1941. Their account of their travels, *The Gobi Desert*, far from being a proselytising text, reveals their liking and respect for the variety of indigenous peoples they encountered, and also their astute realisation that "the visitor can never become intimate in such a circle [i.e. desert societies] until he shows himself able to share its outlook on life, and for this he must be familiar with the language, sayings, customs and traditions of the people" (Cable and French, [1942] 1943: 35). For these three women ("The Trio", as they were known), the honouring of local customs, the adoption of native dress, and the learning of Oriental languages was as much a pragmatic strategy as a gesture of reciprocity.

While they were impelled by religious purpose, however, their writing is not overt propaganda for Western faith. In particular, what to Western eyes might seem childish or ridiculous superstition is presented as meaningful within the foreign culture, although they set the ideal of Christian love against what they perceive as the cruelty and bigotry of Islam. Their most politicised commentary occurs in their discussion of Moslem attitudes towards and treatment of women, a frequent and charged topic among nineteenth-century female visitors to the Middle East and India, as we have shown. Cable and French observe the pitiable status of women in the harem menage of a Moslem inn, for instance, noting how the inmates "spoke of each other as sisters, but eyed each other as rivals" (Cable and French, [1942] 1943: 74). The life of the oasis wife, her only horizons the preparation of food and the bearing of children, is described as equally deplorable. Only the Gospel message, it is suggested, can raise them above the level of animals.

As women, Cable and French were able to create bonds of sympathy between themselves and the native women, some of whom "found, perhaps for the first time, women with heart-leisure to sympathise with them in their sorrows and sufferings" (Cable and French, [1942] 1943: 171–172). But there is a strain of anger in their textual representation of female exploitation within a system in which a woman's "only place in the scheme of existence is to be satellite to some man who has bought her for use as he would buy a chattel for his household" (Cable and French, [1942] 1943: 167). Particularly notable is Cable's depiction of a group of painted and elaborately dressed young Chinese girls, "helpless victims" who have been sold by their parents and who are part of the "hideous and revolting [. . .] traffic in women and girls". Cable's "impotent rage burning in my heart" (Cable and French, [1942] 1943: 178–179) both voices a Western woman's sense of moral outrage on behalf of her own sex, and implicitly sets a culture of female devaluation against one which, in its emphasis on the spiritual worth of every individual, offers the only possible redress. Cable and French do not represent themselves as typical of their nation or gender— indeed, as they often point out, their singleness and childlessness, combined with their rootless existence, make them objects of wonder to their English friends as much as to the indigenous people. But in their abhorrence of creeds which denigrate and degrade women they make a political statement about the superiority of their own cultural values.

Women's friendships

If women travellers were able at all to break down or re-define the differences between self and other, one of the obvious areas where this might be achieved was in their relationship with members of their own sex. In some cases, actual friendships developed, although cultural barriers were always problematic and the association was usually short-lived.

Anna Jameson's friendship with Mrs Schoolcraft, the half American Indian wife of the Indian government agent in Upper Canada (now northern Michigan), is emblematic of the possibilities of contact between women of differing races, untramelled by constricting cultural ideologies on either side. On her first meeting with this woman, who was unwell, Jameson immediately felt linked to her: "all my sympathies were enlisted in her behalf . . . there are a thousand quiet ways in which woman may be kind and useful to her sister woman" (Jameson, [1838] 1990: 378). Mrs Schoolcraft offered Jameson new views of the Indian character and way of life, and the bonding between them was strengthened when they travelled together on a canoe trip to see the former's family in Sault Ste Marie; symbolically, the little boat united "two women, differing in clime, nation, complexion, strangers to each other but a few days ago" (Jameson, [1838] 1990: 444). In Sault Ste Marie, Mrs School-craft's mother acted towards Jameson as a kind of surrogate maternal figure, eventually "adopting" her; after being initiated into the Indian race by shooting the rapids in a canoe, Jameson was given a new Indian name and was welcomed into her new "family". Though a few days later she had to return to Toronto, her readiness to take on the identity of the other race, in an act of female bonding, suggests both a genuinely empathetic impulse and a challenge to her own society's ideologies.

Fanny Parks's friendship with the Baiza Bai, an elite member of Indian society, offers a different example of amity between Western and indigenous women. Perhaps the elite position of this Indian woman made it possible for Parks to accept her as an equal (and for Baiza Bai to accept her) in a way which had not been possible with other Indian women, both those in the harem and those outside, whom Parks had encountered. However, we need to note that the representation of a close relationship with a female member of the Indian elite also served to authenticate Parks's account and helped to bolster her representation of herself as an expert on Indian culture and society (Parks, 1850).

The relations between Western women and their indigenous counterparts were of course complex, and never a simple matter of mutual attraction or affection. Political concerns, such as those outlined above, inevitably coloured Western female responses and determined the parameters within which such a relationship could operate. Their own self-interest also came into play and made it likely, for example, that those friendships which would gain them the closest entry into the foreign culture and society would seem most desirable. Such friendships were, too, difficult to maintain in view of the fact that the British women's residence abroad was generally of a temporary nature (the situation of a visitor such as Lucie Duff Gordon, who was forced to spend all the latter part of her life in Egypt because of her health, presents a different case (Gordon, [1902] 1983)). Links between women, established through the common ground of domestic concerns and social interests, albeit short-lived, were however a valuable kind of reciprocity, a means of opening up, and then beginning to overcome, difference.

Frances Trollope

Domestic Manners of the Americans
(1832)

I conceive that no place in the known world can furnish so striking a proof of the immense value of literary habits as the United States, not only in enlarging the mind, but what is of infinitely more importance, in purifying the manners. During my abode in the country I not only never met a literary man who was a tobacco chewer or a whiskey-drinker, but I never met any who were not, that had escaped these degrading habits. On the women, the influence is, if possible, still more important; unfortunately, the instances are rare, but they are to be found. One admirable example occurs in the person of a young lady of Cincinnati; surrounded by a society totally incapable of appreciating, or even of comprehending her, she holds a place among it, as simply and unaffectedly as if of the same species; young, beautiful and gifted by nature with a mind singularly acute and discriminating, she has happily found such opportunities of cultivation as might distinguish her in any country; it is, indeed, that best of all cultivation which is only to be found in domestic habits of literature, and in that hourly education which the daughter of a man of letters receives when she is made the companion and friend of her father. This young lady is the more admirable as she contrives to unite all the multifarious duties which usually devolve upon American ladies, with her intellectual pursuits. The companion and efficient assistant of her father's literary labours, the active aid in all the household cares of her mother, the tender nurse of a delicate infant sister, the skilful artificer of her own always elegant wardrobe, ever at leisure, and ever prepared to receive with the sweetest cheerfulness her numerous acquaintance, the most animated in conversation, the most indefatigable in occupation, it was impossible to know her, and study her character, without feeling that such women were "the glory of all lands," and, could the race be multiplied, would speedily become the reformers of all the grossness and ignorance that now degrade her own. Is it to be imagined that, if fifty modifications of this charming young woman were to be met at a party, the men would dare to enter it reeking with whiskey, their lips blackened with tobacco, and convinced, to the very centre of their hearts and souls, that women were made for no other purpose than to fabricate sweetmeats and gingerbread, construct shirts, dark stockings, and become mothers of possible presidents? Assuredly not. Should the women of America ever discover what their power might be, and compare it with what it is, much improvement might be hoped for. While, at Philadelphia, among the handsomest, the wealthiest, and the most distinguished of the land, their comparative influence in society, with that possessed in Europe by females holding the same station, occurred forcibly to my mind.

Let me be permitted to describe the day of a Philadelphian lady of the first class, and the inference I would draw from it will be better understood.

It may be said that the most important feature in a woman's history is her maternity. It is so; but the object of the present observation is the social, and not the domestic influence of woman.

This lady shall be the wife of a senator and a lawyer in the highest repute and practice. She has a very handsome house, with white marble steps and doorposts, and a delicate silver knocker and door-handle; she has very handsome drawing rooms (very handsomely furnished, there is a sideboard in one of them, but it is very handsome, and has very handsome decanters and cut glass water-jugs upon it); she has a very handsome carriage, and a very handsome free black coachman; she is always very handsomely dressed; and, moreover, she is very handsome herself.

She rises, and her first hour is spent in the scrupulously nice arrangement of her dress; she descends to her parlour neat, stiff, and silent; her breakfast is brought in by her free black footman; she eats her fried ham and her salt fish, and drinks her coffee in silence, while her husband reads one newspaper, and puts another under his elbow; and then, perhaps, she washes the cups and saucers. Her carriage is ordered at eleven; till that hour she is employed in the pastryroom, her snow-white apron protecting her mouse-coloured silk. Twenty minutes before her carriage should appear, she retires to her chamber, as she calls it, shakes, and folds up her still snow-white apron, smooths her rich dress, and with nice care, sets on her elegant bonnet, and all her handsome *et cætera*; then walks down stairs, just at the moment that her free black coachman announces to her free black footman that the carriage waits. She steps into it, and gives the word: "Drive to the Dorcas society." Her footman stays at home to clean the knives, but her coachman can trust his horses while he opens the carriage door, and his lady not being accustomed to a hand or an arm, gets out very safely without, though one of her own is occupied by a work-basket, and the other by a large roll of all those indescribable matters which ladies take as offerings to Dorcas societies. She enters the parlour appropriated for the meeting, and finds seven other ladies, very like herself, and takes her place among them; she presents her contribution, which is accepted with a gentle circular smile, and her parings of broad cloth, her ends of ribbon, her gilt paper, and her minikin pins, are added to the parings of broad cloth, the ends of ribbon, the gilt paper, and the minikin pins with which the table is already covered; she also produces from her basket three ready-made pincushions, four ink-wipers, seven paper matches, and a past-board watch-case; these are welcomed with acclamations, and the youngest lady present deposits them carefully on shelves, amid a prodigious quantity of similar articles. She then produces her thimble, and asks for work; it is presented to her, and the eight ladies all stitch together for some hours. Their talk is of priests and of missions; of the profits of their last sale, of their hopes from the next; of the doubt whether young Mr This, or young Mr That should receive the fruits of it to fit him out for Liberia; of the very ugly bonnet seen at church on Sabbath morning, of the very handsome preacher who performed on Sabbath afternoon, and of the very large collection made on Sabbath evening. This lasts till three, when the carriage again appears, and the lady and her basket return home; she mounts to her chamber, carefully sets aside her bonnet and its appurtenances, puts on her scolloped black silk apron, walks into the kitchen to see that all is right, then into the parlour, where, having cast a careful glance over the table prepared for dinner, she sits down, work in hand, to await her spouse. He comes, shakes hands with her, spits, and dines. The conversation is not much, and ten minutes suffice for the dinner; fruit and toddy, the newspaper and the work-bag succeed. In the evening the gentleman, being a savant, goes to the Wister society, and afterwards plays a snug rubber at a neighbour's. The lady receives at tea a young missionary and three members of the Dorcas society.—And so ends her day.

For some reason or other, which English people are not very likely to understand, a great number of young married persons board by the year, instead of "going to houskeeping", as they call having an establishment of their own. Of course this statement does not include persons of large fortune, but it does include very many whose rank in society would make such a mode of life quite impossible with us. I can hardly imagine a contrivance more effectual for ensuring the insignificance of a woman, than marrying her at seventeen and placing her in a boarding-house. Nor can I easily imagine a life of more uniform dulness for the lady herself; but this certainly is a matter of taste. I have heard many ladies declare, that it is "just quite the perfection of comfort to have nothing to fix for oneself". Yet despite these assurances, I always experienced a feeling which hovered between pity and contempt, when I contemplated their mode of existence.

How would a newly-married Englishwoman endure it, her head and her heart full of the one dear scheme:

Well-ordered home, *his* dear delight to make?

She must rise exactly in time to reach the boarding-table at the hour appointed for breakfast, or she will get a stiff bow from the lady president, cold coffee, and no egg. I have been sometimes greatly amused upon these occasions by watching a little scene in which the bye-play had much more meaning than the words uttered. The fasting, but tardy lady, looks round the table, and having ascertained that there is no egg left, says distinctly: "I will take an egg, if you please." But as this is addressed to no one in particular, no one in particular answers it, unless it happen that her husband is at table before her, and then he says, "There are no eggs, my dear." Whereupon the lady president evidently cannot hear, and the greedy culprit who has swallowed two eggs (for there are always as many eggs as noses) looks pretty considerably afraid of being found out. The breakfast proceeds in sombre silence, save that sometimes a parrot, and sometimes a canary bird, ventures to utter a timid note. When it is finished, the gentlemen hurry to their occupations, and the quiet ladies mount the stairs, some to the first, some to the second, and some to the third stories, in an inverse proportion to the number of dollars paid, and ensconce themselves in their respective chambers. As to what they do there it is not very easy to say; but I believe they clear-starch a little, and iron a little, and sit in a rocking-chair, and sew a great deal. I always observed that the ladies who boarded wore more elaborately worked collars and petticoats than any one else. The plough is hardly a more blessed instrument in America than the needle. How could they live without it? But time and the needle wear through the longest morning, and happily the American morning is not very long, even though they breakfast at eight.

It is generally about two o'clock that the boarding gentlemen meet the boarding ladies at dinner. Little is spoken, except a whisper between the married pairs. Sometimes a sulky bottle of wine flanks the plate of one or two individuals, but it adds nothing to the mirth of the meeting, and seldom more than one glass to the good cheer of the owners. It is not then, and it is not there, that the gentlemen of the Union drink. Soon, very soon, the silent meal is done, and then, if you mount the stairs after them, you will find from the doors of the more affectionate and indulgent wives, a smell of cigars steam forth, which plainly indicates the felicity of the couple within. If the gentleman be a very polite husband, he will, as soon as he has done smoking and drinking his toddy, offer his arm to his wife, as far as the corner of the street where his store, or his office is situated, and there he will leave her to turn which way she likes. As this is the hour for being full dressed, of course she turns the way she can be most seen. Perhaps she pays a few visits; perhaps she goes to chapel; or, perhaps, she enters some store where her husband deals, and ventures to order a few notions; and then she goes home again—no, not home—I will not give that name to a boarding-house, but she re-enters the cold heartless atmosphere in which she dwells, where hospitality can never enter, and where interest takes the management instead of affection. At tea they all meet again, and a little trickery is perceptible to a nice observer in the manner of partaking the pound-cake, etc. After this, those who are happy enough to have engagements, hasten to keep them; those who have not, either mount again to the solitude of their chamber, or, what appeared to me much worse, remain in the common sitting room, in a society cemented by no tie, endeared by no connexion, which choice did not bring together, and which the slightest motive would break asunder. I remarked that the gentlemen were generally obliged to go out every evening on business, and, I confess, the arrangement did not surprise me.

It is not thus that the women can obtain that influence in society which is allowed to them in Europe, and to which both sages and men of the world have agreed in ascribing such salutary effects. It is in vain that "collegiate institutes" are formed for young ladies, or that "academic degrees" are conferred upon them. It is after marriage, and when these young attempts upon all the sciences are forgotten, that the lamentable insignificance of the American woman appears; and till this be remedied, I venture to prophesy that the tone of their drawing-rooms will not improve.

Lady Mary Wortley Montagu

Turkish Embassy Letters
(1718)

To Lady—,   *Adrianople, 1 April 1717*

I am now got into a new world, where everything I see appears to me a change of scene, and I write to your ladyship with some content of mind, hoping at least that you will find the charm of novelty in my letters, and no longer reproach me that I tell you nothing extraordinary. I won't trouble you with a relation of our tedious journey, but I must not omit what I saw remarkable at Sofia, one of the most beautiful towns in the Turkish empire, and famous for its hot baths, that are resorted to both for diversion and health. I stopped here one day on purpose to see them. Designing to go incognito I hired a Turkish coach. There voitures are not at all like ours, but much more convenient for the country, the heat being so great that glasses would be very troublesome. They are made a good deal in the manner of the Dutch coaches, having wooden lattices painted and gilded, the inside being also painted with baskets and nosegays of flowers, intermixed commonly with little poetical mottos. They are covered all over with scarlet cloth, lined with silk, and very often richly embroidered and fringed. This covering entirely hides the persons in them, but may be thrown back at pleasure and the ladies peep through the lattices. They hold four people very conveniently, seated on cushions, but not raised.

In one of these covered waggons, I went to the bagnio about ten o'clock. It was already full of women. It is built of stone in the shape of a dome, with no windows but in the roof, which gives light enough. There was five of these domes joined together, the outmost being less than the rest and serving only as a hall, where the portress stood at the door. Ladies of quality generally give this woman the value of a crown or ten shillings and I did not forget that ceremony. The next room is a very large one paved with marble, and all round it raised two sofas of marble one above another. There were four fountains of cold water in this room, falling first into marble basins, and then running on the floor in little channels made for that purpose, which carried the streams into the next room, something less than this, with the same sort of marble sofas, but so hot with steams of sulphur proceeding from the baths joining to it, 'twas impossible to stay there with one's clothes on. The two other domes were the hot baths, one of which had cocks of cold water turning into it to temper it to what degree of warmth the bathers have a mind to.

I was in my travelling habit, which is a riding dress, and certainly appeared very extraordinary to them. Yet there was not one of them that showed the least surprise or impertinent curiosity, but received me with all the obliging civility possible. I know no European court where the ladies would have behaved themselves in so polite

Greeks and Turks have a custom of putting round their eyes on the inside a black tincture that, at a distance, or by candlelight, adds very much to the blackness of them. I fancy many of our ladies would be overjoyed to know this secret, but 'tis too visible by day. They dye their nails rose colour; I own I cannot enough accustom myself to this fashion to find any beauty in it.

As to their morality or good conduct, I can say, like Harlequin, that 'tis just as 'tis with you, and the Turkish ladies don't commit one sin the less for not being Christians. Now that I am a little acquainted with their ways I cannot forbear admiring either the exemplary discretion or extreme stupidity of all the writers that have given accounts of them. 'Tis very easy to see they have more liberty than we have, no woman, of what rank so ever being permitted to go in the streets without two muslins, one that covers her face all but her eyes and another that hides the whole dress of her head, and hangs half way down her back and their shapes are also wholly concealed by a thing they call a *ferace* which no woman of any sort appears without. This has straight sleeves that reaches to their fingers ends and it laps all round them, not unlike a riding hood. In winter 'tis of cloth and in summer plain stuff or silk. You may guess then how effectually this disguises them, that there is no distinguishing the great lady from her slave and 'tis impossible for the most jealous husband to know his wife when he meets her, and no man dare either touch or follow a woman in the street.

This perpetual masquerade gives them entire liberty of following their inclinations without danger of discovery. The most usual method of intrigue is to send an appointment to the lover to meet the lady at a Jew's shop, which are as notoriously convenient as our Indian houses, and yet, even those that don't make use of them do not scruple to go to buy pennyworths and tumble over rich goods, which are chiefly to be found amongst that sort of people. The great ladies seldom let their gallants know who they are, and 'tis so difficult to find it out that they can very seldom guess at her name they have corresponded with above half a year together. You may easily imagine the number of faithful wives very small in a country where they have nothing to fear from their lovers' indiscretion, since we see so many that have the courage to expose themselves to that in this world, and all the threatened punishment of the next, which is never preached to the Turkish damsels. Neither have they much to apprehend from the resentment of their husbands, those ladies that are rich having all their money in their own hands, which they take with them upon a divorce with an addition which he is obliged to give them. Upon the whole, I look upon the Turkish women as the only free people in the empire. The very Divan pays respect to them and the Grand Signor himself, when a pasha is executed, never violates the privileges of the harem (or women's apartment) which remains unsearched entire to the widow. They are queens of their slaves, which the husband has no permission so much as to look upon, except it be an old woman or two that his lady chooses. 'Tis true, their law permits them four wives, but there is no instance of a man of quality that makes use of this liberty, or of a woman of rank that would suffer it. When a husband happens to be inconstant, as those things will happen, he keeps his mistress in a house apart and visits her as privately as he can, just as 'tis with you. Amongst all the great men here, I only know the *tefterdar* (ie treasurer) that keeps a number of she-slaves for his own use (that is, on his own side of the house, for a slave once given to serve a lady is entirely at her disposal) and he is spoke of as a libertine, or what we should call a rake, and his wife won't see him, though she continues to live in his house.

Thus you see, dear sister, the manners of mankind do not differ so widely as our voyage writers would make us believe. Perhaps it would be more entertaining to add a few surprising customs of my own invention, but nothing seems to me so agreeable as truth, and I believe nothing so acceptable to you. I conclude with repeating the great truth of my being, dear sister etc.

[. . .]

Now do I fancy that you imagine I have entertained you all this while with a relation that has, at least, received many embellishments from my hand. This is but too like, says you, the Arabian tales; these embroidered napkins, and a jewel as large as a turkey's egg! You forget, dear sister, those very tales were writ by an author of this country and, excepting the enchantments, are a real representation of the manners here. We travellers are in very hard circumstances. If we say nothing but what has been said before us we are dull and we have observed nothing. If we tell anything new, we are laughed at as fabulous and romantic, not allowing for the difference of ranks, which afford difference of company, more curiosity, or the changes of customs that happen every twenty year in every country. But people judge of travellers exactly with the same candour, good nature and impartiality they judge of their neighbours upon all occasions. For my part, if I live to return amongst you I am so well acquainted with the morals of all my dear friends and acquaintance that I am resolved to tell them nothing at all, to avoid the imputation, which their charity would certainly incline them to, of my telling too much. But I depend upon your knowing me enough to believe whatever I seriously assert for truth, though I give you leave to be surprised at an account so new to you. But what would you say if I told you that I have been in a harem where the winter apartment was wainscoted with inlaid work of mother of pearl, ivory of different colours and olive wood, exactly like the little boxes you have seen brought out of this country; and those rooms designed for summer, the walls all crusted with japan china, the roofs gilt and the floors spread with the finest Persian carpets. Yet there is nothing more true, such is the palace of my lovely friend, the fair Fatima, who I was acquainted with at Adrianople. I went to visit her yesterday and, if possible, she appeared to me handsomer than before. She met me at the door of her chamber and, giving me her hand with the best grace in the world: "You Christian ladies," said she with a smile that made her as handsome as an angel, "have the reputation of inconstancy, and I did not expect, whatever goodness you expressed for me at Adrianople, that I should ever see you again; but I am now convinced that I have really the happiness of pleasing you, and if you knew how I speak of you amongst our ladies you would be assured that you do me justice if you think me your friend." She placed me in the corner of the sofa and I spent the afternoon in her conversation with the greatest pleasure in the world.

Anne Elwood

Narrative of a Journey Overland to India
(1830)

In C——'s absence, I always remained in my own room; but one evening, as I went upon my terrace to enjoy the fresh sea-breeze which was just setting in, a casement which I had never before observed slowly opened, and a black hand appeared waving significantly at me. Impressed with some degree of fear, I immediately retreated, but on looking again, the waving was repeated; and several women peeping out, beckoned me to them, making signs that the men were all out of the way. Whilst I was hesitating, a Negro woman and a boy came out upon another terrace, and vehemently importuned me by signs to go to them. I had just been reading Lady Mary Wortley Montague's description of a Turkish Haram—an opportunity might never again occur of visiting an Arab one.—After some conflict between my fears and my curiosity, the latter conquered, and down I went, the boy meeting me at the foot of the stairs; and, lifting up a heavy curtain, he introduced me into a small interior court, at the door of which were a number of women's slippers, and inside were about a dozen females clothed in silk trowsers, vests closely fitting the figure, and fastening in front, and turbans very tastefully put on. They received me with the utmost cordiality and delight, the principal lady, Zaccara, as I found she was called, making me sit down by her side, caressingly taking my hand, presenting me with a nosegay, and, after previously tasting it, offering me coffee, which was brought on a silver tray, in the usual beautiful little china cups. It was, however, so perfumed that I could scarcely drink it. She did the honours, and appeared as superior to the others in manners and address, as an English lady would be to her maid-servants. Her figure was light and slender—her features pretty and delicate—her countenance lively and intelligent,—whilst her manners, which were peculiarly soft and pleasing, were at the same time both affectionate and sprightly. The other women crowded round me with great *empressement*; by signs we kept up a very animated conversation, and when we could not quite comprehend each other's meaning, we all laughed heartily. They asked me where I came from, whether I had many ornaments, any children, &c. exhibiting theirs with great glee. They were amazingly struck with my costume, which they examined so minutely, that I began to think I should have had to undress to satisfy their curiosity;—but what most amused them, was, the circumstance of my gown fastening *behind*, which mystery they examined over and over again, and some broad French tucks at the bottom seemed much to astonish them, as they could not discover their use. They asked me the names of every thing I had on, and when, to please them, I took off my cap, and let down my long hair, Zaccara, following my example, immediately took off her turban and showed me hers: the Negro woman, who seemed the wit of the party, in the mean time holding up the lace cap upon her broad fat hand, and exhibiting it to all around, apparently with great admiration, exclaiming "caap, caap," and also endeavouring, much to their detriment, to put on my gloves, with which they were particularly amused. I sat with them some time, and it was with difficulty they consented to allow me to leave them at last; indeed, not till I made them understand my "Cowasjee" wanted me. Cowasjee's claims they seemed to understand completely, and, on my rejoining the gentlemen, if I were amused with their description of the tournament, you may conceive how astonished they were to learn that I had been actually visiting the Haram!

On the following morning I had an invitation, in form, to repeat my visit, and I was conducted up a very handsome collegiate-looking staircase, near which was stationed the master of the house, apparently at his devotions, but evidently intending to have a furtive peep at me, without my being aware of his so doing. I was now received *in state* in the interior apartments, and all the ladies were much more splendidly dressed than on the preceding evening. Zaccara had on handsome striped silk drawers, and a silk vest descending to her feet, richly trimmed with silver lace. All their hands and feet were dyed with henna, and they were much surprised to see mine of their natural colour. The furniture consisted principally of couches ranged round the room, upon which they invited me to sit cross-legged, after their own mode, and seemed astonished at my preferring our European style. On the walls was a sentence of the Koran framed and glazed, and in a recess was an illuminated Koran, which they showed me. An interesting-looking young woman, seated in a low chair, was employed in making silver lace, the process of which she explained to me, as also its use to trim vests and turbans. My costume underwent the same minute investigation as on the yesterday, and as at this time I had on no cap, they were much struck with the manner in which my hair was dressed, and my shoes and stockings created universal astonishment. Refreshments were brought, but every thing was carefully tasted before it was offered to me,—I suppose to show no treachery was intended,—and I was again interrogated as to my ornaments, children, &c. They told me all their names, and endeavoured, but in vain, to accomplish mine.

Suddenly there was a shriek of joy, laughing and clapping of hands. They drew me quickly to the window, from whence I saw C——walking in the streets, with one of his servants holding an umbrella over his head, surrounded by an immense concourse of people; and very foreign he certainly did look in the streets of Hodeida, with his English dress and hat. The delight of my fair, or rather of my dusky friends, was beyond description; but it was redoubled, when they found it was *my* Cowasjee. The master of the house then came in: he treated me with the greatest deference and respect, and, bringing me a little baby with gold rings in its nose and ears, with all a father's pride he informed me it was his, and that Zaccara was its mother.

He also asked me about my children and my ornaments, the two things always apparently foremost in an Oriental imagination. My wedding-ring catching the eyes of the women, I made them partly understand its signification, but they evidently seemed to consider it as *a charm*.

Zaccara then taking my hand with a very caressing air, invited me to accompany her, and she showed me all over the house. It was completely "upstairs, downstairs, in my lady's chamber," and I saw a number of small rooms, with loopholes and windows in every direction, where they could see without being seen. They pointed out to me our Ship, the Bazaar, the Mosque, from whence the Dowlah was just returning in grand procession; and they then exhibited to me all their ornaments and trinkets. In return, I showed them such as I had about me. My friend the negro woman, poor black Zacchina as she was called, was the only one who ventured to smell to my salts, and this she did with so much eagerness, that the tears were forced into her eyes in consequence, to the great amusement of her companions.

We parted with mutual expressions of regard; and though I had met with neither the beauty of Fatima, nor the luxury of a Turkish Haram, yet I was well pleased with the simplicity, mirth, and happiness, that apparently reigned in the Arab one; and I should have been churlish indeed had I not been gratified with their friendly and artless attempts to please me. Indeed, I flatter myself I made a conquest, for a great boy of twelve or fourteen took such a fancy to me, that he volunteered to accompany me to "Hindy" in the "Merkab," or ship, and he really appeared anxious for me to accept of his services. What should you have thought of my Arab page? The women in Arabia are, apparently, allowed more liberty than in Egypt, for they seemed to be permitted to walk out together whenever they pleased; and once, as we were setting out for, and they were returning from a promenade, we met in the court. They were so carefully veiled, that I had some difficulty to recognize my friends of the Haram again, but they affectionately seized my hand, and caressingly invited me to return with them to their apartments. All the gentlemen were with me, and I cannot help thinking that the Arab ladies prolonged their interview purposely, in order to have a better view of the Fringee Cowasjees, my companions.

Harriet Martineau

Eastern Life, Present and Past
(1848)

I saw two Hareems in the East; and it would be wrong to pass them over in an account of my travels; though the subject is as little agreeable as any I can have to treat. I cannot now think of the two mornings thus employed without a heaviness of heart greater than I have ever brought away from Deaf and Dumb Schools, Lunatic Asylums, or even Prisons. As such are my impressions of hareems, of course I shall not say whose they were that I visited. Suffice it that one was at Cairo and the other at Damascus.

The royal hareems were not accessible while I was in Egypt. The Pasha's eldest daughter, the widow of Defterdar Bey, was under her father's displeasure, and was, in fact, a prisoner in her own house. While her father did not visit her, no one else could: and while she was secluded, her younger sister could not receive visitors: and thus, their hareems were closed.—The one which I saw was that of a gentleman of high rank; and as good a specimen as could be seen. The misfortune was that there was a mistake about the presence of an interpreter. A lady was to have met us who spoke Italian or French: but she did not arrive; and the morning therefore passed in dumb show: and we could not repeat our visit on a subsequent day, as we were invited to do. We lamented this much at the time: but our subsequent experience of what is to be learned in a hareem with the aid of an intelligent and kind interpretess convinced us that we had not lost much.

Before I went abroad, more than one sensible friend had warned me to leave behind as many prejudices as possible; and especially on this subject, on which the prejudices of Europeans are the strongest. I was reminded of the wide extent, both of time and space, in which Polygamy had existed; and that openness of mind was as necessary to the accurate observation of this institution as of every other. I had really taken this advice to heart: I had been struck by the view taken by Mr. Milnes in his beautiful poem of "the Hareem;" and I am sure I did meet this subject with every desire to investigate the ideas and general feelings involved in it. I learned a very great deal about the working of the institution; and I believe I apprehend the thoughts and feelings of the persons concerned in it: and I declare that if we are to look for a hell upon earth, it is where polygamy exists: and that, as polygamy runs riot in Egypt, Egypt is the lowest depth of this hell. I always before believed that every arrangement and prevalent practice had some one fair side,—some one redeeming quality: and diligently did I look for this fair side in regard to polygamy: but there is none. The longer one studies the subject, and the deeper one penetrates into it,—the more is one's mind confounded with the intricacy of its iniquity, and the more does one's heart feel as if it would break.

I shall say but little of what I know. If there were the slightest chance of doing any good, I would speak out at all hazards;—I would meet all the danger, and endure all the disgust. But there is no reaching the minds of any who live under the accursed system. It is a system which belongs to a totally different region of ideas from ours: and there is nothing to appeal to in the minds of those who, knowing the facts of the institution, can endure it: and at home, no one needs appealing to and convincing. Any plea for liberality that we meet at home proceeds from some poetical fancy, or some laudable desire for impartiality in the absence of knowledge of the facts. Such pleas are not operative enough to render it worth while to shock and sadden many hearts by statements which no one should be required needlessly to endure. I will tell only something of what I saw; and but little of what I thought and know.

At ten o'clock, one morning, Mrs. Y. and I were home from our early ride, and dressed for our visit to a hareem of a high order. The lady to whose kindness we mainly owed this opportunity, accompanied us, with her daughter. We had a dis- agreeable drive in the carriage belonging to the hotel, knocking against asses, horses and people all the way. We alighted at the entrance of a paved passage leading to a court which we crossed: and then, in a second court, we were before the entrance of the hareem.

A party of eunuchs stood before a faded curtain, which they held aside when the gentlemen of our party and the dragoman had gone forward. Retired some way behind the curtain stood, in a half circle, eight or ten slave girls, in an attitude of deep obeisance. Two of them then took charge of each of us, holding us by the arms above the elbows, to help us upstairs.—After crossing a lobby at the top of the stairs, we entered a handsome apartment, where lay the chief wife,—at that time an invalid.—The ceiling was gaily painted; and so were the walls,—the latter with curi- ously bad attempts at domestic perspective. There were four handsome mirrors; and the curtains in the doorway were of a beautiful shawl fabric, fringed and tasselled. A Turkey carpet not only covered the whole floor, but was turned up at the corners. Deewáns extended round nearly the whole room,—a lower one for ordinary use, and a high one for the seat of honour. The windows, which had a sufficient fence of blinds, looked upon a pretty garden, where I saw orange trees and many others, and the fences were hung with rich creepers.

On cushions on the floor lay the chief lady, ill and miserable-looking. She rose as we entered; but we made her lie down again: and she was then covered with a silk counterpane. Her dress was, as we saw when she rose, loose trowsers of blue striped cotton under her black silk jacket: and the same blue cotton appeared at the wrists, under her black sleeves. Her headdress was of black net, bunched out curiously behind. Her hair was braided down the sides of this headdress behind, and the ends were pinned over her forehead. Some of the black net was brought round her face, and under the chin, showing the outline of a face which had no beauty in it, nor traces of former beauty, but which was interesting to-day from her manifest illness and unhappiness. There was a strong expression of waywardness and peevishness about the mouth, however. She wore two handsome diamond rings; and she and one other lady had watches and gold chains. She complained of her head; and her left hand was bound up: she made signs by pressing her bosom, and imitating the dandling of a baby, which, with her occasional tears, persuaded my companions that she had met with some accident and had lost her infant. On leaving the hareem, we found that it was not a child of her own that she was mourning, but that of a white girl in the hareem: and that the wife's illness was wholly from grief for the loss of this baby;—a curious illustration of the feelings and manners of the place! The chil- dren born in large hareems are extremely few: and they are usually idolised, and sometimes murdered. It is known that in the houses at home which morally most resemble these hareems (though little enough externally) when the rare event of the birth of a child happens, a passionate joy extends over the wretched household:— jars are quieted, drunkenness is moderated, and there is no self-denial which the poor creatures will not undergo during this gratification of their feminine instincts. They will nurse the child all night in illness, and pamper it all day with sweetmeats and toys; they will fight for the possession of it, and be almost heartbroken at its loss: and lose it they must; for the child always dies,—killed with kindness, even if born healthy. This natural outbreak of feminine instinct takes place in the too pop-ulous hareem, when a child is given to any one of the many who are longing for the gift: and if it dies naturally, it is mourned as we saw through a wonderful conquest of personal jealousy by this general instinct. But when the jealousy is uppermost,—what happens then?—why, the strangling the innocent in its sleep,—or the letting it slip from the window into the river below,—or the mixing poison with its food;—the mother and the murderess, always rivals and now fiends, being shut up together for life. If the child lives, what then? If a girl, she sees before her from the beginning the nothingness of external life, and the chaos of interior existence, in which she is to dwell for life. If a boy, he remains among the women till ten years old, seeing things when the eunuchs come in to romp, and hearing things among the chatter of the ignorant women which brutalise him for life before the age of rationality comes. But I will not dwell on these hopeless miseries.

A sensible looking old lady, who had lost an eye, sat at the head of the invalid: and a nun-like elderly woman, whose head and throat were wrapped in unstarched muslin, sat behind for a time, and then went away, after an affectionate salutation to the invalid.—Towards the end of the visit, the husband's mother came in,—looking like a little old man in her coat trimmed with fur. Her countenance was cheerful and pleasant. We saw, I think, about twenty more women,—some slaves,—most or all young—some goodlooking, but none handsome. Some few were black; and the rest very light:—Nubians or Abyssinians and Circassians, no doubt. One of the best figures, as a picture, in the hareem, was a Nubian girl, in an amber-coloured watered silk, embroidered with black, looped up in festoons, and finished with a black boddice. The richness of the gay printed cotton skirts and sleeves surprised us: the finest shawls could hardly have looked better. One graceful girl had her pretty figure well shown by a tight-fitting black dress. Their heads were dressed much like the chief lady's. Two, who must have been sisters, if not twins, had patches between the eyes. One handmaid was barefoot, and several were without shoes. Though there were none of the whole large number who could be called particularly pretty indi-vidually, the scene was, on the whole, exceedingly striking, as the realisation of what one knew before, but as in a dream. The girls went out and came in, but, for the most part, stood in a half circle. Two sat on their heels for a time: and some went to play in the neighbouring apartments.

Coffee was handed to us twice, with all the well-known apparatus of jewelled cups, embroidered tray cover, and gold-flowered napkins. There were chibouques, for course: and sherbets in cut glass cups. The time was passed in attempts to have conversation by signs; attempts which are fruitless among people of the different ideas which belong to different races. How much they made out about us, we do not know: but they inquired into the mutual relationships of the party, and put the extraordinary questions which are always put to ladies who visit the hareems.—A young lady of my acquaintance, of the age of eighteen, but looking younger, went with her mother to a hareem in Cairo (not the one I have been describing) and excited great amazement when obliged to confess that she had not either children or a husband. One of the wives threw her arms about her, intreated her to stay for ever, said she should have any husband she liked, but particularly recommended her own, saying that she was sure he would soon wish for another wife, and she had so much rather it should be my young friend, who would amuse her continually, than anybody else that she could not be so fond of. Everywhere they pitied us European women heartily, that we had to go about travelling, and appearing in the streets without being properly taken care of,—that is watched. They think us strangely neglected in being left so free, and boast of their spy system and imprisonment as tokens of the value in which they are held.

The mourning worn by the lady who went with us was the subject of much speculation: and many questions were asked about her home and family. To appease the curiosity about her home, she gave her card. As I anticipated, this did not answer. It was the great puzzle of the whole interview. At first the poor lady thought it was to do her head good: then, she fidgetted about it, in the evident fear of omitting some observance: but at last, she understood that she was to keep it. When we had taken our departure, however, a eunuch was sent after us to inquire of the dragoman what "the letter" was which our companion had given to the lady.

The difficulty is to get away, when one is visiting a hareem. The poor ladies cannot conceive of one's having anything to do; and the only reason they can understand for the interview coming to an end is the arrival of sunset, after which it would, they think, be improper for any woman to be abroad. And the amusement to them of such a visit is so great that they protract it to the utmost, even in such a case as ours to-day, when all intercourse was conducted by dumb show. It is certainly very tiresome; and the only wonder is that the hostesses can like it. To sit hour after hour on the deewán, without any exchange of ideas, having our clothes examined, and being plied with successive cups of coffee and sherbet, and pipes, and being gazed at by a half-circle of girls in brocade and shawls, and made to sit down again as soon as one attempts to rise, is as wearisome an experience as one meets with in foreign lands.—The weariness of heart is, however, the worst part of it. I noted all the faces well during our constrained stay; and I saw no trace of mind in any one except in the homely one-eyed old lady. All the younger ones were dull, soulless, brutish, or peevish. How should it be otherwise, when the only idea of their whole lives is that which, with all our interests and engagements, we consider too prominent with us? There cannot be a woman of them all who is not dwarfed and withered in mind and soul by being kept wholly engrossed with that one interest,— detained at that stage in existence which, though most important in its place, is so as a means to ulterior ends. The ignorance is fearful enough; but the grossness is revolting.

At the third move, and when it was by some means understood that we were waited for, we were permitted to go,—after a visit of above two hours. The sick lady rose from her cushions, notwithstanding our opposition, and we were conducted forth with much observance. On each side of the curtain which overhung the outer entrance stood a girl with a bottle of rose water, some of which was splashed in our faces as we passed out.

We had reached the carriage when we were called back:—his Excellency was waiting for us. So we visited him in a pretty apartment, paved with variegated marbles, and with a fountain in the centre. His Excellency was a sensible-looking man, with gay, easy and graceful manners. He lamented the mistake about the interpreter, and said we must go again, when we might have conversation. He insisted upon attending us to the carriage, actually passing between the files of beggars which lined the outer passage. The dragoman was so excessively shocked by this degree of condescension, that we felt obliged to be so too, and remonstrated; but in vain. He stood till the door was shut, and the whip was cracked. He is a liberal-minded man; and his hareem is nearly as favourable a specimen as could be selected for a visit; but what is this best specimen? I find these words written down on the same day, in my journal: written, as I well remember, in heaviness of heart. "I am glad of the opportunity of seeing a hareem: but it leaves an impression of discontent and uneasiness which I shall be glad to sleep off. And I am not conscious that there is prejudice in this. I feel that a visit to the worst room in the Rookery in St. Giles's would have affected me less painfully. There are there at least the elements of a rational life, however perverted; while here humanity is wholly and hopelessly baulked. It will never do to look on this as a case for cosmopolitan philosophy to regard complacently, and require a good construction for. It is not a phase of natural early manners. It is as pure a conventionalism as our representative monarchy, or German heraldry, or Hindoo caste; and the most atrocious in the world."

And of this atrocious system, Egypt is the most atrocious example. It has unequalled facilities for the importation of black and white slaves; and these facilities are used to the utmost; yet the population is incessantly on the decline. But for the importation of slaves, the upper classes, where polygamy runs riot, must soon die out,—so few are the children born, and so fatal to health are the arrangements of society. The finest children are those born of Circassian or Georgian mothers; and but for these, we should soon hear little more of an upper class in Egypt.—Large numbers are brought from the south,—the girls to be made attendants or concubines in the hareem, and the boys to be made, in a vast proportion, those guards to the female part of the establishment whose mere presence is a perpetual insult and shame to humanity. The business of keeping up the supply of these miserable wretches,—of whom the Pasha's eldest daughter has fifty for her exclusive service,—is in the hands of the Christians of Asyoot. It is these Christians who provide a sufficient supply, and cause a sufficient mortality to keep the number of the sexes pretty equal: in consideration of which we cannot much wonder that Christianity does not appear very venerable in the eyes of Mohammedans.

These eunuchs are indulged in regard to dress, personal liberty, and often the possession of office, domestic, military, or political. When retained as guards of the hareem, they are in their master's confidence,—acting as his spies, and indispensable to the ladies, as a medium of communication with the world, and as furnishing their amusements,—being at once playmates and servants. It is no unusual thing for the eunuchs to whip the ladies away from a window, whence they had hoped for amusement; or to call them opprobrious names; or to inform against them to their owner: and it is also no unusual thing for them to romp with the ladies, to obtain their confidence, and to try their dispositions. Cases have been known of one of them becoming the friend of some poor girl of higher nature and tendencies than her companions; and even of a closer attachment, which is not objected to by the proprietor of both. It is a case too high for his jealousy, so long as he knows that the cage is secure. It has become rather the fashion to extenuate the lot of the captive of either sex: to point out how the Nubian girl, who would have ground corn and woven garments, and nursed her infants in comparative poverty all her days, is now surrounded by luxury, and provided for for life: and how the Circassian girl may become a wife of the son of her proprietor, and hold a high rank in the hareem: and how the wretched brothers of these slaves may rise to posts of military command or political confidence; but it is enough to see them to be disabused of all impressions of their good fortune. It is enough to see the dull and gross face of the handmaid of the hareem, and to remember at the moment the cheerful, modest countenance of the Nubian girl busy about her household tasks, or of the Nubian mother, with her infants hanging about her as she looks, with face open to the sky, for her husband's return from the field, or meets him on the river bank. It is enough to observe the wretched health and abject, or worn, or insolent look of the guard of the hareem, and to remember that he ought to have been the head of a household of his own, however humble: and in this contrast of what is with what ought to have been, slavery is seen to be fully as detestable here as anywhere else. These two hellish practices, slavery and polygamy, which, as practices, can clearly never be separated, are here avowedly connected; and in that connected, are exalted into a double institution, whose working is such as to make one almost wish that the Nile would rise to cover the tops of the hills, and sweep away the whole abomination. Till this happens, there is, in the condition of Egypt, a fearful warning before the eyes of all men. The Egyptians laugh at the marriage arrangements of Europe, declaring that virtual polygamy exists everywhere, and is not improved by hypocritical concealment. The European may see, when startled by the state of Egypt, that virtual slavery is indispensably required by the practice of polygamy; virtual proprietorship of the women involved, without the obligations imposed by actual proprietorship; and cruel oppression of the men who should have been the husbands of these women. And again, the Carolina planter, who knows as well as any Egyptian that polygamy is a natural concomitant of slavery, may see in the state of Egypt and the Egyptians what his country and his children must come to, if either of those vile arrangements is permitted which necessitates the other.

It is scarcely needful to say that those benevolent persons are mistaken who believe that Slavery in Egypt has been abolished by the Pasha, and the importation of slaves effectually prohibited. Neither the Pasha nor any other human power can abolish slavery while Polygamy is an institution of the country, the proportion of the sexes remaining in Egypt what it is, there and everywhere else.

41

The reason assigned by Montesquieu for polygamy throughout the East has no doubt something in it:—that women become so early marriageable that the wife cannot satisfy the needs of the husband's mind and heart: and that therefore he must have both a bride and a companion of whom he may make a friend. How little there is in this to excuse the polygamy of Egypt may be seen by an observation of the state of things there and in Turkey, where the same religion and natural laws prevail as in Egypt. In Egypt, the difficulty would be great of finding a wife of any age who could be the friend of a man of any sense: and in Turkey, where the wives are of a far higher order, polygamy is rare, and women are not married so young. It is not usual there to find such disparity of years as one finds in Egypt between the husband and his youngest wife. The cause assigned by Montesquieu is true in connexion with a vicious state of society: but it is not insuperable, and it will operate only as long as it is wished for. If any influence could exalt the ideas of marriage, and improve the training of women in Egypt, it would soon be seen that men would prefer marrying women of nearly their own age, and would naturally remain comparatively constant: but before this experiment can be tried, parents must have ceased to become restless when their daughter reaches eleven years old, and afraid of disgrace if she remains unmarried long after that.

I was told, while at Cairo, of one extraordinary family where there is not only rational intercourse and confidence at home, and some relaxation of imprisonment, but the young ladies read!—and read French and Italian! I asked what would be the end of this: and my informant replied that whether the young ladies married or not, they would sooner or later sink down, he thought, into a state even less contented than the ordinary. There could be no sufficient inducement for secluded girls, who never saw anybody wiser than themselves, to go on reading French and Italian books within a certain range. For want of stimulus and sympathy, they would stop; and then, finding themselves dissatisfied among the nothings which fill the life of other women, they would be very unhappy. The exceptional persons under a bad state of things, and the beginners under an improving system must ever be sufferers,—martyrs of their particular reformation. To this they may object less than others would for them, if they are conscious of the personal honour and general blessing of their martyrdom.

The youngest wife I ever saw (except the swathed and veiled brides we encountered in the streets of Egyptian cities) was in a Turkish hareem which Mrs. Y. and I visited at Damascus. I will tell that story now, that I may dismiss the subject of this chapter. I heartily dreaded this second visit to a hareem, and braced myself up to it as one does to an hour at the dentist's, or to an expedition into the City to prove a debt. We had the comfort of a good and pleasant interpreter; and there was more mirth and nonsense than in the Cairo hareem; and therefore somewhat less disgust and constraint: but still it was painful enough. We saw the seven wives of three gentlemen, and a crowd of attendants and visitors. Of the seven, two had been the wives of the head of the household, who was dead: three were the wives of his eldest son, aged twenty-two; and the remaining two were the wives of his second son, aged fifteen. The youngest son, aged thirteen, was not yet married; but he would be thinking about it soon.—The pair of widows were elderly women, as merry as girls, and quite at their ease. Of the other five, three were sisters:—that is, we conclude, half-sisters;—children of different mothers in the same hareem. It is evident at a glance what a tragedy lies under this; what the horrors of jealousy must be among sisters thus connected for life;—three of them between two husbands in the same house! And we were told that the jealousy had begun, young as they were, and the third having been married only a week.—This young creature, aged twelve, was the bride of the husband of fifteen. She was the most conspicuous person in the place, not only for the splendour of her dress, but because she sat on the deewán, while the others sat or lounged on cushions on the raised floor. The moment we took our seats I was struck with compassion for this child,—she looked so grave, and sad and timid. While the others romped and giggled, pushing and pulling one another about, and laughing at jokes among themselves, she never smiled, but looked on listlessly. I was determined to make her laugh before we went away; and at last she relaxed somewhat,—smiling, and growing grave again in a moment: but at length she really and truly laughed; and when we were shown the whole hareem, she also slipped her bare and dyed feet into her pattens inlaid with mother-of-pearl, and went into the courts with us, nestling to us, and seeming to lose the sense of her new position for the time: but there was far less of the gaiety of a child about her than in the elderly widows. Her dress was superb;—a full skirt and boddice of geranium-coloured brocade, embossed with gold flowers and leaves; and her frill and ruffles were of geranium-coloured gauze. Her eyebrows were frightful,—joined and pro-longed by black paint. Her head was covered with a silk net, in almost every mesh of which were stuck jewels or natural flowers: so that her head was like a bouquet sprinkled with diamonds. Her nails were dyed black; and her feet were dyed black in chequers. Her complexion, called white, was of an unhealthy yellow: and indeed we did not see a healthy complexion among the whole company; nor anywhere among women who were secluded from exercise, while pampered with all the luxuries of eastern living.

Besides the seven wives, a number of attendants came in to look at us, and serve the pipes and sherbet; and a few ladies from a neighbouring hareem; and a party of Jewesses, with whom we had some previous acquaintance. Mrs. Y. was compelled to withdraw her lace veil, and then to take off her bonnet: and she was instructed that the street was the place for her to wear her veil down, and that they expected to see her face. Then her bonnet went round, and was tried on many heads,—one merry girl wearing it long enough to surprise many new comers with the joke.—My gloves were stretched and pulled all manner of ways, in their attempts to thrust their large, broad brown hands into them, one after another. But the great amusement was my trumpet. The eldest widow, who sat next me, asked for it, and put it to her ear; when I said "Bo!" When she had done laughing, she put it into her next neighbour's ear, and said "Bo!" and in this way it came round to me again. But in two minutes, it was asked for again, and went round a second time,—every body laughing as loud as ever at each "Bo!"—and then a third time! Could one have conceived it!—The next joke was on behalf of the Jewesses, four or five of whom sat in a row on the deewán. Almost everybody else was puffing away at a chibouque or a nargeeleh, and the place was one cloud of smoke. The poor Jewesses were obliged to decline joining us; for it happened to be Saturday: they must not smoke on the sabbath. They were naturally much pitied: and some of the young wives did what was possible for them. Drawing in a long breath of smoke, they puffed it forth in the faces of the Jewesses, who opened mouth and nostrils eagerly to receive it. Thus was the sabbath observed, to shouts of laughter.

A pretty little blue-eyed girl of seven was the only child we saw. She nestled against her mother; and the mother clasped her closely, lest we should carry her off to London. She begged we would not wish to take her child to London, and said she "would not sell her for much money."—One of the wives was pointed out to us as particularly happy in the prospect of becoming a mother; and we were taken to see the room in which she was to lie in, which was all in readiness, though the event was not looked for for more than half a year. She was in the gayest spirits, and sang and danced. While she was lounging on her cushions, I thought her the handsomest and most graceful, as well as the happiest, of the party: but when she rose to dance, the charm was destroyed for ever. The dancing is utterly disgusting. A pretty Jewess of twelve years old danced, much in the same way; but with downcast eyes and an air of modesty. While the dancing went on, and the smoking, and drinking coffee and sherbet, and the singing, to the accompaniment of a tambourine, some hideous old hags came in successively, looked and laughed, and went away again. Some negresses made a good back ground to this thoroughly Eastern picture. All the while, romping, kissing and screaming went on among the ladies, old and young. At first, I thought them a perfect rabble; but when I recovered myself a little, I saw that there was some sense in the faces of the elderly women.—In the midst of all this fun, the interpretess assured us that "there is much jealousy every day;" jealousy of the favoured wife; that is, in this case, of the one who was pointed out to us by her companions as so eminently happy, and with whom they were romping and kissing, as with the rest. Poor thing! even the happiness of these her best days is hollow: for she cannot have, at the same time, peace in the hareem and her husband's love.

They were so free in their questions about us, and so evidently pleased when we used a similar impertinence about them, that we took the opportunity of learning a good deal of their way of life. Mrs. Y. and I were consulting about noticing the bride's dress, when we found we had put off too long: we were asked how we liked her dress, and encouraged to handle the silk. So I went on to examine the bundles of false hair that some of them wore; the pearl bracelets on their tattooed arms, and their jewelled and inlaid pattens.—In answer to our question what they did in the way of occupation, they said "nothing:" but when we inquired whether they never made clothes or sweetmeats, they replied "yes."—They earnestly wished us to stay always; and they could not understand why we should not. My case puzzled them particularly. I believe they took me for a servant; and they certainly pitied me extremely for having to go about without being taken care of. They asked what I did: and Mrs. Y., being anxious to do me all honour, told them I had written many books: but the information was thrown away, because they did not know what a book was. Then we informed them that I lived in a field among mountains, where I had built a house; and that I had plenty to do; and we told them in what way: but still they could make nothing of it but that I had brought the stones with my own hands, and built the house myself. There is nothing about which the inmates of hareems seem to be so utterly stupid as about women having any thing to do. That time should be valuable to a woman, and that she should have any business on her hands, and any engagements to observe, are things quite beyond their comprehension.

The pattens I have mentioned are worn to keep the feet and flowing dress from the marble pavement, which is often wetted for coolness. I think all the ladies here had bare feet. When they left the raised floor on which they sat, they slipped their feet into their high pattens, and went stumping about, rather awkwardly. I asked Dr. Thompson, who has admission as a physician into more houses than any other man could familiarly visit, whether he could not introduce skipping-ropes upon these spacious marble floors. I see no other chance of the women being induced to take exercise. They suffer cruelly from indigestion,—gorging themselves with sweet things, smoking intemperately, and passing through life with more than half the brain almost unawakened, and with scarcely any exercise of the limbs. Poor things! our going was a great amusement to them, they said; and they showed this by their intreaties to the last moment that we would not leave them yet, and that we would stay always.—"And these," as my journal says, "were human beings, such as those of whom Christ made friends!—The chief lady gave me roses as a farewell token.— The Jewish ladies, who took their leave with us, wanted us to visit at another house: but we happily had not time.—I am thankful to have seen a hareem under favourable circumstances; and I earnestly hope I may never see another."

I kept those roses, however. I shall need no reminding of the most injured human beings I have ever seen,—the most studiously depressed and corrupted women whose condition I have witnessed: but I could not throw away the flowers which so found their way into my hand as to bespeak for the wrongs of the giver the mournful remembrance of my heart.

[Emilia Bithynia] Lady Hornby

Constantinople During the Crimean War
(1863)

But for our Harem visit. We said good-bye to our friends at Mysseri's, stepped each into a sedan-chair (painted on the back with two comical-looking British lions shaking hands in the most violent manner), and with M. Robolli, mounted on a gallant grey, as our escort, passed up and down hill in the steep side-streets of Pera. Our stout Armenian chairmen hurried the three sedans through still more crowded streets, over the Bridge of Boats, and soon into the silent regions of Stamboul, where veiled women were stealing noiselessly along, and the closely-latticed windows and high walls gave one an idea of a vast convent. Many of these dark-eyed ladies had a veiled black slave behind them, carrying small baskets of hyacinths, jonquils, and other flowers, from the flower-markets. At last, after interminable windings and turnings, we arrived at the half-open gates of an immense courtyard, surrounded by a wall which would have graced a castle of old. I almost expected to see a horn hanging at the gate, with the challenge of the giant within, written in letters of brass. However, M. Robolli rode in without interruption, and the three sedans followed. Some Turks mending the pavement, stared at us with great curiosity: I dare say they thought the Pasha had bought three English slaves.

We were set down in a large circular hall, covered with matting, and were immediately surrounded by numbers of the Pasha's retainers, principally cavasses (a kind of freelance footmen) and chibouquejees (pipe-bearers). These gentlemen were entertaining themselves with a most minute inspection of us, when down the vast staircase (with two flights, *à la Fontainebleau*) came the Chief of the Eunuchs, as hideous and as angry as a Black could possibly be. He dispersed the mob right and left, evidently claiming us as Harem visitors. M. Robolli was conducted with us as far as the first suite of rooms, and he then retired to the apartments of the Pasha, leaving us in the hands of this "bird of night," who was now joined by two others.

At last our conductor stopped on the third and last floor, which is always the principal in Turkish houses, on account of the view. He lifted up the crimson arras, and with a hideous grin invited us to enter. Madame de Souci and Mrs. Brown, who are both very new arrivals at Constantinople, were rather nervous, and begged me to go in first. I had seen how sweetly gentle and kind the Turkish women are, and lifted up the charmed curtain with much more confidence and pleasure than I should have entered an assembly of Englishwomen. I shall not easily forget the sight which presented itself. We were in the midst of a vast apartment, with a lofty, dome-like roof, carved with gigantic wreaths of flowers and pomegranates. An immense staircase was on the other side, lighted by a window which reached from roof to floor,

and in the projecting half-moon of the balusters was a beautiful white-marble fountain. The whole was covered with the same gold-coloured matting. Rich crimson
divans under each enormous window at either end, and raised three steps. The
window looking towards the streets of Stamboul was latticed, with round peep-holes;
but the other was free from even a blind, and the beautiful blue Bosphorus and Sea
of Marmora, with many stately ships upon them, the mountains in the distance, still
glittering here and there with snow,—and nearer, the dark cypresses, and the
minarets of Santa Sophia and numerous other mosques, lay in a grand picture of
quite inconceivable beauty below it. Here, evidently in a dreamy kind of reverie, sat
the principal wife of—Pasha, surrounded by her slaves, some sitting on the steps
beneath the divan, at her feet, others laughing together and strolling about. She rose
as we approached, and gave her hand, after the English fashion, to each. The slaves
all crowded round to look at us, and I assure you that the variety and brilliancy of
their costumes was almost dazzling.

But I must first tell you the dress of the great lady. Her selma, or wide-sleeved
under dress, (trousers, etc.) was of a delicate violet-colour, bound round the waist
by a richly embroidered scarf; her shirt of silvery Broussa gauze. Over this was a magnificent jacket of amber-coloured cashmere, lined with the richest sable. On her head
she wore a fez, bound round with a large plait of hair, which was fastened every here
and there with immense rose-diamonds. A purple lily-flower was stuck straight down
this plait, and shaded her forehead. Her earrings were of a single pendant emerald,
set in a small spray of brilliants. She must have been of surpassing beauty, and was
still strikingly handsome, with perfectly regular features, and skin dark but clear, a
brow and upper-lip which would have graced a Roman Empress. Indeed we made
up our minds at once that it was a Roman Empress she was like.

Rising, she motioned us to follow her, and the principal slaves officiously lifted
the hangings of one of the numerous doorways surrounding this immense apartment. We entered a charming room, evidently a Turkish boudoir, with an immense
window, divans all round it, and the same enchanting view. Here we three poor
Englishwomen sat in a row, distressingly anxious to converse and make ourselves
agreeable, and knowing about a dozen words between us, including the detestable
"*bono*" and "*no bono*," which we were heartily sick and ashamed of. I tried Italian;
Madame Ayesha, I will call her, shook her majestic head; Madame de Souci murmured a few graceful words of thanks in French; at which Madame Ayesha solemnly
uttered the word "*Oui*," and all the slaves, black men included, laughed with joy
and pride at their mistress's accomplishments. This was accounted for by—Pasha
having been Minister at Vienna, and his speaking French.[1]

The hangings of the two doors were constantly being lifted, and more women as
constantly trooping in to peep at us. Some giggled and ran away; others advanced
boldly up the room, and evidently spoke to their mistress about us. Some sat them-

---

[1] As the Turks so particularly forbid any sort of portraits of their women, I have in this edition left out
the real name of the Pasha and of the ladies.

selves down cross-legged at the further end of the room, staring at us to their heart's content, and talking about us in whispers. We, meantime, were talking to each other about them. But presently a splendidly dressed black slave lifted the arras, and behind her appeared a most lovely young Circassian lady, who was, as we afterwards found out, the Pasha's second wife, and a present from the Sultan. She was very tall; but it is impossible to describe her winning beauty, or the exquisite grace of her movements. We were all three instantly charmed with her, and no longer regretted their not understanding English; it was such a pleasure to exclaim every now and then, "Oh you pretty creature!" "Did you ever see such a figure?" "Do look at the shape of her head and throat." "What a lovely mouth! and just listen to her voice." "There's a plait of glossy hair! quite down to her feet it must be when unbound!" This pretty creature, whom we instantly named "the fair Circassian," seemed to be on excellent terms with her majestic colleague. They saluted each other after their usual fashion, and she bowed to us very gracefully when we rose to do her honour, saying something which seemed to be a welcome. I must now tell you her dress. Her trousers, and the robe which twists round the feet, and trails behind, were of the most brilliant blue, edged with a little embroidery of white. Her cashmere jacket was of pale lilac (like the double primroses), lined with a gold-coloured fur. A delicate lilac gauze handkerchief was twined round her head; among the fringe of which, diamond heart-seases, of the natural size, glittered on golden stalks which trembled at the slightest movement. Lilac slippers, embroidered with seed-pearls, completed her toilet. No, I must not forget the shining plaits of black hair which escaped from the handkerchief and hung down behind, and a diamond of enormous size and great beauty, which glittered on one of her white fingers. We decided that this must be a present from the Sultan, and that it must also be one of the stones spoken of in Eastern fairy lore as "lighting the chamber," etc.

The two wives now began a little consultation, and from the word *chibouque* being frequently mentioned, we easily understood the question to be, as to the propriety of offering them to us. Both Madame de Souci and Mrs. Brown declared they should die in the attempt (they are both very delicate); but I, having been taught by no less a person than the Chief of the Bashi-Bazouks, declared that I could take five or six whiffs, not only with resignation, but with pleasure. However, we were not put to the test, for it was evidently decided in the negative; and on the principal wife clapping her hands, some richly-dressed slaves brought in trays of conserves, and water in crystal cups. On the first tray is a glass vase of the conserve, with a beautiful silver basket on either side of it, one of which is filled with spoons of the same metal. You take a spoonful of sweetmeat, and then place the spoon which you have used, in the empty basket on the other side. Then another slave presents you with a richly-cut cup of water. After that the coffee-bearers enter. One of them holds a tray of a semicircular form, from which hangs a magnificently embroidered and fringed cloth of gold. Other slaves then take the coffee and present it to each guest. The outer cup is exactly like an egg-cup; inside this, is one of the finest china, which contains the beverage. We admired their outer cups immensely; they were of richly-chased gold, encircled with diamonds about an inch apart and the size of a large pea.

After drinking coffee with great gravity and decorum, the empty cups being carried away by the other attendants, the principal wife again made an attempt at conversation; but after having thanked her, and said what a beautiful view it was, in pretty decent Turkish, I came to a standstill, although our gestures expressive of regret, were extraordinarily eloquent, I must think, for Englishwomen and children of the North. "Madame Ayesha," as I must still call her, wanted to know if Madame de Souci was English (Inglis). She laughed and nodded; but still our hostess was evidently not satisfied, having no doubt heard the Vicomte spoken of as a Frenchman. We were sadly puzzled how to explain to her, but at last I held up two of my fingers, making them look as much like a loving couple as possible. One of them, I showed, was intended to represent Madame de Souci,—and touching it I repeated the word "Inglis," they all nodded and laughed. The other larger and more imposing one, I touched with great gravity and respect, uttering at the same time the words "Adam (man), fez, Français," or "Her man, her fez, is French." If I had but known the Turkish word "kòja" (husband) then, it would have been all right.

This making of signs was very vexing and tantalizing, and the fair ladies of Stamboul evidently thought so too, for they made signs to us again that it was very grievous to them. Thereupon arose another little murmured consultation; the slaves laughed and clapped their hands, and two or three of the principal ones rushed out of the room. We could not think what they were about, and poor Madame de Souci became very nervous. "I hope to goodness they won't undress us," said she, colouring up, and every ringlet shaking with fright; "I was told that perhaps they would." "Never mind if they do," said I, laughing; "the room is very warm, and it would not hurt us. We must look out though that they do not divide our garments among them, and that they turn out these black men." Just at this moment, unluckily for the fears of poor Madame de Souci, our hostess made a sign to be allowed to look at her dress, which she pronounced to be "*chok ghuzel*"—"very pretty"; the fair Circassian then quietly lifted up Mrs. Brown's dress to look at her petticoats. Poor Madame de Souci certainly thought that the dreaded moment had arrived. "But they are such pretty creatures," said I, jesting; "it will be like being undressed by fairies."

So now the heavy arras was lifted once more, and the slaves who had just left, entered, bearing three magnificent chibouques, and two large shawls. Which of us was to be rolled up in them when stripped of our close-fitting European garments? But to our relief, yet bewilderment, the slaves threw the shawls over their mistresses, over head and all, so that they, holding the thick folds beneath their chins, only showed bright eyes and the least tip of nose.

We were excessively diverted by an old lady (an ugly likeness of Liston, in green trousers and jacket) wrapping her head and shoulders up with extraordinary care and anxiety. "Evidently something in the shape of mankind is coming," said we; "can it be the Pasha? That third chibouque is evidently intended for some one of consequence." "I suppose he won't offer to buy us before his wives." "I wonder if he is good-looking?" "I promised my husband to be home at four o'clock," said Mrs. Brown rather nervously.

All the young and pretty slaves had now disappeared, as silently and swiftly as so many mice, behind one of the hangings. Only the old and plain ones remained. Two huge black men entered, and stood, like sentinels, mute and upright, by the white fountain in the recess. "What dangerous person is coming?" said one of us: "with no cashmeres to protect us, how are we to stand such a blaze of manly beauty?" "Woe is me! is it the Paris, the Adonis, the Butes of the Turks?" said another. We could not help laughing, in spite of ourselves, when again the curtain was lifted, and, guarded by another Black, entered the meek, white-whiskered little beau of seventy-five, our kind escort M. Robolli. After he had kissed the ladies' hands, held out to him beneath the cashmeres, we said, "O dangerous Giaour, for our peace of mind, pray don't stay too long, nor attempt to peep under that yellow and green handker-chief!" The old lady however seemed determined not to run any risk of inspiring a hopeless attachment, for nothing but the tip of a rubicund nose was visible.

And now began an animated conversation. The presence of an interpreter was indeed a relief. And he took joyfully to the jewelled chibouque presented him, the ladies breathing out clouds of smoke in concert, and with a most wonderful grace. It was certainly a very striking scene,—the women-slaves standing and sitting around, in their bright and varied costumes, the Blacks watching our venerable Adonis and listening with the might of their enormous ears, and innumerable laugh-ing eyes peeping from behind the arras, which was in a constant state of agitation. M. Robolli seemed quite to enjoy the state of excitement into which his presence had thrown the harem. He sipped coffee out of his jewelled cup, and evidently said many "obliging things" to the ladies, who received them very graciously, and then begged of him to tell us how welcome we were, and what pleasure our presence gave them, they touching their lips and forehead at the same time. We of course expressed ourselves very sensible of their goodness. They then begged we would take off our bonnets and make ourselves perfectly at home, which we did. They then asked us which we liked best, Stamboul, or London and Paris. I replied that Stamboul was most beautiful, but that at Paris and London we had more liberty, and the streets were better to walk about in. Then a little murmur of delight from the slaves ran round the apartment: "She says Stamboul is most beautiful!" They asked how many children we had, and said that Edie's blue eyes and fair hair must be very pretty,— why did I leave her? I begged M. Robolli to tell them that I feared the variable climate, and also that she was left with my mother. "Don't let them think that we English are unnatural mothers." We all entreated this.

"Madame Ayesha" then said how sorry she was not to be able to present her own daughter to us. It seems that she is a lovely girl of sixteen; her health is usually good, but she is subject at times to fits of depression and nervousness, amounting almost to insanity. These attacks usually lasted about three days, and this was one of these distressing visitations. She was lying quite alone; her mind, the poor mother said, strangely wandering, speaking of places which she had never seen as if she were there. Her old nurse was the only person whom she could bear to see near her. The mother seemed deeply afflicted when speaking of her beautiful but unhappy daughter, who, M. Robolli says, is charming when well, full of grace and liveliness. While he was talking of her and condoling with the mother, whose whole countenance changed to an expression of profound sorrow, the slaves sitting at her feet moaned and beat their breasts, and even the black men expressed the greatest sympathy: I assure you I saw tears in their yellow eyes.

It was impossible not to be much touched, in listening to this account of the beauty and gentleness and goodness of the poor young girl, alone in her misfortune, and seemingly beyond cure (at least here at Stamboul). Her mother looked the image of sorrowful despair, her lips trembled, and she could not utter another word. Wrapping her rich mantle round her, she sat in an attitude of queenly dejection, which Mrs. Siddons might have envied. These Eastern women are wonderful for grace. Of course we felt for, as well as admired her, and begged M. Robolli to say how sorry we were to hear of her sweet young daughter's affliction. She thanked us very earnestly and with a simple grace quite indescribable, a grace which makes you feel at once that you never beheld anything like it before. I said, "It is a very great sorrow for you, but there are others in the world still more unhappy: many who have lost all their children, and many also have ungrateful ones." She replied: "I often think that, and blame myself for giving way to so much grief. My child is good and lovely when she is well. I still have her with me, and Allah may one day please to restore her health and mind entirely." Here she puffed away vigorously at her chibouque, and, putting her hand on her heart, said that it was the very best of comforters in sorrow. We told her the story of poor Sir Edmund Lyons, losing his brave son just in the moment of victory; and two or three even sadder still of this war. She said, "How much England has suffered!" and several of the slaves cried (or pretended).

We then changed the conversation which was becoming so melancholy; and they spoke of their summer palace on the Bosphorus, hoping that when they removed there we should visit them. "It is very lovely," they said; "there are hanging gardens with a stream leaping from rock to rock amongst the orange-trees; and the birds are always singing in the shade. There are also beautiful fountains, and rose-gardens; and we think you will like it." We were just saying what pleasure it would give us to visit them in their little Paradise, when a slave, richly attired, entered. She kissed the hem of "Madame Ayesha's" garment, touched her forehead with it, and then standing upright, with her arms folded over her breast, evidently delivered a message. "Madame Ayesha" explained to M. Robolli. "I am sorry to say I must go," he said; "another Turkish lady is coming to pay a visit, and although Madame admits me with her husband's consent, he being accustomed to European manners, any other Pasha might object to it; and she would not risk getting her friend into trouble." So off went M. Robolli, and off went the fair ladies' cashmeres, and "Madame Liston's" yellow and green handkerchief, and in ran all the pretty young slaves again, like a troop of fawns. I never saw so many women together in my life before; there seemed to be no end of them.

There was one little girl of extraordinary beauty, about twelve, and another a little older, almost as lovely. I never saw any living being, or any picture, so beautiful as the youngest. They told us that she was a daughter of the Pasha, by a slave who died last year, and who was also very lovely. The wives seemed as fond of this little houri as if she had been their own child, and were quite pleased at our great admiration of her. Poor child! I wonder what her fate will be.

While I was holding her little hand in mine, and looking at her lovely dark eyes with their deep fringes (you learn what "eyelashes" mean here), in came the belle, for whose sake M. Robolli was banished from the women's apartments. Although not beautiful, I think she was one of the most striking persons I ever beheld. She had none of the almost invariable softness of the Turkish women, but a face of the most marked talent and decision, and satire, and with a decisive, authoritative manner to correspond, and yet perfectly courtly, and with that exquisite case and grace which is so enchanting in Turkish women. She had piercing black eyes, of immense size and lustre, with thick eyebrows; and hair of so raven a hue that I instantly thought of the younger and more flattering portraits of Charles II. A large, dark mole on the somewhat sallow cheek, made the picture still more striking, and added to this she had tied a rich lace handkerchief round her neck, just after the fashion of a beau of the Vandyke school, the ends hanging down. She held a lighted Havannah cigar between her fingers, and we admired her rich lace and muffles as she smoked with the air of a Rochester. Her dress and trousers were of amber-coloured silk, her waistcoat blue, embroidered richly in silver; round her slight waist she wore a many-coloured cashmere scarf, into which a massive gold chain and Turkish watch was comfortably tucked. Her hair was dressed in what they tell me is the old Turkish fashion, cut in steps, as it were, down the forehead; about an inch long by the parting, below that a little longer, by the ear longer still,—which has a very curious effect, and gives a rather masculine look. A light-blue handkerchief was twisted gracefully round her head, fastened on with six or seven splendid stars of brilliants. Between the two centre ones, on the forehead, was a long piece of white muslin, about the breadth of one's hand, which, thrown back over the head, fell nearly to her heels behind. A ruby of enormous size flashed and glistened on the finger.

To us she seemed a striking "picture of the East," as she sat pleasantly chatting with——Pasha's wives. She and the chief wife sat, or rather reclined, on the divan. The beautiful Circassian seemed to feel cold, and half sat, half knelt by the enormous *mangale* (a kind of brazen tripod, filled with charcoal) in the centre of the room. I thought I had never seen anything more lovely and graceful, as she dreamily smoked her chibouque, and her great diamond flashed on her white hand, and she lifted up her head now and then to join in the conversation of the other two, or to laugh in the low, musical tone which had charmed us so much at first.

Our visit seemed very like a tale of the Arabian Nights, especially when the slaves entered with tambourines, and, sitting down cross-legged at the further end of the apartment, entertained us with a concert of "music." A more dreadful noise it is scarcely possible to imagine: you hardly know whether to laugh or to cry. A slave beats the tambourine, and leads the discord with her harsh and grating voice. The rest take up the howl one after another, and yell louder and louder as the story which they were reciting progresses. The fair Circassian seemed to take especial delight in the performance, and, whilst searching for bright little bits of charcoal in the mangale to re-light her chibouque, kept prompting them with verses which they seemed to have forgotten,—to our great misery and regret; for ears, teeth, and hair were set on edge and bristling up the wrong way, at this excruciating "treat."

It was at last put a stop to by two things: first, by Mrs. Brown's sinking back on the divan, pale as death, overcome by the noise and the mingled fumes of charcoal and chibouques; and secondly, by the entrance of a very fine baby with his two nurses. He looked so odd to us in his little trousers and fur jacket, and wearing a tiny fez, ornamented with a loop of diamonds. This young gentleman belonged to the visitor lady, and stretched out his arms to her very prettily. He was not at all shy with the Turkish ladies, or with the slaves, but evidently considered us veritable "Giaours," and would not come near us. The nurse who carried him was a lovely young woman: she was dressed in trousers and jacket of a bright green, and wore on her head a pale-yellow handkerchief, fastened with a large diamond. The other was an immense black woman, dressed entirely in scarlet silk, with a little edging of white, and a snow-white handkerchief bound round her woolly head. These two "nurses" would certainly create a sensation in Hyde Park. They appeared devoted to the baby.

But now our imperial-looking hostess made signs that we were to eat, at which announcement we were not at all sorry, the fresh air of the Bosphorus having given us famous appetites. We followed her accordingly into the lofty apartment, with the dome-like painted roof; the fair Circassian leading me affectionately by the hand, and the Pasha's lovely little daughter gently conducting Madame de Souci and Mrs. Brown. The principal slaves went before to lift the arras, and a motley group followed behind. We could hardly believe the scene to be real: "It is so like an Arabian Night!" we kept exclaiming, as we crossed with the brilliant group over the golden matting of that vast apartment.

At the entrance of the dining-room stood two Arab slaves, richly attired. To each lady, as she entered, one of these held a beautiful silver bowl, while the other poured rose-water over her hands from a vase of the same richly-chased material. Two little slave-girls presented fine napkins, the ends embroidered in gold, on which we each shook the rose-water from our fingers. The dining-room was a most luxurious apartment, closely latticed, for it looked into the streets of Stamboul, but cheerful, and rich in crimson divans and carved and painted flowers on walls and ceiling. All had been done that was possible to make the cage bearable.——Pasha's harem is, I am told, one of the most "fashionable," which accounted for our seeing a European dining-table, adorned with a handsome centre-piece, and four beautiful vases of flowers and fruit, after the French fashion.

The dinner-service was of rare and beautiful china; the silver knives and forks were extremely handsome; the *servietti* delicately fine; the flowers exquisitely arranged, and mingled with oranges and lemons, in the Eastern fashion; the slaves were standing round, three or four deep, awaiting our slightest sign: we felt still more in the land of dreams.

First of all they placed to each guest a sparkling water-bottle and glass. Then a fine china plate containing a flat roll of a kind of rye-bread, called *semeet*, quite new and warm, and covered with a small seed, which, not being a canary or a linnet, I objected to. Then soup was served,—a great novelty in a harem: it was most excellent,—chicken and vermicelli. Then came a dish of pilauf, of chicken and rice, done brown. I sat next to the chief wife, on her right hand; as the slave held the dish, she pointed out the nicest pieces, begging of me to take them. The fair Circassian sat opposite to me. I was curious to see if they really seemed to like the modern innovation of knives and forks. For the first few minutes they used them,— evidently to do as we did; but the Circassian beauty, failing to secure the particular piece of chicken she coveted with a troublesome fork and spoon, threw those incompetent auxiliaries down, and grubbed successfully, and to her entire satisfaction, with her fingers. She then looked at me and laughed; and showing me how to take a piece of bread between my fingers, begged us to eat *à la Turque*, which they were all doing themselves, fast and furious; and, to please them, we accordingly picked a few chicken-bones with our fingers.

We had all three been enchanted with the fair Circassian, as I have told you,— with her beauty, her winning, yet lofty manners, and exquisite grace; we had seen her smoke, and admired her still; we had even forgiven her for loving the barbarous noise in the "concert of music:" but to see her lick her fingers up to the last joint after each dish,—to see her lick her favourite tortoiseshell spoon bright after successive, and never-to-be-believed enormous platefuls of sweet pancakes daubed with honey, and tarts too luscious for the Knave of Hearts!—this was too much for Venus herself to have done with impunity: we were perfectly disenchanted long before the feast was over. The rest were not quite so bad (excepting "Madame Liston," who might as well have had a trough at once); but we began to feel rather sick after the first few dishes were dispatched, and the animal passions of some of the ladies began to be roused by their favourite sweets and jellies, which they tore to pieces with their fingers, and threw down their throats in large lumps. The jester waited at table, presenting the principal dishes with jokes which caused bursts of laughter from the ladies and the slaves in attendance, who seem perfectly at home, and on very free-and-easy terms with their mistresses, notwithstanding their complete submission to them. The jester was a wild and most extraordinary-looking woman, with an immensity of broad humour and drollery in her face. We thought it quite as well that we could not understand the jokes at which the fair Circassian, between the intervals of licking her fingers and spoon, and popping tit-bits on our plates, laughed so complacently, and which sometimes obliged the Arabs and eunuchs at the door to dive under the arras to conceal their uncontrollable fits of mirth.

It was certainly a most singular dinner-party. The dishes of course were innumerable; the chicken and rice, and the *cabeb*, we enjoyed; the rest were very sweet, and very fat; and we were delighted when our hostess rose, and again the refreshing rose-water was handed to us.

We then returned to the luxurious divan of the smaller room. Again the slaves handed coffee in jewelled cups; again the fair Circassian looked dreamy and lovely, hanging fondly over her chibouque; again we admired the blue Bosphorus, and the distant mountains, and the dark cypresses of Stamboul; again we asked for M.

Robolli, and again the fair ladies were enveloped in their cashmeres; the blacks standing mute, watchful, and listening. We repeated our thanks and adieus; the slaves lifted the arras. M. Robolli kissed the hands of the kind and veiled ladies. The Blacks conducted us down the broad staircase, crowding boisterously around us, and muttering the word *bakshish*.

Our visit to the Harem was over. M. Robolli mounted his "gallant grey," and rode back with us through the latticed streets and over the Bridge of Boats to Pera. It seemed as if we had had a dream.

Emmeline Lott

The Governess in Egypt
(1865)

Her Highness, who takes precedence of all the wives, who stand in awe of her, had not yet risen from her downy couch, and so there the young Princesses waited like a band of slaves until their imperious grandmother had finished her toilette, as she never would receive them in her chamber. Why or wherefore I know not. Perhaps there were other visitors there, whom it did not suit the Validè Princess to allow her granddaughters to see; perhaps her Grand Eunuch, a shrewd, cunning, crafty individual, who was a very sinister looking personage, but who appeared thoroughly to understand the ways of his Viceregal mistress, was closeted with Her Highness, communing with her on affairs of state, or private matters. At all events there I found them squatting down at the door-sill.

But His Highness the Grand Pacha, (who was her pet—her Ibrahim—the very prototype of her lamented husband, the gallant yet cruel Ibrahim Pacha,) broke through all ceremony; and I soon found that this "dot of humanity's" word was law here as well as at Ghezire; for, passing by the Princesses, he exclaimed, "Come along, Madame," pulled aside the dismal funeral-looking black curtain, ornamented with a silver crescent in the centre, which hung across the doorway, and bounded like a gazelle into the apartment, where he remained some time with the Validè Princess, as I did not presume to enter her presence.

I stood talking to the young Princesses, all of whom were rather intelligent, tractable, and amiable girls, and would, had we remained longer together, have become considerably Europeanized, as I found them anxious to learn, and particularly attached to me, poor dear neglected creatures! a circumstance not to be wondered at, as, extraordinary as it may appear, neither Turkish fathers nor mothers seem to like having a posey of daughters. Perhaps it is from avaricious motives; for with them they are obliged to give dowries suitable to their position in society; whereas boys, so to speak, are made to shift for themselves. Thus the Viceroy, or their mother, the Lady Paramount—whose first child was a son, who had been dead many years, but who would have been eighteen years old had he lived—(for they were her children,) took not the slightest interest in them. Consequently they were allowed to grow wild and uncared for; but as I thought it was a pity that such noble females should be brought up in that barbarous manner, I took an interest in them, and began to teach them English, and to cause them to adopt many European modes and customs.

As soon as H.H. the Viceroy's mother had finished her morning toilette, she came forth out of her chamber.

She was a short elderly person, a most courtly dame, and perfect lady in the fullest acceptation of the term, with grey hair, and large piercing black eyes, but commanding in her manner, often too imperious and stately in her carriage. Her manners were courtly, at which I was surprised; in short, I never beheld anything but what was ladylike in her behaviour. She appeared to have sprung from quite a different stock to that of H.H. the *Baba's* three wives. Perhaps she was brought up at the Imperial Court of *Is-tam-bol,* "Constantinople;" but I never could learn any thing reliable about her history, except that Ibrahim Pacha, when desperately in love with her, wrote some beautiful verses to her at the old palace of Bebek, a copy of which I have given elsewhere. That perhaps may account for H.M. the Sultan naming the Palace of Bebek as that Princess's residence during her visit to the Imperial Court in 1864, and which was considered by her as a very great compliment. About these grounds she must have rambled with infinite delight, but perhaps mingled with sorrow for the loss of Ibrahim Pacha, to whom she was devotedly attached; all appeared to be mystery, doubt, and conjecture. All I know is that at first I found her exceedingly imperious towards me; she even went so far as to expect that I should kneel at her feet and squat down at her door like a slave.

I had often, when a child, been found by Her Most Gracious Majesty the Queen and the late Prince Consort playing about in the private grounds at Frogmore and Windsor; and when I had encountered that royal pair, who took flowers from my basket which I had gathered in the grounds and smiled, I had stepped aside, stood still, and curtseyed—no more. I did the same to H.H. the Validè Princess of Egypt, and I thought that was quite sufficient respect to show her, and I never did anything more; nay, I positively refused to do more.

Gradually, as we became better acquainted with each other, her haughtiness diminished; still there was a lack of that amiability and suavity of manner about her which most certainly characterised their Highnesses, the three wives, always making you uncomfortable in her presence. She was a fitting partner for such a prince as Ibrahim Pacha. She possessed great intellectual activity; hence there is no doubt but that she meddled indirectly in the weightiest affairs of the State; weightiest, I repeat, because I suppose Her Highness considered, in her eyes, the relations between the Sultan and the Viceroy to be such; in those matters she appeared at home, as I shall afterwards have occasion to explain.

She was extremely penurious—nay, mean would be the more appropriate expression—and, as an illustration, I need only adduce the fact of her Harem being the most beggarly arranged of any I ever entered. Her staff of attendants was very limited; her habits were frugal; her attire, upon ordinary occasions, extremely plain, while on grand ones it was regal and queenlike. She was avaricious to a degree, imperious in her manner, and exacting in the extreme.

The finest trait in her character was her devoted affection for her son, the Viceroy, which was truly reciprocal. She loved H.H. the Grand Pacha with the same enthusiasm, and spoilt and indulged him in every way possible. As regards myself, when Her Highness began to understand my European ways better, she treated me with respect. I never received a present, or baksheesh, of any kind from her, although to others she distributed gold and jewels with no sparing hand; but when illness overtook me, she manifested great sympathy—in short, did everything in her power to contribute to my comfort, so far as she understood how, and Heaven knows that was little enough about our European ways and habits; for she had never been in England, although Ibrahim Pacha, when he visited London, took with him some women. They were Armenians, and not Turkish, whom European travellers, because the former adopt at pleasure that mask, *the veil,* always take for the latter, a most common error.

The Validè Princess was attired in a robe of white satin on this occasion (for be it remembered that it was the *Bairam,* the Turks' greatest festival), having a breadth in front and behind, about two yards longer than the rest of the dress, which was on this day, being a state occasion, held up by four of the ladies of the Harem, or four of her *Ikbals,* but which, on ordinary times, is turned back like a three-cornered handkerchief, one of the corners being tucked in the waist-belt. Over that was placed a blue satin paletot, trimmed with sable fur. On her head she wore a small handkerchief; and in the centre of the forehead was a large diamond fly. In her hand she carried her small gold watch, encircled with diamonds; and her feet were encased in white satin shoes.

When she reached the landing-place, the young Princesses and myself salaamed her. Her Highness then descended the staircase (the slaves holding up her train in front and behind) which led into the room where we had found the Belgian lady, passed between two rows of the ladies of her Harem (many of whom were very aged), and then walked majestically through four rows of slaves, and sat herself down in the centre of the divan, under the window (the Belgian lady had vacated the apartment). Then she took her darling pet, the Prince, placed him beside her on the right hand, while on the left sat a lady, whom I was afterwards informed was the widow of Said Pacha, the late Viceroy. By the side of H.H. the Grand Pacha sat his sisters, and then, lower down, a bevy of Princesses belonging to other members of the Viceregal family.

After all were seated in due order, according to their rank, each of the ladies of the Harem approached this Viceregal dame. Those of the highest rank kissed her right hand, and bowed their foreheads upon it, exclaiming, "*Allaha emanet oloun!*" "May God be with you!" The others kissed the hem of her robe; upon which all the slaves bowed their foreheads.

After this ceremony had been gone through, coffee and pipes were handed round (to the Princesses only) by six slaves, dressed in black cloth jackets, wearing black trousers, embroidered shirts, like men, and black silk neckties, over which were turned white collars. Their heads were covered with fezes; their feet were encased in patent leather shoes, with bows of black ribbon. All were of the same height, and, what was singular, their complexions were nearly alike.

H.H. the Grand Pacha then kindly took me on a tour of inspection through the whole suite of apartments. They were large, noble, lofty rooms, but all carpetless, and destitute of every kind of furniture, except divans, having suspended from the centre of the ceilings chandeliers, quite as large and elegant as that which hangs from the roof of the Italian Opera House, in London.

Before H.H. the Grand Pacha took his leave, Her Highness filled his pockets with several packets of gold coin, as *backsheesh*, of which he was despoiled by the head-nurse, on his return to the Harem, who on that occasion must have pocketed upwards of twenty to thirty pounds.

This visit to the Harem in the Citadel had initiated me into some of the secrets of Harem life, and I failed not to profit by them. I learned that the Messrs. H. were the *Inan divan end*, the Genii of those "Abodes of Bliss," and that Madame Caroline was, or more properly speaking, I should say, had been, at one time, their Highnesses, the three wives, *Karagueuz*, "Evil Eye."

I now looked upon Egypt as a strange country. I regarded my own position as a dangerous one. I had to guard against being looked upon by the Princesses as an "Evil Eye;" for although H.H. the Viceroy only treated me with that consideration which my position entitled me to receive, still, as one European woman had supplanted them in the *Baba's* affection for a time, I had no desire that a similar mark of his favour (honour, all in the Harem consider it to be) should be shown to me. I had been engaged to take charge of the heir presumptive to all his wealth, as I had been led to suppose, to educate the Prince, and prepare him for a preceptor. I had thought it rather singular when the Viceroy and his reported partners had told me not to care about his instruction; but now I thought it more so than ever. I resolved to keep my standing in that character. I trusted that my own habitual reservedness of manner would save me from any advances being made, and determined not to become a loadstone of attraction to H.H. the Viceroy.

I had remarked how dull, melancholy, ah! and even dejected, Madame Caroline looked when I glanced at her, and my curiosity was naturally wakened to know what really were her feelings at being "caged up," as it were, in the Harem of the Citadel.

Had she been entrapped, "caught," bought or sold like a parrot? If so, who were the white slave-dealers? Thereby hung a tale. In after times I obtained, at Constantinople, a solution of all these queries which now floated on my imagination; and now I believe that Turks, Jews, and Europeans, who have become domiciled in the East, are not only traffickers in every kind of merchandise, but also in *live* as well as dead stock. Did she ever think of her European home? What a dull, monotonous life she must have led there! Poor creature! I wondered how H.H. the Validè Princess treated her and her sons, noble intelligent European-looking boys, also called Princes. I recalled to mind the imperious look of that haughty dame. I longed to know her antecedents, her manners were so stately and court-like.

Above all other beings in the world, I, who had always been accustomed to have my own will, and to enjoy my liberty, should not have liked to be at her beck and call. Oh! no, indeed; I had, before I saw Her Highness "at home," witnessed enough of the proud Validè Princess.

I had no idea of being treated like an *abject* slave, by the widow of that over-bearing ruler, Ibrahim Pacha, nor to be at Her Highness's command, nor by her caressed, flattered, and then cast off as whim or fancy led her. I was H.H. the Grand Pacha's *Institutrice*, and not the Validè Princess's slave nor subject. I had no idea of passing the best years of my existence within such "a gilded cage;" and so I always kept at a respectful distance from H.H. the Viceroy's mother, as I knew her to be a most shrewd and accomplished intriguante, one who, to advance the interest of her son and grandson, would "stick at nothing," absolutely nothing.

Lucie Duff Gordon

Letters from Egypt
(1875)

LUXOR, *January* 13, 1864.

We spent all the afternoon of Saturday at Keneh, where I dined with the English Consul, a worthy old Arab, who also invited our captain, and we all sat round his copper tray on the floor and ate with our fingers, the captain, who sat next me, picking out the best bits and feeding me and Sally with them. After dinner the French Consul, a Copt, one Jesus Buktor, sent to invite me to a fantasia at his house, where I found the Mouniers, the Moudir, and some other Turks, and a disagreeable Italian, who stared at me as if I had been young and pretty, and put Omar into a great fury. I was glad to see the dancing-girls, but I liked old Seyyid Achmet's patriarchal ways much better than the tone of the Frenchified Copt. At first I thought the dancing queer and dull. One girl was very handsome, but cold and uninteresting; one who sang was also very pretty and engaging, and a dear little thing. But the dancing was contortions, more or less graceful, *very* wonderful as gymnastic feats, and no more. But the captain called out to one Latifeh, an ugly, clumsy-looking wench, to show the Sitt what she could do. And then it was revealed to me. The ugly girl started on her feet and became the 'serpent of old Nile,'—the head, shoulders and arms eagerly bent forward, waist in, and haunches advanced on the bent knees—the posture of a cobra about to spring. I could not call it *voluptuous* any more than Racine's *Phèdre*. It is *Venus toute entière à sa proie attachée*, and to me seemed tragic. It is far more realistic than the 'fandango,' and far less coquettish, because the thing represented is *au grande sérieux*, not travestied, *gazé*, or played with; and like all such things, the Arab men don't think it the least improper. Of course the girls don't commit any indecorums before European women, except the dance itself. Seyyid Achmet would have given me a fantasia, but he feared I might have men with me, and he had had a great annoyance with two Englishmen who wanted to make the girls dance naked, which they objected to, and he had to turn them out of his house after hospitably entertaining them.

Our procession home to the boat was very droll. Mme. Mounier could not ride an Arab saddle, so I lent her mine and *enfourché'd* my donkey, and away we went with men running with 'meshhaals' (fire-baskets on long poles) and lanterns, and the captain shouting out 'Full speed!' and such English phrases all the way—like a regular old salt as he is. We got here last night, and this morning Mustapha A'gha and the Nazir came down to conduct me up to my palace. I have such a big rambling house all over the top of the temple of Khem. How I wish I had you and the chicks to fill it! We had about twenty *fellahs* to clean the dust of three years' accumulation, and my room looks quite handsome with carpets and a divan. Mustapha's little girl found her way here when she heard I was come, and it seemed quite pleasant to have her playing on the carpet with a dolly and some sugar-plums, and making a feast for dolly on a saucer, arranging the sugar-plums Arab fashion. She was monstrously pleased with Rainie's picture and kissed it. Such a quiet, nice little brown tot, and curiously like Rainie and walnut-juice.

The view all round my house is magnificent on every side, over the Nile in front facing north-west, and over a splendid range of green and distant orange buff hills to the south-east, where I have a spacious covered terrace. It is rough and dusty to the extreme, but will be very pleasant. Mustapha came in just now to offer me the loan of a horse, and to ask me to go to the mosque in a few nights to see the illumination in honour of a great Sheykh, a son of Sidi Hosseyn or Hassan. I asked whether my presence might not offend any Muslimeen, and he would not hear of such a thing. The sun set while he was here, and he asked if I objected to his praying in my presence, and went through his four *rekahs* very comfortably on my carpet. My next-door neighbour (across the courtyard all filled with antiquities) is a nice little Copt who looks like an antique statue himself. I shall *voisiner* with his family. He sent me coffee as soon as I arrived, and came to help. I am invited to El-Moutaneh, a few hours up the river, to visit the Mouniers, and to Keneh to visit Seyyid Achmet, and also the head of the merchants there who settled the price of a carpet for me in the bazaar, and seemed to like me. He was just one of those handsome, high-bred, elderly merchants with whom a story always begins in the Arabian Nights. When I can talk I will go and see a real Arab hareem. A very nice English couple, a man and his wife, gave me breakfast in their boat, and turned out to be business connections of Ross's, of the name of Arrowsmith; they were going to Assouan, and I shall see them on their way back. I asked Mustapha about the Arab young lady, and he spoke very highly of her, and is to let me know if she comes here and to offer hospitality from me: he did not know her name—she is called 'el *Hággeh*' (the Pilgrimess).

Thursday.—Now I am settled in my Theban palace, it seems more and more beautiful, and I am quite melancholy that you cannot be here to enjoy it. The house is very large and has good thick walls, the comfort of which we feel to-day for it blows a hurricane; but indoors it is not at all cold. I have glass windows and doors to some of the rooms. It is a lovely dwelling. Two funny little owls as big as my fist live in the wall under my window, and come up and peep in, walking on tip-toe, and looking inquisitive like the owls in the hieroglyphics; and a splendid horus (the sacred hawk) frequents my lofty balcony. Another of my contemplar gods I sacrilegiously killed last night, a whip snake. Omar is rather in consternation for fear it should be 'the snake of the house,' for Islam has not dethroned the *Dii lares et tutelares.*

I have been 'sapping' at the *Alif Bey* (A B C) today, under the direction of Sheykh Yussuf, a graceful, sweet-looking young man, with a dark brown face and such fine manners, in his *fellah* dress—a coarse brown woollen shirt, a *libdeh*, or felt skull-cap, and a common red shawl round his head and shoulders; writing the wrong way is very hard work. Some men came to mend the staircase, which had fallen in and which consists of huge solid blocks of stone. One crushed his thumb and I had to operate on it. It is extraordinary how these people bear pain; he never winced in the least, and went off thanking God and the lady quite cheerfully. Till to-day the weather has been quite heavenly; last night I sat with my window open, it was so warm. If only I had you all here! How Rainie would play in the temple, Maurice fish in the Nile, and you go about with your spectacles on your nose. I think you would discard Frangi dress and take to a brown shirt and a *libdch*, and soon be as brown as any *fellah*. It was so curious to see Sheykh Yussuf blush from shyness when he came in first; it shows quite as much in the coffee-brown Arab skin as in the fairest European—quite unlike the much lighter-coloured mulatto or Malay, who never change colour at all. A photographer who is living here showed me photographs done high up the White Nile. One negro girl is so splendid that I must get him to do me a copy to send you. She is not perfect like the Nubians, but so superbly strong and majestic. If I can get hold of a handsome *fellahah* here, I'll get her photographed to show you in Europe what a woman's breast can be, for I never knew it before I came here—it is the most beautiful thing in the world. The dancing-girl I saw moved her breasts by some extraordinary muscular effort, first one and then the other; they were just like pomegranates and gloriously independent of stays or any support.

I have been reading Miss Martineau's book; the descriptions are excellent, but she evidently knew and cared nothing about the people, and had the feeling of most English people here, that the difference of manners is a sort of impassable gulf, the truth being that their feelings and passions are just like our own. It is curious that all the old books of travels that I have read mention the natives of strange countries in a far more natural tone, and with far more attempt to discriminate character, than modern ones, *e.g.*, Niebuhr's Travels here and in Arabia, Cook's Voyages, and many others. *Have* we grown so *very* civilized since a hundred years that outlandish people seem like mere puppets, and not like real human beings? Miss M.'s bigotry against Copts and Greeks is droll enough, compared to her very proper reverence for 'Him who sleeps in Philæ,' and her attack upon hareems outrageous; she implies that they are brothels. I must admit that I have not seen a Turkish hareem, and she apparently saw no other, and yet she fancies the morals of Turkey to be superior to those of Egypt. It is not possible for a woman to explain all the limitations to which ordinary people do subject themselves. Great men I know nothing of; but women can and do, without blame, sue their husbands-in-law for the full 'payment of debt,' and demand a divorce if they please in default. Very often a man marries a second wife out of duty to provide for a brother's widow and children, or the like. Of course licentious men act loosely as elsewhere. *Kulloolum Beni Adam* (we are all sons of Adam), as Sheykh Yussuf says constantly, 'bad-bad and good-good'; and modern travellers show strange ignorance in talking of foreign natives *in the lump*, as they nearly all do.

I think you would enjoy, as I do, the peculiar sort of social equality which prevails here; it is the exact contrary of French *égalité*. There are the great and powerful people, much honoured (outwardly, at all events), but nobody has *inferiors*. A man comes in and kisses my hand, and sits down *off* the carpet out of respect; but he smokes his pipe, drinks his coffee, laughs, talks and asks questions as freely as if he were an Effendi or I were a fellahah; he is not my inferior, he is my poor brother. The servants in my friends' houses receive me with profound demonstrations of respect, and wait at dinner reverently, but they mix freely in the conversation, and take part in all amusements, music, dancing-girls, or reading of the Koran. Even the dancing-girl is not an outcast; she is free to talk to me, and it is highly irreligious to show any contempt or aversion. The rules of politeness are the same for all. The passer-by greets the one sitting still, or the one who comes into a room those who are already there, without distinction of rank. When I have greeted the men they always rise, but if I pass without, they take no notice of me. All this is very pleasant and graceful, though it is connected with much that is evil. The fact that any man may be a Bey or a Pasha to-morrow is not a good fact, for the promotion is more likely to fall on a bad slave than on a good or intelligent free man. Thus, the only honourable class are those who have nothing to hope from the great—I won't say anything to fear, for all have cause for that. Hence the high respectability and *gentility* of the merchants, who are the most independent of the Government. The English would be a little surprised at Arab judgments of them; they admire our veracity and honesty, and like us on the whole, but they blame the men for their conduct to women. They are shocked at the way Englishmen talk about Hareem among themselves, and think the English hard and unkind to their wives, and to women in general. English Hareemát is generally highly approved, and an Arab thinks himself a happy man if he can marry an English girl. I have had an offer for Sally from the chief man here for his son, proposing to allow her a free exercise of her religion and customs as a matter of course. I think the influence of foreigners is much more real and much more useful on the Arabs than on the Turks, though the latter show it more in dress, etc. But all the engineers and physicians are Arabs, and very good ones, too. Not a Turk has learnt anything practical, and the dragomans and servants employed by the English have learnt a strong appreciation of the value of a character for honesty, deserved or no; but many to deserve it. Compared to the couriers and *laquais de place* of Europe, these men stand very high. Omar has just run in to say a boat is going, so good-bye, and God bless you.

Frances Trollope

Domestic Manners of the Americans
(1832)

There is something in the system of breeding and rearing negroes in the Northern States, for the express purpose of sending them to be sold in the South, that strikes painfully against every feeling of justice, mercy, or common humanity. During my residence in America I became perfectly persuaded that the state of a domestic slave in a gentleman's family was preferable to that of a hired American "help", both because they are more cared for and valued, and because their condition being born with them, their spirits do not struggle against it with that pining discontent which seems the lot of all free servants in America. But the case is widely different with such as, in their own persons or those of their children "loved in vain", are exposed to the dreadful traffic above-mentioned. In what is their condition better than that of the kidnapped negroes on the coast of Africa? Of the horror in which this enforced migration is held, I had a strong proof during our stay in Virginia. The father of a young slave, who belonged to the lady with whom we boarded, was destined to this fate, and within an hour after it was made known to him, he sharpened the hatchet with which he had been felling timber, and with his right hand severed his left from the wrist.

But this is a subject on which I do not mean to dilate; it has been lately treated most judiciously by a far abler hand.[1] Its effects on the moral feelings and external manners of the people are all I wish to observe upon, and these are unquestionably most injurious. The same man who beards his wealthier and more educated neighbour with the bullying boast "I'm as good as you," turns to his slave, and knocks him down, if the furrow he has ploughed or the log he has felled, please not this stickler for equality. This is a glaring falsehood on the very surface of such a man's principles that is revolting. It is not among the higher classes that the possession of slaves produces the worst effects. Among the poorer class of landholders, who are often as profoundly ignorant as the negroes they own, the effect of this plenary power over males and females is most demoralising; and the kind of coarse, not to say brutal, authority which is exercised, furnishes the most disgusting moral spectacle I ever witnessed. In all ranks, however, it appeared to me that the greatest and best feelings of the human heart were paralysed by the relative positions of slave and owner. The characters, the hearts of children, are irretrievably injured by it. In Virginia we boarded for some time in a family consisting of a widow and her four daughters, and I there witnessed a scene strongly indicative of the effect I have men-

---

[1] See Captain Hall's *Travels in America*.

tioned. A young female slave, about eight years of age, had found on the shelf of a cupboard a biscuit, temptingly buttered, of which she had eaten a considerable portion before she was observed. The butter had been copiously sprinkled with arsenic for the destruction of rats, and had been thus most incautiously placed by one of the young ladies of the family. As soon as the circumstance was known, the lady of the house came to consult me as to what had best be done for the poor child; I immediately mixed a large cup of mustard and water (the most rapid of all emetics), and got the little girl to swallow it. The desired effect was instantly produced, but the poor child, partly from nausea and partly from the terror of hearing her death proclaimed by half-a-dozen voices round her, trembled so violently that I thought she would fall. I sat down in the court where we were standing, and, as a matter of course, took the little sufferer in my lap. I observed a general titter among the white members of the family, while the black stood aloof and looked stupefied. The youngest of the family, a little girl about the age of the young slave, after gazing at me for a few moments in utter astonishment, exclaimed: "My! if Mrs Trollope has not taken her in her lap, and wiped her nasty mouth! Why, I would not have touched her mouth for two hundred dollars!"

The little slave was laid on a bed, and I returned to my own apartments; some time afterwards I sent to inquire for her, and learnt that she was in great pain. I immediately went myself to inquire farther, when another young lady of the family, the one by whose imprudence the accident had occurred, met my anxious inquiries with ill-suppressed mirth—told me they had sent for the doctor—and then burst into uncontrollable laughter. The idea of really sympathizing in the sufferings of a slave appeared to them as absurd as weeping over a calf that had been slaughtered by the butcher. The daughters of my hostess were as lovely as features and complexion could make them; but the neutralizing effect of this total want of feeling upon youth and beauty must be witnessed to be conceived.

Anna Jameson

Winter Studies and Summer Rambles in Canada
(1838)

Celibacy in either sex is almost unknown among the Indians; equally rare is all profligate excess. One instance I heard of a woman who had remained unmarried from choice, not from accident or necessity. In consequence of a dream in early youth, (the Indians are great dreamers,) she not only regarded the sun as her manito or tute-lary spirit, (this had been a common case,) but considered herself especially dedi-cated, or in fact married, to the luminary. She lived alone; she had built a wigwam for herself, which was remarkably neat and commodious; she could use a rifle, hunt, and provided herself with food and clothing. She had carved a rude image of the sun, and set it up in her lodge; the husband's place, the best mat, and a portion of food, were always appropriated to this image. She lived to a great age, and no one ever interfered with her mode of life, for that would have been contrary to all their ideas of individual freedom. Suppose that, according to our most approved Euro-pean notions, the poor woman had been burnt at the stake, corporeally or metaphor-ically, or hunted beyond the pale of the village, for deviating from the law of custom, no doubt there would have been directly a new female sect in the nation of the Chippewas, an order of *wives of the sun*, and Chippewa vestal virgins; but these wise people trusted to nature and common sense. The vocation apparently was not generally admired, and found no imitators.

Their laws, or rather their customs, command certain virtues and practices, as truth, abstinence, courage, hospitality; but they have no prohibitory laws whatever that I could hear of. In this respect their moral code has something of the spirit of Christianity, as contrasted with the Hebrew dispensation. Polygamy is allowed, but it is not common; the second wife is considered as subject to the first, who remains mistress of the household, even though the younger wife should be the favourite. Jealousy, however, is a strong passion among them: not only has a man been known to murder a woman whose fidelity he suspected, but Mr. Schoolcraft mentioned to me an instance of a woman, who, in a transport of jealousy, had stabbed her husband. But these extremes are very rare.

Some time ago, a young Chippewa girl conceived a violent passion for a hunter of a different tribe, and followed him from his winter hunting-ground to his own village. He was already married, and the wife, not being inclined to admit a rival, drove this love-sick damsel away, and treated her with the utmost indignity. The girl, in desperation, offered herself as a slave to the wife, to carry wood and water, and lie at her feet—anything to be admitted within the same lodge and only look upon the object of her affection. She prevailed at length. Now, the mere circumstance of her residing within the same wigwam made her also the wife of the man, according to the Indian custom; but apparently she was content to forego all the privileges and honours of a wife. She endured, for several months, with uncomplaining resigna-tion, every species of ill usage and cruelty on the part of the first wife, till at length this woman, unable any longer to suffer even the presence of a rival, watched an opportunity as the other entered the wigwam with a load of fire-wood, and cleft her skull with the husband's tomahawk.

"And did the man permit all this?" was the natural question.

The answer was remarkable. "What could *he* do? he could not help it: a woman is always absolute mistress in her own wigwam!"

In the end, the murder was not punished. The poor victim having fled from a distant tribe, there were no relatives to take vengeance, or do justice, and it concerned no one else. She lies buried at a short distance from the Sault Ste. Marie, where the murderess and her husband yet live.

Women sometimes perish of grief for the loss of a husband or a child, and men have been known to starve themselves on the grave of a beloved wife. Men have also been known to give up their wives to the traders for goods and whisky; but this, though forbidden by no law, is considered disreputable, or as my informant expressed it, "only bad Indians do so."

I should doubt, from all I see and hear, that the Indian squaw is that absolute slave, drudge, and non-entity in the community, which she has been described. She is despotic in her lodge, and everything it contains is hers; even of the game her husband kills, she has the uncontrolled disposal. If her husband does not please her, she scolds and even cuffs him; and it is in the highest degree unmanly to answer or strike her. I have seen here a woman scolding and quarrelling with her husband, seize him by the hair, in a style that might have become civilised Billingsgate, or christian St. Giles's, and the next day I have beheld the same couple sit lovingly together on the sunny side of the wigwam, she kneeling behind him, and combing and arranging the hair she had been pulling from his head the day before; just such a group as I remember to have seen about Naples, or the Campagna di Roma, with very little obvious difference either in costume or complexion.

There is no law against marrying near relations, but it is always avoided; it is contrary to their customs: even first cousins do not marry. The tie of blood seems considered as stronger than that of marriage. A woman considers that she belongs more to her own relatives than to her husband or his relatives; yet, notwithstanding this and the facility of divorce, separations between husband and wife are very rare. A couple will go on "squabbling and making it up" all their lives, without having recourse to this expedient. If from displeasure, satiety, or any other cause, a man sends his wife away, she goes back to her relations, and invariably takes her children with her. The indefeasible right of the mother to her offspring is Indian law, or rather, the contrary notion does not seem to have entered their minds. A widow remains subject to her husband's relations for two years after his death; this is the decent period of mourning. At the end of two years, she returns some of the presents made to her by her late husband, goes back to her own relatives, and may marry again.

You will understand that these particulars, and others which may follow, apply to the Chippewas and the Ottawas around me; other tribes have other customs. I speak merely of those things which are brought under my own immediate observation and attention.

During the last American war of 1813, the young widow of a chief who had been killed in battle, assumed his arms, ornaments, wampum, medal, and went out with several war parties, in which she distinguished herself by her exploits. Mrs. Schoolcraft, when a girl of eleven or twelve years old, saw this woman, who was brought into the Fort at Mackinaw and introduced to the commanding officer; and retains a lively recollection of her appearance, and the interest and curiosity she excited. She was rather below the middle size, slight and delicate in figure, like most of the squaws;—covered with rich ornaments, silver armlets, with the scalping-knife, pouch, medals, tomahawk—all the insignia, in short, of an Indian warrior, except the war-paint and feathers. In the room hung a large mirror, in which she surveyed herself with evident admiration and delight, turning round and round before it, and laughing triumphantly. She was invited to dine at the officer's mess, perhaps as a joke, but conducted herself with so much intuitive propriety and decorum, that she was dismissed with all honour and respect, and with handsome presents. I could not learn what became of her afterwards.

Heroic women are not rare among the Indians, women who can bravely suffer—bravely die; but Amazonian women, female amateur warriors, are very extraordinary; I never heard but of this one instance. Generally, the squaws around me give me the impression of exceeding feminine delicacy and modesty, and of the most submissive gentleness. Female chiefs, however, are not unknown in Indian history. There was a famous *Squaw Sachem*, or chief, in the time of the early settlers. The present head chief of the Ottawas, a very fine old man, succeeded a female, who, it is further said, abdicated in his favour.[1]

Even the standing rule or custom that women are never admitted to councils has been evaded. At the treaty of Butte des Morts, in 1827,[2] an old Chippewa woman, the wife of a super-annuated chief, appeared in place of her husband, wearing his medal, and to all intents and purposes representing him. The American commissioners treated her with studied respect and distinction, and made her rich presents in cloth, ornaments, tobacco, &c. On her return to her own village, she was way-laid and murdered by a party of Menomonies. The next year two Menomonie women were taken and put to death by the Chippewas: such is the Indian law of retaliation.

[. . .]

Yet a word more before I leave my Indians.

There is one subject on which all travellers in these regions—all who have treated of the manners and modes of life of the north-west tribes, are accustomed to expatiate with great eloquence and indignation, which they think it incumbent on the gallantry and chivalry of Christendom to denounce as constituting the true badge and distinction of barbarism and heathenism, opposed to civilisation and Christianity:—I mean the treatment and condition of their women. The women, they say, are "drudges," "slaves," "beasts of burthen," victims, martyrs, degraded, abject, oppressed; that not only the cares of the household and maternity, but the cares and labours proper to the men, fall upon them; and they seem to consider no

---

[1] Major Anderson.

[2] This was a treaty arranged by the American government, for settling the boundary line between the territories of the Menomonies and Chippewas, who had previously disturbed the frontiers by their mutual animosities.

expression of disapprobation, and even abhorrence, too strong for the occasion; and if there be any who should feel inclined to modify such objurgations, or speak in excuse or mitigation of the fact, he might well fear that the publication of such opinions would expose him to have his eyes scratched out, (metaphorically,) or die, in every female coterie, in every review, the death of Orpheus or Pentheus.

Luckily I have no such risk to run. Let but my woman's wit bestead me here as much as my womanhood, and I will, as the Indians say, "tell you a piece of my mind," and place the matter before you in another point of view.

Under one aspect of the question, all these gentlemen travellers are right: they are right in their estimate of the condition of the Indian squaws—they *are* drudges, slaves: and they are right in the opinion that the condition of the women in any community is a test of the advance of moral and intellectual cultivation in that community; but it is not a test of the virtue or civilisation of the man; in these Indian tribes, where the men are the noblest and bravest of their kind, the women are held of no account, are despised and oppressed. But it does appear to me that the woman among these Indians holds her true natural position relatively to the state of the man and the state of society; and this cannot be said of all societies.

Take into consideration, in the first place, that in these Indian communities the task of providing subsistence falls solely and entirely on the men. When it is said, in general terms, that the men do nothing but *hunt* all day, while the women are engaged in perpetual *toil,* I suppose this suggests to civilised readers the idea of a party of gentlemen at Melton, or a turn-out of Mr. Meynell's hounds;—or at most a deer-stalking excursion to the Highlands—a holiday affair;—while the women, poor souls! must sit at home and sew, and spin, and cook victuals. But what is the life of an Indian hunter?—one of incessant, almost killing toil, and often danger.[1] A hunter goes out at dawn, knowing that, if he returns empty, his wife and his little ones must *starve*—no uncommon predicament! He comes home at sunset, spent with fatigue, and unable even to speak. His wife takes off his moccasins, places before him what food she has, or, if latterly the chase has failed, probably no food at all, or only a little parched wild rice. She then examines his hunting-pouch, and in it finds the claws, or beak, or tongue of the game, or other indications by which she knows what it is, and where to find it. She then goes for it, and drags it home. When he is refreshed, the hunter caresses his wife and children, relates the events of his chase, smokes his pipe, and goes to sleep—to begin the same life on the following day.

Where, then, the whole duty and labour of providing the means of subsistence, ennobled by danger and courage, fall upon the man, the woman naturally sinks in importance, and is a dependent drudge. But she is not therefore, I suppose, so *very*

---

[1] I had once a description of an encounter between my illustrious grandpapa Waub-Ojeeg and an enormous elk, in which he had to contend with the infuriated animal for his very life for a space of three hours, and the snows were stained with his blood and that of his adversary for a hundred yards round. At last, while dodging the elk round and round a tree, he contrived to tear off the thong from his moccasin, and with it to fasten his knife to the end of a stick, and with this he literally hacked at the creature till it fell from loss of blood.

miserable, nor, relatively, so very abject; she is sure of protection; sure of mainte-
nance, at least while the man has it; sure of kind treatment; sure that she will never
have her children taken from her but by death; sees none better off than herself, and
has no conception of a superior destiny; and it is evident that in such a state the
appointed and necessary share of the woman is the household work, and all other
domestic labour. As to the necessity of carrying burthens, when moving the camp
from place to place, and felling and carrying wood, this is the most dreadful part
of her lot; and however accustomed from youth to the axe, the paddle, and the
carrying-belt, it brings on internal injuries and severe suffering—and yet it *must* be
done. For a man to carry burthens would absolutely incapacitate him for a hunter,
and consequently from procuring sufficient meat for his family. Hence, perhaps, the
contempt with which they regard it. And an Indian woman is unhappy, and her
pride is hurt, if her husband should be seen with a load on his back; this was strongly
expressed by one among them who said it was "unmanly;" and that "she could not
bear to see it!"

Hence, however hard the lot of woman, she is in no *false* position. The two sexes
are in their natural and true position relatively to the state of society, and the means
of subsistence.

The first step from the hunting to the agricultural state is the first step in the
emancipation of the female. I know there are some writers who lament that the introduction of agriculture has not benefited the Indian women, rather added to their
toils, as a great proportion of the hoeing and planting has devolved on them; but
among the Ottawas, where this is the case, the women are decidedly in a better state
than among the hunting Chippewas; they can sell or dispose of the produce raised
by themselves, if there be more than is necessary for the family, and they take some
share in the bargains and business of the tribe: and add, that among all these tribes,
in the division of the money payments for the ceded land, every woman receives her
individual share.

Lewis and Clarke, in exploring the Missouri, came upon a tribe of Indians who,
from local circumstances, kill little game, and live principally on fish and roots; and
as the women are equally expert with the men in procuring subsistence, they have
a rank and influence very rarely found among Indians. The females are permitted to
speak freely before the men, to whom indeed they sometimes address themselves in
a tone of authority. On many subjects their judgment and opinion are respected,
and in matters of trade their advice is generally asked and pursued; the labours of
the family too are shared equally.[1] This seems to be a case in point.

Then, when we speak of the *drudgery* of the women, we must note the equal division of labour; there is no class of women privileged to sit still while others work.
Every squaw makes the clothing, mats, moccasins, and boils the kettle for her own
family. Compare her life with the refined leisure of an elegant woman in the higher
classes of our society, and it is wretched and abject; but compare her life with that
of a servant-maid of all work, or a factory girl,—I do say that the condition of the

[1] Travels up the Missouri.

squaw is gracious in comparison, dignified by domestic feelings, and by equality with all around her. If women are to be exempted from toil in reverence to the sex, and as *women*, I can understand this, though I think it unreasonable; but if it be merely a privilege of station, and confined to a certain set, while the great primeval penalty is doubled on the rest, then I do not see where is the great gallantry and consistency of this our Christendom, nor what right we have to look down upon the barbarism of the Indian savages who make *drudges* of their women.

I will just mention here the extreme delicacy and personal modesty of the women of these tribes, which may seem strange when we see them brought up and living in crowded wigwams, where a whole family is herded within a space of a few yards: but the lower classes of the Irish, brought up in their cabins, are remarkable for the same feminine characteristic: it is as if true modesty were from within, and could hardly be outwardly defiled.

But to return. Another boast over the Indian savages in this respect is, that we set a much higher value on the chastity of women. We are told (with horror) that among some of the north-west tribes the man offers his wife or sister, nothing loth, to his guest, as a part of the duty of hospitality; and this is, in truth, *barbarism!*— the heartless brutality on one side, and the shameless indifference on the other, may well make a woman's heart shrink within her. But what right have civilised *men* to exclaim, and look sublime and self-complacent about the matter? If they do not exactly imitate this fashion of the Indians, their exceeding and jealous reverence for the virtue of women is really indulged at a very cheap rate to themselves. If the chastity of women be a virtue, and respectable in the eyes of the community for its own sake, well and good; if it be a mere matter of expediency, and valuable only as it affects property, guarded by men just as far as it concerns their honour—as far as regards ours, a jest,—if this be the masculine creed of right and wrong—the fiat promulgated by our lords and masters, then I should be inclined to answer, as the French girl answered the Prince de Conti, "Pour Dieu! monseigneur, votre altesse royale est par trop insolente!" There is no woman, worthy the name, whose cheek does not burn in shame and indignation at the thought.

Such women as those poor perverted sacrificed creatures who haunt our streets, or lead as guilty lives in lavish splendour, are utterly unknown among the Indians.

With regard to female right of property, there is no such thing as real property among them, except the hunting-grounds or territory which are the possession of the tribe. The personal property, as the clothing, mats, cooking and hunting apparatus, all the interior of the wigwam, in short, seems to be under the control of the woman; and on the death of her husband the woman remains in possession of the lodge, and all it contains, except the medal, flag, or other insignia of dignity, which go to his son or male relatives. The corn she raises, and the maple sugar she makes, she can always dispose of as she thinks fit—they are *hers*.

It seems to me a question whether the Europeans, who, Heaven knows, have much to answer for in their intercourse with these people, have not, in some degree, injured the cause of the Indian women:—first, by corrupting them; secondly, by checking the improvement of all their own peculiar manufactures. They prepared deer-skins with extraordinary skill; I have seen dresses of the mountain sheep and young buffalo skins, richly embroidered, and almost equal in beauty and softness to a Cashmere shawl; and I could mention other things. It is reasonable to presume that as these manufactures must have been progressively improved, there might have been farther progression, had we not substituted for articles they could themselves procure or fabricate, those which we fabricate; we have taken the work out of their hands, and all motive to work, while we have created wants which they cannot supply. We have clothed them in blankets—we have not taught them to weave blankets. We have substituted guns for the bows and arrows—but they cannot make guns: for the natural progress of arts and civilisation springing from within, and from their own intelligence and resources, we have substituted a sort of civilisation from without, foreign to their habits, manners, organisation: we are making paupers of them; and this by a kind of terrible necessity. Some very economical members of our British parliament have remonstrated against the system of Indian presents as too *expensive*; one would almost suppose, to hear their arguments, that pounds, shillings, and pence were the stuff of which life is made—the three primal elements of all human existence—all human morals. Surely they can know nothing of the real state of things here. If the issue of the presents from our government were now to cease, I cannot think without horror of what must ensue: trifling as they are, they are an Indian's existence; without the rifle he must die of hunger; without his blanket, perish of cold. Before he is reduced to this, we should have nightly plunder and massacre all along our frontiers and back settlements; a horrid brutalising contest like that carried on in Florida, in which the white man would be demoralised, and the Red man exterminated.

The sole article of traffic with the Indians, their furs, is bartered for the necessaries of life; and these furs can *only* be procured by the men. Thus their only trade, so far from tending to the general civilisation of the people, keeps up the wild hunting habits, and tells fearfully against the power and utility of the women, if it be not altogether fatal to any amelioration of their condition. Yet it should seem that we are ourselves just emerging from a similar state, only in another form. Until of late years there was no occupation for women by which a subsistence could be gained, except servitude in some shape or other. The change which has taken place in this respect is one of the most striking and interesting signs of the times in which we live.

I must stop here: but do you not think, from the hints I have rather illogically and incoherently thrown together, that we may assume as a general principle, that the true importance and real dignity of woman is everywhere, in savage and civilised communities, regulated by her capacity of being useful; or, in other words, that her condition is decided by the share she takes in providing for her own subsistence and the well-being of society as a productive labourer? Where she is idle and useless by privilege of sex, a divinity and an idol, a victim or a toy, is not her position quite as lamentable, as false, as injurious to herself and all social progress, as where she is the drudge, slave, and possession of the man?

The two extremes in this way are the Indian squaw and the Turkish sultana; and

I would rather be born the first than the last:—and to carry out the idea, I would rather, on the same principle, be an Englishwoman or a Frenchwoman than an American or a German woman,—supposing that the state of feeling as regards women were to remain stationary in the two last countries—which I trust it will NOT.

Frances Kemble

Journal of a Residence on a Georgian Plantation
(1863)

Soon after this visit, I was summoned into the wooden porch or piazza of the house, to see a poor woman who desired to speak to me. This was none other than the tall, emaciated-looking Negress who, on the day of our arrival, had embraced me and my nurse with such irresistible zeal. She appeared very ill today, and presently unfolded to me a most distressing history of bodily afflictions. She was the mother of a very large family, and complained to me that, what with childbearing and hard field labor, her back was almost broken in two. With an almost savage vehemence of gesticulation, she suddenly tore up her scanty clothing, and exhibited a spectacle with which I was inconceivably shocked and sickened. The facts, without any of her corroborating statements, bore tolerable witness to the hardships of her existence. I promised to attend to her ailments and give her proper remedies; but these are natural results, inevitable and irremediable ones, of improper treatment of the female frame; and, though there may be alleviation, there cannot be any cure when once the beautiful and wonderful structure has been thus made the victim of ignorance, folly, and wickedness.

After the departure of this poor woman, I walked down the settlement toward the infirmary or hospital, calling in at one or two of the houses along the row. These cabins consist of one room, about twelve feet by fifteen, with a couple of closets smaller and closer than the staterooms of a ship, divided off from the main room and each other by rough wooden partitions, in which the inhabitants sleep. They have almost all of them a rude bedstead, with the gray moss of the forests for mattress, and filthy, pestilential-looking blankets for covering. Two families (sometimes eight and ten in number) reside in one of these huts, which are mere wooden frames pinned, as it were, to the earth by a brick chimney outside, whose enormous aperture within pours down a flood of air, but little counteracted by the miserable spark of fire, which hardly sends an attenuated thread of lingering smoke up its huge throat. A wide ditch runs immediately at the back of these dwellings, which is filled and emptied daily by the tide. Attached to each hovel is a small scrap of ground for a garden, which, however, is for the most part untended and uncultivated.

Such of these dwellings as I visited today were filthy and wretched in the extreme, and exhibited that most deplorable consequence of ignorance and an abject condition, the inability of the inhabitants to secure and improve even such pitiful comfort as might yet be achieved by them. Instead of the order, neatness, and ingenuity which might convert even these miserable hovels into tolerable residences, there was the careless, reckless, filthy indolence which even the brutes do not exhibit in their lairs and nests, and which seemed incapable of applying to the uses of existence the few miserable means of comfort yet within their reach. Fire-wood and shavings lay littered about the floors, while the half-naked children were cowering round two or three smouldering cinders. The moss with which the chinks and crannies of their ill-protecting dwellings might have been stuffed was trailing in dirt and dust about the ground, while the back door of the huts, opening upon a most unsightly ditch, was left wide open for the fowls and ducks, which they are allowed to raise, to travel in and out, increasing the filth of the cabin by what they brought and left in every direction.

In the midst of the floor, or squatting round the cold hearth, would be four or five little children from four to ten years old, the latter all with babies in their arms, the care of the infants being taken from the mothers (who are driven afield as soon as they recover from child labor), and devolved upon these poor little nurses, as they are called, whose business it is to watch the infant, and carry it to its mother whenever it may require nourishment. To these hardly human little beings I addressed my remonstrances about the filth, cold, and unnecessary wretchedness of their room, bidding the older boys and girls kindle up the fire, sweep the floor, and expel the poultry. For a long time my very words seemed unintelligible to them, till, when I began to sweep and make up the fire, etc., they first fell to laughing, and then imitating me. The incrustations of dirt on their hands, feet, and faces were my next object of attack, and the stupid Negro practice (by-the-by, but a short time since nearly universal in enlightened Europe) of keeping the babies with their feet bare, and their heads, already well capped by nature with their woolly hair, wrapped in half a dozen hot, filthy coverings.

Thus I traveled down the "street," in every dwelling endeavoring to awaken a new perception, that of cleanliness, sighing, as I went, over the futility of my own exertions, for how can slaves be improved? Nathless, thought I, let what can be done; for it may be that, the two being incompatible, improvement may yet expel slavery; and so it might, and surely would, if, instead of beginning at the end, I could but begin at the beginning of my task. If the mind and soul were awakened, instead of mere physical good attempted, the physical good would result, and the great curse vanish away; but my hands are tied fast, and this corner of the work is all that I may do. Yet it cannot be but, from my words and actions, some revelations should reach these poor people; and going in and out among them perpetually, I shall teach, and they learn involuntarily a thousand things of deepest import. They must learn, and who can tell the fruit of that knowledge alone, that there are beings in the world, even with skins of a different color from their own, who have sympathy for their misfortunes, love for their virtues, and respect for their common nature—but oh! my heart is full almost to bursting as I walk among these most poor creatures.

The infirmary is a large two-story building, terminating the broad orange-planted space between the two rows of houses which form the first settlement; it is built of whitewashed wood, and contains four large-sized rooms. But how shall I describe to you the spectacle which was presented to me on entering the first of these? But half the casements, of which there were six, were glazed, and these were obscured with dirt, almost as much as the other windowless ones were darkened by the dingy shutters, which the shivering inmates had fastened to in order to protect themselves from the cold. In the enormous chimney glimmered the powerless embers of a few sticks of wood, round which, however, as many of the sick women as could approach were cowering, some on wooden settles, most of them on the ground, excluding those who were too ill to rise; and these last poor wretches lay prostrate on the floor, without bed, mattress, or pillow, buried in tattered and filthy blankets, which, huddled round them as they lay strewed about, left hardly space to move upon the floor. And here, in their hour of sickness and suffering, lay those whose health and strength are spent in unrequited labor for us—those who, perhaps even yesterday, were being urged on to their unpaid task—those whose husbands, fathers, brothers, and sons were even at that hour sweating over the earth, whose produce was to buy for us all the luxuries which health can revel in, all the comforts which can alleviate sickness. I stood in the midst of them, perfectly unable to speak, the tears pouring from my eyes at this sad spectacle of their misery, myself and my emotion alike strange and incomprehensible to them. Here lay women expecting every hour the terrors and agonies of childbirth, others who had just brought their doomed offspring into the world, others who were groaning over the anguish and bitter disappointment of miscarriages—here lay some burning with fever, others chilled with cold and aching with rheumatism, upon the hard cold ground, the draughts and dampness of the atmosphere increasing their sufferings, and dirt, noise, and stench, and every aggravation of which sickness is capable, combined in their condition— here they lay like brute beasts, absorbed in physical suffering; unvisited by any of those Divine influences which may ennoble the dispensations of pain and illness, forsaken, as it seemed to me, of all good; and yet, O God, Thou surely hadst not forsaken them! Now pray take notice that this is the hospital of an estate where the owners are supposed to be humane, the overseer efficient and kind, and the Negroes remarkably well cared for and comfortable.
[. . .]

You cannot conceive anything more grotesque than the Sunday trim of the poor people, their ideality, as Mr. Combe would say, being, I should think, twice as big as any rational bump in their head. Their Sabbath toilet really presents the most ludicrous combination of incongruities that you can conceive—frills, flounces, ribbons; combs stuck in their woolly heads, as if they held up any portion of the stiff and ungovernable hair; filthy finery, every color in the rainbow, and the deepest possible shades blended in fierce companionship round one dusky visage; head hand-kerchiefs, that put one's very eyes out from a mile off; chintzes with sprawling patterns, that might be seen if the clouds were printed with them; beads, bugles, flaring sashes, and, above all, little fanciful aprons, which finish these incongruous toilets with a sort of airy grace, which I assure you is perfectly indescribable. One young man, the oldest son and heir of our washerwoman Hannah, came to pay his respects to me in a magnificent black satin waistcoat, shirt gills which absolutely engulfed his black visage, and neither shoes nor stockings on his feet.

[. . .]

There were two very aged women, who had seen different, and, to their faded recollections, better times, who spoke to me of Mr. [Butler]'s grandfather, and of the early days of the plantation, when they were young and strong, and worked as their children and grandchildren were now working, neither for love nor yet for money. One of these old crones, a hideous, withered, wrinkled piece of womanhood, said that she had worked as long as her strength had lasted, and that then she had still been worth her keep, for, said she: "Missus, tho' we no able to work, we make little niggers for massa." Her joy at seeing her present owner was unbounded, and she kept clapping her horny hands together and exclaiming: "While there is life there is hope; we seen massa before we die." These demonstrations of regard were followed up by piteous complaints of hunger and rheumatism, and their usual requests for pittances of food and clothing, to which we responded by promises of additions in both kinds; and I was extricating myself as well as I could from my petitioners, with the assurance that I would come by-and-by and visit them again, when I felt my dress suddenly feebly jerked, and a shrill cracked voice on the other side of me exclaimed: "Missus, no go yet—no go away yet; you no see me, missus, when you come by-and-by; but," added the voice, in a sort of wail, which seemed to me as if the thought was full of misery, "you see many, many of my offspring." These melancholy words, particularly the rather unusual one at the end of the address, struck me very much. They were uttered by a creature which *was* a woman, but looked like a crooked, ill-built figure set up in a field to scare crows, with a face infinitely more like a mere animal's than any human countenance I ever beheld, and with that peculiar, wild, restless look of indefinite and, at the same time, intense sadness that is so remarkable in the countenance of some monkeys. It was almost with an effort that I commanded myself so as not to withdraw my dress from the yellow, crumpled, filthy claws that gripped it, and it was not at last without the authoritative voice of the overseer that the poor creature released her hold of me.

We have, as a sort of under nursemaid and assistant of my dear M[argery], whose white complexion, as I wrote you, occasioned such indignation to my Southern fellow travelers, and such extreme perplexity to the poor slaves on our arrival here, a much more orthodox servant for these parts, a young woman named Psyche, but commonly called Sack, not a very graceful abbreviation of the divine heathen appellation. She cannot be much over twenty, has a very pretty figure, a graceful, gentle deportment, and a face which, but for its color (she is a dingy mulatto), would be pretty, and is extremely pleasing, from the perfect sweetness of its expression; she is always serious, not to say sad and silent, and has always an air of melancholy and timidity, that has frequently struck me very much, and would have made me think some special anxiety or sorrow must occasion it, but that God knows the whole condition of these wretched people naturally produces such a deportment, and there is no necessity to seek for special or peculiar causes to account for it. Just in proportion as I have found the slaves on this plantation intelligent and advanced beyond the general brutish level of the majority, I have observed this pathetic expression of countenance in them, a mixture of sadness and fear, the involuntary exhibition of the two feelings, which I suppose must be the predominant experience of their whole lives, regret and apprehension, not the less heavy, either of them, for being, in some degree, vague and indefinite—a sense of incalculable past loss and injury, and a dread of incalculable future loss and injury.

[. . .]

As I was cantering along the side of one of the cotton fields I suddenly heard some inarticulate vehement cries, and saw what seemed to be a heap of black limbs tumbling and leaping toward me, renewing the screams at intervals as it approached. I stopped my horse, and the black ball bounded almost into the road before me, and, suddenly straightening itself up into a haggard hag of a half-naked Negress exclaimed, with panting, eager breathlessness: "Oh, missis, missis, you no hear me cry, you no hear me call. Oh, missis, me call, me cry, and me run; make me a gown like dat. Do, for massy's sake, only make me a gown like dat." This modest request for a riding habit in which to hoe the cotton fields served for an introduction to sundry other petitions for rice, and sugar, and flannel, all which I promised the petitioner, but not the "gown like dat"; whereupon I rode off, and she flung herself down in the middle of the road to get her wind and rest.

The passion for dress is curiously strong in these people, and seems as though it might be made an instrument in converting them, outwardly at any rate, to something like civilization; for, though their own native taste is decidedly both barbarous and ludicrous, it is astonishing how very soon they mitigate it in imitation of their white models. The fine figures of the mulatto women in Charleston and Savannah are frequently as elegantly and tastefully dressed as those of any of their female superiors; and here on St. Simons, owing, I suppose, to the influence of the resident lady proprietors of the various plantations, and the propensity to imitate in their black dependents, the people that I see all seem to me much tidier, cleaner, and less fantastically dressed than those on the rice plantation, where no such influences reach them.

I have been long promising poor old House Molly to visit her in her own cabin, and so the day before yesterday I walked round the settlement to her dwelling, and a most wretched hovel I found it. She has often told me of the special directions left by her old master for the comfort and well-being of her old age, and certainly his charge has been but little heeded by his heirs, for the poor faithful old slave is most miserably off in her infirm years. She made no complaint, however, but seemed overjoyed at my coming to see her. She took me to the hut of her brother, old Jacob, where the same wretched absence of every decency and every comfort prevailed; but neither of them seemed to think the condition that appeared so wretched to me one of peculiar hardship—though Molly's former residence in her master's house might reasonably have made her discontented with the lot of absolute privation to which she was now turned over—but, for the moment, my visit seemed to compensate for all sublunary sorrows, and she and poor old Jacob kept up a duet of rejoicing at my advent, and that I had brought "de little missis among um people afore they die."

Leaving them, I went on to the house of Jacob's daughter Hannah, with whom Psyche, the heroine of the rice island story, and wife of his son Joe, lives. I found their cabin as tidy and comfortable as it could be made, and their children, as usual, neat and clean; they are capital women, both of them, with an innate love of cleanliness and order most uncommon among these people. On my way home I overtook two of my daily suppliants, who were going to the house in search of me, and meat, flannel, rice, and sugar, as the case might be; they were both old and infirm-looking women, and one of them, called Scylla, was extremely lame, which she accounted for by an accident she had met with while carrying a heavy weight of rice on her head; she had fallen on a sharp stake, or snag, as she called it, and had never recovered the injury she had received. She complained also of falling of the womb. Her companion (who was not Charybdis, however, but Phœbe) was a cheery soul who complained of nothing, but begged for flannel. I asked her about her family and children; she had no children left, nothing but grandchildren; she had had nine children, and seven of them died quite young; the only two who grew up left her to join the British when they invaded Georgia in the last war, and their children, whom they left behind, were all her family now.

In the afternoon I made my first visit to the hospital of the estate, and found it, as indeed I find everything else here, in a far worse state even than the wretched establishments on the rice island, dignified by that name; so miserable a place for the purpose to which it was dedicated I could not have imagined on a property belonging to Christian owners. The floor (which was not boarded, but merely the damp hard earth itself) was strewn with wretched women, who, but for their moans of pain, and uneasy, restless motions, might very well each have been taken for a mere heap of filthy rags; the chimney refusing passage to the smoke from the pine-wood fire, it puffed out in clouds through the room, where it circled and hung, only gradually oozing away through the windows, which were so far well-adapted to the purpose that there was not a single whole pane of glass in them. My eyes, unaccustomed to the turbid atmosphere, smarted and watered, and refused to distinguish at first the different dismal forms, from which cries and wails assailed me in every corner of the place. By degrees I was able to endure for a few minutes what they were condemned to live their hours and days of suffering and sickness through; and, having given what comfort kind words and promises of help in more substantial forms could convey, I went on to what seemed a yet more wretched abode of wretchedness.

This was a room where there was no fire because there was no chimney, and where the holes made for windows had no panes or glasses in them. The shutters being closed, the place was so dark that, on first entering it, I was afraid to stir lest I should fall over some of the deplorable creatures extended upon the floor. As soon as they perceived me, one cry of "Oh missis!" rang through the darkness; and it really seemed to me as if I was never to exhaust the pity, and amazement, and disgust which this receptacle of suffering humanity was to excite in me. The poor dingy supplicating sleepers upraised themselves as I cautiously advanced among them; those who could not rear their bodies from the earth held up piteous beseeching hands, and as I passed from one to the other I felt more than one imploring clasp laid upon my dress, to solicit my attention to some new form of misery. One poor woman, called Tressa, who was unable to speak above a whisper from utter weakness and exhaustion, told me she had had nine children, was suffering from incessant flooding, and felt "as if her back would split open." There she lay, a mass of filthy tatters, without so much as a blanket under her or over her, on the bare earth in this chilly darkness. I promised them help and comfort, beds and blankets, and light and fire—that is, I promised to ask Mr. [Butler] for all this for them; and, in the very act of doing so, I remembered with a sudden pang of anguish that I was to urge no more petitions from his slaves to their master. I groped my way out, and, emerging on the piazza, all the choking tears and sobs I had controlled broke forth, and I leaned there crying over the lot of these unfortunates till I heard a feeble voice of "Missis, you no cry; missis, what for you cry?" and, looking up, saw that I had not yet done with this intolerable infliction. A poor crippled old man, lying in the corner of the piazza, unable even to crawl toward me, had uttered this word of consolation, and by his side (apparently too idiotic, as he was too impotent, to move) sat a young woman, the expression of whose face was the most suffering, and, at the same time, the most horribly repulsive I ever saw. I found she was, as I supposed, half-witted; and, on coming nearer to inquire into her ailments and what I could do for her, found her suffering from that horrible disease—I believe some form of scrofula—to which the Negroes are subject, which attacks and eats away the joints of their hands and fingers—a more hideous and loathsome object I never beheld; her name was Patty, and she was granddaughter to the old crippled creature by whose side she was squatting.

Margaret Brooke

My Life in Sarawak
(1913)

The Rajah and I had only been a few weeks in Kuching when he had to leave me and go on an expedition to the interior, and I was left alone in the Astana with a maid whom I had brought from England. She was an ordinary sort of woman, with no capacity for enjoying anything that was not European. She left me soon after, for, as she said, she did not like living in such an outlandish place. With this solitary exception there was, at this time, no one in the Astana with whom I could speak, as I did not know Malay. There was, however, the Rajah's butler, a Sarawak Malay, who had been with the first Rajah Brooke for some years. At the Rajah's death, my husband took this man into his service. He was called Talip (a name signifying light). Talip knew a few words of English, and he and I became great friends. He was good-looking, taller than most Malays, with dark, intelligent eyes, a black moustache, and an abundant crop of hair forming a short curly fringe under his head-handkerchief, which he folded round his head with consummate skill. He was a bit of a dandy, and very neat in appearance. He wore a white jacket, under which appeared the folds of his yellow and black sarong, white trousers, and he walked about with bare feet. He was a favourite with all classes in Kuching, for his many years in the first Rajah's service had endeared him to the people.

During the Rajah's absence I got a great deal of information out of Talip, and the way he managed to make himself understood in his broken English was wonderful. One day I said to him, "I want to see the Malay women of Kuching. Ask them to come here." Talip answered, "Certainly. I bring my two wives play with you!" I gently suggested that, together with the two wives, the ministers' and chiefs' wives and daughters might be included in the invitation. After talking the matter over, Talip and I settled that I should hold a reception—my first reception in Sarawak—and that he should be the chamberlain on the occasion and invite, in my name, the principal women of the place.

My life now began to be interesting, for Talip and I had a great many preparations to make and plans to talk over. The dining-room of the Astana was large, and could accommodate about two hundred and fifty guests. I kept impressing on Talip that none of the ministers' and chiefs' lady relations should be forgotten, as it would never do to create jealousy on this my first introduction to the women of the country. I found out that the Datu Bandar, the Datu Imaum, the Datu Temanggong, and the other chiefs all had wives, sons, daughters, and grandchildren galore. "They must all be invited," I said; "for I must know them and make friends with them." I was then initiated by Talip into the proper manner of giving parties in Malayland.

First of all, the question of refreshments had to be considered. Talip invested in dozens and dozens of eggs, pounds and pounds of sugar, and I cannot remember the bewildering quantity of cocoa-nuts and of various other ingredients he deemed necessary for making Malay cakes. These he judiciously parcelled out to the houses of the people I was going to invite, so that they could make the cakes with which I was to present them when they came to call. Talip also borrowed from them cups, saucers, plates, and many other things wanted for such an important occasion.

Some days before the party, on looking out of my sitting-room window towards the landing-place and the path leading up from it to our door, I saw a number of little boys staggering under the weight of numerous round, red lacquer boxes. These were very large, and I sent for Talip and asked him what they were. He informed me that they were to be used for the various cakes and fruit in the same way as we use silver dishes. Talip arranged that on this great occasion we should all sit on the floor round the room, and that the place occupied by the chiefs' wives, with myself in their midst, should be set out with piles of gorgeous cushions covered with gold brocade—also borrowed from the houses of my guests.[1] A fortnight or so was occupied in the preparations, and at last the day came to which I had been looking forward so much. I glanced into the dining-room in the morning, and thought how pretty a meal laid out for Malay ladies looked—very much prettier than the table arrangements at our dinner-parties in England. Great strips of white and red material, bought for the occasion in the Bazaar, were laid down both sides of the room with cross pieces at each end. The red boxes were put at equal distances on these strips, and between the boxes were dishes with the fruits of the country—mangosteens, mangoes, oranges, pineapples, etc. The red lacquer boxes made beautiful notes of colour all round the room.

The tea-party was supposed to begin at 4 o'clock, so accordingly, I dressed myself in my best garments and was quite ready to enter the dining-room and receive my guests. I had heard a great deal of noise going on outside my rooms since 2 o'clock in the afternoon: the rustle of silks, bare feet pattering up and down the verandah, and, becoming curious, I looked over the partitions and saw women in silken draperies flitting about. But Talip was on guard, and every time I came out, or even looked over the partitions, he said to me, "You must not show yourself too soon." However, at 4 o'clock I was dressed, and determined to go out, when Talip again, like the angel with the flaming sword at the gate of Paradise, waved me back. He made me understand that I ought not to show myself before 5.30 on account of Malay etiquette, and went on to explain that the Rajah's subjects should await my pleasure. In his opinion, 9 o'clock would have been preferable for our meeting, but considering my impatience he would allow me to enter the dining-hall at half-past five! So another hour and a half went by whilst I patiently waited to make the acquaintance of my guests, on account of inexorable Malay etiquette. I felt a little

---

[1] There is no greater pleasure one can give Malays than that of borrowing their things. Women, however, ungrudgingly lend their golden ornaments to each other, and the same may be said of their crockery, their furniture, their clothes, etc.

anxious, for I did not know a word of Malay, so I took Marsden's Dictionary with me, and armed with the great volume, at 5.30 punctually, made my entrance into the hall. I was quite taken aback by the charming sight that awaited me as I entered the dining-hall. The rows of women and young girls seated on the floor round the room, with their silken brocades and gauzy veils of rose, green, blue, and lilac, reminded me of an animated bed of brightly coloured flowers. I noticed what beautiful complexions most of these women had, of the opaque pale yellow kind, like the petals of a fading gardenia. Their dark eyes and long eyelashes, their arched eyebrows, their magnificent black hair, their lovely feet and hands, and their quiet manners, were to me quite entrancing. As I came into the room, Talip told them to get up, and the sound of their rustling silks, all moving together, was like a gentle wind sighing through the branches of a bamboo forest. Datu Isa and Datu Siti, the wives of the principal Malay chiefs, came forward one on each side of me, and, each placing one hand under my elbows and the other under my finger-tips, led me to the seat prepared for me against the wall, in the middle of a row of women. My pile of cushions was uncomfortably high, so I asked Talip whether I could not have two pillows taken away, but he said: "No, that could not be. Rajah Ranee must have three cushions more than the chiefs' wives." Therefore, once again I gave way to the conventions of Malaya.

Talip and his satellites appeared with huge jugs of lukewarm coffee, made sweet as syrup to suit the taste of my guests. It was, however, devoid of milk, as the Malays of Sarawak are unaccustomed to the use of that liquid.[1] It took some time to help us all, but when each guest's cup was full, Talip stood in the middle of the room and shouted out: "Makan! la. . . . Minum! la. . . . Jangan malu!" (Eat. Drink. Don't be ashamed).

After coffee, the real business of the day began. Talip told me to say something to my guests, and that he would translate my words into Malay. "Datus, Daiangs, my friends," I said, "I have sent for you because I feel lonely without you. I have come to live here and to make friends with you all. I have waited for this day with great impatience, because I know we shall love one another, and I feel sure if women are friends to one another they can never feel lonely in any country." Talip translated my speech at great length, and when he had finished, Datu Isa, the wife of Datu Bandar the chief minister, bent forward, her eyes cast down, her hands palm downwards on her knees, and replied, "Rajah Ranee, you are our father, our mother, and our grandmother. We intend to take care of you and to cherish you, but don't forget that you are very young, and that you know nothing, so we look upon you as our child. When the Rajah is away, as I am the oldest woman here, I will look after you. There is one thing you must not do: I have heard of Englishwomen taking the hands of gentlemen by the roadside. Now, Rajah Ranee, you must not do that, and when you are sad you must come to me, and I will help to lighten your heart." Talip translated this to me, and I smiled in response. But all the women kept that

---

[1] Some Malay women confided in me that they would not drink it, as by so doing they might get to resemble animals.

gravity which never leaves Malays when they are shy or nervous, or in the presence of strangers. I thought I would try a little conversation on my own account. I looked out some words in Marsden's Dictionary, and meant to inquire of Datu Isa how many sons she had. This remark thawed the ice, for a ripple of laughter went over the room. Instead of saying "sons" I had used the words "baby boys"—the old lady being seventy, no explanation is required! After that, we became very friendly. I consulted Marsden for the rest of the afternoon, and got on beautifully with my guests.

It is strange, even now, how well I remember that party: it might all have happened yesterday. From that eventful day my home-sickness completely vanished, for I felt I had found my friends.

Then began a very agreeable time, such as usually comes with a new and interesting friendship. I think the Malay women as well as myself were mutually interested in one another, and I encouraged the frequent morning visits that one or another of the chieftains' lady relations paid to me. I somehow managed to make myself understood, although my Malay must have sounded strange to them. Indeed, in their strenuous endeavours to understand what I said, I sometimes noticed a strained—I might almost say painful—expression flit across their faces. They were much too kind, however, to laugh or smile, or even to show a moment's impatience. Little by little matters mended, and in a few weeks I became more fluent.

That mighty question of "chiffons," which is usually thought to belong only to European womenkind, seemed to me to play quite as important a part in the minds of my new friends. One day, as I was admiring their beautiful silks, satins, and golden ornaments, Datu Isa (who was, you remember, the lady who had undertaken the care of me during the Rajah's absence) said to me in a very ceremonious manner, "You are the wife of our Rajah, and you ought to wear our dress." I was simply delighted, and at once agreed. Lengthy discussions then took place as to what colours I should choose, and where the things should be made. Finally, the matter resolved itself into the Malay ladies joining together, and insisting on providing me with the whole dress, and I must say it was a beautiful one. The garment called "kain tape" (the Malay name for a woman's skirt) consists of a narrow sheath; this was folded and tucked under my armpits, and made to cover my feet. It was woven in red-and-gold brocade. My jacket was of dark blue satin, and had gold rosettes sewn over it. The collar of the jacket was edged with plaques of gold, fastening in front with a larger clasp, shaped like outstretched wings. All down the sleeves of the jacket, which were slashed up to the elbow, were tiny buttons of gold that jingled like bells. A gauzy scarf of white and gold, obtained from Mecca, covered my head, and a wide wrap of green silk and gold brocade was flung over the left shoulder ready to cover my head and face when wearing the dress in my walks abroad. According to Datu Isa, my right eye alone should peep forth from the golden wrap on such occasions.

Datu Isa had a great many things to say as to the wearing of these garments. "You are my child, Rajah Ranee," she said, "and I have thought a good deal as to whether, being a married woman, you ought to wear golden ornaments, because it is the custom in our country for virgins only to be thus decorated, but as you are the wife of our Rajah, I think that your Malay dress should be as splendid as possible, and we all agree that it will suit you well." I did not share in this opinion. I loved wearing the dress, because of its beauty, but if the truth were told, a tall Englishwoman cannot expect to wear it with the grace which belongs to those tiny frail-looking daughters of the sun. They are all very small indeed, and the noiseless way they move about lends additional beauty to the dress. No European woman, accustomed as she is to freedom, exercise, and somewhat abrupt movements, can possibly imitate with any degree of success the way in which they glide about and manipulate their silken and gauzy draperies.

It is interesting to know the ideas Malay women entertain about the wearing of these clothes. I was somewhat embarrassed with the length of my sarong, ordered by Datu Isa, and arranged by her so that it should fall in folds draggling on the ground. "Never mind, Rajah Ranee," she would say, "you will get accustomed to it by and by, and you must remember that the Rajah's wife never shows her feet." "But why?" I said to Datu Isa. "Because," she answered, "she is never supposed to walk about. She must have servants and subjects at her call every moment of the day. Now, if you wear that dress properly, you would not fasten it in very securely anywhere, but you would sit on cushions almost motionless, because at the slightest movement your clothes would fall off. The wives of the Sultan of Brunei never secure their kain tapes." This was all very well; moreover, it must be remembered that Datu Isa was strictly conservative. Her ideas concerning ceremonial dress and deportment in Sarawak were as rigid as were those of aristocratic old ladies in Early Victorian days. But Datu Isa's daughter-in-law, Daiang Sahada, who is about my own age, reassured me when I felt a little anxious as to whether I could play my part satisfactorily and not derogate from the exalted position Datu Isa was always striving to put me in. "We understand, Rajah Ranee," she would say. "You must not be too anxious; we all know Datu Isa; she is kind and good and you must humour her. Little by little, she will understand, and will not mind if you wear your kain tape so as to allow you to walk a yard or so."

[. . .]

Some months had gone by since the day of my first arrival in Kuching and, odd as it may seem, Europe and all its ways were relegated as it were to an almost imperceptible background in my memory. The charm of the people, the wonderful beauty of the country, the spaciousness, and the absence of anything like conventionality, all enchanted me. Moreover, the people were my own, and every day that passed— and I am not ashamed to own it—little by little I lost some of my European ideas, and became more of a mixture between a Dyak and a Malay. The extraordinary idea which English people entertain as to an insuperable bar existing between the white and coloured races, even in those days of my youth, appeared to me to be absurd and nonsensical. Here were these people, with hardly any ideas of the ways of Europeans, who came to me as though they were my own brothers and sisters.

They must have thought some of my ways curious and strange, but instead of finding fault with them, they gave way to me in everything. I suppose they saw how ready I was to care for them and consider them as members of my family, and as the country became more familiar to me, little by little, much as when one develops photographic plates, some hitherto unperceived trait in their character came out and charmed me.

2

Women and knowledge

The nineteenth century in particular was a period when the accumulation of information about other cultures was seen to be a task of national importance (Richards, 1993). Such information had to be presented according to representational formats which were in the process of becoming inflexible. These formats have persisted in a modified form into the present day. The production of knowledge about other cultures, because of its national characteristic, and because the position of the national was already implicitly coded as masculine, was necessarily also the site for the production of particular types of gendered subjects. Thus, the taking up of a position in relation to information and knowledge was at the same time a taking up of a stand in relation to gendered identity. During the eighteenth and nineteenth centuries it was deemed to be important for women implicitly or explicitly to take such a stand to make their politics or respectability open to public scrutiny.

As we suggested in the general Introduction, women writers in the eighteenth and nineteenth centuries had to write against or be complicit with textual parameters which marked out areas of "womanly" or "feminine" subject matter for them. That certain topics were considered appropriate for treatment by women is borne out by Anthony Trollope's comment on his mother's notoriously acerbic *Domestic Manners of the Americans* (1832): "Thirty years ago my mother wrote a book about the Americans . . . That was essentially a woman's book. She saw with a woman's keen eye, and described with a woman's light but graphic pen, the social defects and absurdities which our near relatives had adopted into their domestic life . . . she did not regard it as part of her work to dilate on the nature and operation of those political arrangements which had produced the social absurdities which she saw . . . Such a work is fitter for a man than for a woman" (Trollope, [1862] 1987, I: 2). Indeed the restrictiveness outlined here in the nineteenth century in some ways set paradigms for later female commentators; twentieth-century women travel writers still have to negotiate a world in which certain kinds of knowledge are considered more "manly" than "womanly".

The posited "difference" of gender here (which, as Fanny Trollope's text ably demonstrates, is a question of perceived voice, not of actual production) derives from the notion that the separate sphere of female existence prescribed by nineteenth-century ideologies of gender roles should extend to female texts. In the case of travel writing, this produces the expectation that women will treat those aspects of the foreign environment which seem to have a particularly feminine resonance or interest. In textual terms, this difference may be notable more in the particular objects of the female gaze than in the subject position and site of enunciation themselves, in contrast to areas of narrative such as landscape description or the recounting of challenging exploits. The presentation of topics such as social mores, domestic and family life, dress, culinary and eating habits—in other words, the observable life of the female Other—suggests how approaches to the materiality of the foreign environment can be considered within the wider gendered discourse of travel writing, itself forming part of the debate on what constitutes "female" or, more accurately, appropriately "feminine" knowledge.

A woman writer in the eighteenth and nineteenth centuries who ventured into the "masculine" side of literary activity, whether through the use of political or scientific discourse, was to a considerable extent risking her secure gendered position. As has been indicated, however, the frequent disclaimers in female travel texts of competence in these spheres of knowledge fail to disguise the fact that many women did engage with topics generally considered inappropriate for their sex. In the introductory section on "Women writing about women" above, we have shown, for example, how female travellers to North America usually took up a political stance towards slavery, incorporating discussion of it into their narratives. We have also mentioned those travellers who focused on issues such as women's rights and education in the context of their travel accounts. In addition to the political, the main areas of knowledge beyond the more overtly acceptable domestic, in which women could and did operate, are science, aesthetics, and race. These areas will be discussed in turn.

Women and scientific knowledge

Women travellers had to make difficult decisions about the tone that they would adopt in writing about another culture, its topography, flora and fauna. They had a choice to make about taking up a scientific posture, adopting a scientific voice, and using Linnean typologies and Latin names for plants, which would set them within a system of knowledge and a tradition of scientific endeavour in Britain (a body of knowledge from which they were explicitly barred until 1913 when women were allowed into the Royal Geographic Society and other scientific academies). This adoption of a scientific stance does not only involve making explicit allegiances to authoritative bodies within Britain, but it also involves implicitly or explicitly making claims to competence within a masculine sphere. Although women could and did engage in scientific study, they did so largely as amateurs, for whom such study could only be considered a hobby. It should be noted that botanising was a seen as an appropriate and safe occupation for nineteenth-century young ladies and the acquisition of a technical vocabulary was part of this process. Furthermore, as Pratt has argued, in the nineteenth century claiming scientific knowledge involved setting oneself in a particular relation to the indigenous culture: the taking up of a Eurocentric position of knowledge in relation to the flora and fauna of a country entailed the virtual and actual removal of plants and animals from their environment in order to locate them instead within a Western and hence global system of knowledge (Mills, 1994; Pratt, 1992). Such a strategy is particularly observable with those nineteenth-century women travellers who were specifically interested in plants and who went abroad to collect them. In such cases, their use of scientific terminology may be considered both an expression of individual engagement with scientific discourse and a voicing of, or interpellation into, a Eurocentric position of knowledge. In some women's travel texts, however, there is certainly a sense that the writer is attempting to situate herself within a scholarly discursive tradition which foregrounds knowledge rather than personal response. A good example of this is Amelia

Murray who, in describing the flora she saw in the United States and Cuba, widely uses Latin names, thus representing herself as scientifically knowledgeable (Murray, [1856] 1969). Fanny Parks, however, is quite different from other writers, for, in describing plants in India, she uses not only the Latin and vernacular British classification where appropriate, but she also includes the indigenous names for the plant; furthermore, she writes very detailed accounts of the way the plant is gathered, classified and used in indigenous herbal medicine, religion and culture (Parks, [1850] 2000).

The ignoring of the local environmental conditions, the local names, the conditions of use and symbolic use of plants and animals for the inhabitants involves implicitly a rejection of the values of that culture. Thus, adopting a scientific voice is not a simple choice. It has benefits for British women travellers in that it allies them to those in positions of high status and indeed situates them within a hegemonic scientific tradition. It also distances the women writers from charges of "nativism" (Mills, 1992). But implicitly adopting such a voice has implications for the claims that the text is making and for its relation to the indigenous culture.

The same is true for those nineteenth-century women who chose a scientific or scholarly discourse to write about the material aspects of the foreign culture. This is notably the case with Amelia Edwards. Edwards, wholly eschewing the assumption that a scholarly treatment of the foreign is inappropriate for and unattainable by women writers, adopts a consistently factual and learned approach to her trip to Egypt, undertaken in 1853. (It should be noted, however, that the trip itself is represented as having been made almost on a whim, in the same way that Mary Kingsley depicts her expedition as a "lark".) Her *A Thousand Miles up the Nile* ([1888] 1997) contains a wealth of information about the background to the sites she visited; her account, as well as being colourfully descriptive and witty, is substantially re-inforced by details such as actual measurements of tombs and statistics, and is illustrated by diagrams and reproductions of hieroglyphics, in addition to more conventional "romantic" engravings. Edwards authorises her own scholarly status by the extensive use of explanatory notes, citing earlier and contemporary Egyptologists; as her comments in the Preface to the first edition indicate, in so doing she is both deferring to a (male) position of knowledge and inserting herself into that professional arena: "the writer who seeks to be accurate, has frequently to go for his [sic] facts, if not actually to original sources . . . at all events to translations and commentaries locked up in costly folios, or dispersed far and wide among the pages of scientific journals and the transactions of learned societies" (Edwards, 1997: xi). Significantly, her emphasis on the precarious future of many of the Egyptian antiquities awakened public concern and helped her to establish the Egyptian Exploration Fund; she also left her own Egyptian collection and library to University College, London, together with a fund to establish the first Chair in Egyptology in Britain, thus inscribing herself, nominally if not actually, into the male world of academia.

The discourse of aesthetics

When describing a landscape, it is possible to set one's description within a scientific discourse, or to employ the language of aesthetics. Both of these strategies would serve to ally women travellers with those in positions of some power within Britain. However, it has a similar distancing effect, in that, as Bohls has argued, "aesthetic discourse disclosed a heightened potential for contributing to the colonial project . . . as travellers began to inscribe the concept of disinterested contemplation on the landscape through scenic tourism. The effect was to distance spectators from their surroundings and obscure the connection between topography and people's material needs' (Bohls, 1995: 48). Conventionally, descriptive writing about landscape was, however, less obviously a "colonial" project than a means of ordering it by establishing a common ground of evaluation drawing on previously authorised high status discourses. This position of aestheticising the landscape involved emptying it of people except as structural elements within a composition, or as signifiers of the rustic.

The aesthetic vocabulary of the sublime is often invoked by travellers in the nineteenth century: the sublime moment in a text for the traveller is one where the focus of attention is less on the landscape than on the emotions which it evokes in the narrator (Mills, 2000). This is especially true of encounters with landscapes which were most unlike anything at home. Descriptions of the sublime were overdetermined for Western women; at one and the same time the sublime combined high status aesthetic discourse (often a kind of Romantic poetic language) together with "feminine" emotional response. Female authored descriptions of Niagara provide a good example, especially since Niagara had already become established by the nineteenth century as a place where extreme responses were common and in some senses socially sanctioned (McGreevy, 1992). It is rare for scientific details of height or volume of water to be given, and instead the response implements a discourse of emotionalism and analogy. Even largely dispassionate and analytical commentators such as Frances Wright ([1821] 1963) and Harriet Martineau move into a different language register when describing "the thundering floor" and "the foaming whirlpool and rushing flood" of the Falls (Martineau, 1837, I: 108). Some observers express an almost obsessive desire to identify with the scene before them—even to throw themselves into the water— suggesting suppressed passion which reads its own frustrations into the turbulence of the environment. Fanny Kemble, in particular, describes the cascade in characteristically dramatic and hyperbolic terms of release from restraint and submission to chaos, which both replicate her own confessed attempts to jump over the edge and articulate a personal urge for self-abandonment: she watches "each mountainous mass of water, as it reached the dreadful brink, recoiling, as in horror, from the abyss; and after rearing backwards in helpless terror, as it were hurling itself down to be shattered in the inevitable doom" (Kemble, 1878, III: 310).

As well as drawing on the descriptive vocabulary of the sublime, many nineteenth-century women travel writers employed the vocabulary of the picturesque. Like the sublime, drawing on the picturesque involved describing the landscape in terms of its compositional elements. Given that landscape sketching and painting, and the display of technical artistic knowledge which this involved, were considered in the late eighteenth and nineteenth centuries particularly appropriate accomplishments for young middle-class women, it is not surprising that artistic metaphors or analogies are such a common feature of female-authored travel texts in this period. Female descriptions of landscape are also often filled with references to Claude Lorrain, Nicolas Poussin and Salvator Rosa, artists commonly associated with the picturesque, thus allowing them to claim a certain discursive authority. The work of these painters was taken as a standard of evaluation, as well as a means of familiarising the scenery for the readers, until well into the nineteenth century. The middle-class status of most nineteenth-century Western women travellers would have enabled them to gain acquaintance with this art through books of engravings (the domestic sphere) and galleries and museums (part of the public sphere to which women had access, albeit limited), and "copying" was an established part of this learning process. In using the painters as points of reference, then, they are arguably taking on a male voice as the locus of authority, in order to give authenticity to the scene being described. Claude, for instance, is often mentioned in connection with skies and sunsets: Fanny Kemble, describing a Roman evening sky in 1846, exclaims, "If we had only been Claude Lorrain, what a sunset we should have painted!" (Kemble, 1882, III: 26). Poussin is usually recalled in connection with more solid nature, mountains, trees and rural scenes. Colourful groups of figures in the landscape are equated with those in Salvator Rosa's work: the guides who take Frances Trollope to the Camaldoli monastery near Florence are described as being out of a Salvator painting, while another striking figure, an Apennine mountaineer in local costume, could, Trollope claims, also have been depicted by Rosa (Trollope, 1842). Other painters who are called up in order to verify the artistic "truth" of the Italian scene include Turner, Correggio, Canaletto and Murillo.

This application of aesthetic knowledge, especially avowed familiarity with well-known painters, had links with the Grand Tour, a feature of eighteenth-century upper-class life exclusive to men, whose aims and aspirations—especially in its foregrounding of the cultural and environmental riches of southern Europe—established an essentially male tradition of artistic and geographical experience (Black, 1985; Chard, 1999; Hibbert, 1969). Nineteenth-century women travellers, particularly those who went to Italy and wrote about it in terms of aesthetic familiarisation, were thus almost inevitably replicating a male model of itinerary and discourse.

While the source of the knowledge is male, however, the application of artistic criteria has a particularly feminine resonance. As has already been suggested, nineteenth-century women were particularly disposed to "seeing" nature through an artistic medium, since they had been taught that imitation or copying were particularly feminine accomplishments. Encouraged to "fix" external reality in this way, women travellers not only wrote of the landscape in pictorial terms, but also sometimes illustrated their texts with their own sketches, often suitably "mastered" to conform with the notions of beauty formulated in relation to landscape composition: among these included in this anthology are Emily Lowe in Scandinavia (1857), Amelia Edwards in the Dolomites and Egypt (1873, 1888), Emily Eden in India (1920), and perhaps the best known commentator/illustrator, Marianne North (1892, 1893), who not only constantly describes the landscape in visual terms, but also painted the scenes and botanical features she observed (the paintings later formed the collection housed in the Marianne North gallery in Kew Gardens).

As well as this visual and compositional framework, the picturesque also involved a certain strategy of textual description which some women found useful; it allowed them to assert that they were not organising the accounts of their travels at all but were simply amassing detail of the objects and sights which they had seen to give an overall impression of the country. Fanny Parks's writing explicitly refers to the picturesque in the title of her book *A Pilgrim in Search of the Picturesque* (1850), and her writing flits from subject to subject without any overt organising principle. This form of seemingly unorganised writing was often drawn on strategically by women writers who did not wish to claim authority for their texts by organising their information according to scientific or logical categories, whilst at the same time allowing them to include material about a country which might be read as authoritative.

This aestheticising discourse often marked out a particular class position for women, indicating their education and the leisure necessary for acquiring this knowledge of the vocabulary of the aesthetic; it also signified that they were tourists rather than missionaries or explorers, since this particular stance in relation to the landscape signalled to the reader that their concerns were with exploring their own psyches and perceptions rather than presenting information about the indigenous peoples or their country. It is therefore not surprising that in some women's texts, there is little interest in impressionistic description of the landscape, particularly amongst those who wished to signal that they were not tourists. As Miller says of Annie Taylor, a missionary writing about Tibet: "she mentioned a primula or two and the herds of wild animals but she scarcely noticed the terrain and was indifferent to geography" (Miller, 1976: 49). Whereas many male explorers both feel that it is their duty to chart an unexplored territory and have been formally educated and equipped with the skills necessary to do so, women travellers often have different interests and skills; in this case, Taylor was more concerned with establishing her place within a missionary expedition to Tibet.

More iconoclastic female travel writers were also often disposed to ironise reliance on the discursive convention which the picturesque had become. Mary Shelley, for example, while frequently employing terms such as "picturesque", "fantastic", and "sublime" to portray Italian scenery, at the same time both notes the inadequacy of language itself as a descriptive tool, and calls attention to the way in which outworn cliché has become a substitute for experience: at the Falls of the Rhine, she writes ironically that it "is always satisfactory to get a picturesque adjunct or two to add interest when, with toil and time, one has reached a picturesque spot" (1844, I: 50).

The language of aesthetics in women's travel texts is not confined to representations of landscape. In both colonial and non-colonial contexts, their depictions of indigenous peoples draw on the discourse of "civilised" European society, in the form of artistic reference and metaphor. In the introductory section of "Women writing about women" above, we have already referred to this process at work in accounts of the harem, where beautiful Oriental women are described in terms of painting and statuary. It becomes even more noticeable in descriptions of Native American Indians, in which the European trope of the Noble Savage—a figure deemed to be close to nature and untouched by degradation—is brought into play, drawing on Old World aesthetic models. In "reading" the American Indian as a figure of perfection (against its opposite, the figure of degeneration, which they implement in other discursive contexts including writing about Black American people), the women travellers are thus engaging with a discursive tradition which situates them within class and race, rather than gender, parameters. This tradition depends on a notion of cultural supremacy: the observer establishes a position of superiority over the observed, shared with the readers, while the subject of observation becomes iconised as an idealised Other. Moreover, since most such depictions of Native Americans in the nineteenth century drew on a pre-existent terminology, a set of images already within the lexis of travel writing, the process of observation itself became an aesthetic and textual act which sought to assimilate the natives to European cultural paradigms.

In these texts, the "difference" of American Indians is constructed as exoticism, as distanced from the subject of enunciation as the art by which it is referenced. So, for Anna Jameson, an impressive six-foot tall Ottawa chief is a figure that "a sculptor might have envied" (Jameson, [1838] 1990: 386), while another young warrior "reminded me of a young Mercury, or of Thorwaldsen's 'Shepherd Boy'" (Jameson, [1838] 1990: 436).[1] Comparisons are frequently made to classical statues, as well as to other visual arts: both Susanna Moodie and her sister, Catherine Parr Traill, who emigrated to Upper Canada in the early 1830s and wrote about their experiences of travelling across the continent, observe that Native Americans would make splendid subjects for a painter (Moodie, [1852] 1986; Traill, [1846] 1989).

It is also important to note that women travel writers in North America use the discourse of aesthetics in a reverse strategy of belittlement, albeit less destructively than some of their male counterparts. In this process, American Indianness is defined by the constituents of a superior European culture, but in such a way as to make it look ridiculous, foregrounding the "differences that fall outside the [European] paradigms' by deliberately focusing on the inappropriateness of the analogies (Pratt, 1992: 44). In this respect, female texts are not transgressive but part of a self-validating cultural hegemony. For example, in Jameson's description of the "dandyism" of a Pottowottomie warrior, whom she refers to as "Beau Brummel", the referential context makes absurd the conjunction of apparent native vanity, curious ornamentations, and semi-nakedness. Other instances of a "high" linguistic register, however, seem designed more to reinforce appreciation of aesthetic difference than to ridicule it. References to the hair of pretty young squaws arranged "à *la Greque*" (Jameson, [1838] 1990: 382), or to the beauty of American Indian womanhood as 'the very *beau idéal* of savage life and unadorned nature' (Moodie, [1852] 1986: 283) suggest a more sympathetic reception of indigenous culture, even while the use of French terms here is a discursive means of establishing the cultural superiority of the observer and her complicity with an educated readership.

Women and domestic knowledge

In his article on commodity and identity in women's travel writing, Tim Youngs (1997) proposes a special relation between femininity and material objects, and argues that the representation of certain objects such as buttons in colonialist female texts has a particular significance in the process of self-construction initiated by the foreign experience. As Youngs himself notes, such an essentialist claim needs quali-fication, and we have throughout the general Introduction above pointed out the dangers of labelling discursive strategies "male" or "female". It is nevertheless the case, as we have noted in the introductory section to "Women writing about women", that what may be termed the domestic is often foregrounded in women's texts, espe-cially those of the nineteenth century. The focus of observation, moreover, is itself frequently gendered in terms of particular female resonance: food is often discussed in the context of its preparation as well as consumption; clothes are noted for their practicality as well as their aesthetic appearance; children are observed in relation to their health and upbringing.

The production of meaning here would seem to depend not only upon a kind of knowledge or experience which is predominantly coded as feminine but also upon a readership which shares this knowledge. In an alien or threatening environment, the woman traveller may seek to re-affirm her own cultural identity by positioning the (European) domestic as a signifier of civilisation in opposition to the unfamil-iarity of the native Other. Cultural disorientation may thus be countered by the re-iteration of the known—here, established gender roles and concerns. In this process the relation between women's domestic activities and the hegemonic struc-tures which have formulated such activities as peculiarly female becomes problema-tised: for women travellers to engage with the domestic abroad is both to accede to their own culture's restraints on them and to enable questioning or re-visioning. (It is also worth pointing out that since most of the nineteenth-century travellers were middle class, the foreign experience may have brought them closer to the funda-mentals of domestic activity than they encountered at home, where, in more afflu-ent households at least, servants did much of the basic work.) Such engagement may facilitate both a critique of their own cultural patterns and a validation of them. For example, negative comments on the upbringing of children, or of particular culinary and gastronomic customs may be a means of re-inforcing a conviction of the superiority of the observer's life-style. Conversely, details of unfamiliar dishes and willingness to try, even to enjoy, them may express a challenge to cultural hegemonies (Kingsley, [1897] 1982). As Melman has argued, the description of enormous harem banquets—apparently relished—by some nineteenth-century visitors to the Middle East—subverts the myth of the Western woman being without physical appetite (Melman, 1995). Similarly, approval of domestic arrangements may reflect a readiness to embrace alternative—and more satisfactory—roles for women. The domestic arena, then, like the other areas of observation which we have discussed, is a potential site of destabilisation as well as of cultural exchange. Like these areas, too, it shows how responses to the foreign are refracted through the interlinked determinants of gender and class.

Women and racism

We have already shown that women travellers engage with patriarchal discourses in their representations of the foreign Other, whether it be the high status discourse of aesthetics or the colonialist discourse of Orientalism. Implicit in our discussion, however, has been the notion that women commentators often subvert these discourses in various ways so as to provide a female-oriented slant on their observations, thus modifying the more ideologically constraining or self-aggrandising elements of male accounts. But if the we/they dichotomies of representation are to some extent dependent on the writer's gender, it must also be stressed that female accounts of indigenous peoples are by no means free from the discursive constraints of racism and nationalism, with the accompanying assumptions of superiority which these often entail (Wetherill and Potter, 1992). Like their male counterparts, when nineteenth-century British women travellers came into contact with racial and cultural difference their responses were coloured by the historical and socio-political contexts of their own (dominant) culture. Racist statements set these women very firmly within their own culture with all the privileges which that position entailed. And although this is largely a nineteenth-century phenomenon, such racism persists, even if only implicitly, in texts written in the present day.

Despite their largely anti-slavery stance, many nineteenth-century Western women commentators articulate the same kind of distancing strategies found in male texts such as H.M. Stanley's and Thomas Parke's writings on Africa (Youngs, 1992, 1994). Distance is established and maintained by the use of racial stereotypes which draw on the notion of Black people as animalistic, filthy and ignorant. In the context of the supposedly more civilised Black Americans, rather than African tribes, the emphasis is more on their ridiculousness as they appear to mimic the customs and culture of their white "superiors". In a more specifically ideological context—such as direct encounters with slavery—contempt, hostility and fear subtextually co-exist with overt sympathy or indignation. Racism, as this suggests, thus took a variety of forms; while few women travellers were as directly antagonistic as Mrs Basil Hall who distinguished American Black people as a whole as smelly and dirty, "so stupid and so indolent, always in the way when not wanted" (Hall, 1931: 217), or Isabella Trotter who objected to seeing Black hands on the plates of food offered her by slaves (Trotter, 1859), more subtle—and perhaps less conscious—kinds of prejudice are observable even among those travellers most inclined to adopt the Black Americans' cause.[2]

Staying at Charleston, on her way to her husband's Georgia plantation (and before she had seen the worst conditions of slavery), Kemble noted with ironic amusement that "it is impossible to conceive anything funnier, and at the same time more provokingly stupid, dirty, and inefficient, than the tribe of black-faced heathen divinities and classicalities who make believe to wait upon us here—the Dianas, Phyllises, Floras, Caesars, etc., who stand grinning in wonderment and delight round our table, and . . . [keep] poking their woolly heads and white grinders in at the door every five minutes" (Kemble, [1863] 1961: 40–41). Similarly, Martineau draws on a discourse of mockery, reliant on stereotype, when she describes the antics of the Black servants at a wayside hotel: "little impish blacks peep and grin . . . [one] serves with a most ostentatious bustle, his eyes wide open, his row of white teeth all in sight" (Martineau, 1838, II: 41–42). As with Kemble's description, the metonymic emphasis on bodily elements here is predicated on the assumed superiority of the white gaze, and is a commonplace of much nineteenth-century writing on Black people.

Racism in relation to Native Americans takes a somewhat different form. Generally, those Indians who fall shortest of the ideal of the Noble Savage, mentioned earlier in this section, are represented in a most obviously racist—that is, derogatory— manner. Isabella Bird's revulsion at the "flat noses, wide mouths, and black hair, cut straight above the eyes and hanging lank and long at the back and sides" (Bird, [1879] 1983: 4) of some Californian Indians establishes her sense of her own cultural and anthropological superiority. Less obviously prejudiced, but equally indicative of an assumed we/they binary, is the patronisingly humorous approach exemplified by Matilda Houston's description of an Indian child (which she calls a "little red thing") wrapped tightly in a papoose: "it has all the appearance of a gigantic carrot, with something resembling a human head on the thick end of it" (Houston, 1850, I: 129). In both these instances, the writers position themselves as observers distinct from the objects of their observation, whom they reify by a process of reductiveness; there is no evident desire to bridge the perceived gap between them.

In conclusion, in producing information about other cultures, women travel writers also produce a position for themselves as gendered subjects. They are forced by discursive paradigms within which they write to take up positions on a range of issues which seem far removed from the subjects about which they write. Because of the impact of feminism on eighteenth- and nineteenth-century gender relations, Western women writers have had to define themselves in relation to femininity and they have also had to establish their position with regards to their own culture. When each woman writer negotiates her own position out of the discursive range available to her, each choice entails other assumptions and necessitates other statements. Thus, the act of describing another culture entails situating the woman travel writer in minute detail in relation to her own culture. The gendered travel text itself becomes, then, a reflection and mediation of the society which has produced it.

Notes

1 Bertel Thorwaldsen (1770–1844) was a Danish sculptor, born in Copenhagen, who settled in Rome for most of his life and became a highly acclaimed artist. He was one of the most

successful imitators of classical sculpture; many of his statues represented the pagan deities. Various of his best works were exhibited in England, some remaining here in private collections.

2 Here, class factors may well be interacting with racial stereotyping to produce this prejudice.

Marianne Baillie

First Impressions on a Tour Upon the Continent in the Summer of 1818
(1819)

[. . .] we soon arrived at the tremendous ascent, known under the very appropriate name of *Les Eschelles de Savoy.* Here we stopped at a lone hovel, to add a couple of oxen to our usual three horses; but these animals being at work at the plough, we were obliged to be satisfied with the assistance of another horse. A girl accordingly brought him out, helped to arrange the traces, &c., and ran by his side half way up the mountain, till we had attained the most arduous pass, and then returned with him to her cottage. She wore her hair gathered in a knot at the back of the head, in the true Italian style. As we toiled along, we observed a *paysanne*, with a load upon her head (most probably on her early way to some village market), stop to pay her morning devotions at a shrine of the Virgin, rudely carved in wood, and placed in a niche by the road-side. How shall I describe the wonderful manner in which we climbed these frightful eschelles? We seemed to be drawn up by our straining, labouring horses almost in a perpendicular direction, and at a foot's pace. On our left was a yawning chasm of immense magnitude, among a gloomy pile of frowning rocks, which might well be the abode of some ancient giant or geni; while further on, these same rocks, extending their mighty barriers on every side, seemed to hang tremulously over head, threatening to crush the hapless traveller, should sudden wind or storm arise to shake them from their precarious-looking base. The blue heaven above us was nearly shut from our sight by their dark and shadowy projections. Our guides (three or four in number, and resembling, in their wild, strange attire and features, a group of *Salvator Rosa's* banditti) pointed out to us the ancient road, passable, even in its best days, by mules alone. It was a narrow ledge, with no defence whatever from the precipice on one side, winding in serpentine mazes through deep grottos, or chasms, in the bowels of the mountain. We saw a prodigious monument of Bonaparte's daring genius in a tunnel, which had been cut through the heart of these solid rocks, and beneath which a fine road was to have been made; but his career of power having been so suddenly and awfully checked, the work remains unfinished. After shuddering amid the sublimity of these scenes for some time, their rugged character gradually softened upon us, and the tender green of the fern, mingling richly with the tangled underwood, began to make its welcome appearance. Far above our heads, also, dark forests of lofty pine were occasionally visible, although the lower crags of overhanging rock generally hid them from our view. At length the prospect expanded into verdant pastures (where cows and goats were peacefully browsing), shaded by beech, elm, chestnut, and apple trees, and skirted by softly-swelling banks, covered with a rich and mossy vegetation. The blue smoke wreath, frequently rising above the tufted foliage, marked the vicinity of hamlets, and the little orchards and inclosed patches of well-cultivated garden ground (seen here and there), and the groups of women spinning at their cottage doors, gave the whole an indescribable air of pastoral comfort and beauty.

[. . .]

Here we crossed a ferry over the river Tessin, which divides the dominions of Austria from those of Sardinia. The richness and grace of the wooded banks, which fringed this fine stream, delighted us; and the face of the whole country gradually smiled and brightened, till it at last expanded into the most glorious burst of exquisite loveliness that the imagination can conceive: for now we first beheld the *Lago Maggiore*, embosomed in romantic hills, with the superb Alps rising beyond them, and its shores studded with innumerable hamlets, villas, and cottages. The declining sun shed a warm colouring of inexpressible beauty upon the calm surface of this celebrated lake, whose waters, smooth and glassy, pure and tranquil, seemed indeed, in the words of Byron, to be a fit

> Mirror and a bath
> For Beauty's youngest daughters.

It was impossible not to kindle into enthusiasm as we gazed upon a scene of such Armida-like fascination. Why should I attempt a description of the Borromean Isles, the Isola Madre, Isola Bella, and other fairy-green gems, which adorned the bosom of this queen of waters? They have been already so celebrated by the pencil and the lyre, that my efforts would be those of presumption. I find it quite too much even to relate the effect they produced upon our minds; for no words can adequately express our feelings of admiration and surprise!

We were now once more in Piedmont, and the road led us through the town of Arona, built upon the shores of the lake, which is full forty miles in length. We saw a picturesque figure of a peasant girl kneeling upon the banks, and laving (like a young naiad) her long tresses in the stream. There is a fine grey ruin of a castle upon the left, as you enter Arona, and a chain of bold cliffs covered with vineyards, with several cottages, peeping out from amid bowers of fragrance, near their craggy summits. A refreshing breeze tempered the still ardent heat of day: it seemed to rise upon us, in a gale of balmy softness, from the water, whose placid waves are some-times, however, ruffled into sudden anger, by storms of wind from the surrounding Alps; and many unfortunate accidents to boatmen, &c. arise in consequence. It would be difficult to imagine any thing in nature more luxuriantly beautiful than the hanging gardens belonging to the little villas in this neighbourhood; where stan-dard peach-trees, olives, filberts, grapes, figs, Turkey wheat, orange blossoms, carna-tions, and all the tribe of vegetables, are mingled together in rich confusion, and the vines trained upon low trellises slope down to the water's edge; while, among the grass at the feet of the taller trees, the pumpkin trails her golden globes and flowers. We remarked several pretty faces, in a style neither wholly Italian nor French, but which formed an agreeable and happy mixture of both. The ever odious *goître*, nevertheless, sometimes obtruded its horrid deformity among them; and it was an equal mortification to our dreams of perfection to observe, that even in the little towns, built in the very heart of all this sweetness and purity, the most disgusting smells (indicative of innately filthy habits) perpetually issued forth, poisoning every street, and mingling their pollutions with the fragrant breath of the mountain gale. But now the fanciful crags on the opposite side of the lake began to assume a pur-plish blue tint, deeply influenced by, and half lost in, the shadow of lowering clouds, which (fast gathering round their summits in dark and misty volumes) foreboded an approaching storm. Bright and catching lights, however, still lingered upon the bright sails of distant boats, and upon the no less white walls of the little villages; which were built so close upon the shore as to seem as if they sprung from the bosom of the waves.

[. . .]

The colour of the rocks in those places which were not covered with snow was sin-gular, being of a light *aqua marine*, occasioned by the lichens which grew upon them. Large eagles, formidable from their strength and boldness, are frequently seen amidst these dreary wastes. I was soon quite wearied by the bleak spectacle of such wide desolation, my eyes ached with the dazzling brightness of the snows, and I began sincerely to wish the passage over. The ascent and descent altogether is forty-two miles; coming down from a height of seven thousand feet, we could not see three yards before us, being completely enveloped in a thick dense fog. It seemed like plunging into a fearful gulf of vapours! Such a mist I never could have *imagined*.

The road now led us though tall forests of pine, darkly magnificent, which grew upon the shelving sides of the precipitous descent. Upon the jutting crags, we occa-sionally beheld the fearless goat, bounding about, enjoying the sense of liberty, and snuffing the keen air of his native mountains; a child or two, also, sometimes appeared in almost equally dangerous situations, at the door of a wooden hut, called a *chalet*, built of timber (of a reddish tint), and much in the form of an ark. A little thinly scattered underwood of birch, &c. with colts-foot twining round the roots, now began to evince our approach to more hospitable regions, and the sensation of piercing cold in some measure abated. The sun made several felicitous attempts to struggle through the heavy and obscuring clouds; and a prospect (of which we caught a transient glimpse between two enormous rocks) seemed to open like an enchanted vision of ineffable brightness and beauty. During this interval of a moment, we beheld a narrow but fertile valley, a river, with hills of vivid green rising beyond, bounded in the distant horizon by mountains of glowing purple, and smiled upon by a summer sky of the clearest blue. Suddenly it was brilliantly illuminated by a partial gleam of sun, and thus discovered, (sparkling through a thin veil of still lingering mist) it seemed to break upon us like a lovely dream. I could have fancied it Voltaire's Eldorado, or the gay, unreal show of fairy land, seen by Thomas the Rhymer, in Scott's Minstrelsy of the Border. Indeed sober language has no words or terms to describe its singular effect. Apropos to sobriety of language: Although there is nothing so wearing as hyperbolical and exaggerated expressions, applied on common or insignificant occasions, and although I consider them in that case to be the resource of a weak capacity, which is incapable of judicious restraint and discrimination, it is equally insupportable to hear the real wonders and charms of nature or art spoken of with tame and tasteless apathy. Those persons who have soul enough to feel and appreciate them must either vent their just enthusiasm, in terms which to common minds sound romantic and poetical, or else resolve to be wholly silent.

Frances Kemble

Journal
(1835)

My mind was eagerly dwelling on what we were going to see: that sight which—— said was the only one in the world which had not disappointed him. I felt absolutely nervous with expectation. The sound of the cataract is, they say, heard within fifteen miles when the wind sets favourably: to-day, however, there was no wind; the whole air was breathless with the heat of midsummer, and, though we stopped our waggon once or twice to listen as we approached, all was profoundest silence. There was no motion in the leaves of the trees, not a cloud sailing in the sky; every thing was as though in a bright, warm death. When we were within about three miles of the Falls, just before entering the village of Niagara,——stopped the waggon; and then we heard distinctly, though far off, the voice of the mighty cataract. Looking over the woods, which appeared to overhang the course of the river, we beheld one silver cloud rising slowly into the sky,—the everlasting incense of the waters. A perfect frenzy of impatience seized upon me: I could have set off and run the whole way; and when at length the carriage stopped at the door of the Niagara house, waiting neither for my father, D——, nor——, I rushed through the hall, and the garden, down the steep footpath cut in the rocks. I heard steps behind me;——was following me: down, down I sprang, and along the narrow footpath, divided only by a thicket from the tumultuous rapids. I saw through the boughs the white glimmer of that sea of foam. "Go on, go on; don't stop," shouted——, and in another minute the thicket was passed: I stood upon Table Rock.——seized me by the arm, and, without speaking a word, dragged me to the edge of the rapids, to the brink of the abyss. I saw Niagara.—Oh, God! who can describe that sight?

Frances Kemble

Records of a Girlhood
(1878)

You must not expect any description of Niagara from me, because it is quite unspeakable, and, moreover, if it were not, it would still be quite unimaginable. The circumstances under which I saw it I can tell you, but of the great cataract itself, what can be told except that it is water?

I confess the sight of it reminded me, with additional admiration, of Sir Charles Bagot's daring denial of its existence; having failed to make his pilgrimage thither during his stay in the United States, he declared on his return to England that he had never been able to find it, that he didn't believe there was any such thing, and that it was nothing but a bragging boast of the Americans.

[. . .]

We reached Queenstown, on the Niagara river, below the falls, at about twelve o'clock, and had three more miles to drive to reach them. The day was serenely bright and warm, without a cloud in the sky, or a shade in the earth, or a breath in the air. We were in an open carriage, and I felt almost nervously oppressed with the expectation of what we were presently to see. We stopped the carriage occasionally to listen for the giant's roaring, but the sound did not reach us until, within three miles over the thick woods which skirted the river, we saw a vapoury silver cloud rising into the blue sky. It was the spray, the breath of the toiling waters ascending to heaven. When we reached what is called the Niagara House, a large tavern by the roadside, I sprang out of the carriage and ran through the house, down flights of steps cut in the rock, and along a path skirted with low thickets, through the boughs of which I saw the rapids running a race with me, as it seemed, and hardly faster than I did. Then there was a broad, flashing sea of furious foam, a deafening rush and roar, through which I heard Mr. Trelawney, who was following me, shout, "Go on, go on; don't stop!" I reached an open floor of broad, flat rock, over which the water was pouring. Trelawney seized me by the arm, and all but carried me to the very brink; my feet were in the water and on the edge of the precipice, and then I looked down. I could not speak, and I could hardly breathe; I felt as if I had an iron band across my breast. I watched the green, glassy, swollen heaps go plunging down, down, down; each mountainous mass of water, as it reached the dreadful brink, recoiling, as in horror, from the abyss; and after rearing backwards in helpless terror, as it were, hurling itself down to be shattered in the inevitable doom over which eternal clouds of foam and spray spread an impene-trable curtain. The mysterious chasm, with its uproar of voices, seemed like the watery mouth of hell. I looked and listened till the wild excitement of the scene took such possession of me that, but for the strong arm that held me back, I really think I should have let myself slide down into the gulf. It was long before I could utter, and as I began to draw my breath I could only gasp out, "O God! O God!" No words can describe either the scene itself, or its effect upon me.

We stayed three days at Niagara, the greater part of which I spent by the water, under the water, on the water, and more than half in the water. Wherever foot could stand I stood, and wherever foot could go I went. I crept, clung, hung, and waded; I lay upon the rocks, upon the very edge of the boiling cauldron, and I stood alone under the huge arch over which the water pours with the whole mass of it, thun-dering over my rocky ceiling, and falling down before me like an immeasurable curtain, the noonday sun looking like a pale spot, a white wafer, through the dense thickness. Drenched through, and almost blown from my slippery footing by the whirling gusts that rush under the fall, with my feet naked for better safety, grasp-ing the shale broken from the precipice against which I pressed myself, my delight was so intense that I really could hardly bear to come away.

The rock over which the rapids run is already scooped and hollowed out to a great extent by the action of the water; the edge of the precipice, too, is constantly crumbling and breaking off under the spurn of its downward leap. At the very brink the rock is not much more than two feet thick, and when I stood under it and thought of the enormous mass of water rushing over and pouring from it, it did not seem at all improbable that at any moment the roof might give way, the rock break off fifteen or twenty feet, and the whole huge cataract, retreating back, leave a still wider basin for its floods to pour themselves into. You must come and see it before you die, dear H——.

After our short stay at Niagara, we came down Lake Ontario and the St. Lawrence to Montreal and Quebec. Before I leave off speaking of that wonderful cataract, I must tell you that the impression of awe and terror it produced at first upon me completely wore away, and as I became familiar with it, its dazzling brightness, its soothing voice, its gliding motion, its soft, thick, furry beds of foam, its veils and draperies of floating light, and gleaming, wavering diadems of vivid colours, made it to me the perfection of loveliness and the mere magnificence of beauty. It was certainly not the "familiarity" that "breeds contempt," but more akin to the "perfect love" which "casteth out fear;" and I began at last to understand Mr. Trelawney's saying that the only impression it produced on him was that of perfect repose; but perhaps it takes Niagara to mesmerize him.

[The first time I attempted to go under the cataract of Niagara I had a companion with me, and one of the local guides, who undertook to pilot us safely. On reaching the edge of the sheet of water, however, we encountered a blast of wind so violent that we were almost beaten back by it. The spray was driven against us like a furious hailstorm, and it was impossible to open our eyes or draw our breath, and we were obliged to relinquish the expedition. The next morning, going down to the falls alone, I was seduced by the comparative quietness and calm, the absence of wind or atmospheric disturbance, to approach gradually the entrance to the cave behind the water, and finding no such difficulty as on the previous day, crept on, step by step, beneath the sheet, till I reached the impassable jutting forward of the rock where it meets the full body of the cataract. My first success emboldened me to two subsequent visits, the small eels being the only unpleasant incident I encountered. The narrow path I followed was a mere ledge of shale and broken particles of the rock, which is so frayable and crumbling, either in its own nature, or from the constant action of the water, that as I passed along and pressed myself close against it, I broke off in my hands the portions of it that I grasped.]

A few miles below the falls is a place called the whirlpool, which, in its own kind, is almost as fine as the fall itself. The river makes an abrupt angle in its course, when it is shut in by very high and rocky cliffs—walls, in fact—almost inaccessible from below. Black fir trees are anchored here and there in their cracks and fissures, and hang over the dismal pool below, most of them scathed and contorted by the fires or the blasts of heaven. The water itself is of a strange colour, not transparent, but a pale blue-green, like a discoloured turquoise, or a stream of verdigris, streaked with long veins and angry swirls of white, as if the angry creature couldn't get out of that hole, and was foaming at the mouth; for, before pursuing its course, the river churns round and round in the sullen, savage, dark basin it has worn for itself, and then, as if it had suddenly found an outlet, rushes on its foaming, furious way down to Ontario. We had ridden there and alighted from our horses, and sat on the brink for some time. It was the most dismal place I ever beheld, and seemed to me to grow horribler every moment I looked at it: drowning in that deep, dark, wicked-looking whirlpool would be hideous, compared to being dashed to death amid the dazzling spray and triumphant thunder of Niagara.

[There are but three places I have ever visited that produced upon me the appalling impression of being accursed, and empty of the presence of the God of nature, the Divine Creator, the All-loving Father: this whirlpool of Niagara, that fiery, sulphurous, vile-smelling wound in the earth's bosom, the crater of Vesuvius, and the upper part of the Mer de Glace at Chamouni. These places impressed me with horror, and the impression is always renewed in my mind when I remember them: God-forsaken is what they looked to me.]

Anna Jameson

Winter Studies and Summer Rambles in Canada
(1838)

[. . .]

Niagara in summer

Between the town of Queenston and the cataract of Niagara lies the pretty village of Stamford, (close to Lundy Lane, the site of a famous battle in the last war,) and celebrated for its fine air. Near it is a beautiful house with its domain, called Stamford Park, built and laid out by a former governor (Sir Peregrine Maitland.) It is the only place I saw in Upper Canada combining our ideas of an elegant, well-furnished English villa and ornamented grounds, with some of the grandest and wildest features of the forest scene. It enchanted me altogether. From the lawn before the house, an open glade, commanding a park-like range of broken and undulating ground and wooded valleys, displayed beyond them the wide expanse of Lake Ontario, even the Toronto light-house, at a distance of thirty miles, being frequently visible to the naked eye. By the hostess of this charming seat I was conveyed in a light pony carriage to the hotel at the Falls, and left, with real kindness, to follow my own devices. The moment I was alone, I hurried down to the Table Rock. The body of water was more full and tremendous than in the winter. The spray rose, densely falling again in thick showers, and behind those rolling volumes of vapour the last gleams of the evening light shone in lurid brightness, amid amber and crimson clouds; on the other side, night was rapidly coming on, and all was black, impenetrable gloom, and "boundless contiguity of shade." It was very, very beautiful, and strangely awful too! For now it was late, and as I stood there, lost in a thousand reveries, there was no human being near, no light but that reflected from the leaping, whirling foam; and in spite of the deep-voiced continuous thunder of the cataract, there was such a stillness that I could hear my own heart's pulse throb—or did I mistake feeling for hearing?—so I strayed homewards, or housewards I should say, through the leafy, gloomy, pathways—wet with the spray, and fairly tired out.

Two or three of my Toronto friends are here, and declare against my projects of solitude. To-day we had a beautiful drive to Colonel Delatre's. We drove along the road *above* the Falls. There was the wide river spreading like a vast lake, then narrowing, then boiling, foaming along in a current of eighteen miles an hour, till it swept over the Crescent Rock in a sheet of emerald green, and threw up the silver clouds of spray into the clear blue sky. The fresh luxurious verdure of the woods, relieved against the dark pine forest, added to the beauty of the scene. I wished more than ever for those I love most!—for some one who would share all this rapture of admiration and delight, without the necessity of speaking—for, after all, what are words! They express nothing, reveal nothing, avail nothing. So it all sinks back into my own heart, there to be kept quiet. After a pleasant dinner and music, I returned to the hotel by the light of a full moon, beneath which the Falls looked magnificently mysterious, part glancing silver light, and part dark shadow, mingled with fleecy folds of spray, over which floated a soft, sleepy gleam; and in the midst of this tremendous velocity of motion and eternity of sound, there was deep, deep repose, as in a dream. It impressed me for the time like something supernatural—a vision, not a reality.

The good people, travellers, describers, poets, and others, who seem to have hunted through the dictionary for words in which to depict these cataracts under every aspect, have never said enough of the rapids above—even for which reason, perhaps, they have struck me the more; not that any words in any language would have prepared me for what I now feel in this wondrous scene. Standing to-day on the banks above the Crescent Fall, near Mr. Street's mill, gazing on the rapids, they left in my fancy two impressions which seldom meet together—that of the sublime and terrible, and that of the elegant and graceful—like a tiger at play. I could not withdraw my eyes; it was like a fascination.

The verge of the rapids is considerably above the eye; the whole mighty river comes rushing over the brow of a hill, and as you look up, it seems coming down to overwhelm you. Then meeting with the rocks, as it pours down the declivity, it boils and frets like the breakers of the ocean. Huge mounds of water, smooth, transparent, and gleaming like the emerald, or rather like the more delicate hue of the chrysopaz, rise up and bound over some unseen impediment, then break into silver foam, which leaps into the air in the most graceful fantastic forms; and so it rushes on, whirling, boiling, dancing, sparkling along, with a playful impatience, rather than overwhelming fury, rejoicing as if escaped from bondage, rather than raging in angry might—wildly, magnificently beautiful! The idea, too, of the immediate danger, the consciousness that anything caught within their verge is inevitably hurried to a swift destination, swallowed up, annihilated, thrills the blood; the immensity of the picture, spreading a mile at least each way, and framed in by the interminable forests, adds to the feeling of grandeur; while the giddy, infinite motion of the headlong waters, dancing and leaping, and revelling and roaring, in their mad glee, gave me a sensation of rapturous terror, and at last caused a tension of the nerves in my head, which obliged me to turn away.

The great ocean, when thus agitated by conflicting winds or opposing rocks, is a more tremendous thing, but it is merely tremendous—it makes us think of our prayers; whereas, while I was looking on these rapids, beauty and terror, and power and joy, were blended, and so thoroughly, that even while I trembled and admired, I could have burst into a wild laugh, and joined the dancing billows in their glorious, fearful mirth—

Leaping like Bacchanals from rock to rock,
Flinging the frantic Thyrsus wild and high!

I shall never see again, or feel again, aught like it—never! I did not think there was an object in nature, animate or inanimate, that could thus overset me *now!*

Mrs Charles Meredith

Notes and Sketches of New South Wales
(1844)

The crew of the harbour-master's boat were New Zealanders, fine intelligent-looking, copper-coloured fellows, clad in an odd composite style, their national dress and some British articles of apparel being blended somewhat grotesquely. The New Zealanders are much the noblest specimens of "savages" that I have ever met with. During our residence in Sydney I saw a chief walking along one of the principal streets, with his wife following him. I had often heard of and seen what is called majestic demeanour, but this untutored being, with his tattooed face and arms, and long shaggy mantle, fairly outdid even my imaginings of the majestic, as he paced deliberately along, planting his foot at every step as if he had an emperor's neck beneath it, and gazing with most royal indifference around him. There was the concentrated grandeur of a hundred regal mantles of velvet, gold, and ermine in the very sway of his flax-fringed cloak; I never beheld anything so truly stately. I cannot say so much for his lady, a black-haired, brown-faced body, in a gaudy cotton-print grown, and (so far as I could judge) nothing else. She trotted after her lordly better-half, staring with unsophisticated curiosity at everything, apparently quite a novice in the busy scene; but I verily believe, had you placed the man amidst the coronation splendours of Westminster Abbey, that he would not have been so "vulgar" as to betray surprise. Nor is their courtesy of manner in any degree inferior to their magnificent demeanour. I have heard my husband say, that when at New Zealand, he was treated by the chiefs with such kind, anxious hospitality, and true gentlemanly bearing, as might put to shame many an educated but less civilized European.

Mary Shelley

Rambles in Germany and Italy
(1844)

The inn at Schaffhausen is large and good, without being first-rate. We engaged a *voiturier* to take us the next day to Zurich, and bargained to visit the Falls of the Rhine on our way. We wished to reach them by water, as the best approach; but Murray had by a misprint in his Hand-book put seventeen francs instead of seventeen batz, as the price asked for a boat; and as we, as you well know, are perforce economical travellers, we demurred. This misapprehension being set right by the very civil master of the hotel, we engaged a boat, and the carriage was to meet us at the Falls. We embarked in a rough canoe; a man held an oar at the stern, and a woman one at the prow. We sped speedily down the rapid river, and at one point a little apprehension of danger, just enough to make the heart beat, was excited. We approached the Falls, we were hurrying towards the ledge of rocks; it seemed as if we must go right on, when, by a dexterous use of the oars, we found ourselves with one stroke in the calm water of a little cove; the moment was just agreeably fearful; and at the crisis, an eagle had soared majestically above our heads. It is always satisfactory to get a picturesque adjunct or two to add interest when, with toil and time, one has reached a picturesque spot.

The cottage built to let out the Falls as a show is the contrary of all this; but it has some advantages. You see the sight from various points of view, being first on a level with the upper portion of the river, and by degrees, as you descend to other windows and balconies, reach the level of the lower part. The falls of Terni is the finest cataract I have seen: I believe it to be the grandest in Europe; but it is altogether of a different character from the falls of the Rhine. The waters of the Velino are contracted into a narrow channel, and fall in one stream down a deep precipice The falls of the Rhine are broken into many, and are spread wide across the whole breadth of the river; their descent is never so great, but they are varied by many rocks, which they clothe fantastically with transparent waves, or airy spray.

What words can express—for indeed, for many ideas and emotions there are no words—the feelings excited by the tumult, the uproar and matchless beauty of a cataract, with its eternal, ever-changing veil of misty spray? The knowledge of its ceaseless flow; there, before we were born; there, to be after countless generations have passed away; the sense of its power, that would dash us to atoms without altering the tenor of its way, which gives a shiver to the frame even while we gaze in security from its verge; the radiance of its colouring, the melody of its thunder—can these words convey the impression which the mind receives, while the eye and ear seem all too limited in their powers of perception? No! for as painting cannot picture forth motion, so words are incapable of expressing commotion in the soul. It stirs, like passion, the very depths of our being; like love allied to ruin, yet happy in possession, it fills the soul with mingled agitation and calm. A portion of the cataract arches over the lowest platform, and the spray fell thickly on us, as standing on it and looking up, we saw wave, and rock, and cloud, and the clear heavens through its glittering ever-moving veil. This was a new sight, exceeding anything I had ever before seen; however, not to be wet through, I was obliged quickly to tear myself away.

[. . .]

SEPTEMBER 4

We did not go to bed till nearly twelve. We were to rise at two; and at the blast of a trumpet we were awakened. You must know, besides its glass, Prague is famous for the manufacture of brass wind instruments, and P——bought a trumpet for sixteen florins (thirty-two shillings): to prevent all possibility of any of the party not shaking off slumber at the right moment, he blew a blast which must have astonished all the sleepers in the inn.

We again traversed the ghostly-looking white market-place of Budweis by the light of the unset moon, and took our places in one of the carriages on the railroad. Day soon struggled through the shades of night, quenched the moonbeams, and disclosed the face of earth. I never recollect a more delightful drive than the hundred miles between Budweis and Linz: each hour the scene gains in beauty—from fertile and agreeable, it becomes interesting, then picturesque; and at last it presents a combination of beauty which I never saw equalled. I hurry over the miles, as our carriages were hurried along the railroad, which having an inclination down toward Linz, went very fast—I hurry on, and speak briefly of the ever-varying panorama of distant mountain, wood-clothed upland and fertile plain, all gay in sunshine, which we commanded as we were whirled along the brink of a chain of hills. I never can forget the glorious sunset of that evening. We were on the height of a mountain,

> "At whose verdant feet
> A spacious plain, outstretched in circuit wide,
> Lay pleasant."—[1]

As we descended towards Linz, the sun dropped low in the heavens. The prospect was extensive; varied by the lines of wooded hills and majestic mountains, and towering above, on the horizon, was stretched the range of the Salzburg and Styrian Alps. The Danube wound through the varied plain below; the town of Linz was upon the banks, and a bridge spanned the river; above, it swept under high precipices—below, it flowed majestically on: its glittering waves were seen afar giving that life and sublimity to the landscape which it never acquires without the addition of ocean, lake, or river—water, in short, in some magnificent form. Golden and crimson, the clouds waited on the sun, now dazzling in brightness; and now, as that

---

[1] *Paradise Regained.*

sunk behind the far horizon, stretching away in fainter and fainter hues, reflected by the broad river below. The town of Linz was a point or resting place for the eye, which added much to the harmony and perfection of the landscape. I held my breath to look. My heart had filled to the brim with delight, as, sitting on a rock by the lake of Como, I had watched the sunlight climb the craggy mountains opposite. The effect of this evening—when instead of *up*, I looked *down* on a widespread scene of glorious beauty, was different; yet so poor is language, that I know not how to paint the difference in words. I had never before been aware of all the awe the spirit feels when we are taken to a mountain top, and behold the earth spread out fair at our feet: nor of the delight a traveller receives when, at the close of a day's travel, he—

> Obtains the brow of some high-climbing hill,
> Which, to his eye, discovers unawares
> The goodly prospect of some foreign land
> First seen; or some renowned metropolis,
> With glistening spires and pinnacles adorned,
> Which now the *setting* sun gilds with his beams.[1]

Catherine Parr Traill

The Backwoods of Canada
(1846)

Some of our party, who were younger and lighter of foot than we sober married folks, ran on before; so that when the blanket, that served the purpose of a door, was unfastened, we found a motley group of the dark skins and the pale faces reposing on the blankets and skins that were spread round the walls of the wigwam.

The swarthy complexions, shaggy black hair, and singular costume of the Indians formed a striking contrast with the fair-faced Europeans that were mingled with them, seen as they were by the red and fitful glare of the wood-fire that occupied

---

[1] Milton. Do these lines, in the "Paradise Lost," refer in the poet's mind to his first view of Florence? It seems very probable.

the centre of the circle. The deer-hounds lay stretched in indolent enjoyment, close to the embers, while three or four dark-skinned little urchins were playing with each other, or angrily screaming out their indignation against the apish tricks of the hunchback, my old acquaintance Maquin, that Indian Flibberty-gibbet, whose delight appeared to be in teazing and tormenting the little papouses, casting as he did so side-long glances of impish glee at the guests, while as quick as thought his features assumed an impenetrable gravity when the eyes of his father or the squaws seemed directed towards his tricks.

There was a slight bustle among the party when we entered one by one through the low blanket-doorway. The merry laugh rang round among our friends, which was echoed by more than one of the Indian men, and joined by the peculiar half-laugh or chuckle of the squaws. "*Chippewa*" was directed to a post of honour beside the hunter Peter; and squaw Peter, with an air of great good humour, made room for me on a corner of her own blanket; to effect which two papouses and a hound were sent lamenting to the neighbourhood of the hunchback Maquin.

The most attractive persons in the wigwam were two Indian girls, one about eighteen,—Jane, the hunter's eldest daughter, and her cousin Margaret. I was greatly struck with the beauty of Jane; her features were positively fine, and though of gipsey darkness the tint of vermilion on her cheek and lip rendered it, if not beautiful, very attractive. Her hair, which was of jetty blackness, was soft and shining, and was neatly folded over her forehead, not hanging loose and disorderly in shaggy masses, as is generally the case with the squaws. Jane was evidently aware of her superior charms, and may be considered as an Indian belle, by the peculiar care she displayed in the arrangement of the black cloth mantle, bound with scarlet, that was gracefully wrapped over one shoulder, and fastened at her left side with a gilt brooch. Margaret was younger, of lower stature, and though lively and rather pretty, yet wanted the quiet dignity of her cousin; she had more of the squaw in face and figure. The two girls occupied a blanket by themselves, and were busily engaged in working some most elegant sheaths of deer-skin, richly wrought over with coloured quills and beads: they kept the beads and quills in a small tin baking-pan on their knees; but my old squaw (as I always call Mrs. Peter) held her porcupine-quills in her mouth, and the fine dried sinews of the deer, which they make use of instead of thread in work of this sort, in her bosom.

On my expressing a desire to have some of the porcupine-quills, she gave me a few of different colour that she was working a pair of mocassins with, but signified that she wanted "'*bead*' to work mocsin," by which I understood I was to give some in exchange for the quills. Indians never give since they have learned to trade with white men.

She was greatly delighted with the praises I bestowed on Jane. She told me Jane was soon to marry the young Indian who sat on one side of her in all the pride of a new blanket coat, red sash, embroidered powder-pouch, and great gilt clasps to the collar of his coat, which looked as warm and as white as a newly washed fleece. The old squaw evidently felt proud of the young couple as she gazed on them, and often repeated, with a good-tempered laugh, "Jane's husband—marry by and by."

We had so often listened with pleasure to the Indians singing their hymns of a Sunday night that I requested some of them to sing to us; the old hunter nodded assent; and, without removing his pipe, with the gravity and phlegm of a Dutchman, issued his commands, which were as instantly obeyed by the younger part of the community, and a chorus of rich voices filled the little hut with a melody that thrilled to our very hearts.

The hymn was sung in the Indian tongue, a language that is peculiarly sweet and soft in its cadences, and seems to be composed with many vowels. I could not but notice the modest air of the girls; as if anxious to avoid observation that they felt was attracted by their sweet voices, they turned away from the gaze of the strangers, facing each other and bending their heads down over the work they still held in their hands. The attitude, which is that of the Eastern nations; the dress, dark hair and eyes, the olive complexion, heightened colour, and meek expression of face, would have formed a study for a painter. I wish you could have witnessed the scene; I think you would not easily have forgotten it. I was pleased with the air of deep reverence that sat on the faces of the elders of the Indian family, as they listened to the voices of their children singing praise and glory to the God and Saviour they had learned to fear and love.

[. . .]

I was much pleased with the simple piety of our friend the hunter Peter's squaw, a stout, swarthy matron, of most amiable expression. We were taking our tea when she softly opened the door and looked in; an encouraging smile induced her to enter, and depositing a brown papouse (Indian for baby or little child) on the ground, she gazed round with curiosity and delight in her eyes. We offered her some tea and bread, motioning to her to take a vacant seat beside the table. She seemed pleased by the invitation, and drawing her little one to her knee, poured some tea into the saucer, and gave it to the child to drink. She ate very moderately, and when she had finished, rose, and, wrapping her face in the folds of her blanket, bent down her head on her breast in the attitude of prayer. This little act of devotion was performed without the slightest appearance of pharisaical display, but in singleness and simplicity of heart. She then thanked us with a face beaming with smiles and good humour; and, taking little Rachel by the hands, threw her over her shoulder with a peculiar sleight that I feared would dislocate the tender thing's arms, but the papouse seemed well satisfied with this mode of treatment.

In long journeys the children are placed in upright baskets of a peculiar form, which are fastened round the necks of the mothers by straps of deer-skin; but the *young* infant is swathed to a sort of flat cradle, secured with flexible hoops, to prevent it from falling out. To these machines they are strapped, so as to be unable to move a limb. Much finery is often displayed in the outer covering and the bandages that confine the papouse.

There is a sling attached to this cradle that passes over the squaw's neck, the back of the babe being placed to the back of the mother, and its face outward. The first thing a squaw does on entering a house is to release herself from her burden, and stick it up against the wall or chair, chest or any thing that will support it, where the passive prisoner stands, looking not unlike a mummy in its case. I have seen the picture of the Virgin and Child in some of the old illuminated missals, not unlike the figure of a papouse in its swaddling-clothes.

The squaws are most affectionate to their little ones. Gentleness and good humour appear distinguishing traits in the tempers of the female Indians.

Elizabeth M. Sewell

Impressions of Rome, Florence and Turin
(1862)

I never yet heard any one describe Civita Vecchia, and certainly I am not able to do so myself. From the moment we drove under the archway of the large rambling hotel, till we left it the next morning, our thoughts were concentrated in Rome, and so I imagine it must be with most persons. The place looked to me like a set of barracks. I have no recollection of shops, and scarcely of a street. There was a railway station; but I scarcely noticed how it was reached. Perhaps, however, that arose from the fact of our pressing anxiety lest we should be too late for the train. We had gone on all the morning in a dreaming fashion—lingering over our breakfast, taking but little thought of our bags and boxes, trusting all to Giuseppe, and only thinking how satisfactory it was to be on *terra firmâ*, and how pleasant to be journeying to Rome, when a sudden rush of the porter, the waiter, and the landlord startled us with the conviction that we had not a minute to lose. How we hurried to the chamber of the one member of our party, who being over-tired had breakfasted in her own room,— how we collected gloves, ribands, brooches, and every miscellaneous article of the toilette, and thrust them into our bags and pockets,—how mercilessly we turned and twisted about our unhappy friend, throwing her garments upon her stringless and unbuttoned, and how we bemoaned ourselves, and reproached Giuseppe, and professed to give up at once any hope of being in time—and in the midst of all the confusion, what dreary visions arose of a long day at Civita Vecchia, may very easily be imagined! And after all what was our condition? We found ourselves quietly seated in the railway carriage, with time to settle ourselves comfortably, to make every arrangement for our luggage, and to laugh at our folly in having suffered ourselves to be so frightened. That is a very common experience in continental railway travelling. English and Americans are the only people who rush through life, and delight

113

in braving and just escaping a great annoyance. "Not a minute to lose," means ten minutes to spare in France and Italy, but it is long before one can fully comprehend and accept this fact.

And of all railways, that from Civita Vecchia to Rome would seem to be the least likely to hurry and leave you behind. It partakes of the genius of the country: by the word "country" meaning the Papal States. It is not absolutely retrograde, but its advances are made in the most careful and least exciting manner. You do not rush over the Campagna, upon which you enter immediately after leaving the fortifications; you progress soberly by the side of the Mediterranean. There is full opportunity for watching the extent of the blue waters, the curling and crisping of the waves, and the white foam, so sparkling and free. You may see a steamer in the distance which left Naples the evening before, and is now coming up to Civita Vecchia to take in passengers; and you may congratulate yourself most heartily that you are not going on board. Or you may turn to the Campagna. The very name has an untold charm. What you see is, you are informed, the most uninteresting portion of the whole tract; and certainly, if you were passing over such an extent of uncultivated land in England, you might be inclined to call it so; but how can the Roman Campagna ever be uninteresting? It stretches away like a raised map; but beneath those uneven mounds, upon which flocks of sheep and herds of dark-eyed, light-coloured buffalo-oxen are grazing, what treasures of antiquity, what ruins of houses, temples, statues, columns, lie buried! It requires faith indeed to believe it; the present has so completely obliterated the past. Only the towers of a few old fortified stone houses on the shore, recall the contests of the mediæval age. The shepherds, with their rough sheepskin coats and pointed hats; the sickly peasants who here and there lie stretched upon the green bank, are now the sole possessors of the Campagna; at least, so far as life and employment can be called possession. The land itself is the property of the great nobles of Rome; but they have no connexion with it, except through the suffering, emaciated, and scattered population who are condemned to cultivate it. There are railway stations between Civita Vecchia and Rome; but what need there is of any, is a question which it is easier for a traveller to ask than to answer. No roads are to be seen, and no villages. In the distance there may be a solitary farmhouse, surrounded by a group of stunted trees; but even this is little better than a hospital. At certain seasons of the year, if great precautions are taken, it may be occupied, and some persons doubtless do occupy it; but what their lives are, and how soon they may be brought to an end, is seen by the condition of the miserable beggars, who creep up to the carriage piteously asking for money, which it would seem they can have no means of expending.

The train rolls on, and you draw nearer to Rome. Away to the north-east, a shadowy outline is seen on the horizon; its form is undulating, its tint a pale grey, deepened with blue. There is something singularly graceful in it, as it stands apart from the long line of soft and jagged hills which so nearly approach it. You could almost say that it was conscious of beauty and individuality; and when you hear that you are looking upon the "lone Soracte," which

> ——from out the plain
> Heaves like a long-swept wave about to break,
> And on the curl hangs pausing,

you feel that, apart from all associations, the solitary mountain has gained a place in your memory for ever.

And those jagged hills!—there is snow on their summits, and behind the openings of the foremost ridge a glistening mass is seen, which must be very far off. They are the Sabine mountains,—and though now they may seem strange to you, recalling by their names only the days of mythical barbarism, you will ere long learn to linger with delight upon the grey tints of their stony peaks,—blending exquisitely with the rich purple shadows of their deep recesses, until in idea they have become one with Rome itself,—so softening the sternness of its past, and the desolation of its present condition, that any description, or any thought which separates the ruins from the mountains, will be felt to be an untruthfulness,—an ungrateful denial of the beauty bestowed upon the Eternal City.

But you are hurrying forward, and there are indications of a close approach to a town. Cottages are more frequent, and looking to the right, a cultivated country is seen, ascending gradually to the foot of a remarkably-shaped square-topped hill, which may lay some claim to the dignity of a mountain. On its highest elevation, a convent of the Passionists has been erected, and the form of the building can almost be distinguished. The sides of this hill sink into the Campagna, which stretches away from it like the flat sea-coast—there is no visible line of separation. The Alban Mount—for it is that which you are regarding—is, as it were, a mighty upheaving of the Campagna, and having from its elevation escaped the desolating malaria, it has gathered around its base white towns and villages, glittering amongst pines, olives, and chestnuts. Marino, Grotta Ferrata, Rocca di Papa, will all in time become familiar to you; now, you scarcely look at them, for your eye is wandering beyond the Alban Mount to the far-extending slopes rich in beauty and cultivation, which spread away to the east, and where you may seek for places, in thought familiar to you from childhood—Frascati and Tivoli. It is very difficult to understand it all. That same Alban Mount stood looking upon the Campagna before Rome was founded; the very stones of Alba Longa are, so it is said by some, still resting upon its declivity overhanging the Alban Lake; and on the summit—Monte Cavo, as it is now called—was the great temple of Jupiter, to which the Roman generals directed their triumphal march when they had gained some splendid victory. It is so impossible to think, much more to feel at this, as you are carried along in a railway carriage, that, in very despair, you turn away and dwell only upon what is visibly before you. There is nothing grand or exciting, or in the least satisfying, in that. Before you have had time to know that you must be approaching Rome, you are there—at the railway station—nothing better than a railway station, bustling, dusty, most matter-of-fact. Neither carriages nor porters have anything peculiar about them; and though the Papal gendarmes strut about with cocked hats, and a good deal of silver upon their coats, and have fierce and surly faces, they are not therefore so very unlike gendarmes all over the world.

I had one great advantage myself in entering Rome; I was placed in a carriage with a friend who had seen it before, and who did not wish to talk. If I had been called upon to express enthusiasm or admiration, I should have been greatly disturbed; for, in truth, I felt but little of either. A first view of any place, of which one has for years formed to oneself a definite picture, must necessarily be a shock, even if it does not prove a disappointment. To enter Rome by the Porta Portese on your way to the Via Sistina, is to pass by the high, bare walls of the hospital of Or San Michele, and then thread your course through a number of narrow streets, flanked by dilapidated houses, and thronged with beggars, too sickly and degraded to be picturesque, till you reach the banks of the Tiber. Looking across the river, you may then see a small building, encircled by columns, and roofed with what appear to be wooden tiles, which you are told is the Temple of Vesta. It excites no poetical feeling by its beauty, and you pass it too rapidly to summon imagination to your assistance. The Tiber is crossed by the "Ponte di quattro Capi;" you have not yet learnt that it is the old Pons Fabricius, and its name is but an amusement and a wonder. So are many of the names of the streets, but beauty and grandeur are still not to be found. Only the grand, decayed, circular building—the theatre of Marcellus—upon which you stumble unexpectedly in the midst of some most decayed and beggarly streets, gives you a certain thrill—a suspicion that after all you are not going to be disappointed, that there may be something in Rome to awaken a new and an intense interest. And there are glimpses of nobler and more imposing thoroughfares as you proceed, but only glimpses—you seem to skirt them all. In and out, through lanes and alleys, you proceed, till suddenly—you could almost start from your seat and entreat the driver to pause—in a small open "Place" is an immense deep basin of clear water; behind it, rocks and statues, Neptune, Tritons, and horses, are mingled together in such confusion, that you cannot attempt to distinguish them. They are backed by the façade of a Roman Palazzo, with its columns, pilasters, and bas-reliefs; and from a central niche, and from every projection at the side, profuse streams gush out, pouring down the rocks in foaming lines, till they fall glittering and dancing into the vast stone reservoir. It is such a contrast to the dirt and poverty, the hopeless, abject decay from which you have just escaped, that it comes before you as a marvel of magic. The taste which designed it may be objectionable, the details may be faulty in the extreme, but the effect is undoubted. You cannot wonder that Roman superstition attaches a peculiar power to the Fountain of Trevi, and bids those who are about to depart from Rome, but would fain return to it again, drink of its charmed waters, and their wish will receive its fulfilment.

The Fountain of Trevi is but a short distance from the Via Sistina, and the Via Sistina demands but a short description. It is neither ancient nor modern, neither handsome nor decayed. It dates, as one-half of Rome appears to date, from Sixtus the Fifth; and it has some good houses in it, and some very bad. That there are no porticoes to the doorways, no steps, no ornaments, is not surprising; for who can find anything like architectural beauty in an Italian house? In England, certainly, I should have been surprised to see opposite the door of a large private dwelling a dark archway, looking like the entrance to a coal-cellar, and in which, unhappy, poverty-stricken people had gathered, watching for an opportunity to beg; but so, also, I should not, in England, have expected to ascend to my suite of rooms by a stone staircase, so dirty that one could only gather up one's dress and step carefully, and be thankful that one was near-sighted. The small door flat against the wall might have been the entrance to a closet, but the bell-handle and the tinkling bell indicated something more dignified; and there was a marble tablet inserted near, with an inscription, commemorating the fact, that Thorwaldsen, the sculptor, during his residence in Rome, inhabited the same *appartment.* That was the first little romance which awaited me. There were to be many more before I said good-bye to Rome, although they were scarcely to be found in the drawing-room, dining-room, and bed-rooms, opening from an ante-room, and communicating with each other, which were to constitute our home for the next two months. Continental rooms, and continental furniture, are all very much alike; there may be less cotton velvet in Italy than in France, the fashion of the sofas may be more cumbersome, there may be a greater medley of colour,—yellow and green may predominate over crimson,—and the beds may partake rather of the quality of straw than feathers, but these are very slight differences. It is when you look out of your window into the little garden below, that you are conscious of a change. The orange-trees, the luxuriant flowers, the little rippling fountains, tell you then that you are in Italy, even before you have caught the musical language of the servants, who are chattering and calling to each other, rejoicing in the brilliant sunshine, and perhaps more indifferent than yourself to the sharp wind which accompanies it.

There was a collection of these little gardens filling the space between the backs of the houses of the Via Sistina and the Via Gregoriana; and there were some mysterious connexion between them, and a way through an archway and a courtyard, by which persons could go privately from one street to the other. The houses also seemed to have some unknown means of communication. It was difficult to tell whether the balcony at which you were looking belonged to yourself or your neighbour.

The distinction between *meum* and *tuum* was by no means clear, especially when it dawned upon you, that persons inhabiting an *appartement* on the floor above you, reached it by some courtyard quite removed from the public entrance. All this was very perplexing and rather exciting, when eventually there came a fear of robbers, and I lay awake at night thinking of the staircase between the dining and drawing rooms, which led down into unpenetrated regions, and the little door in the wall outside our ante-room, marked "studio," but leading to I knew not what.

That, however, was an after-fear. I slept undisturbed my first night in Rome—at least, when I had become accustomed to my straw bed.

Anna Jameson

Winter Studies and Summer Rambles in Canada
(1838)

In the afternoon, Mr. Johnson informed me that the Indians were preparing to dance, for my particular amusement. I was, of course, most thankful and delighted. Almost in the same moment, I heard their yells and shrieks resounding along the shore, mingled with the measured monotonous drum. We had taken our place on an elevated platform behind the house—a kind of little lawn on the hill-side;—the precipitous rocks, clothed with trees and bushes, rose high like a wall above us: the glorious sunshine of a cloudless summer's day was over our heads—the dazzling blue lake and its islands at our feet. Soft and elysian in its beauty was all around. And when these wild and more than half-naked figures came up, leaping, whooping, drumming, shrieking, hideously painted, and flourishing clubs, tomahawks, javelins, it was like a masque of fiends breaking into paradise! The rabble of Comus might have boasted themselves comely in comparison, even though no self-deluding potion had bleared their eyes and intellect. It was a grotesque and horrible phantas-magoria. Of their style of clothing, I say nothing—for, as it is wisely said, nothing can come of *nothing:*—only if "all symbols be clothes," according to our great modern philosopher—my Indian friends were as little symbolical as you can dare to imagine:—*passons par là.* If the blankets and leggings were thrown aside, all the resources of the Indian toilette, all their store of feathers, and bears' claws, hawks' bells, vermilion, soot, and verdigris, were brought into requisition as decoration: and no two were alike. One man wore three or four heads of hair, composed of the manes and tails of animals; another wore a pair of deers' horns; another was *coiffé* with the skin and feathers of a crane or some such bird—its long bill projecting from his fore-head; another had the shell of a small turtle suspended from his back, and dangling behind; another used the skin of a polecat for the same purpose. One had painted his right leg with red bars, and his left leg with green lines: particoloured eyes and faces, green noses, and blue chins, or *vice versâ*, were general. I observed that in this grotesque deformity, in the care with which everything like symmetry or harmony in form or colours was avoided, there was something evidently studied and artisti-cal. The orchestra was composed of two drums and two rattles, and a chorus of voices. The song was without melody—a perpetual repetition of three or four notes, melancholy, harsh, and monotonous. A flag was stuck in the ground, and round this they began their dance—if dance it could be called—the movements consisting of the alternate raising of one foot, then the other, and swinging the body to and fro. Every now and then they paused, and sent forth that dreadful, prolonged, tremu-lous yell, which re-echoed from the cliffs, and pierced my ears and thrilled along my nerves. The whole exhibition was of that finished barbarism, that it was at least complete in its way, and for a time I looked on with curiosity and interest. But that innate loathing which dwells within me for all that is discordant and deformed, rendered it anything but pleasant to witness. It grated horribly upon all my perceptions. In the midst, one of those odd and unaccountable transitions of thought caused by some mental or physical reaction—the law which brings extremes in contrast together, came across me. I was reminded that even on this very day last year I was seated in a box at the opera, looking at Carlotta Grisi and Perrot dancing, or rather flying through the galoppe in "Benyowsky." The oddity of this sudden association made me laugh, which being interpreted into the expression of my highest approbation, they became every moment more horribly ferocious and animated; redoubled the vigour of their detestably awkward movements and the shrillness of their savage yells, till I began involuntarily to look about for some means of escape—but this would have been absolutely rude, and I restrained myself.

I presume it was in consequence of these new arrivals that we had a grand *talk* or council after breakfast this morning, at which I was permitted to be present, or, as the French say, to *assist*.

There were fifty-four of their chiefs, or rather chief men, present, and not less than two hundred Indians round the house, their dark eager faces filling up the windows and doorways; but they were silent, quiet, and none but those first admitted attempted to enter. All as they came up took my hand: some I had seen before, and some were entire strangers, but there was no look of surprise, and all was ease and grave self-possession: a set of more perfect gentlemen, in *manner*, I never met with.

The council was convened to ask them if they would consent to receive goods instead of dollars in payment of the pensions due to them on the sale of their lands, and which, by the conditions of sale, were to be paid in money. So completely do the white men reckon on having everything their own way with the poor Indians, that a trader had contracted with the government to supply the goods which the Indians had not yet consented to receive, and was actually now on the island, having come with me in the steamer.

As the chiefs entered, they sat down on the floor. The principal person was a venerable old man with a bald head, who did not speak. The orator of the party wore a long gray blanket-coat, crimson sash, and black neckcloth, with leggings and moccasins. There was also a well-looking young man dressed in the European fashion, and in black; he was of mixed blood, French and Indian; he had been carried early to Europe by the Catholic priests, had been educated in the Propaganda College at Rome, and was lately come out to settle as a teacher and interpreter among his people. He was the only person besides Mr. Schoolcraft who was seated on a chair, and he watched the proceedings with great attention. On examining one by one the assembled chiefs, I remarked five or six who had good heads—well developed, intellectual, and benevolent. The old chief, and my friend the Rain, were conspicuous among them, and also an old man with a fine square head and lofty brow, like the picture of Red-jacket, and a young man with a pleasing countenance, and two scalps hung as ornaments to his belt. Some faces were mild and vacant, some were stupid and coarse, but in none was there a trace of insolence or ferocity, or of that vile expression I have seen in a depraved European of the lowest class. The worst physiognomy was that of a famous medicine-man—it was mean and cunning. Not only the countenances but the features differed; even the distinct characteristics of the Indian, the small deep-set eye, breadth of face and high cheek-bones, were not universal: there were among them regular features, oval faces, aquiline noses. One chief had a head and face which reminded me strongly of the Marquis Wellesley. All looked dirty, grave, and pictur-esque, and most of them, on taking their seats on the ground, pulled out their tobacco-pouches and lighted their wooden pipes.

Nearly opposite to me was a famous Pottowottomi chief and conjuror, called the Two Ears. He was most fantastically dressed and hideously painted, and had two large clusters of swansdown depending from each ear—I suppose in illustration of his name. There were three men with their faces blacked with grease and soot, their hair dishevelled, and their whole appearance studiously squalid and miserable: I was told they were in mourning for near relations. With these exceptions the dresses were much what I have already described; but the chief whom I immediately distinguished from the rest, even before I knew his name, was my cousin, young Waub-Ojeeg, the son of Wayish,ky; in height he towered above them all, being about six feet three or four. His dress was equally splendid and tasteful; he wore a surtout of fine blue cloth, under which was seen a shirt of gay colours, and his father's medal hung on his breast. He had a magnificent embroidered belt of wampum, from which hung his scalping-knife and pouch. His leggings (metasses) were of scarlet cloth beauti-fully embroidered, with rich bands or garters depending to his ankle. Round his head was an embroidered band or handkerchief, in which were stuck four wing-feathers of the war-eagle, two on each side—the testimonies of his prowess as a warrior. He held a tomahawk in his hand. His features were fine, and his countenance not only mild, but almost femininely soft. Altogether he was in dress and personal appear-ance the finest specimen of his race I had yet seen; I was quite proud of my adopted kinsman.

He was seated at some distance; but in far too near propinquity, for in truth they almost touched me, sat a group of creatures—human beings I must suppose them—such as had never been seen before within the lines of civilisation. I had remarked them in the morning surrounded by a group of *Ottawas*, among whom they seemed to excite as much wonder and curiosity as among ourselves: and when I inquired who and what they were, I was told they were *cannibals* from the Red River, the title being, I suspect, quite gratuitous, and merely expressive of the disgust they excited. One man had his hair cut short on the top of his head, and it looked like a circular blacking-brush, while it grew long in a fringe all round, hanging on his shoulders. The skins thrown round them seemed on the point of rotting off; and their attitude when squatted on the ground was precisely that of the larger apes I have seen in a menagerie. More hideous, more pitiable specimens of humanity in its lowest, most degraded state, can hardly be conceived; melancholy, squalid, stupid—and yet not fierce. They had each received a kettle and a gun by way of encouragement.

The whole number of chiefs assembled was seventy-five; and take notice that the half of them were smoking, that it was blazing noontide, and that every door and window was filled up with the eager faces of the crowd without, and then you may imagine that even a scene like this was not to be enjoyed without some drawbacks; in fact, it was a sort of purgatory to more senses than one, but I made up my mind to endure, and did so. I observed that although there were many hundreds round the house, not one woman, outside or inside, was visible during the whole time the council lasted.

I should not forget to mention that the figures of most of the men were superb; more agile and elegant, however, than muscular—more fitted for the chase than for labour, with small and well formed hands and feet. When the dance was ended, a young warrior, leaving the group, sat himself down on a little knoll to rest. His spear lay across his knees, and he reposed his head upon his hand. He was not painted, except with a little vermilion on his chest—and on his head he wore only the wing of the osprey: he sat there—a model for a sculptor. The perfection of his form, the graceful abandonment of his attitude, reminded me of a young Mercury, or of Thorwaldsen's "Shepherd Boy." I went up to speak to him, and thanked him for his exertions in the dance, which indeed had been conspicuous: and then, for want of something else to say, I asked him if he had a wife and children? The whole expression of his face suddenly changed, and with an air as tenderly coy as that of a young girl listening to the first whisper of a lover, he looked down and answered softly, "Kah-ween!"—No, indeed! Feeling that I had for the first time embarrassed an Indian, I withdrew, really as much out of countenance as the youth himself. I did not ask him his name, for that were a violation of the Indian form of good breeding, but I learn that he is called *the Pouncing Hawk*—and a fine creature he is—like a blood horse or the Apollo; West's comparison of the Apollo Belvedere to a young Mohawk warrior has more of likelihood and reasonableness than I ever believed or acknowledged before.

A keg of tobacco and a barrel of flour were given to them, and they dispersed as they came, drumming, and yelling, and leaping, and flourishing their clubs and war-hatchets.

Not far from this, and almost immediately in front of our house, stands another wigwam, a most wretched concern. The owners have not mats enough to screen them from the weather; and the bare poles are exposed through the "looped and windowed raggedness" on every side. The woman, with her long neglected hair, is always seen cowering despondingly over the embers of her fire, as if lost in sad reveries. Two naked children are scrambling among the pebbles on the shore. The man wrapt in a dirty ragged blanket, without a single ornament, looks the image of savage inebriety and ferocity. Observe that these are the two extremes, and that between them are many gradations of comfort, order, and respectability. An Indian is *respectable* in his own community, in proportion as his wife and children look fat and well fed; this being a proof of his prowess and success as a hunter, and his consequent riches.

I was loitering by the garden gate this evening, about sunset, looking at the beautiful effects which the storm of the morning had left in the sky and on the lake. I heard the sound of the Indian drum, mingled with the shouts and yells and shrieks of the intoxicated savages, who were drinking in front of the village whisky-store;— when at this moment a man came slowly up, whom I recognised as one of the Ottawa chiefs, who had often attracted my attention. His name is Kim,e,wun, which signifies the Rain, or rather "it rains." He now stood before me, one of the noblest figures I ever beheld, above six feet high, erect as a forest pine. A red and green handkerchief was twined round his head with much elegance, and knotted in front, with the two ends projecting; his black hair fell from beneath it, and his small black piercing eyes glittered from among its masses, like stars glancing through the thunder clouds. His ample blanket was thrown over his left shoulder, and brought under his right arm, so as to leave it free and exposed; and a sculptor might have envied the disposition of the whole drapery—it was so felicitous, so richly graceful.[1] He stood in a contemplative attitude, evidently undecided whether he should join his drunken companions in their night revel, or return, like a wise man, to his lodge and his mat. He advanced a few steps, then turned, then paused and listened—then turned back again. I retired a little within the gate, to watch, unseen, the issue of the conflict. Alas! it was soon decided—the fatal temptation prevailed over better thoughts. He suddenly drew his blanket round him, and strided onwards in the direction of the village, treading the earth with an air of defiance, and a step which would have become a prince. On returning home, I mentioned this scene to Mr. and Mrs. Schoolcraft, as I do everything which strikes me, that I may profit by their remarks and explanations. Mr. S. told me a laughable anecdote.

A distinguished Pottowottomie warrior presented himself to the Indian agent at Chicago, and observing that he was a very good man, very good indeed—and a good friend to the Long-knives, (the Americans,) requested a dram of whisky. The agent replied, that he never gave whisky to *good* men,—good men never asked for whisky; and never drank it. It was only *bad* Indians who asked for whisky, or liked to drink it. "Then," replied the Indian quickly in his broken English, "me damn rascal!"

[. . .] suddenly the windows were darkened, and looking up, I beheld a crowd of faces, dusky, painted, wild, grotesque—with flashing eyes and white teeth, staring in upon me. I quickly threw down the paper and hastened out. The porch, the little lawn, the garden walks, were crowded with Indians, the elder chiefs and warriors sitting on the ground, or leaning silently against the pillars; the young men, women,

---

[1] While among the Indians, I often had occasion to observe that what we call the *antique* and the *ideal* are merely free, unstudied nature. Since my return from Canada, I have seen some sketches made by Mr. Harvey when in Ireland—figures of the Cork and Kerry girls, folded in their large blue cloaks; and I remember, on opening the book, I took them for drawings after the antique—figures brought from Herculaneum or Pompeii, or some newly-discovered Greek temple.

and boys lounging and peeping about, with eager and animated looks, but all perfectly well conducted, and their voices low and pleasing to the ear. They were chiefly Ottawas and Pottowottomies, two tribes which "call brother," that is, claim relationship, and are usually in alliance, but widely different. The Ottawas are the most civilised, the Pottowottomies the least so of all the lake tribes. The Ottawa I soon distinguished by the decency of his dress, and the handkerchief knotted round the head—a custom borrowed from the early French settlers, with whom they have had much intercourse: the Pottowattomie by the more savage finery of his costume, his tall figure, and a sort of swagger in his gait. The dandyism of some of these Pottowottomie warriors is inexpressibly amusing and grotesque; I defy all Regent Street and Bond Street to go beyond them in the exhibition of self-decoration and self-complacency. One of these exquisites, whom I distinguished as Beau Brummel, was not indeed much indebted to a tailor, seeing he had neither a coat nor any thing else that gentlemen are accustomed to wear; but then his face was most artistically painted, the upper half of it being vermilion, with a black circle round one eye, and a white circle round the other; the lower half of a bright green, except the tip of his nose, which was also vermilion. His leggings of scarlet cloth were embroidered down the sides, and decorated with tufts of hair. The band, or garter, which confines the leggings, is always an especial bit of finery; and his were gorgeous, all embroidered with gay beads, and strings and tassels of the liveliest colours hanging down to his ankle. His moccasins were also beautifully worked with porcupine quills; he had armlets and bracelets of silver, and round his head a silver band stuck with tufts of moose-hair, dyed blue and red; and conspicuous above all, the eagle feather in his hair, showing he was a warrior, and had taken a scalp—*i.e.* killed his man.

Over his shoulders hung a blanket of scarlet cloth, very long and ample, which he had thrown back a little, so as to display his chest, on which a large outspread hand was painted in white. It is impossible to describe the air of perfect self-complacency with which this youth strutted about. Seeing my attention fixed upon him, he came up and shook hands with me, repeating "Bojou! bojou!" Others immediately pressed forward also to shake hands, or rather take my hand, for they do not *shake* it; and I was soon in the midst of a crowd of perhaps thirty or forty Indians, all holding out their hands to me, or snatching mine, and repeating "bojou" with every expression of delight and good-humour.

This must suffice in the way of description, for I cannot further particularise dresses; they were very various, and few so fine as my young Pottowottomie. I remember another young man, who had a common black beaver hat, all round which, in several silver bands, he had stuck a profusion of feathers, and long tufts of dyed hair, so that it formed a most gorgeous helmet. Some wore the hair hanging loose and wild in elf-locks, but others again had combed and arranged it with much care and pains.

The men seemed to engross the finery; none of the women that I saw were painted. Their blankets were mostly dark blue; some had strings of beads round their necks, and silver armlets. The hair of some of the young women was very prettily arranged, being parted smooth upon the forehead, and twisted in a knot behind, very much *à la Grecque*. There is, I imagine, a very general and hearty aversion to cold water.

[. . .]

There was not a figure among them that was not a study for a painter; and how I wished that my hand had been readier with the pencil to snatch some of those picturesque heads and attitudes!

Marianne North

Some Further Recollections of a Happy Life
(1892)

The flowers about Darjeeling seemed endless. I found new ones every day. The *Thunbergia coccinca* was perhaps the most striking; it twined itself up to the tops of the oaks, and hung down in long tresses of brilliant colour, the oak itself having leaves like the sweet chestnut, and great acorns as big as apricots almost hidden in their cups. There was another lovely creeper peculiar to Darjeeling,—the sweet-scented cluster ipomœa, of a pure pink or lilac colour. The wild hydrangea with its tricolour blooms was also much more beautiful than the tame one. I worked so hard and walked so much that, after a dinner or two with Sir Ashley Eden and other grandees, I refused any more invitations. I could not keep awake in the evening.

How I longed to spend a spring in Darjeeling, and to see all the wonderful rhododendrons and magnolias in flower! They were such great old trees there, and of so many different varieties. One hairy magnolia was then in flower, and the Lieutenant-Governor had a branch cut down for me one day; it was very sweet. Major Lewin, the head of the police, was kind enough to lend me his interpreter— a most grave and responsible character, with long eyes and a pigtail. He wore a brown dressing-gown and a Chinese cap turned up like a beef-eater, and whenever I made the slightest remark, he got out his note-book and made a memorandum of it, like an M.P. in search of facts. His name was Laddie. He spoke excellent English, and declared it necessary for me to have twelve coolies and a cook to go about the hills with me, bringing up my expenses to over thirty shillings a day. I started in a dandy the Governor lent me, carried by a fine band of ragamuffins; it was almost worth the extra pay to see their picturesque figures and independent air of insolence. One of them had nothing on but a striped blue and white scarf worn under one arm and over the other shoulder, where it was fastened by a skewer with a great silver ring in its head. Even the dirtiest were covered with bangles, and had turquoise in their ears. All had the flat Chinese face and long eyes. I had to take an old cook, with all his machinery and food, which made the luggage much heavier.

It was late in the morning before we got started, and ascended the steep hill through the camp, when the young officers darted after me, "Where are you going to now, Miss North?" for they all knew me by sight, though I did not know them. Much of our way led through the forest. At one place a great fallen tree filled up the path, covered with rhododendrons and other parasites, and I saw my old friend the aralia again. Rangerom is a mere clearing in the forest on the steep hillside, which some insane governor had once made to grow cinchona in. It was then turned into a botanic garden of native plants and pines, and a poor Scotch gardener was slowly dwindling away with fever and ague among them. There was only the one small bungalow besides, which was used for picnics chiefly, and was quite quiet at night. There was a grand view of Kinchinjanga when it showed itself, and the forest-studies all round were endless.

While hard at work at that fairy dell I felt it was raining, and before I could get over the fifty yards of steep descent to the bungalow with my things, I was soaked through and through, and came back through a running stream of water to find the house occupied by a large picnic party—a regular ball-supper, cooks, coolies, and other litter all over the passage floor, and half a dozen ladies all drying their things and themselves in my room, using my towel and soap, almost too much company to be pleasant. I escaped as soon as I could to my poor soaked painting. "You only sketch it on the spot and paint it indoors?" one beauty said, pointing to the poor thing which was so covered with raindrops that it looked as if it had the smallpox. "Yes," I said, "that's what I do. Then I take it out to be rained on, which makes the colours run faster, and that's the way I paint, as you say, so quickly." Those unthinking, croqueting-badminton young ladies always aggravated me, and I could hardly be civil to them. I had not met a single person at Darjeeling who had seen the great mountain at sunrise, and few of them had seen it at all that year. Kinchinjanga did not keep fashionable hours.

There seemed to be a superabundance of the foxglove and snapdragon kind of flower. One balsam was of a cream-yellow, with a deep claret-coloured throat inside and out, and there were lovely turquoise berries on another plant, shaded from blue to green, as the real turquoise is. I found, higher up, a beautiful blue creeper, like a gentian—*Crawfurdia speciosa*, with its buds set between two leaves. The bells were two inches long, shaded into white at the neck like the common gentians, and of the same waxy material. Another new idea to me was the poppy, *Meconopsis Wallichii*, the flowers as large as our field-poppy, but of the most lovely pale blue with a gold centre, growing on branches from a central stem of brown velvet a yard or more high. As they faded, all the leaves and stalks turned from green to gold and brown, and were covered with hairs.

From the hill above Jonboo one saw the plains of Bengal like a sea, and mountains on the other three sides. The clouds rolling in and out of the valleys and up into the sky at sunset, quite took one's breath away with their beauty and colours. They were perfect pillars of fire on some evenings, and one thick cloud with a gold edge, just in front of the setting sun, cast wonderful shadows and rays opposite; but the sky was entirely clear overhead on both nights. The road up passed through grand rhododendrons with gigantic leaves with brown and white linings. The hydrangea, too, grew into quite a tree here. All the rhododendron trunks were pinkish, some of them quite satin-like and smooth; no moss or ferns could find a hold for their roots in them. Others were covered with creeping things, and the dwarf bamboo came up to the very tops.

Anne Elwood

Narrative of a Journey Overland to India
(1830)

Probably the climate indisposes Europeans from making exertions, but it is surprising that there is not more attention paid to horticulture, and ornamental planting by the inhabitants of Bombay. A few cabbages and English vegetables seem to bound their ambition. In general, the excuse is, that gardening, on account of the immense quantity of water which is requisite, is very expensive. It is difficult, however, to believe that irrigation would be more costly than the fuel which is used in our hot-houses and conservatories in England, and which however does not prevent individuals from indulging in exotic flowers and fruits. In India, seeds and plants are generally raised by laying them positively under water; small trenches are made round the roots, or the ground is laid out in small compartments, which are surrounded with mounds of earth, and it is the chief occupation of the cultivator, or the Mollee, as the gardener is called, to fill these with water; he makes a small opening to admit the stream, and when the ground of one enclosure is completely filled and saturated, he then conducts it to another and another, either using a hoe for the purpose, or with his foot forming the aperture, and reminding one of Moses' description of a similar custom in Egypt, 1451 years before Christ; and which, such are the unchangeable manners of Oriental Countries, is still practised there as well as in India, though more than three thousand years have elapsed since the Lawgiver of the Jews flourished.

"The Land of Egypt from whence ye came out, where thou sowedst thy seed, and wateredst it with thy foot, as a garden of herbs."—Deut. chap. xi. v. 10.

The circumstance of the European inhabitants not being allowed to settle in India, must of course necessarily very much impede their either building or planting; for it is a mortifying thing to think that their labours may be all thrown away upon a stranger, whose first act may possibly be to pull down the edifices, and to root up plants which have given them so much trouble to raise, and which they have viewed with parental fondness. Among the denunciations of Divine vengeance upon the Jews for disobedience, it is expressly specified, that "They shall build a house, and not dwell therein; they shall plant a vineyard, and shall not gather the grapes thereof." This is, however, very frequently the case in India, and it would consequently be an act of folly to expend much care or money on possessions of such uncertain tenure.

In Bombay, however, where the principal civilians chiefly reside, and also those favoured few among the military who obtain staff appointments, and lucrative situations, and who probably intend to remain several years in India, it is surprising that more attention is not paid to gardening; for in ten or twenty years, which is a moderate calculation of time for a residence in India, they would have a chance of seeing trees of their own planting come to perfection. At present, with the exception of a few individuals who have better taste, a few flowering shrubs immediately in front of the Bungalow, are all that are to be seen on the Island of Bombay in general, and sometimes not even so much.

Among those frequently cultivated in ornamental gardening in the Island of Bombay, is the golden Mohur, which with its light acacia-like leaves, showy blossoms, and long and airy anthers, rising some inches above the corolla, now of deep crimson, now of orange hue, with golden variety, or with light yellow flowers, surprises and delights the beholder with the multiplicity of its colours.

The beautiful oleander, or almond-tree, which, even in Italy, seems to be considered as a somewhat delicate plant, here flourishes as a common garden shrub. The magnificent hibiscus, with its deep-hued double crimson blossoms, which show so gaily amongst its green foliage, or with its delicately white flowers, at once astonishes by its grandeur, and pleases by its beauty. There are also the Malabar creeper, with its palmated leaves, and bell-shaped corolla, hanging in elegant festoons, and tapestrying the walls of buildings with its delicate foliage,—the Ceylon creeper, with its beautiful blossoms of brilliant blue,—and occasionally China and other rose trees, which take the imagination to the Islands of the West.

The Gloriosa superba, and the Hoya carnosa, the inhabitants of our hothouses, are here to be seen flourishing in open air; also the Mogrey, or the Indian jessamine, with its powerful and almost overcoming perfumes, with which the Hindoos love to adorn themselves; the men ornamenting their turbans, and the women decorating their hair therewith, or wearing chains of them as necklaces round their throats.

There are also the Indian fig, with its prickly leaves; the Palma Christi, or Ricinus communis, from which the castor oil is extracted, and whose seeds are given to female buffaloes to increase their milk; here too is the milk bush, a species of Euphorbia, of which impenetrable and impervious fences are composed.

The Neem is most peculiarly light and elegant in its appearance, somewhat resembling a young acacia or mountain ash, whilst its clusters of flowers are not dissimilar to those of the lilac, and are delightfully fragrant; as are the yellow tufts of the Baubool (Acacia Arabica), from which tree a gum is obtained, which is highly nutritious, and which is eaten by the poorer natives as food. Tulip trees, with their massy foliage, and variously-coloured corollas, that with purple and golden magnificence delight the eye, are planted on each side of many of the public roads, and will in time form noble avenues. The Mango (Mangifera Indica), is not unlike an ilex in appearance, and its leaves are of the deepest green. The tops of this tree form a considerable feature in Indian landscapes, and it is considered a charity to plant them; an act of benevolence which is frequently performed by the pious. Hindoo. The fruit is something between a plum and an apricot, and has not unfrequently, to use Dr. Borthwick Gilchrist's grandiloquous phrase, "a sad terebenthine taste," which is, at first, very disagreeable. Those who are partial to them, on first landing, sometimes exceed in the use of them, and prickly heat, and other disorders ensue in consequence. The mango of Mazagong, a town or village in Bombay, is famed throughout the East. In the reign of Shah Jehan, an abundant and fresh supply of this fruit was ensured for his use by couriers, who were stationed between Delhi and the Mahratta coast; and it is said, that the parent-tree of this fine species, from which all the others have been grafted, is, during the fruit season, honoured by a guard of Sepoys. Moore's fascinating Lalla Rookh, has given them equal celebrity in the West. Who could ever hear or eat a mango of Mazagong, without thinking of the disappointment of the learned Chamberlain Fadlaleen when the couriers failed in their duty, and when the constant supply of mangoes for the royal table, by some cruel irregularity was not forthcoming: for "to eat any mangoes but those of Mazagong, was, of course, impossible."

The tamarind is a beautiful tree, something resembling an elm, and it has all the lightness and elegance of a youthful acacia. Its fruit is of a darker colour and is drier than the West Indian; its pods are twice as long,—and, as seen hanging upon the tree, they are not unlike those of beans in appearance. The sea-loving cocoanut-tree (Cocos nucifera,) forms a striking feature in the Island of Bombay; and as there are numerous plantations of it, and every individual plant pays a tax to government, a considerable revenue must be thereby produced. To the natives it is invaluable, as its fruit is constantly introduced in their curries—coir cordage is manufactured from the fibrous covering of the nut, it furnishes oil for their lamps, thatch for their huts, a cloak in rainy weather, and the spirit so well known, toddy. It is curious of a morning to see this last article collected. Small steps are cut in the tree, up which the toddy-gatherer clambers quite to the top with the utmost ease, the liquor being produced by an incision made there, and it is not unpleasant in an unfermented state before sunrise. Rafters, water-pipes, fuel, and a substitute for paper, are also afforded by certain species of palms. Some people do not admire the cocoanut-tree, and perhaps on the Malabar shores, as a vessel slowly coasts up and down, it is almost tiring to see so much of it; but the tall and airy cocoa, either singly dancing aloft in the air, or presenting, *en masse*, a continuous shade, the stems resembling the pillars of a gothic cathedral, must always be interesting, and nothing can exceed the beauty of the more youthful ones, just throwing out its branchy leaves, with a graceful and coquettish air, like a young belle in the pride of her charms, claiming, and ready to receive the homage of mankind, to her light and wavy elegance. The taller palmyra, or brab-tree, with its broad fan-shaped leaves standing on high, and crowning the exalted summits of the hills, seems proudly to aspire to reach to heaven; but the date tree here is apparently of an inferior species, seldom bears fruit, and has not the lofty character it assumes in Egypt and Arabia. The areca palm, or betelnut-tree, (areca catechu)[1] which is cultivated in many parts of India, but which flourishes particularly in the Tiperah district in Bengal, on the banks of the Megna, and grows spontaneously on the hills in the Concan and North Canara, furnishes the nut, which, mixed with betel leaf (piper betel,) and quick lime (or chunam,) forms the composition which the Hindoos are constantly masticating. The bamboos, (Bambusa arundinecea,) which are, in reality, nothing but reeds, in the space of a few months grow to an enormous height, and have somewhat the appearance of osiers. The famous walking-sticks are formed of the first and smaller shoots, and the larger are employed in the construction of buildings, and in furniture. The plantain, or banana, with its broad and gracefully hanging leaf, two or three yards long, when first opened, is of the most delightfully fresh and vivid green imaginable. The youthful foliage is wrapt up so carefully, that as it gradually unfolds, it presents a pleasing spectacle of the care Nature takes of her productions. But the glory of India is the Sacred Banyan, the Indian fig-tree, Ficus Indica, or the Ficus Religiosa of Linnæus. This giant of the forest, or rather forest in itself, charitably extends its branches in every direction, and throwing out new shoots, which fall to the ground and there take root, without separating from the parent tree, it forms a continuous and a delightful shade, and provides a home and a shelter for the houseless native. It is said to derive its name of Banyan from the adoration which that caste pays to it, who paint it daily, make offerings of rice, and pray to it. Pennant says, it is called the pagod tree, and tree of councils, because idols are placed under its shade, and councils held beneath its branches. In some places it is believed to be the haunt of spectres, as the ancient oaks of Wales have been of fairies. Pillars of stone, and posts elegantly carved, and ornamented with the most beautiful porcelain to supply the use of mirrors, are occasionally placed under its shade.

Universal veneration is also paid all over India to the Peepul-tree, or wild fig-tree, (Ficus Religiosus,) which, though it has no connection with the Banyan, is called and considered by the natives as its wife. A late traveller mentions, that his suite, who were in want of fire-wood, were not allowed to touch its sacred branches, and a considerable dispute arose between them and the natives in consequence. Spirits

---

[1] The extract called *Cult* by the natives, *Cutch* by the English, is obtained from the inner wood of the Acacia Catechu.

are supposed to delight in the Peepul, and he was informed that an earthen pot hanging on the tree, was brought thither by some person whose father was dead, that the ghost might drink! But I must have tired you with this enumeration, and I will therefore defer any farther account of Hindoostanee productions till another letter. Adieu!

Bombay is famed all over the East for its onions, which are certainly of a very superior species to our western ones. They are of immense size, and so mild as to be by no means unpleasant in taste, and they have not that very disagreeable and almost unbearable smell that the English onions have. The sweet potato is much used, and the common potato, though of late introduction, is gaining ground in India, and it is said, that the prejudice once entertained against it by the natives is quickly passing away. The yam (Dioscorea), and the brinjal, or egg-plant, (Solanum Melongena,) together with the banda, or bendy, (Hibiscus esculentus) frequently make their appearance at table. This last is a very excellent and delicate vegetable; it is a pod, or rather capsule, three or four inches in length, and the seeds within are quite equal to our young peas, which they somewhat resemble. Cardamoms (Amomum repens) and Chili pepper (Græcum Capsacum) are put down as things of course, to eat at pleasure, with that never-failing dish the curry.

"Plantains, the golden and the green," are amongst the fruits in most common use among the natives. I have described the tree in my last letter; the flower, of the class Pentandria, is comparatively small; the fruit is from three to six inches long, and when the exterior skin is stripped off, the interior presents a yellowish white substance, very nutritive and wholesome, something between an apricot and a pear in taste, but perhaps superior to either; eaten with or without milk, it forms an excellent breakfast for those who cannot take heavier food in this hot country. The custard-apple, in the opinion of many, should rank next in delicacy. It is a curious-looking fruit, with a green and rough-coated exterior; but the interior contains a number of dark seeds, imbedded in a cream-like substance, very much resembling custard in taste. The pompelmose, or shaddock, (Malus aurantia,) the sweet-lime, and the pomegranate, are very grateful and refreshing in so sultry a climate. The oranges, principally of the species which is sometimes termed mandarine, are of an inferior sort, and the grapes are not particularly good, though up the country they are remarkably fine. There are also water-melons (Angurca Citrullus), guavas (Psiduim), something like pears in appearance, and the papaw. The Jaca, or Jack-tree (Artocarpus integrifolia), is of considerable size, and the fruit is of enormous dimensions. Of its wood, very pretty furniture is made, in colour resembling satin-wood when quite new, and afterwards assuming the appearance of light mahogany.

The paddy, or rice fields, make a considerable figure at Bombay, and are of a most beautiful vivid green, but it is not considered to be wholesome to live in their vicinity. From the common hemp, the intoxicating liquor called *bang* is produced, and the Juarree (Holcus Sorghum) and Bajaree (Holcus spicatus) are used in various ways. But, I am ashamed to say, I know but little of the Indian agriculture, and I will therefore not attempt to give you information, which might prove erroneous.

Amelia Murray

Letters from the United States, Cuba and Canada
(1856)

This is a fine day; several ladies and gentlemen of this place called on me, and I received Mr. and Mrs. H——, who forestalled my intention, by coming to me. Professor and Mrs. Gibbs took me to make a sketch of the Ettewan and Yemassee Rivers from the Battery, at White Point. There I saw the first palmetto I ever yet met with in the open air; and, on my return to the hotel, a gentleman told me the *Isabel* steamer had just brought a cargo of oranges from Cuba. In one garden this morning, I saw a standard orange tree, with some fruit upon it, but it was supposed not to be sweet; and since that I have found several of the same, bearing only what we should call Seville oranges. The timber-trees of Magnolia grandiflora all about this place are fine, and must be beautiful in summer, but this severe winter renders vegetation very backward; and I see some of the live oaks (*Quercus virens*) rather cut by the cold. The Tillandsia usnoides (called everywhere here by the name of hanging moss), having the appearance, at a little distance, of our hair-like lichens, dresses most of the trees, but especially the live oak, with its graceful pendulous bunches, sometimes hanging a yard and a half long; the stem is not larger than a thread, set with small, rounded, frosted white leaves; the little sweet-scented, reddish, purplish flowers come out at the end of the rope-like stems which swing about in the breeze. They steep this Tillandsia in water, and use its black, hair-like fibres for stuffing mattresses and pillows; the seeds being light, are carried about by the wind, and stick and fructify in all the trees around; yet it seems difficult to cultivate, for I have never seen it in our English Epiphyte houses. The temperature of any greenhouse would suit its constitution, but I imagine it requires to be blown about; and a still atmosphere is probably uncongenial to the habits of this pretty waving plant. I have seen a live oak as large as any of our British oaks, having upon it as many tufts of Tillandsia as leaves; it does not appear to be injurious like the mistletoe, but adds to the beauty of its adopted parent without shortening the life of whatever sustaining tree may support it. I drank tea at Mrs. R——'s, and spent a pleasant evening with Mr. and Mrs. H——.

January 30.—Professor and Mrs. Gibbs called for me at eleven in the morning, and we had a delightful day in the open air, botanizing, &c. Dr. Gibbs knew every plant and seed. For the first time I found yarras and cactuses in the hedge-rows; ferns, such as Polypodium incanum, plentifully on ancient live oaks, Asplenium ebeneum, and Botrychium Virginiacum, in an English looking lane; the beautiful little Houstonia serpyllifolia and Mitchella repens, with scarlet twin berries; Prunus Carolinian; and the Jasmine-coloured Gelseminium sempervirens twining up it, and through the hedges of Ilex Cassine. I often feel in this country as if I had been removed to a new heavens and a new earth, and as if my enjoyments now are a fore-taste of worlds where space and time will open out fresh delights, in a fuller com-prehension of the mighty Creator and his mighty works.

[. . .]

This is a very pretty town; the sea runs into a deep bay, filled by ships of many nations, come to be laden with sugar; it is a cleaner place than Havana, and the blacks and mulattos less numerous. I did not leave the house last evening, but occu-pied myself in making a sketch of the bay from hence. We left Havana by the six o'clock train the day before yesterday; reached Guines by nine; went to see a cave in a chalky hill three miles from the village—a fatiguing and difficult expedition, but I found numerous flowers known in our gardens and hot-houses; among them the pretty Asclepias tuberosa, Ipomœas of all colours and sizes, a lilac, a scilla, a sola-mena, and other things new to me, and the whole country was dotted over by cocoa-nut trees. That neighbourhood has little other foliage, although during our journey by rail I saw fine mango and other trees—among them a palmetto as tall as the Chamærops of Florida; it looks something like the same species. We passed many haciendas, the plantations belonging to which were in high cultivation, great herds of cattle and many horses feeding about them; and there were tall chimneys indi-cating steam-engines for crushing sugar.

On Sunday last, we went to the service on board the *Vestal*, commanded by Captain Thompson, then moored in the harbour of Havana; the *Buzzard* steamer left a day or two before, and the *Argus* will remain, while the *Vestal* is expected at this place. It is curious to hear the watchmen belonging to the towns in Cuba. They sing out the hours and the state of the weather in a stentorian tone, always preced-ing their announcement by a shrill and prolonged whistle. I observe that their voices are tuned nearly to the same intervals, though of course one is rather more musical than another. A thick fog obscures the view this morning—it was the same yester-day; it indicates that the day will be a hot one. Yesterday the thermometer stood at 86°, unusually high for this month, but I do not find the heat so oppressive as when at 80° in England.

Matanzas is situated in an almost circular basin, formed by low hills of a nearly even height, except when broken by a chasm through which flows the River Yamorri—to the north-west. The houses, like those of Havana, are almost all low, having usually not more than one, or at most two storeys, some of them with flat roofs, and others heavily tiled by circular shaped tiles, as if rows of chimney-pots were strung together, and laid half a foot apart. In a garden just below my window I see a magnificent Oleander, and a fine yellow Bignonia (*stans ?*), in full bloom. I heard an amusing anecdote with reference to botanical ignorance; as a lady had heard the name of Hedysarum gyrans, next day she gravely informed a gentleman, "that plant is the harum scarum gatherum." So little attention is paid to natural history here, that I can get no assistance as to the botanical names of either trees, flowers, or shrubs, and as many of the former are yet without bloom, it is difficult to make them out even with the assistance of Loudon; it is the same with out-of-the-way fruits—one is a *pappy* and another is a *mammy*, and so on; but the local terms do not help one the least.

Mr. Da Costa, the Consul, was so obliging as to take us an interesting drive last evening up heights to the north-east, from whence I was able to sketch the Pau of Matanza, and a fine valley beneath, dotted in all directions with cocoa-nut trees, but I observed few trees of any other kind. By a road impracticable for any other vehicle than a volante, with its giant wheels, we reached a villa and plantation belonging to one of the proprietors here. The foliage all round appeared so strange; Tree Euphorbias, Shrubby Cactus, immense Cannas, and thickets of Coffee, Bananas, &c. For the first time I saw cocoa-nuts; some were gathered, and I drank some of the juice which looked like clear water, and tasted nearly the same, with a slight *soupçon* of sugar. I was quite surprised to see a green nut (placed with a hole in it over a tumbler) pouring forth such a bright, innocent-looking liquid. I supposed it would always have a milky hue. The nuts enlarge by degrees; but it was a long time before I could find out which of the palms was the true cocoa-nut tree. Some said this was, and others doubted, and said it was a tree resemblsng the one that produces the nut, whereas, there is only that single cocoa that I have yet seen here. There are tall Arecas and Palmettos, which are probably the same as those of Florida; and there is the Date (*Phœnix*), and the Sago Palm, and Bactris, but two kinds of cocoas I have not yet seen here. At this plantation of Mr. Jinks's I for the first time saw sugar crushing. It was, in this instance, not done by steam, but by horses and mules, negro boys sitting as postilions, laughing and shouting, and the whole affair having such a wild, unearthly look, though it seemed a case of enjoyment to all except the poor beasts concerned in this kind of merry-go-round, that I could fancy the employment might have been selected by Dante for one of the punishments of his *Inferno*. The driver, who received us and showed us every hospitality, was a handsome, good-humoured, intelligent-looking Cuban creole. At Guines, where I saw a large plantation, all the sugar was distilling for rum, a spirit which bears a high price at this moment, and is therefore more profitable than sugar. Coolies were employed there as well as negroes, but they do not seem equally fitted for labour, and are more to be pitied than the negro slaves, for their masters are indifferent about their comfort. The sun set as a more magnificent globe of fire than I had ever before seen it. There was just enough twilight when we left the plantation for me to watch that we went safely down a long and steep white chalky descent into the valley below; and I regretted that afterwards I could see nothing of the beauties of our drive, excepting fire-flies, which sparkled among the aloes, and yuccas, and coffee bushes, as we proceeded along a track, which, if the Consul and the other gentleman on horseback had not assured me was free from danger, I should have thought could hardly have been safely traversed; but with the exception of every now and then sinking in ruts, and passing over rocks, large enough to have overset an English vehicle, we had no difficulties, and the negro postilion and his two little white horses, appeared quite at their ease. We passed by two haciendas, in our road to the pass through which the Yamorri River makes its way to the town, and into the sea beyond. The name "Yamorri" is by tradition derived from the dying exclamation of a native warrior who

fell into the stream. It does not seem very deep. Another river flows along the opposite side of this place, and there is also the Cardinas a short distance down the coast
to the south, but I believe none of them are navigable. I have lost time here in looking
about, owing to the early mornings having been thick and foggy ever since we came,
an unusual circumstance. It is too hot to stir in the middle of the day, and the
evenings are very short, so that I shall accomplish less here in four days than I should
do in two elsewhere.

Matanzas, March 16.—I saw some nice plants in small gardens yesterday. The
Copaiba is a very pretty tree, and I hope to get a bulb of a gigantic lily, some Crinum
or Amaryllis, which they tell me has a purple and white flower. A Ceanothus-looking
shrub has here the name of tree mignonette from its fragrance. I went in a volante
to draw from the Yamorri Pass. There are caves in the cretaceous rocks above, one
of which is so extensive that it is believed to pass under the whole of the town of
Matanzas. Looking up from below, I saw some stalactitic pillars supporting rocks
above. I sketched one of them. In some places here the rocks look as if they had all
been submitted to the action of fire, and this more completely than in Florida; for
in these I see no organic remains. I think they must all have been burnt up, while
at Ocala they seem only to have been warmed up. I suppose Cuba to be older land
than the most southern part of the United States, although from Havana to
Matanzas, I see only cretaceous formations—but coal is found not very distant from
Havana, and the hundreds of miles farther south allow space enough for anything.
This morning I am going to a plantation a few miles down the coast, south; to-
morrow we return to Havana, and I shall have one more week there before crossing
over to New Orleans.

Your affectionate

A. M. M.

Amelia B. Edwards

A Thousand Miles up the Nile
(1888)

The first glimpse that most travellers now get of the Pyramids is from the window
of the railway carriage as they come from Alexandria; and it is not impressive. It does
not take one's breath away, for instance, like a first sight of the Alps from the high

level of the Neufchâtel line, or the outline of the Acropolis at Athens as one first recognises it from the sea. The well-known triangular forms look small and shadowy, and are too familiar to be in any way startling. And the same, I think, is true of every distant view of them,—that is, or every view which is too distant to afford the means of scaling them against other objects. It is only in approaching them, and observing how they grow with every foot of the road, that one begins to feel they are not so familiar after all.

But when at last the edge of the desert is reached, and the long sand-slope climbed, and the rocky platform gained, and the Great Pyramid in all its unexpected bulk and majesty towers close above one's head, the effect is as sudden as it is overwhelming. It shuts out the sky and the horizon. It shuts out all the other Pyramids. It shuts out everything but the sense of awe and wonder.

Now, too, one discovers that it was with the forms of the Pyramids, and only their forms, that one had been acquainted all these years past. Of their surface, their colour, their relative position, their number (to say nothing of their size), one had hitherto entertained no kind of definite idea. The most careful study of plans and measurements, the clearest photographs, the most elaborate descriptions, had done little or nothing, after all, to make one know the place beforehand. This undulating table-land of sand and rock, pitted with open graves and cumbered with mounds of shapeless masonry, is wholly unlike the desert of our dreams. The Pyramids of Cheops and Chephren are bigger than we had expected; the Pyramid of Mycerinus is smaller. Here, too, are nine Pyramids, instead of three. They are all entered in the plans and mentioned in the guide-books; but, somehow, one is unprepared to find them there, and cannot help looking upon them as intruders. These six extra Pyramids are small and greatly dilapidated. One, indeed, is little more than a big cairn.

Even the Great Pyramid puzzles us with an unexpected sense of unlikeness. We all know, and have known from childhood, that it was stripped of its outer blocks some five hundred years ago to build Arab mosques and palaces; but the rugged, rock-like aspect of that giant staircase takes us by surprise, nevertheless. Nor does it look like a partial ruin, either. It looks as if it had been left unfinished, and as if the workmen might be coming back to-morrow morning.

The colour again is a surprise. Few persons can be aware beforehand of the rich tawny hue that Egyptian limestone assumes after ages of exposure to the blaze of an Egyptian sky. Seen in certain lights, the Pyramids look like piles of massy gold.

Having but one hour and forty minutes to spend on the spot, we resolutely refused on this first occasion to be shown anything, or told anything, or to be taken anywhere—except, indeed, for a few minutes to the brink of the sand-hollow in which the Sphinx lies couchant. We wished to give our whole attention, and all the short time at our disposal, to the Great Pyramid only. To gain some impression of the outer aspect and size of this enormous structure,—to steady our minds to something like an understanding of its age,—was enough, and more than enough, for so brief a visit.

For it is no easy task to realise, however imperfectly, the duration of six or seven thousand years; and the Great Pyramid, which is supposed to have been some four thousand two hundred and odd years old at the time of the birth of Christ, is now in its seventh millennary. Standing there close against the base of it; touching it; measuring her own height against one of its lowest blocks; looking up all the stages of that vast, receding, rugged wall, which leads upward like an Alpine buttress and seems almost to touch the sky, the Writer suddenly became aware that these remote dates had never presented themselves to her mind until this moment as anything but abstract numerals. Now, for the first time, they resolved themselves into something concrete, definite, real. They were no longer figures, but years with their changes of season, their high and low Niles, their seed-times and harvests. The consciousness of that moment will never, perhaps, quite wear away. It was as if one had been snatched up for an instant to some vast height overlooking the plains of Time, and had seen the centuries mapped out beneath one's feet.

To appreciate the size of the Great Pyramid is less difficult than to apprehend its age. No one who has walked the length of one side, climbed to the top, and learned the dimensions from Murray, can fail to form a tolerably clear idea of its mere bulk. The measurements given by Sir Gardner Wilkinson are as follows:—length of each side, 732 feet; perpendicular height, 480 feet 9 inches; area 535,824 square feet.[1] That is to say, it stands 115 feet 9 inches higher than the cross on the top of St. Paul's, and about 20 feet lower than Box Hill in Surrey; and if transported bodily to London, it would a little more than cover the whole area of Lincoln's Inn Fields. These are sufficiently matter-of-fact statements, and sufficiently intelligible; but, like most calculations of the kind, they diminish rather than do justice to the dignity of the subject.

More impressive by far than the weightiest array of figures or the most striking

---

[1] Since the first edition of this book was issued, the publication of Mr. W. M. Flinders Petrie's standard work, entitled *The Pyramids and Temples of Gizeh*, has for the first time placed a thoroughly accurate and scientific description of the Great Pyramid at the disposal of students. Calculating from the rock-cut sockets at the four corners, and from the true level of the pavement, Mr. Petrie finds that the square of the original base of the structure, in inches, is of these dimensions:—

	Length.	Difference from Mean.		Azimuth.	Difference from Mean.	
N	9069.4	+	.6	−3′20″	+	23″
E	9067.7	−	1.1	−3′57″	−	14″
S	9069.5	+	.7	−3′41″	+	2″
W	9068.6	−	.2	−3′54″	−	11″
Mean	9068.8		.65	−3′43″		12″

For the height, Mr. Petrie, after duly weighing all data, such as the thickness of the three casing-stones yet *in situ*, and the presumed thickness of those which formerly faced the upper courses of the masonry, gives from his observations of the mean angle of the Pyramid, a height from base to apex of 5776.0 ± 7.0 inches. See *The Pyramids and Temples of Gizeh*, chap. vi. pp. 37 to 43. [Note to the Second Edition.]

comparisons, was the shadow cast by the Great Pyramid as the sun went down. That mighty Shadow, sharp and distinct, stretched across the stony platform of the desert and over full three-quarters of a mile of the green plain below. It divided the sunlight where it fell, just as its great original divided the sunlight in the upper air; and it darkened the space it covered, like an eclipse. It was not without a thrill of something approaching to awe that one remembered how this self-same Shadow had gone on registering, not only the height of the most stupendous gnomon ever set up by human hands, but the slow passage, day by day, of more than sixty centuries of the world's history.

It was still lengthening over the landscape as we went down the long sand-slope and regained the carriage. Some six or eight Arabs in fluttering white garments ran on ahead to bid us a last good-bye. That we should have driven over from Cairo only to sit quietly down and look at the Great Pyramid had filled them with unfeigned astonishment. With such energy and despatch as the modern traveller uses, we might have been to the top, and seen the temple of the Sphinx, and done two or three of the principal tombs in the time.

"You come again!" said they. "Good Arab show you everything. You see nothing this time!"

So, promising to return ere long, we drove away; well content, nevertheless, with the way in which our time had been spent.

The Pyramid Bedouins have been plentifully abused by travellers and guidebooks, but we found no reason to complain of them now or afterwards. They neither crowded round us, nor followed us, nor importuned us in any way. They are naturally vivacious and very talkative; yet the gentle fellows were dumb as mutes when they found we wished for silence. And they were satisfied with a very moderate bakhshîsh at parting.

As a fitting sequel to this excursion, we went, I think next day, to see the mosque of Sultan Hassan, which is one of those mediæval structures said to have been built with the casing-stones of the Great Pyramid.

[. . .]

Now the camel-riding that is done at Assûan is of the most commonplace description, and bears to genuine desert travelling about the same relation that half-an-hour on the Mer de Glace bears to the passage of the Mortaretsch glacier [. . .]

We mounted and rode away; two imps of darkness following at the heels of our camels, and Salame performing the part of bodyguard. Thus attended, we found ourselves pitched, swung, and rolled along at a pace that carried us rapidly up the slope, past a suburb full of cafés and grinning dancing girls, and out into the desert. Our way for the first half-mile or so lay among tombs. A great Mohammedan necropolis, part ancient, part modern, lies behind Assûan, and covers more ground than the town itself. Some scores of tiny mosques, each topped by its little cupola, and all more or less dilapidated, stand here amid a wilderness of scattered tombstones. Some are isolated; some grouped picturesquely together. Each covers, or is supposed to cover, the grave of a Moslem Santon; but some are mere commemorative chapels dedicated to saints and martyrs elsewhere buried. Of simple head-stones defaced, shattered, overturned, propped back to back on cairns of loose stones, or piled in broken and dishonoured heaps, there must be many hundreds. They are for the most part rounded at the top like ancient Egyptian stelæ, and bear elaborately-carved inscriptions, some of which are in the Cufic character, and more than a thousand years old. Seen when the sun is bending westward and the shadows are lengthening, there is something curiously melancholy and picturesque about this City of the Dead in the dead desert.

Leaving the tombs, we now strike off towards the left, bound for the obelisk in the quarry, which is the stock sight of the place. The horizon beyond Assûan is bounded on all sides by rocky heights, bold and picturesque in form, yet scarcely lofty enough to deserve the name of mountains. The sandy bottom under our camel's feet is strewn with small pebbles, and tolerably firm. Clustered rocks of black and red granite profusely inscribed with hieroglyphed records crop up here and there, and serve as landmarks just where landmarks are needed. For nothing would be easier than to miss one's way among these tawny slopes, and to go wandering off, like lost Israelites, into the desert.

Winding in and out among undulating hillocks and tracts of rolled boulders, we come at last to a little group of cliffs, at the foot of which our camels halt unbidden. Here we dismount, climb a short slope, and find the huge monolith at our feet.

Being cut horizontally, it lies half buried in drifted sand, with nothing to show that it is not wholly disengaged and ready for transport. Our books tell us, however, that the under-cutting has never been done, and that it is yet one with the granite bottom on which it seems to lie. Both ends are hidden; but one can pace some sixty feet of its yet visible surface. That surface bears the tool-marks of the workmen. A slanting groove pitted with wedge-holes indicates where it was intended to taper towards the top. Another shows where it was to be reduced at the side. Had it been finished, this would have been the largest obelisk in the world. The great obelisk of Queen Hatshepsu at Karnak, which, as its inscriptions record, came also from Assûan, stands ninety-two feet high, and measures eight feet square at the base;[1] but this which lies sleeping in the desert would have stood ninety-five feet in the shaft, and have measured over eleven feet square at the base. We can never know now why it was left here, nor guess with what royal name it should have been inscribed. Had the king said in his heart that he would set up a mightier obelisk than was ever yet seen by eyes of men, and did he die before the block could be extracted from the quarry? Or were the quarrymen driven from the desert, and the Pharaoh from his throne, by the hungry hordes of Ethiopia, or Syria, or the islands beyond the sea? The great stone may be older than Rameses the Great, or as modern as the last of the Romans; but to give it a date, or to divine its history, is impossible. Egyptology,

---

[1] These are the measurements given in Murray's Handbook. The new English translation of Mariette's *Itinéraire de la Haute Egypte* gives the obelisk of Hatshepsu 108 feet 10 inches in height. See *The Monuments of Upper Egypt*, translated by Alphonse Mariette: London, 1877.

which has solved the enigma of the Sphinx, is powerless here. The obelisk of the quarry holds its secret safe, and holds it for ever.

Ancient Egyptian quarrying is seen under its most striking aspect among extensive limestone or sandstone ranges, as at Turra and Silsilis; but the process by which the stone was extracted can nowhere be more distinctly traced than at Assûan. In some respects, indeed, the quarries here, though on a smaller scale than those lower down the river, are even more interesting. Nothing surprises one at Silsilis, for instance, more than the economy with which the sandstone has been cut from the heart of the mountain; but at Assûan, as the material was more precious, so does the economy seem to have been still greater. At Silsilis, the yellow cliffs have been sliced as neatly as the cheeses in a cheesemonger's window. Smooth, upright walls alone mark the place where the work has been done; and the amount of débris is altogether insignificant. But at Assûan, when extracting granite for sculptural purposes, they attacked the form of the object required, and cut it out roughly to shape. The great obelisk is but one of many cases in point. In the same group of rocks, or one very closely adjoining, we saw a rough-hewn column, erect and three-parts detached, as well as the semi-cylindrical hollow from which its fellow had been taken. One curious recess from which a quadrant-shaped mass had been cut away puzzled us immensely. In other places the blocks appeared to have been coffer-shaped. We sought in vain, however, for the broken sarcophagus mentioned in Murray.

But the drifted sands, we may be sure, hide more precious things than these. Inscriptions are probably as abundant here as in the breccia of Hamamat. The great obelisk must have had a fellow, it we only knew where to look for it. The obelisks of Queen Hatshepsu, and the sarcophagi of many famous kings, might possibly be traced to their beds in these quarries. So might the casing stones of the Pyramid of Menkara, the massive slabs of the Temple of the Sphinx, and the walls of the sanctuary of Philip Aridæus at Karnak. Above all, the syenite Colossus of the Ramesseum and the monster Colossus of Tanis,[1] which was the largest detached statue in the world, must each have left its mighty matrix among the rocks close by. But these, like the song of the sirens or the alias of Achilles, though "not beyond all conjecture," are among the things that will never now be discovered.

As regards the process of quarrying at Assûan, it seems that rectangular granite blocks were split off here, as the softer limestone and sandstone elsewhere, by means of wooden wedges. These were fitted to holes already cut for their reception; and, being saturated with water, split the hard rock by mere force of expansion. Every quarried mass hereabouts is marked with rows of these wedge-holes.

---

[1] For an account of the discovery of this enormous statue and the measurements of its various parts, see *Tanis*, Part I, by W.M. Flinders Petrie, chap. ii. pp. 22 *et seq.* published by the Egypt Exploration Fund, 1885. [Note to Second Edition.]

Marianne North

Some Further Recollections of a Happy Life
(1892)

From my verandah or sitting-room I could see up and down the steep valley covered with trees and woods; higher up were meadows, and Newcastle 4000 feet above me, my own height being under a thousand above the sea. The richest foliage closed quite up to the little terrace on which the house stood; bananas, rose-apples[1] (with their white tassel flowers and pretty pink young shoots and leaves), the gigantic bread-fruit, trumpet-trees (with great white-lined leaves), star-apples (with brown and gold plush lining to their shiny leaves), the mahogany-trees (with their pretty terminal cones), mangoes, custard apples, and endless others, besides a few dates and cocoanuts. A tangle of all sorts of gay things underneath, golden-flowered allamandas, bignonias, and ipomœas over everything, heliotropes, lemon-verbenas, and geraniums from the long-neglected garden running wild like weeds: over all a giant cotton-tree quite 200 feet high was within sight, standing up like a ghost in its winter nakedness against the forest of evergreen trees, only coloured by the quantities of orchids, wild pines, and other parasites which had lodged themselves in its soft bark and branches. Little negro huts nestled among the "bush" everywhere, and zigzag paths led in all directions round the house. The mango-trees were just then covered with pink and yellow flowers, and the daturas, with their long white bells, bordered every stream. I was in a state of ecstasy, and hardly knew what to paint first. The black people too were very kind, and seemed in character with the scenery. They were always friendly, and ready for a chat with "missus." The population seemed enormous, though all scattered. There was a small valley at the back of the house which was a marvel of loveliness, bananas, daturas, and great *Caladium esculentum* bordering the stream, with the *Ipomœa bona nox*, passion-flower, and *Tacsonia Thunbergii* over all the trees, giant fern-fronds as high as myself, and quantities of smaller ferns with young pink and copper-coloured leaves, as well as the gold and silver varieties. I painted all day, going out at daylight and not returning until noon, after which I worked at flowers in the house, as we had heavy rain most afternoons at that season; before sunset it cleared again, and I used to walk up the hill and explore some new path, returning home in the dark.

[. . .]

The view from the dining-room was like an opal: the sea-line generally lost in a blue haze, the promontories of St. Augusta, and Port Royal with its long coral reef,

---

[1] *Eugenio jambos*, native of East Indies. Fruit the size of a hen's egg, rose-scented, with the flavour of an apricot.

stretching out into it all salmon-coloured, then the blue sea again, Kingston amid its gardens, and the great Vega all rich green, with one corner of purest emerald-green sugar-cane, the whole set between rich hillsides, with bananas and mangoes full of flowers, and the beautiful gold-brown star-apple[1] tree taking the place in the landscape which the copper-beech does in England. The mahoe is the hardest and blackest wood in the island, and its velvety leaves and trumpet-flowers of copper and brass tints made a fine study: all the flowers seemed so big. The poinsettias were often a foot across, one passion-flower covered two large trees, the dracænas were ten feet high, the gardenias loaded with sweet flowers. One day the captain started Agnes Wilberforce and myself on two horses with a groom for Newcastle, where he had arranged that Dr. S. should meet us and show us the famous Fern Walk. It was a glorious day. We rode up the steep hills straight into the clouds, and found rain in the great village of barracks, but we went on in spite of it. The scarlet geraniums and zinnias of former soldiers' gardens had seeded themselves all about, and above them we came to patches of wild alpinia, called by the English ginger and cardamom, with lovely waxy flowers smelling like their names. Great branches of *Oncidium* orchids were pushing their way through the bushes, and creepers in abundance, huge white cherokee roses, and quantities of begonias.

At last we turned into the forest at the top of the hill, and rode through the Fern Walk; it almost took away my breath with its lovely fairy-like beauty; the very mist which always seemed to hang among the trees and plants there made it the more lovely and mysterious. There were quantities of tree-ferns, and every other sort of fern, all growing piled on one another; trees with branches and sterms quite covered with them, and with wild bromeliads and orchids, many of the bromeliads with rosy centres and flowers coming out of them. A close waxy pink ivy was running up everything as well as the creeping fern, and many lycopodiums, mosses, and lichens. It was like a scene in a pantomime, too good to be real, the tree-fern fronds crossing and recrossing each other like net-work. One saw dozens at the one view, their slender stems draped and hidden by other ferns and creeping things. There were tall trees above, which seemed to have long fern-like leaves also hanging from them, when really it was only a large creeping fern which had found its way over them up to the very tops. They were most delicious to look at, and, my horse thought, to eat also, for he risked my life on a narrow ledge by turning his head to crop the leaves from the bank, when his hind-legs slipped over the precipice. I said "Don't," and the Doctor and Agnes laughed, while the good horse picked his legs up again and went on munching in a more sensible position. We rode back by a lower fern walk, still lovelier because it was even damper.

[. . .]

After leaving the sea the atmosphere got more and more like a hot fern-house, till we reached Bath, where the inn was kept by a decent kind of white woman. It

---

[1] *Chrysophyllum Cainito.* Fruit the size of a large apple; the inside divided in two cells, each containing a black seed surrounded by gelatinous pulp.

was really hot and without air; so I worked at home in slight clothing till four o'clock, and then walked up two miles of marvellous wood scenery to the baths, which were slightly sulphurous and very hot and delicious. Two large nutmegs, male and female, grew close to them, with the beautiful outer fruit just opening and showing the nut and the crimson network of mace round it. The flowers are like those of the arbutus. Lower down bamboos were growing in great magnificence, their great curves of cane arching overhead and interlacing like some wonderful Gothic crypt. Large marrow-fat palms were there too, with their whole trunks and heads covered with hanging ferns, and tangled up with creepers. The cabbage-palm was in abundance, with its leaves very much uncombed, and a yard or more of fleshy green shoots, the flowers and fruit under them, many of the former being then still folded tight in the green bract which sticks out at right angles from the stem: to cut open one of these palm flower-sheaths and shake out the contents like a tassel of the finest ivory-work was a great pleasure and never-ending wonder to me.

The town of Bath consists of one long street of detached houses, having an avenue down it of alternate cabbage-palms and Otaheite apples. The old botanical garden had long since been left to the care of nature; but to my mind no gardener could have treated it better, for everything grew as it liked, and the ugly formal paths were almost undiscoverable. The most gorgeous trees were tangled up with splendid climbing plants, all seeding and flowering luxuriantly; the yellow fruit of the gamboge strewed the ground under them, and the screw-pine rested on its stilted roots, over which hoya plants were twining, covered with their sweet star-flowers. I longed for some one to tell me the names of many other plants which I have since learned to know in their native lands; but it was delightful to have time to study them and not feel hurried.

I asked why I saw no snakes, and was told they had all gone up into the trees to drink out of the wild bromeliads! Those pretty parasites often held quite a pint of water in the cornucopias which form their centres, as I found to my cost one day when bending one down to look at its flower, and it emptied its contents up my sleeve. I drove into the more open country in the dusk, and saw a large acacia-leaved tree full of deep pink flowers and shaking leaves, and was told "Thorley's food for cattle" was made from it; the natives called it the guangatree. I saw the two marenga-trees, from the berries of which the oil of Ben used by watchmakers is pressed; they are both very sweet, especially the one with a lilac flower which they call Jamaica lilac. The chocolate plant is also much cultivated at Bath: it has large leaves which rustle like paper when touched; the younger ones are of all sorts of tender tints, from pink to yellow; its tiny flowers and huge pods hang directly from the trunk and branches under the leaves, and the pods are coloured, according to their degree of ripeness, from green to purple, red, or orange. The flowers, small bunches of gray stars about the size of a fourpenny piece, are scarcely visible close to the bark of the tree. The nuts are buried in a rather acid white pulp in rows inside the pod.

[. . .]

From that flat-topped, isolated hill, one saw a long stretch of wild mountain coast, and many islands, some 2000 feet below, across which long-tailed boatswain-birds were always flying; behind it, the highest peak of Mahé frowned down on us, often inky-black under the storm-clouds. They were gathering round it when I came up on the 7th of January, and for a whole fortnight the rains came down day and night, showing me wonderful cloud-effects, dark as slate, with the dead white capucin trees sticking through like pins in a pincushion. There were few living specimens of any age, but those were noble ones, the young leaves a foot in length, looking like green satin lined with brown velvet, and growing in terminal bunches at the ends of the woody branches. They seemed to me much like the gutta-percha trees of Borneo, but I could make out nothing certain of the flowers, and was told "it had no flower," or a "red flower," or a "white one," each statement most positive, from those who lived actually under the trees! The nuts every one knew, and collected them as curiosities. Flowers were sent afterwards to England, and Sir J. Hooker declared it a new genus, and named it *Northea seychellana*, after me. Under the capucins were abundance of tree-ferns; noble palms with pink young leaves, salmon-coloured fading ones, and orange and scarlet fruits, some drooping and some standing erect, high above the leaves; tall stiff trees of *Wormia ferruginea*, with white flowers and brown furry buds, whose young leaves of the deepest carmine tints are nearly as long as those of the capucin. These are most remarkable for the joined petioles to the leaves, forming cups in which I always found a reservoir of water in the early morning to nourish the young succulent leaves. The more mature and woody ones did not require them, and they were dispensed with.

Many other trees were there, whose names no one knew, with unobtrusive white flowers, scarcely any coloured, one of the few exceptions being a colea, whose yellow trumpet-flowers grew straight out of its trunk and woody branches. Under them were great starry leaves belonging to evil-smelling brown arums, and an endless variety of ferns, including the great bird's-nest. One day we had a fine morning. Mr. W. sent boys out to cut a way, and we scrambled up and down valleys of boulders, through the wet forests, and up to the top of the Nun's Nose Mountain. The hanging roots of the pandanus were a great help in pulling ourselves up the walls of mud and granite; but the palms and many other growing things were so full of long thorns that my hands were bleeding and torn before we reached the top. Just round the summit we found the pitcher-plants festooned and trailing over the shrubs; but a dozen feet below this there was not one. The stems were crimson, and as thick as my finger, and the habit so different that a London nurseryman would possibly have given it a different name from the dense mat which covered the top of the mountain. But I traced some of these stems and found they joined the others, and that they had only "adapted themselves to circumstances." The top of the mountain consisted of one smooth granite boulder covered with carpets of nepenthes and creeping grass. The nepenthes was matted together, and could be lifted up by the yard without coming to any root-hold, every lid of its pitchers the brightest crimson, like a green carpet with red dots, as I looked down on it; and hundreds of male flowers

143

stood up from it. Among them I found some of the missing female flowers, which every one in the Seychelles said were as yet unknown. Near the edge of the summit were fine tufts of brown flowering grass, as high as pampas grass, and quantities of the lovely *Angræcum eburneum.* I saw one of these exquisite orchids perched on a root in a stream looking at its face in the water, surrounded by pink begonia and maiden-hair fern.

Mrs Charles Meredith

Notes and Sketches of New South Wales
(1844)

About three miles from Bathurst, near a pretty cottage on the Macquarie (in a district chiefly granite), is a singular group of low rocks rising abruptly from the turf of the plains, and perfectly white; they appeared to me to be masses of pure quartz, of which many specimens occur a few miles higher up the river. Pebbles of very clear quartz crystal are sometimes found in the neighbourhood, but the natives search for them so successfully, that I only picked up one or two small ones.

These crystals, although by no means rare, are preserved as "charms" by the Aborigines, being given to them by their doctors, or "Crodjees," after a variety of ceremonies, which Mr. Meredith describes to me as highly absurd, he having been present at the rites, when performed by a tribe at Dundunemawl on the Macquarie, about forty miles below Wellington Valley. Great preparations were made, as for a grand Corrobbory, or festival, the men divesting themselves of even the portions of clothing commonly worn, and painting their naked black bodies in a hideous manner with pipe-clay. After dark they lit their fires, which are small, but kept blazing with constant additions of dry bark and leaves, and the sable gentry assembled by degrees as they completed their evening toilettes, *full dress* being painted nudity. A few began dancing in different parties, preparatory to the grand display, and the women, squatting on the ground, commenced their strange monotonous chant, each beating accurate time with two boomerangs. Then began the grand corrobbory, and all the men joined in the dance, leaping, jumping, bounding about in the most violent manner, but always in strict unison with each other, and keeping time with the chorus, accompanying their wild gesticulations with frightful yells and noises. The whole "tableau" is fearfully grand: the dark wild forest scenery around—the bright fire-light gleaming upon the savage and uncouth figures of the men, their natural dark hue being made absolutely horrible by the paintings bestowed on them, consisting of lines and other marks done in white and red pipe-clay, which give them an indescribably ghastly and fiendish aspect—their strange attitudes, and violent contortions and movements, and the unearthly sound of their yells, mingled with the wild and monotonous wail-like chant of the women, make altogether a very near approach to the horribly sublime, in the estimation of most Europeans who have witnessed an assembly of the kind. In the midst of the performance on this occasion, two men advanced, bearing between them a large piece of bark, about six feet high and three feet wide, rudely painted with red and white clay, the design consisting of a straight line down the middle, and diagonal ones thickly marked on each side. The exhibition of this wonderful and mystic specimen of art caused extreme excitement and admiration, and the bearers held it in the midst of the dancers, who bounded and yelled around it with redoubled energy. Presently the oldest "Crodjee" present approached the charmed bark, and walked slowly round and round, examining it in every part, and then carefully smelling it, up and down, before, behind, and on all sides, with grave and reverential demeanour. This was to "find where the charms lay," which charms, consisting of small crystals, he had of course concealed about his person. After a great deal of smelling and snuffing, he commenced violently sucking a part of the bark, and, after some other manœuvres, spat out a "charm" into his hand, and went on sucking for as many as were then required.

These charmed crystals are kept with great care by the possessor, his wife usually having charge of the treasure, which she carries in the family "wardrobe," and the loss of one is esteemed an awful calamity. The charm-sucking ceremony takes place at the full moon, the time generally chosen by the natives for such celebrations. In this instance that Crodjee's part of the performance was very clumsily done, and Mr. Meredith asked one of the men, the following day, "if he were such a fool as to believe that the Crodjee really sucked the crystals out of the bark?" The fellow winked, nodded, and looked wondrously wise, and intimated that *he* certainly *knew* better, but that it would not do to *say* so. And thus is fraud perpetuated, alike by savage and by civilized men, and thus ever do policy and expediency take the place of truth and honesty!

One of the aboriginal dances is called "the Kangaroo dance," and one man, wearing a long tail, drops down on his hands and feet, pretending to graze, starting to look about, and mimicking the demeanour of the animal as nearly as possible; the others, in the character of dogs and hunters, performing their part of the play in a circle round him, at a very short distance.

The natives I saw at Bathurst were less ugly and better proportioned than I expected; the men being far superior to the women, though none of them are tall or largely made; six feet is a most extraordinary size among them. The sable pican-ninies were naked, long-armed, large-stomached, little bodies, giving one the idea of a new sort of spider; I never had seen a black child before, and did not see enough of them then to familiarize me with the novelty. Several of the men knew Mr.

Meredith, and whilst I was one day making some purchase in a store, one of them accosted him at the door, pointing at the same time to me. "Lady there, that Gin 'long o' you?—Ay, Ay?" "Yes, that's my Gin."—"Ay, Ay?" Then somewhat banter-ingly, "Bel you got Gin (you have no Gin); poor fellow you—you no Gin!" A "poor fellow" meaning a bachelor, and the possession of a wife, among them, being in fact equivalent to keeping a servant, as the unfortunate Gins perform all the labour.

Judging from what I have heard, I imagine that their marriage-customs are as truly *saxage* as any other of their strange ceremonies. Polygamy is general among all who can attain the desirable wealth of several wives, though few have more than two living with them at one time.

Female children are sometimes "promised" in infancy to their future husbands (frequently decrepit old men), and others appear to be taken by means of force and ill usage, as is the case among many savage nations. The men are always tyrannical, and often brutally cruel to their unfortunate wives, who really seem to occupy as miserable and debased a position, in *every* respect, as it is possible for human beings to do. I never before heard of, or could have conceived, any state so pitiable and so utterly degraded. If some of the zealous Missionaries of whom we hear so much were to endeavour to raise the moral and social condition of these wretched creatures, and to teach them a few of the simple principles and virtues of Christianity, they would indeed be worthily employed.

Severe personal chastisement is among the lesser grievances of the poor Gins. One day Mr. Meredith saw one of them crying most bitterly, and asked what was the matter. She replied, that she was going to get a beating because she had accidentally broken her husband's "pyook" (pipe). Mr. Meredith directly went to the fellow, and tried to dissuade him from his brutal purpose; but in vain, unless another pyook were given him, on which condition he would let her off. Unfortunately there was not one to be procured; and notwithstanding all my husband's persuasions, and his representations to the black tyrant of the simple fact, that even if he killed his wife, that would not make him a new pipe, he remained doggedly sulky, and the next morning the poor Gin appeared with her *arm broken*, from the cruel beating he had given her with a thick stick. Such instances are of frequent occurrence.

These poor unhappy wretches are *slaves*, in every social sense, and are not even permitted to feed but at their husband's pleasure, and off the offal he may choose to fling them, although on them devolves the chief care of providing the materials for the repast. Two meals a day is the full allowance of the natives; but as they cook all they have for supper, and gorge themselves then to their utmost ability, breakfast depends on the possible remains of the feast. Their usual food consists of kangaroos and opossums roasted whole, without any portion being rejected; and they greedily devour garbage, entrails, &c. of any kind they can pick up, quantity rather than quality being the desideratum as regards provisions. Sometimes they feed more dain-tily, procuring turtle, fish, wild turkeys' eggs, guanas snakes, and some large kinds of grubs, which are reckoned great luxuries. Occasionally the women dig up a bitter hot root, not unlike a bad radish, which serves them for a meal, in default of better viands.

146

Each family have their own fire, round which they sit to eat. The husband first takes the opossum, &c., tears it to pieces and gnaws off his own favourite morsels from the joints, which he then hands over his shoulder to his wife, who waits patiently behind him; and should food be scarce, her supper is a tolerably light one. The children are "helped" much in the same manner; and when, either from having eaten as much as they can, or all they have, the family have finished their repast, they crouch round the fire and go to sleep.

The single men, emphatically termed "poor fellows," have one fire in common; and with them, as with the family group, it is a point of etiquette to hand round their half-gnawed bones to one another.

Great fondness is usually displayed by parents for their children (if they survive the perils of infancy), and instances have often occurred of a couple, who had several little ones of their own, adopting some poor friendless orphan, and freely bestowing on it an equal share of their scanty food. Such cases I have known frequently among the *poor* at home: they who have least to give, and are consequently most intimate with the misery of want, have the greatest compassion and charity for fellow-sufferers.

Although they appear to treat their children kindly when they can in some measure help themselves, yet infanticide is frequent among the women, who often dislike the trouble of taking care of their babies, and destroy them immediately after birth, saying that "Yahoo," or "Devil-devil," took them. One woman, whom Mr. Meredith saw a day or two after the birth of her baby, on being asked where it was, replied with perfect nonchalance, "I believe Dingo patta!"—*She believed the dog had eaten it!* Numbers of the hapless little beings are no doubt disposed of by their unnatural mothers in a similar manner.

I never could make out anything of their religious ideas, or even if they had a comprehension of a beneficent Supreme Being; but they have an *evil* spirit, which causes them great terror, whom they call "Yahoo," or "Devil-devil:" he lives in the tops of the steepest and rockiest mountains, which are totally inaccessible to all human beings, and comes down at night to seize and run away with men, women, or children, whom he eats up, children being his favourite food; and this superstition is used doubtless as a cloak to many a horrid and revolting crime committed by the wretched and unnatural mothers, who nearly always, when their infants disappear, say "Yahoo" took them. They never can tell which way he goes by his tracks, because he has the power of turning his feet in any direction he pleases, but usually wears them heels first, or, as they express it, "Mundoey that-a-way, cobbra *that*-a-way" (feet going one way, and head or face pointing the other). The name Devil-devil is of course borrowed from our vocabulary, and the doubling of the phrase denotes how terrible or intense a devil he is; that of Yahoo, being used to express a bad spirit, or "Bugaboo," was common also with the aborigines of Van Diemen's Land, and is as likely to be a coincidence with, as a loan from, Dean Swift; just as their word "*coolar*," for anger, very nearly approaches in sound our word *choler*, with a like meaning.

Susanna Moodie

Roughing it in the Bush
(1852)

Tom Nogan, the chief's brother, had a very large, fat, ugly squaw for his wife. She was a mountain of tawny flesh; and, but for the innocent, good-natured expression which, like a bright sunbeam penetrating a swarthy cloud, spread all around a kindly glow, she might have been termed hideous.

This woman they considered very handsome, calling her "a fine squaw—clever squaw—a much good woman;" though in what her superiority consisted, I never could discover, often as I visited the wigwam. She was very dirty, and appeared quite indifferent to the claims of common decency (in the disposal of the few filthy rags that covered her). She was, however, very expert in all Indian craft. No Jew could drive a better bargain than Mrs. Tom; and her urchins, of whom she was the happy mother of five or six, were as cunning and avaricious as herself.

One day she visited me, bringing along with her a very pretty covered basket for sale. I asked her what she wanted for it, but could obtain from her no satisfactory answer. I showed her a small piece of silver. She shook her head. I tempted her with pork and flour, but she required neither. I had just given up the idea of dealing with her, in despair, when she suddenly seized upon me, and, lifting up my gown, pointed exultingly to my quilted petticoat, clapping her hands, and laughing immoderately.

Another time she led me all over the house, to show me what she wanted in exchange for *basket*. My patience was well nigh exhausted in following her from place to place, in her attempt to discover the coveted article, when, hanging upon a peg in my chamber, she espied a pair of trousers belonging to my husband's logging-suit. The riddle was solved. With a joyful cry she pointed to them, exclaiming "Take basket.—Give them!" It was with no small difficulty that I rescued the indispensables from her grasp.

The cunning which they display in their contests with their enemies, in their hunting, and in making bargains with the whites (who are too apt to impose on their ignorance), seems to spring more from a law of necessity, forced upon them by their isolated position and precarious mode of life, than from any innate wish to betray. The Indian's face, after all, is a perfect index of his mind. The eye changes its expression with every impulse and passion, and shows what is passing within as clearly as the lightning in a dark night betrays the course of the stream. I cannot think that deceit forms any prominent trait in the Indian's character. They invariably act with the strictest honour towards those who never attempt to impose upon them. It is natural for a deceitful person to take advantage of the credulity of

148

others. The genuine Indian never utters a falsehood, and never employs flattery (that powerful weapon in the hands of the insidious), in his communications with the whites.

His worst traits are those which he has in common with the wild animals of the forest, and which his intercourse with the lowest order of civilised men (who, in point of moral worth, are greatly his inferiors), and the pernicious effects of strong drink, have greatly tended to inflame and debase.

It is a melancholy truth, and deeply to be lamented, that the vicinity of European settlers has always produced a very demoralising effect upon the Indians. As a proof of this, I will relate a simple anecdote.

Jah, of Rice Lake, a very sensible, middle-aged Indian, was conversing with me about their language, and the difficulty he found in understanding the books written in Indian for their use. Among other things, I asked him if his people ever swore, or used profane language towards the Deity.

The man regarded me with a sort of stern horror, as he replied, "Indian, till after he knew your people, never swore—no bad word in Indian. Indian must learn your words to swear and take God's name in vain."

Oh, what a reproof to Christian men! I felt abashed, and degraded in the eyes of this poor savage—who, ignorant as he was in many respects, yet possessed that first great attribute of the soul, a deep reverence for the Supreme Being. How inferior were thousands of my countrymen to him in this important point!

Amelia Murray

Letters from the United States, Cuba and Canada
(1856)

CHARLESTON, *January* 7, 1855.

MY DEAR FRIENDS,—

The post for England went off to-day unexpectedly; I had only a few minutes' warning, and no time to look at my letter, so that I forget whether I wrote last from Petersburg; but as we reached Wilmington too late at night, and started too early to see anything of that place, I could not have said much about it. White sand and pine barrens made up the whole two hundred and sixty miles of yesterday's journey. It required twenty-two hours' railroad to accomplish that distance. Almost all the pitch pines are disfigured, and most probably will be killed, by the bark being stripped off, that the turpentine may drip from it into a small vessel placed on the ground. The forest looks as if it was planted with white posts; but this is occasionally relieved by thickets of Rhododendron, Kalmia, and Phyllerea, which must be splendid when flowering, in May; and about sixty miles from this place the pitch is superseded by the Pinus palustris. It is pretty to see the long tassel-like looking leaves streaming in the wind; but it makes a very transparent-looking forest, as the branches grow wide apart, and the bunches of foliage are also distant from each other. I begin to mark cotton plantations, and my compassionate feelings are rapidly changing sides. It appears to me our benevolent intentions in England have taken a mistaken direction, and that we should bestow our compassion on the masters instead of on the slaves. The former by no means enjoy the incubus with which circumstances have loaded them, and would be only too happy if they could supersede this black labour by white; but as to the negroes, they are the merriest, most contented set of people I ever saw; of course there are exceptions, but I am inclined to suspect that we have as much vice, and more suffering, than is caused here by the unfortunate institution of Slavery; and I very much doubt if freedom will ever make the black population, in the mass, anything more than a set of grown-up children. Even as to the matter of purchase and sale, it is disliked by masters; and I find compassion very much wasted upon the objects of it. An old lady died here lately, and her negroes were to be parted with; Mrs. S——, an acquaintance of mine, knew these blacks, and shed tears about their change of fate; but when they came to market, and she found all so gay and indifferent about it, she could not help feeling her sorrow was greatly thrown away. Mrs. Stowe's Topsy is a perfect illustration of Darkie's character, and many of the sad histories of which her book is made up may be true as isolated facts; but yet I feel sure that, as a whole, the story, however ingeniously worked up, is an unfair picture; a libel upon the slaveholders as a body. I very much doubt if a real Uncle Tom can often be found in the whole negro race; and if such a being is, or was, he is as great a rarity as a Shakespeare among whites. One particular want appears to me evident in negro minds and character: they have no consciousness of the fitness of things. I suffer now from the cold wintry weather here; and upon my begging Blackie for a better fire in my room, in the civilest, most anxious tone, he asked whether I would not like some iced water? (Knowing this to be a luxury in hot weather, he would never consider that it might be less acceptable in cold.) We have lately had black chambermaids in all hotels. They are perfectly good-natured, and officiously anxious to help us in all matters in which their assistance is not required. "Let I do this, Missus," and "Let I do that," when perhaps it is hard to induce them to do what is really wanted—to light the fire when we are cold, or to bring a little warm water when clean hands would be a luxury. They fairly take possession of us, and unless we lock them out, they stand to watch our proceedings, and curiously to inspect our things. "Adeline," at Lynchburg, saw my sketch of the black cook on board the *Links* canal-boat, at which she burst into a loud laugh, and exclaimed, "He very like a monkey, missus—we very like monkies." And she appeared delighted with her own wit—not at all hurt by the idea. A pretty

Southern lady arrived at the hotel, with a fair infant in the arms of his black nurse. I came out from the tea-room rather sooner than was expected, and found all the Darkies that could get away assembled round the tiny massa, (they are very fond of children, and make capital nurses,—tender, watchful, playful, and yet, I think, firm; but they are firm only with children), jumping and screaming their delight. Upon seeing me an elderly man came forward, with a grin and a bow—"The black population are only enjoying themselves, missus." I said I was glad they were happy, and left them to their happiness. At one of the railroad stations I watched a young and intelligent-looking black man, considerably beyond boyhood, perseveringly keeping up a kind of Highland trot over a number of small pitch barrels with all the zest of a white child from four to six years of age. I begin to doubt whether they ever grow mentally after twenty. They are precocious children, being so imitative; they soon ripen, come to a stand-still, and advance no farther. In this respect Uncle Tom is a myth, but Topsy a reality. I mean to go and see a sale of slaves; my wish is to judge the subject fairly in all its bearings, and this I may be trusted to do even by Abolitionists; for early prejudices and my national and acquired feelings are certainly opposed to slavery; but if countenances are "a history as well as a prophecy," the national expression of faces in the North as contrasted with those of the South tell a strange, and to me an unexpected story, as regards the greatest happiness principle of the greatest number! Of course, it must be borne in mind that no rules are without exception; but, oh, the haggard, anxious, melancholy, restless, sickly, hopeless faces I have seen in the Northern States—in the rail-cars, on the steam-boats, in the saloons, and particularly in the ladies' parlour. There is beauty of feature and complexion, with hardly any individuality of character. Nothing like simplicity, even among children after ten years of age—hot-house, forced impetuous beings, the *almighty dollars*, the incentive and only guide to activity and appreciation. Women care that their husbands should gain gold, that they may spend it in dress and ostentation; and the men like that their wives should appear as queens, whether they rule well, or ill, or at all; yet it is certain that I have made the acquaintance, and that I value the friendship, of superior women in the North, and if I should be thought to have expressed myself with too much severity, I appeal to their candour and judgment; and being American cousins they have the Anglo-Saxon love of Truth, and will not spurn her even in an unveiled form, or receive her ungraciously even when thus presented. I have reason to speak gratefully, and warmly do I feel, and anxiously do I venture these observations, which may seem even harsh and ungrateful. I do not yet know much of the Southern ladies; but from Washington to this place I have been struck by a general improvement of countenance and manner in the white race, and this in spite of the horrors which accompany the misuse of tobacco. If the gentlemen of this part of the country would only acquire habits of self-control and decency in this matter, they would indeed become the *Preux Chevaliers* of the United States, as their hills and valleys may prove the store-houses and gardens of the Union. May their sons and daughters look to these things, and increase in wealth, prosperity, virtue, and happiness!

[. . .]

NEW ORLEANS, *March* 31, 1855.

MY DEAR FRIENDS,—

I left the St. Charles Hotel yesterday. Mr. Robert G——, brother to my Virginian friend, called to bring me to his pleasant and comfortable house, and in what may be called the "West end" of New Orleans. I find myself established, and quite at home, with every luxury and attention that a traveller can require. The weather is still as fresh and cold as an ordinary dreary March with us, though more roses are in bloom than we could find so early in the year in England. Several loquat trees (*Eisobotria Japonica*) placed round the garden are only just beginning to ripen their delicious fruit, with its golden, or rather apricot-coloured hue; in most seasons before April, peas and strawberries are plentiful, but they are not yet to be had. My ideas are rather puzzled about seasons: after the dog days in Cuba, I feel as if this ought to be autumn, not spring; but I have no doubt that an interval of colder weather will be salutary to our constitutions before we pass the approaching summer in the Northern States. Instead of growing thin during my travels, I was beginning to fear that, on my return to England, I should make my appearance in too portly a style; but three weeks at Havana have obviated that fear. In my room here it is pleasant to have a four-post bed, which brings English customs to mind. I never saw anything but French bedsteads in the North. No curtains are required; a full and wide mosquito-net, without opening, and which is put back during the day, and looks like a transparent bonnet-box over the pillows, is drawn forward at night, and protects me completely from the invasion of insects. This is a better contrivance than those at Cuba, where I found a persevering mosquito would often succeed in establishing itself within the curtains. The wood of which the bedstead is made looks like a kind of walnut; the top has a heavy projecting eave—this, I am told, is advantageous, as it gives room for the iron rod underneath upon which the mosquito-net is hung. While I am writing a black woman enters: they walk in and out of your room, just as the fancy takes them, without knocking; and the door must be locked if one does not wish to be intruded on. The negroes are curious, and like to come and ask questions, and see what you are at; so "Emily" inquires if I will let her make the bed while I am in the room; being as well inclined for a little talk as herself, I agree. She tells me the coloured people are well content and happy; that she was "raised in Virginny," and came here from Richmond; that masters and mistresses about are very tender of their people; that she has got her husband and three children, babies almost, the youngest an infant, then in the house; she does odd jobs after dinner, but she says that on the plantations it is not often the people work after dinner (she is munching something all this while); they have usually task-work, which can be quickly done if they choose; that the black population don't like bacon—"they likes to have fresh meat three times a day, and what they likes beside." She seemed utterly astonished when I told her that the English working-people could seldom get meat at all, and that they had not as much firing as they chose, &c. &c. "Lord bless you, missus, that would never do at all here: why, some of the coloured ones have got a'most as much jewellery as their missuses; they gets their own way tolerable somehow; and they very often desires to be sold when they be affronted."

"Emily" thought that in England slaves would have it all their own way entirely; and this is the idea that darkies have of freedom: plenty to eat and drink, finery to their heart's content—no work. Here they despise the free negroes. One woman was offered her freedom in my hearing: she took the offer as an insult, and said, "I know what the free niggers are, missus: they are the meanest niggers as ever was; I hopes never to be a free nigger, missus," A slave quarrelling with another black, after calling him names, at last sums up as the acme of contempt, "You be a d——d nigger without a master!" This is the consequence of the fact, that free negroes being idle and profligate are generally poor and miserable. A common reproach among them is to say, "You be's as bad as a free nigger." I think if any unprejudiced person sees the state of the free black population in Canada, and then makes a tour of a few months in the Southern States, with an open eye and unprejudiced mind, he will come to the conclusion that things are better than names; and that if by a *ukase* he could carry back all the darkies (from ignorance and misrepresentation induced to run away from their masters) he would benefit the blacks, whatever he might do for the whites, who, I believe, would be very much averse to receive these contaminated negroes again, except from motives of duty and compassion.

Mrs. Stowe gives great credit to a young lady who, becoming the heiress of a few slaves, gave them all their freedom. I have heard of a young lady who succeeded to the possession of negroes, and nothing else; by emancipating them she might have gained a fine character from the Abolitionists, and have cast off not only a responsibility, but a heavy expense; instead of which she sought occupation for herself, laboured hard, and earned the means of existence for her poor black dependents, as well as her own living. Which of these two ladies acted the more Christian part? Last night, conversing with a very intelligent gentleman who has travelled in Canada, I remarked that free negroes there were in a much more degraded, suffering, and irreligious state than any slaves I have seen; and that they often reproach the whites with having, by false pretences, inveigled them to their destruction. He said, "I will tell you a circumstance which occurred relative to that matter. A confidential black, who was treated with the greatest kindness by his master, took it in his head one day to run away, with the idea of establishing himself in Canada. When in that country I accidentally fell in with him, acting as waiter in an hotel: we immediately recognized each other; and, with tears in his eyes, he said, "Oh, sir! tell of the family; how is this one, how is that?" I answered his inquiries, and then asked how he got on. "I get on in the season pretty well; I make some money, but very bad in the winter. Oh, sir! beg my dear master for me; beg him to forgive, and take me back again." And I feel sure that these negroes who are not so far gone in drunkenness and profligacy, as to have lost all self-respect, would generally make the same request; exceptions only prove the rule. My woman on the Detroit River was taken care of by a husband, who, having occupation as a black pilot (an employment for which their strong local perception peculiarly fits them), was the only really contented black I met with; but she lost her children, and may, perhaps, end in being motherless; while in slavery, they would have been healthy. As to the separation of families, I see that great pains are taken to avoid that evil. I believe that it hardly occurs more frequently than in England from other causes: and I imagine a law might be enacted to make it less easy here. So in this case, as in every other social abuse, the governing power should regulate, but not wholly forbid, or the result will be the encouragement of twenty evils where there was one before. I have seen a great many visitors to day; among them some very agreeable people.

Frances Trollope

Paris and the Parisians
(1836)

This morning we took possession of half a dozen chairs under the trees which front the beautiful group of Petus and Aria. It was the hour when all the newspapers are in the greatest requisition; and we had the satisfaction of watching the studies of three individuals, each of whom might have sat as a model for an artist who wished to give an idea of their several peculiarities. We saw, in short, beyond the possibility of doubt, a royalist, a doctrinaire, and a republican, during the half hour we remained there, all soothing their feelings by indulging in two sous' worth of politics, each in his own line.

A stiff but gentleman-like old man first came, and having taken a journal from the little octagon stand—which journal we felt quite sure was either "La France" or "La Quotidienne"—he established himself at no great distance from us. Why it was that we all felt so certain of his being a legitimatist I can hardly tell you, but not one of the party had the least doubt about it. There was a quiet, half-proud, half-melancholy air of keeping himself apart; an aristocratical cast of features; a pale care-worn complexion; and a style of dress which no vulgar man ever wore, but which no rich one would be likely to wear today. This is all I can record of him: but there was something pervading his whole person too essentially loyal to be misunderstood, yet too delicate in its tone to be coarsely painted. Such as it was, however, we felt it quite enough to make the matter sure; and if I could find out that old gentleman to be either doctrinaire or republican, I never would look on a human countenance again in order to discover what was passing within.

The next who approached us we were equally sure was a republican: but here the discovery did little honour to our discernment; for these gentry choose to leave no doubt upon the subject of their *clique*, but contrive that every article contributing to the appearance of the outward man shall become a symbol and a sign, a token and a stigma, of the madness that possesses them. He too held a paper in his hand, and without venturing to approach too nearly to so alarming a personage, we scrupled not to assure each other that the journal he was so assiduously perusing was "Le Réformateur."

Just as we had decided what manner of man it was who was stalking so majestically past us, a comfortable-looking citizen approached in the uniform of the National Guard, who sat himself down to his daily allowance of politics with the air of a person expecting to be well pleased with what he finds, but nevertheless too well contented with himself and all things about him to care overmuch about it. Every line of this man's jocund face, every curve of his portly figure, spoke contentment and well-being. He was probably one of that very new race in France, a tradesman making a rapid fortune. Was it possible to doubt that the paper in his hand was "Le Journal des Débats?" was it possible to believe that this man was other than a prosperous doctrinaire?

Thus, on the neutral ground furnished by these delightful gardens, hostile spirits meet with impunity, and, though they mingle not, enjoy in common the delicious privileges of cool shade, fresh air, and the idle luxury of an *al fresco* newspaper, in the midst of a crowded and party-split city, with as much certainty of being unchallenged and uninterrupted as if each were wandering alone in a princely domain of his own.

Such, too, as are not over splenetic may find a very lively variety of study in watching the ways of the little dandies and dandiesses who, at some hours of the day, swarm like so many humming-birds amidst the shade and sunshine of the Tuileries. Either these little French personages are marvellously well-behaved, or there is some superintending care which prevents screaming; for I certainly never saw so many young things assembled together who indulged so rarely in that salutary exercise of the lungs which makes one so often tremble at the approach of

Soft infancy, that nothing can, but cry.

The costumes of these pretty creatures contributes not a little to the amusement; it is often so whimsical as to give them the appearance of miniature maskers. I have seen little fellows beating a hoop in the full uniform of a National Guard; others waddling under the mimicry of kilted Highlanders; and small ladies without number in every possible variety of unbabylike apparel.

The entertainment to be derived from sitting in the Tuileries Gardens and studying costume is, however, by no means confined to the junior part of the company. In no country have I ever seen anything approaching in grotesque habiliments to some of the figures daily and hourly met lounging about these walks. But such vagaries are confined wholly to the male part of the population; it is very rare to see a woman outrageously dressed in any way; and if you do, the chances are five hundred to one that she is not a Frenchwoman. An air of quiet elegant neatness is, I think, the most striking characteristic of the walking costume of the French ladies. All the little minor finishings of the female toilet appear to be more sedulously cared for than the weightier matters of the pelisse and gown. Every lady you meet is *bien chaussée, bien gantée*. Her ribbons, if they do not match her dress, are sure to accord with it; and for all the delicate garniture that comes under the care of the laundress, it should seem that Paris alone, of all the earth, knows how to iron.

The whimsical caprices of male attire, on the contrary, defy anything like general remark; unless, indeed, it be that the air of Paris appears to have the quality of turning all the *imperials, favoris,* and *moustaches* which dwell within its walls to jetty black-ness. At a little distance, the young men have really the air of having their faces tied up with black ribbon as a cure for the mumps; and, handsome as this dark *chevelure* is generally allowed to be, the heavy uniformity of it at present very considerably lessens its striking effect. When every man has his face half covered with black hair, it ceases to be a very valuable distinction. Perhaps, too, the frequent advertisements of compositions infallible in their power of turning the hair to any colour except "what pleases God," may tend to make one look with suspicious eyes at these once fascinating southern decorations; but, at present, I take it to be an undoubted fact, that a clean, close-shaven, northern-looking gentleman is valued at a high premium in every *salon* in Paris.

It is not to be denied that the "glorious and immortal days" have done some injury to the general appearance of the Tuileries Gardens. Before this period, no one was permitted to enter them dressed in a *blouse*, or jacket, or *casquette*; and no one, either male or female, might carry bundles or baskets through these pretty regions, sacred to relaxation and holiday enjoyment. But liberty and unseemly sordiness of attire being somehow or other jumbled together in the minds of the sovereign mob,—not sovereign either—the mob is only vice-regal in Paris as yet;—but the mob, however, such as it is, has obtained, as a mark of peculiar respect and favour to themselves, a new law or regulation, by which it is enacted that these royal precincts may become like unto Noah's ark, and that both clean and unclean beasts may enter here.

Could one wish for a better specimen of the sort of advantage to be gained by removing the restraint of authority in order to pamper the popular taste for what they are pleased to call freedom? Not one of the persons who enter the gardens now, were restricted from entering them before; only it was required that they should be decently clad;—that is to say, in such garments as they were accustomed to wear on Sunday or any other holiday; the only occasions, one should imagine, on which the working classes could wish to profit by permission to promenade in a public garden: but the obligation to appear clean in the garden of the king's palace was an infringe-ment on their liberty, so that formality is dispensed with; and they have now obtained the distinguished and ennobling privilege of being as dirty and ill-dressed as they like.

[Anon.]

The Englishwoman in Russia
(1855)

There was but little to vary the monotony of our life in Archangel, as we had but few opportunities of seeing much of the Russians. In the spring we decided upon paying a visit to Vologda, having received an invitation to pass a few weeks at the house of the governor of the province. In the midst of our busy preparations for the journey, the Starosta or head man of a neighbouring village came to beg the honour of our company at a festival which he proposed giving the next day to celebrate his daughter's marriage. We accepted the invitation, and the following morning hired a boat to take us across the Dwina, for the village was situated on the opposite bank at the distance of about eight versts. We had no sooner landed than the bride's father, the Starosta himself, came out to welcome us, and to conduct us to his house. A great number of people were assembled in front of it; they all seemed very merry, and were gaily dressed in their best attire: we passed through the crowd and followed our host, who ushered us with many profound bows into the best apartment, where we found a numerous company already arrived. There were at the least thirty women, all in their national dress, seated in straight rows round the room; most of them had their arms crossed, and remained almost motionless; their gaily coloured silks and showy head-dresses had a very striking effect. The bride herself, a pretty-looking girl of about seventeen, was seated at the upper end of the room with the bridegroom at her right hand. A table, covered with a white cloth and tastefully ornamented with festoons of artificial flowers and bows of pink ribbon, was before them, on which was placed the wedding-cake made of flour and honey, with almonds on the top; several dishes of sweetmeats, preserves, and dried fruits were arranged around it. It was, as I was told, the etiquette for the bride not to speak even to the bridegroom; but we went up to her, and offered our congratulations, which they both acknowledged by a graceful inclination. The Starosta ordered chairs to be placed just opposite the table, and begged us to be seated, so we had a good opportunity of examining and admiring the bride's dress. It was composed of a coiffure nearly a foot high, somewhat resembling a brimless hat; it was of gold, enriched with pearls and fastened on by a knot of gold tissue behind, which was edged with lace; her ears were decorated with handsome rings, and round her neck were innumerable rows of pearls. I expressed a doubt as to whether they were real; but I was assured they were so, only they were defective in form. Her casackan or jacket was of gold cloth, with a border of pearl embroidery, the sleeves of cambric, short and very full, tied up with blue ribbon and finished by a lace trimming; the skirt of her dress was of crimson flowered silk, having a gold border nearly a foot deep, with gold buttons up the front. This is the national costume, but it varies in different provinces, and is not equally rich. But then the Starosta was well to do; he was not only the head man of the village, but he had shops of his own in Moscow and in St. Petersburg. I noticed that the bride's fingers were loaded with rings; indeed she seemed to have on all the finery the whole family could muster. As for the bridegroom, he was a good-looking young man of twenty-two or so, and very respectably dressed in the costume of a shopkeeper, which consists of a long blue coat called a caftan, closely buttoned up to the throat. We were presented with tea, coffee, wine, bonbons, cakes, fruit, &c., in succession, all of which we were expected to partake of, or the hosts would think themselves slighted, and their hospitality insulted. The spoons I remarked were of Tula work, and had the appearance of being of gold, but were in reality of silver-gilt, with arabesque flowers all over them, which they say are done with some kind of acid: I believe the secret is not known out of Russia. All the Russian women assembled at this festival were of the upper class of petty shopkeepers or farmers, and they were dressed in the same costume as the bride, with perhaps fewer ornaments. During the whole time we were in the room their amusement consisted in singing, one after the other, in a low kind of chant, songs improvised in honour of the occasion, all the rest of the company sitting silent and motionless as statues. As soon as one had exhausted all her available talent on the subject, another took it up and gave us her ideas upon it. According to one, the bride was too young to be married: she wondered how her mother could part with her, and thought she ought to have kept her at home for a long time yet. Another seemed to think she was doing perfectly right to marry her daughter, after bringing her up so prudently, and making her so clever in household affairs. A third wished to settle the matter entirely by praising the bridegroom; "he was so gay of heart, he loved his bride so well." His possessions, it appears, were worth having, and enough to tempt a village-maid; for "he had plenty of cows, pigs, and horses;" and as the climax to all these advantages of estates real and personal, she assured us, "that he could take his wife to church in a droshsky!" The whole of the guests remained quite silent, listening with a serious face to the songs; there was no laughing or chatting; each kept her seat and preserved such an intense gravity all the time, that they evidently considered matrimony as no joke after all, and not in the least amusing. Were I malicious, I would remark that they had every one of them been married themselves. After we had remained a reasonable time in the company of the young couple, we went outside to see the guests assembled in the front of the house; there we found several women dancing a wearisome kind of dance, if such it might be called, which consisted in merely walking to and fro in pairs placed one behind the other in a long line. They moved forwards and then backwards to a monotonous singsong kind of air; on advancing, the first two changed places with the last couple, and so in succession. The amusement seemed to afford them intense delight, and so fond are they of it that they keep it up for hours together. On the opposite side of the yard the men were having a ball amongst themselves; their performance was more entertaining, and we laughed heartily at a comic pas de deux by a couple of young men, who capered about in a very diverting manner. Another peasant danced a solo in very good style. After the dancing the men sang us some national airs; each took the hand or leant on the shoulder of his neighbour, "in order to unite the tones," as they said. We thanked them for their entertainment, and re-entered the house to take our leave of the good Starosta and his family, when we again expressed our wishes for their happiness, but we were not allowed to depart until we had drunk their health in a glass of champagne, a wine which the Russians give upon all extraordinary occasions. As we were stepping into the boat the peasants gave us a parting cheer, and far away, when the village was quite lost to our view in the distance, we heard their wild voices still singing in chorus, their beautiful national airs in honour of the young Russian bride.

Lady Anne Barker

Station Life in New Zealand
(1870)

You know we brought all our furniture out with us, and even papers for the rooms, just because we happened to have everything; but I should not recommend any one to do so, for the expense of carriage, though moderate enough by sea (in a wool ship), is enormous as soon as it reaches Lyttleton, and goods have to be dragged up country by horses or bullocks. There are very good shops where you can buy everything, and besides these there are constant sales by auction where, I am told, furniture fetches a price sometimes under its English value. House rent about Christchurch is very high. We looked at some small houses in and about the suburbs of the town, when we were undecided about our plans, and were offered the most inconvenient little dwellings, with rooms which were scarcely bigger than cupboards, for 200*l.* a year; we saw nothing at a lower price than this, and any house of a better class, standing in a nicely arranged shrubbery, is at least 300*l.* per annum. Cab-hire is another thing which seems to me disproportionately dear, as horses are very cheap; there are no small fares, half-a-crown being the lowest "legal tender" to a cabman; and I soon gave up returning visits when I found that to make a call in a Hansom three or four miles out of the little town cost 1*l.* or 1*l.* 10*s.*, even remaining only a few minutes at the house.

All food (except mutton) appears to be as nearly as possible at London prices; but yet every one looks perfectly well-fed, and actual want is unknown. Wages of all sorts are high, and employment a certainty. The look and bearing of the immigrants appear to alter soon after they reach the colony. some people object to the independence of their manner, but I do not; on the contrary, I like to see the upright gait, the well-fed, healthy look, the decent clothes (even if no.one touches his hat to you), instead of the half-starved, depressed appearance, and too often cringing servility of the mass of our English population. Scotchmen do particularly well out here; frugal and thrifty, hard-working and sober, it is easy to predict the future of a man of this type in a new country. Naturally, the whole tone of thought and feeling is almost exclusively practical; even in a morning visit there is no small-talk. I find no difficulty in obtaining the useful information upon domestic subjects which I so much need; for it is sad to discover, after all my house-keeping experience, that I am still perfectly ignorant. Here it is necessary to know *how* everything should be done; it is not sufficient to give an order, you must also be in a position to explain how it is to be caried out. I felt quite guilty when I saw the picture in *Punch* the other day, of a young and inexperienced matron requesting her cook "not to put any lumps into the melted butter," and reflected that I did not know how lumps should be kept out; so, as I am fortunate enough to number among my new friends a lady who is as clever in these culinary details as she is bright and charming in society, I immediately went to her for a lesson in the art of making melted butter without putting lumps into it.

The great complaint, the never-ending subject of comparison and lamentation among ladies, is the utter ignorance and inefficiency of their female servants. As soon as a ship comes in it is besieged with people who want servants, but it is very rare to get one who knows how to do anything as it ought to be done. Their lack of all knowledge of the commonest domestic duties is most surprising, and makes one wonder who in England did the necessary things of daily cottage life for them, for they appear to have done nothing for themselves hitherto.

As for a woman knowing how to cook, that seems the very last accomplishment they acquire; a girl will come to you as a housemaid at 25*l.* per annum, and you will find that she literally does not know how to hold her broom, and has never handled a duster. When you ask a nurse her qualifications for the care of perhaps two or three young children, you may find, on close cross-examination, that she can recollect having once or twice "held mother's baby," and that she is very firm in her determination that "you'll keep baby yourself o' nights, mem!" A perfectly inexperienced girl of this sort will ask, and get, 30*l.* or 35*l.* per annum, a cook from 35*l.* to 40*l.*; and when they go "up country," they hint plainly they shall not stay long with you, and ask higher wages, stipulating with great exactness how they are to be conveyed free of all expense to and from their place.

Then, on the other hand, I must say they work desperately hard, and very cheerfully: I am amazed how few servants are kept even in the large and better class of houses. As a general rule, they appear willing enough to learn, and I hear no complaints of dishonesty or immorality, though many moans are made of the rapidity with which a nice tidy young woman is snapped up as a wife; but that is a complaint no one can sympathise with. On most stations a married couple is kept; the man either to act as shepherd, or to work in the garden and look after the cows, and the woman is supposed to attend to the indoor comforts of the wretched bachelor-master: but she generally requires to be taught how to bake a loaf of bread, and boil a potato, as well as how to cook mutton in the simplest form. In her own cottage at home, who did all these things for her? These incapables are generally perfectly helpless and awkward at the wash-tub; no one seems to expect servants to know their business, and it is very fortunate if they show any capability of learning.

I must end my long letter by telling you a little story of my own personal experience in the odd ways of these girls. The housemaid at the boarding-house where we have stayed since we left Heathstock is a fat, sonsy, good-natured girl, perfectly ignorant and stupid, but she has not been long in the colony, and seems willing to learn. She came to me the other day, and, without the least circumlocution or hesitation, asked me if I would lend her my riding-habit as a pattern to given the tailor; adding that she wanted my best and newest. As soon as I could speak for amazement, I naturally asked why; she said she had been given a riding-horse, that she had *loaned* a saddle, and bought a hat, so now she had nothing on her mind except the habit; and further added, that she intended to leave her situation the day before the races, and that it was "her fixed intent" to appear on horseback each day, and all day long, at these said races. I inquired if she knew how to ride? No; she had never mounted any animal in her life. I suggested that she had better take some lessons before her appearance in public; but she said her mistress did not like to spare her to "practise," and she stuck steadily to her point of wanting my habit as a pattern. I could not lend it to her, fortunately, for it had been sent up to the station with my saddle, & c.; so had she been killed, as I thought not at all unlikely, at least my conscience would not have reproached me for aiding and abetting her equestrian freak. I inquired from every one who went to the races if they saw or heard of any accident to a woman on horseback, and I most anxiously watched the newspapers to see if they contained any notice of the sort, but as there has been no mention of any catastrophe, I suppose she has escaped safely. Her horse must have been quieter and better broken than they generally are. F——says that probably it was a very old "station screw." I trust so, for her sake!

[. . .]

BROOMIELAW,
September 1866.

I am writing to you at the end of a fortnight of very hard work, for I have just gone through my first experience in changing servants; those I brought up with me four months ago were nice, tidy girls, and as a natural consequence of these attractive qualities they have both left me to be married. I sent them down to Christchurch in the dray, and made arrangements for two more servants to return in the same conveyance at the end of a week. In the meantime we had to do everything for ourselves, and on the whole we found this picnic life great fun. The household consists, besides F—— and me, of a cadet, as they are called—he is a clergyman's son learning sheep-farming under our auspices—and a boy who milks the cows and does odd jobs out of doors. We were all equally ignorant of practical cookery, so the chief responsibility rested on my shoulders, and cost me some very anxious moments, I assure you, for a cookery-book is after all but a broken reed to lean on in a real emergency; it starts by assuming that its unhappy student possesses a knowledge of at least the rudiments of the art, whereas it ought not to disdain to tell you whether the water in which potatoes are to be boiled should be hot or cold. I must confess that some of my earliest efforts were both curious and nasty, but F—— ate my numerous failures with the greatest good-humour; the only thing at which he made a wry face was some soup into which a large lump of washing-soda had mysteriously conveyed itself; and I also had to undergo a good deal of "chaff" about my first omelette, which was of the size and consistency of a roly-poly pudding. Next to these failures I think the bread was my greatest misfortune; it went wrong from the first. One night I had prepared the tin dish full of flour, made a hole in the midst of the soft white heap, and was about to pour in a cupful of yeast to be mixed with warm water (you see I know all about it in theory), when a sudden panic seized me, and I was afraid to draw the cork of the large champagne bottle full of yeast, which appeared to be very much "up." In this dilemma I went for F——. You must know that he possesses such extraordinary and revolutionary theories on the subject of cooking, that I am obliged to banish him from the kitchen altogether, but on this occasion I thought I should be glad of his assistance. He came with the greatest alacrity; assured me he knew all about it, seized the big bottle, shook it violently, and twitched out the cork: there was a report like a pistol-shot, and all my beautiful yeast flew up to the ceiling of the kitchen, descending in a shower on my head; and F—— turned the bottle upside down over the flour, emptyings the dregs of the hops and potatoes into my unfortunate bread. However, I did not despair, but mixed it up according to the directions given, and placed it on the stove; but, as it turned out, in too warm a situation, for when I went early the next morning to look at it, I found a very dry and crusty mass. Still, nothing daunted, I persevered in the attempt, added more flour and water, and finally made it up into loaves, which I deposited in the oven. That bread *never* baked! I tried it with a knife in the orthodox manner, always to find that it was *raw* inside. The crust gradually became several inches thick, but the inside remained damp, and turned quite black at last; I baked it until midnight, and then I gave it up and retired to bed in deep disgust. I had no more yeast and could not try again, so we lived on biscuits and potatoes till the dray returned at the end of the week, bringing, however, only one servant.

Owing to some confusion in the drayman's arrangements, the cook had been left behind, and "Meary," the new arrival, professed her willingness to supply her place; but on trial being made of her abilities, she proved to be quite as inexperienced as I was; and to each dish I proposed she should attempt, the unvarying answer was, "The missis did all that where I come from." During the first few days after her arrival her chief employment was examining the various knick-knacks about the drawing-room; in her own department she was greatly taken with the little cottage mangle. She mangled her own apron about twenty times a day, and after each attempt I found her contemplating it with her head on one side, and saying to herself,

"'Deed, thin, it's as smooth as smooth; how iver does it do it?" A few days later the cook arrived. She is not all I could wish, being also Irish, and having the most extraordinary notions of the use, or rather the abuse, of the various kitchen implements: for instance, she *will* poke the fire with the toasting fork, and disregards my gentle hints about the poker; but at all events she can both roast mutton and bake bread. "Meary" has been induced to wash her face and braid up her beautiful hair, and now shines forth as a very pretty good-humoured girl. she is as clever and quick as possible, and will in time be a capital housemaid. She has taken it into her head that she would like to be a "first-rater," as she calls it, and works desperately hard in the prosecution of her new fancy.

Mrs Edward Millett

An Australian Parsonage
(1872)

It was after a day of intense heat, followed by no night breeze, that I summoned up courage to take a walk with Rosa, just as darkness had fallen and a dull red line was all that marked the west. Our way led past the convict depôt and the house of the colonial surgeon, below which, on a bank sloping towards the river, often stood one or two lonely huts containing sick natives, who were brought thither by their friends for the benefit of medical assistance. A fire was burning here, betokening the presence of an invalid on this particular evening, and as Rosa and I leaned over the bridge watching the flicker of the fire-light in the dry river bed, a man standing near the wooden piers, who had recognized me, looked up, and told me that a native woman lay very ill in a hut below.

On hearing this Rosa and I turned off the bridge, and went down the bank to see if we could offer her any help. We found, to our regret, that the sick woman was one with whom we were well acquainted, and her evidently hopeless state somewhat surprised us, as poor "Kitty" had called at our house in good health not very long before. Her intelligence was above the average, and a stranger from England, whose impressions of Australian natives had been solely derived from books, would have probably supposed, on seeing her neatly dressed and waiting at table, that she was a West Indian mulatto, excepting for the softness of her hair. I had been so much struck with her appearance on one such occasion as afterwards to feel surprised on receiving a visit from her attired in nothing but the native costume of a long fur mantle over one shoulder and under the other; but I found that, just in the same way as European ladies put on their travelling dresses, natives assume the kangaroo skin when about to make a journey.

I came up to the hut where she was now lying on the ground, and the sight of me appeared to gratify the poor creature, for it was plain that she had something to say to me, and that she might the better do so her husband raised her and supported her in a sitting posture, when with much difficulty she pronounced the words, "Will you take my little girl?" The man completed the sentence for her, by explaining that she knew herself to be dying, and wanted me to take charge of Binnahan, their only child. I said at once that I would do so, feeling inwardly certain of my husband's consent, but she seemed at first almost afraid to believe me; and the man tried to reassure her, by saying in the native language, that I "was not telling lies." However, I did not leave her until I had tranquillized her mind with the repeated assurance that in case of her death her little daughter should live with us.

Now it so happened that at the clerical meeting, amongst other subjects of discussion, the duties of Government chaplains towards the natives had occupied much attention, and my husband, amongst others of the clergy, had expressed an opinion that the natives were sadly neglected, and ought to be so no longer. Poor Kitty's request, which I communicated to him on his return, was a speedier test of sincerity than he had anticipated, although it was one from which he had no thought of flinching; he therefore went immediately to the river-side, and telling her he was come to hear her wishes that he might endeavour to fulfil them, she just gasped out the words, "Take Binnahan—make good." She lingered a day or two longer, but on the following morning a little girl, whose only clothing was a small piece of cotton print pinned round her, peeped timidly and without speaking into the room where I was sitting, to let me know that she had arrived.

She was a very slight little creature, with the thin limbs of her wild race, in fact the natives in general were so slim that I remember Khourabene's ideas of art being much offended by a picture of savages in the "Illustrated London News," which had represented them all with large calves to their legs, and he pointed out the defect, perhaps I ought rather to say superfluity, with very great disdain. I supposed that she might be seven years old, but as she had changed all her first teeth, she was evidently older than she looked. Her skin, like that of the children at Albany whom Mrs. Smythe had noticed, was darker than her hair, which was soft and curly, setting off by its lighter colour the line of jet-black eyebrow and the dark expressive eyes below.

She shared the Malay nose and mouth with her countrymen in general, a type of feature which is unfortunately far more commonly found amongst them than fine hair, and which imparts to the countenance a sullen look even when there is no real sullenness in the temper; but nature's even hand makes amends for this by the brilliancy of the teeth and eyes, so that a smile on a native face is like a flash of light. Although she was quite clean, I could not sufficiently divest my mind of home traditions to suppose otherwise than that to wash her must be the first thing to be done, so Rosa and I put her in a bath; but as she had arrived before I had been able to prepare her wardrobe, to dress her on leaving the tub was a matter far more difficult. I had managed, however, by sundown to complete an overall pinafore, in which she immediately started off to exhibit herself to her parents, returning to sleep at our house, which from that day forth became her home.

Two mornings afterwards, just as the sun had risen, a pair of little black cousins appeared at our door; there was no need to ask why they had come so early, as the grief in their faces betrayed their errand, and poor little Binnahan, throwing herself face downwards on Rosa's bed, moaned aloud as though her heart was broken. She went away with the two girls as soon as the first burst of grief was over, and about an hour afterwards some native women came to ask me if I would give them a covering to lay over poor Kitty in her grave. This was the only time that I ever had a similar request, and I sent them away much gratified with a piece of white calico. We had once had a sadder petition preferred to us by some natives; it was for the loan of our wheelbarrow to convey to her grave a woman who had been speared a few hours before, and whom we had seen at our door that morning alive and well, and had noticed as being remarkably handsome.

I went down to the river-side, soon after sending the white covering, that I might see the last of Binnahan's poor mother. I should have known, even at a distance, that there had been a death amongst the natives, from the monotonous wailing noise that is always raised on such occasions until after the funeral, with a view of keeping off the evil spirit Jingy, the official mourner being relieved, when wearied, by others in uninterrupted succession until the grave is closed. A fat old woman, thus enacting the part of exorcist when I got to the place, was doing so with all her might, shaking her hands incessantly from the wrists in a despairing manner, whilst she uttered her cries until the perspiration streamed off her face with heat and fatigue. Altogether she offered as wide a contrast as could be imagined to the mutes who are hired to stand at the doors of the house in a ceremonious English funeral.

The corpse was laid on its side, as if asleep, beneath a bower of green branches, of which the husband, with the tears running down his black cheeks, removed a few, that I might look at his poor dead wife. I should not have known that she was dead as, owing to the dark skin, my unpractised eye could not detect the change in the complexion and appearance caused by death.

It is customary amongst the natives to bury the dead in a sitting posture; the nails of the corpse are also burnt off before burial, and the hands tied together, and Binnahan seemed pleased to tell me that with regard to her mother the ceremony of burning the nails had been omitted; both that and the tying of the hands are said to be measures of precaution lest the deceased should work his or her way up again to the world's surface, and alarm the living not only by "walking," but, if a man, by using his spears (which are always buried with him) upon his former friends. As the funeral follows close upon the death, the practice of burning off the nails must at least possess, one would think, the recommendation of deciding any doubt about life being extinct or merely suspended, and a native, whom we heard of as having shouldered himself out of the ground, above which he lived for some time afterwards, may possibly have owed his revival to these last offices of his somewhat hasty friends.

I now did my best to make a proper suit of clothes for Binnahan, preparatory to sending her to the Government school, during which interval she was constantly visited by her cousins and her aunt, the latter giving me to understand, with the air of a person who makes a family arrangement, that the girls should leave off coming as soon as her niece had recovered her spirits, or, as the good lady expressed it, "when Binnahan never more mother thinkum." I was glad, however, to find that this period of forgetfulness did not arrive. The child's grief soon exhausted itself, but so far from forgetting her mother, she never seemed better pleased than to be reminded of her.

I could not help laughing at myself the first time that my new charge started for school. Rosa's two little sisters good-naturedly came to act as convoy, but the black cousins, whom I had not invited, appeared also, and fell into the ranks of the escort. Now the whole party was barefoot, and Binnahan's preference for going to school as the crow flies necessitated a short cut over stubble fields, from which the white feet instinctively shrank, but which seemed good smooth walking to the hard little hoofs of the others.

I had heard so much of the invincible attractions of the bush, and the impossibility of preventing a native from running back to it, that my mind misgave me on the point about which I had least for fear, namely, that she would not return at dinner-time but rather take pot-luck with her relations on some chance dolghite or opossum. Whilst I stood watching in our verandah, with the anxiety of a hen looking after a foster-duckling, the party divided, adding thereby much to my uncertainties; but afternoon arrived, and with it came Binnahan, in a more than contented frame of mind, for she seemed extremely pleased with the step that she had ascended on life's ladder.

She learned to read very rapidly, the quick sight possessed by all natives no doubt much assisting her; in fact, when her father came to see her after she had been with us for a few months, she read aloud to him at such great length, to convince him of her progress, that his face exhibited in succession the three phases of delight, astonishment, and weariness, reminding me of the sensations ascribed by Johnson to the readers of "Hudibras."

I wish that I could have said that her energy in learning to sew equalled that shown in her efforts to master the mysteries of reading; her backwardness in needle-work being the more provoking as her eye was so correct. She would come in from an hour's play in the garden to exhibit herself to me in a mantle of green leaves, put together in excellent shape with small bits of stick broken to the size of pins, but to construct a piece of dress by making a multitude of neat stitches appeared to require a perseverance in which her disposition was defective. I doubt, however, whether an Anglo-Saxon would have done much better who had spent the first eight or nine years of life without settled occupations or civilized habits.

The same keen sight, that enabled her so quickly to acquire a knowledge of the alphabet, soon made her acquainted with the figures on the clock's face, which at half-past twelve she described as being "cut in two, all same damper" (dampers or bush bread being of a muffin shape), but I found much difficulty in teaching her how to tell the time correctly. I could however always trust to her to bring me an accurate description of the relative positions of the two hands if I wanted to know the hour.

Mrs Algernon St Maur

Impressions of a Tenderfoot
(1890)

We wandered all through China-Town. Several guides offered to take charge of us, but we preferred seeing what we could by ourselves. If it were not for the ordinary style of building the houses, we could fancy ourselves in Pekin or Canton. There is a population of over 40,000 Chinese in San Francisco. They all live in the quarter called "China-Town," apart from every one else, pursuing mostly their own work and trades. We saw Chinese hurrying in every direction, for the Celestial is always busy, and therefore in haste. We passed many stores containing goods of all kinds, and by looking through the doorway we saw how the people were employed. In one shop there were boot-makers at work; in another sewing machines were busy. The Chinese excel in all kinds of labour, and are so frugal that they can undersell the Americans even in cheap tailoring. But here the sweating system is also in vogue, and it is the middleman who is making a profit. A pair of blue overalls (an article of clothing worn by almost every workman) is made by the men employed in these tailors' shops for a quarter-dollar, or one shilling of our money. We passed many provision-shops, and very unpalatable the food looked; thin pieces of meat, dried ducks, bundles of sausages, and stale pork being the principal things we noticed. There were baskets of vegetables of all kinds in front of the windows of these shops, and these seemed to find a ready sale.

Then, through a narrow door far under the level of an ordinary cellar, we saw the barber at work in his shop. The front part of a Chinaman's head is kept shaved; the back is arranged into a pigtail. Where nature has not been bountiful, and I doubt if she is ever sufficiently so—it makes no difference, as all appear to have black silk plaited in with their hair to make the pigtail longer; it usually reaches down the back as far as the knees. In China it is thought disrespectful to roll it round one's head, but in this country the Chinese servants do it in order to get the pigtails out of the

167

way. When the Chinaman's forehead is shaved and his pigtail arranged, he is by no means out of the hands of the barber, for the inside of his ears have also to be shaved. We saw this being done, and rather a disagreeable process it seemed; but I suppose the Celestial must suffer with the rest of the world *pour être beau.*

We found all the Chinese civil and obliging. Before entering their Joss-houses, as they call their places of worship, their shops, or restaurants, we asked permission to do so, which was readily granted. Among the antiChinese party the custom is to treat the Celestials as rudely as possible. We did not wish to do this, nor did the Americans who accompanied us. We went into the shop of a goldsmith, who was beating out gold rings, and we saw some that he had finished. He was working by a small reed lamp, similar to those found in the ruins of Pompeii, and by him also stood a very curious old pair of scales, with which he weighed his rings before selling them by weight. Though we did not buy, as we passed out he raised his head from his work and nodded to us.

Our next visit was to a restaurant, and having bowed to the men in charge, we passed in. Saw two cooks making little square rolls; which, when finished, were stamped with a Chinese mark. These rolls are filled with mincemeat, and are sent to Chinamen all over Canada and America. We did not like the taste of them; and, after seeing them passed into the ovens, we went upstairs. In Chinese restaurants here, the higher up you go the more you pay, and for this reason, the houses not being built on the lines of a Chinaman's ideal, it is only on the upper floor that seclusion, and a garden on the roof with verandahs to sit in, can be obtained. On the first floor we saw an eating-house for the poorer class of workmen; each table being partitioned off from the next with screens. After mounting to the upper-floor, we found ourselves in a charming Chinese house; all the fittings and furniture were of home workmanship, the chairs and tables being of ebony, beautifully inlaid with mother-of-pearl, while valuable carvings, screens, and lamps were tastefully arranged. Both the Chinese and Japanese have certainly perfect taste. Six or eight round tables were neatly laid out for dinner. The dishes were so small, that though there were many of them piled up with fruits, tiny pieces of fish, and other things, it looked to me like a doll's dinner-party, and not a repast prepared for hungry men. Opposite to each guest were tiny plates, a china spoon, a pair of ivory chopsticks, and a small glass bowl, containing some kind of liqueur.

We passed through the kitchen, where several cooks were busily engaged with their tiny pans; but a hungry navvy would have eaten up everything we saw in a very short time. Can this be all the food Celestials need? Is the bird's-nest soup so very sustaining, or do they not eat in the quantities Europeans do? The last question is answered negatively, the problem solved; Chinamen can live on rice, and nothing else, doing the hardest work in mines, or manual labour all the time; and this is how they can save so much where other men must eat to live.

We were attracted by the sounds of merry voices, and passed on, and soon were intently watching a dinner-party from behind a screen. Ten Chinamen were dining together; by their dress we concluded they were well-to-do merchants—some of whom are very wealthy—they were evidently enjoying excellent jokes; as we watched them from our undignified position, we observed that in this, as well as in some of the other private rooms, was an alcove, with the opium pipe; by it, on a luxurious couch, one of the guests was lying in a sort of stupor, apparently unconscious; the other guests seemed to take no notice of him, as if there was nothing unusual in his condition.

We passed into another room, and had tea; it was nicely served in beautiful oriental china cups. In front of each person stood a covered cup on a little stand: and the tea-leaves were placed in each of these; a Chinaman came in and poured boiling water from a bronze kettle over the leaves, the cover was replaced, and in a few minutes the tea was ready; and, with care, was poured into another cup, and the one containing the leaves acted as a kind of tea-pot, and was refilled with boiling water. Excellent tea it was, but somewhat costly; so much so, that our American friends, who bought 1 lb., had $5 to pay for it. Green tea is preferred, the flavour is more flowery and delicate, when infused being of a pale colour. Our tea was served with plates of cakes, nuts, and ginger. During the time we were having it a band played in the verandah, and such a band! The noise made by the five musicians was deafening; but as three of their number had gongs (or something very like them), and the fourth a drum, it was not surprising. The fifth musician had a sort of trumpet, and when the gongs at intervals ceased playing, the trumpet, single-handed, produced most discordant tones, mingled with wails, which were meant for singing. We were thankful when this performance ceased, though, judging by the acclamations of the rest of the audience, the music was considered excellent.

We visited several joss-houses, and were saddened by the rows of idols we saw, some of which were very hideous. The Chinese do not pray to the good spirits, we were told, as they do them no harm, but to the evil ones. All these poor souls seem to be in a state of the greatest spiritual darkness, having few redeeming points in their religion. There is no devoutness in their joss-houses, the men who are in charge sleep about the doors; those who come in to say their prayers write them, and afterwards burn them in an oven.

Looking in at several of the opium dens, we saw as much of them as we wished; we heard enough about the horrors of this vice, and occasionally we passed a Chinaman who looked like a ghost—an unmistakable victim.

Some of the people we met could not reason, nor even speak quietly on the subject of the Chinese question. The moment anything was said about China or the Chinese, they talked without weighing either their words or their arguments. With such a person it was our fate to travel in the cars for three days, coming from Portland. Unsought, he joined in our conversation, which happened to be on the subject of the Chinese; he remarked, "The Chinese are of no use in San Francisco, or, for that matter, in America, and they must go, for they are parasites; dirty, useless, lying, and dishonest." With some difficulty I was able to remark that at Victoria the English people told me they were most valuable as domestic servants, where no other servants were available, and did a great deal of work; he continued his abuse. "They were the curse of his country, and brought over disease and many other dreadful things." I asked him if he had ever been to China-Town. He confessed that, though he had lived in the city of San Francisco twenty years, he had never been there, nor had he ever allowed his wife to go, nor to have any dealings with the Chinese. He then advised Algernon not to allow me to visit China-Town, as it would be at the peril of our lives from small-pox, leprosy, and other horrors.

The subject lapsed, as we did not trouble to talk much more to him, though for two days we travelled onwards in the same dusty and hot cars.

I do not know why it is, but when nearing one's destination, ideas are often exchanged, and he again joined us; but I think he must have forgotten our conversation of the previous day, for to our amusement he began telling us of the best shops in San Francisco, adding, "When my wife wants Chinese bargains, she buys them of a smuggler who calls once a week at our house; our home is full of valuable things we have got from him at cheap prices."

Fancy taking advice from such a creature!

3

Women and space

Women travel writers have had to negotiate with the discursive frameworks of scientific writing, imperialism, aesthetics, and the ideology of the separate spheres in order to represent their travels spatially. These areas of knowledge, which we discuss in the introductory section of "Women and knowledge" above, together with the stereotypes of the proper place for the sexes, play a key role in representing spatiality within travel texts. Much of the constitutive work for these frameworks has been undertaken by male travellers, geographers and artists. Women travel writers have thus had to try to position themselves somewhere in relation to these discourses of aesthetics, science and imperialism and find a voice for themselves amid these authoritative statements of surveying, analysing, assessing and evaluating. Furthermore they have had to challenge the assumption that women within the public sphere are somehow "out of place". Middle-class British women travel writers have to situate themselves textually in relation to their own culture so that they need not necessarily be judged as transgressing that culture's norms about the "place" of women. At the same time, "place" becomes a gendered site in which individual female aspiration can be played out and enterprise enacted.

In this introductory section we will discuss several factors and issues which have gendered space and the representational practices of women travel writers to a significant degree: firstly, the sense of restriction which women have reported feeling in relation to their mobility in the public sphere; secondly, the fear of sexual attack which again has had an impact on women's behaviour and descriptions of their behaviour in the public sphere; thirdly, gender and the sublime; and finally, space and knowledge/looking. We conclude this introductory section, however, by discussing the challenges to the determining force of these factors in the construction of spatial relations. Rather than assuming that women travel writers were positioned passively by social pressures, we would argue that, precisely by travelling unaccompanied, women travellers in the nineteenth century challenged the seeming masculinity of the public sphere.

Restriction

Spatial relations as they pertain to women have generally been analysed in terms of restriction. Thus, Iris Marion Young describes the process whereby through the social constraints acting on their behaviour and thinking about their bodily movements, women see themselves as constrained within space and find it difficult to move freely in the way that men seem to do (Young, 1989). She makes several telling observations about women's movements. Firstly, she tells a personal anecdote of finding herself in some turmoil when in a party of walkers she seemed to be taking the lead much less than some of her male companions; she sees this as due to social conditioning of females which discourages them from taking up leadership roles, but she also suggests that we could see unease in this case as emanating from women's sense of their own spatial locatedness and from society's views of women being unable to orient themselves and navigate in the same way as men. Secondly, she observes that girls are taught that it is acceptable to move and exert themselves in ways which bear connotations of weakness and ineffectualness; this is not done explicitly but, for example, it is seen as permissible for a woman to "throw like a girl", with all the connotations of failure that this phrase bears.

Although Young's analysis of female movement is an important one, as Gillian Rose has shown, it is only a part of the complex negotiation of spatial relations which women undertake (Rose, 1993).[1] It is also true that British middle-class women travellers, particularly in the nineteenth century, experienced a constraint on their movements because of the fear of sexual harassment or attack as well as because of society's pressures on women to see themselves as vulnerable and lady-like, with all of the physical restrictions which lady-like clothing and deportment entailed. In the general Introduction above, we have shown that many nineteenth-century female travellers, when they adopted proto-masculine garments more suitable to the rigours of their undertakings, felt socially compromised and obliged to protest their femininity. These women were encouraged to see that their "proper" sphere was the private domestic sphere, and thus this also led to a pressure on their mobility within the public sphere, which many argue still operates in the present time. But, paradoxically, women in the nineteenth century and in the present have also experienced a degree of freedom travelling in other countries which was not possible for them within Britain. Particularly within countries which were colonised, nineteenth-century women travellers experienced a degree of safety and the possibility of travelling unescorted by white men, or even in the company of "natives", because of the knowledge that they were under the protection of the colonial authority. An attack on them would indicate an attack on the colonial authorities which was, at least at an ideological level, unthinkable within certain periods of colonial rule in Africa and India.

Strangely, perhaps it is only in recent years that it has been possible for women travel writers to represent themselves as ineffectual, so strong has the stereotype of the intrepid woman traveller been. For some women travellers in the twentieth and twenty-first century, it seems as if it is now permissible to admit freely and even unapologetically to their inability to cope with dangerous situations or orient themselves. This type of writing might be seen to signify an extremely conservative femininity, both asserting a right to travel through the public sphere whilst at the same time displaying a feminine failure to manage to travel effectively, as some nineteenth-century women's travel writing did (Mazuchelli, 1876). However, perhaps it could be argued that, although this may be one of the interpretations of this type of writing, it may also be read as meaning differently in the context of nineteenth-century women's writing, signifying instead a move away from the type of adventure heroes of nineteenth-century imperial discourse, to a more human, flawed and ultimately more humorous account of travel.

Fear of sexual attack

Sexual attack is often something which is most marked in women's travel writing paradoxically because of its absence. There is often a sense that the fault would lie with the woman herself if she reported fear of sexual impropriety, and would perhaps draw attention to the problematic nature of her travelling unaccompanied within the public sphere. For Gillian Rose, it is this fear of attack which marks and constitutes the public sphere for middle-class Western women (Rose, 1993).

Whilst nineteenth-century British women in colonial countries sometimes feel protected by their position within the colonial hierarchy, as we mentioned earlier, there is a sense in which they are also perceived to be colonialism's weakest point. Within colonised countries the sexual honour of British women was seen to be of extreme importance (Sharpe, 1993). Colonial rule was often played out on the bodies of Western women, so that extreme acts of retribution for supposed attacks on British women were represented in the British press and by the colonial authorities as morally justified. This obsession with the protection of British women necessarily had an effect on the way they comported themselves within colonised countries and the way that they represented themselves in their travel writing.

Within other countries in the nineteenth century, sexual attack was considered to be such a taboo subject that it could hardly be mentioned at all in women's travel writing. Instead, it constitutes a presence which makes itself felt by its absence. Marianne North, for example, proudly relates how she pre-empted what could easily have been a sexual attack when she was painting in solitude in Safed by picking up a huge stone and telling the three men who were threatening her "In good English to 'be off'". She adds that she refrained from swearing because "that would have been unladylike" (North, 1893: 180) In a very different context, Emmeline Lott, governess to the Grand Pacha, son of the Viceroy of Turkey in the 1860s, describes the dangerous position that she was in with regard to the harem inhabitants: since the Viceroy had had at least one European mistress before, Lott was well aware that he could easily turn his attentions to her, with the result that she would incur the extreme—and possibly fatal—jealousy of the other favourites. Recounting how she dealt with her situation—"I trusted that my own habitual reservedness of manner would save me from any advances being made, and determined not to become a lodestone of attraction to H.H. the Viceroy" (Lott, 1865, II: 34)—she represents herself not as invulnerable but as able to circumvent the possibility of sexual attack, with all its attendant perils, physical as well as moral.

Some women travelling unaccompanied in Europe considered such journeys to be risky; long distance travel by carriage or coach, for example, could entail the threat of unwelcome attentions of fellow male passengers, while incipient, if not actual, threats from strangers in Italian cities caused distress to a woman travelling on her own (Jameson, 1915; Kemble, 1882; Martin, 1828). The kind of freedom and safety experienced within colonised countries was, however, possible in other continents. Nineteenth-century female travellers to the United States frequently comment on the ease and safety with which a woman could move about on her own. Isabella Bird's experiences in the Rocky Mountains confirmed the assurances she had received that a lady alone in the "uncivilised West" would be sure of "respect" (although she carried a loaded revolver with her, she never needed to use it) (Barr, 1985). Harriet

Martineau, travelling with one other female companion, observes that "the national boast (is) a perfectly true one . . . a woman may travel alone from Maine to Georgia without dread of any kind of injury" (Martineau, [1878] 1983, II: 85). And Fanny Kemble notes the contrast with Italy: in America a woman is "certain of assistance, attention, the most respectful civility, the most human protection, from every man she meets without the fear of injury or insult" (Kemble, 1847, I: 66). Bird makes a similar comparison with England, with respect to rail travel. Here, of course, there were no colonial authorities to engender fear of reprisal, and one can only speculate why the protection of being a lady, as Davidson suggests, operated here, unlike in Europe (Davidson, 1889). Perhaps the consciousness of the fragility of a newly established democratic society helped to ensure that social relations in the context of gender as well as of class depended on an erosion or collapse of difference—which sexual attack obviously reinforces. More generally, the lack of reference to sexual attack may have been because women's experience when travelling abroad did not live up to the stereotypes of danger and disaster which they had been led to expect.

An additional factor may have been that in their written accounts of their travels they felt obliged to play down the threat of sexual attack, for fear of being accused of sexual impropriety for having placed themselves in situations of potential danger. Whatever reason prompted the paucity of reference in this respect, the relative freedom which was often experienced abroad does point up quite markedly the sense of restrictedness which middle-class women experienced in Britain.

Because of the sense in European society during the nineteenth century that women were or should be restricted to the domestic sphere in order for them to be considered sexually "safe", when women travelled alone in other countries they were seen as strange, eccentric and sexualised. They often had to combat in their writing the idea that they had no place within the public sphere; they also had to counter criticism when they travelled through places which it seemed unnatural or dangerous for them to visit. This constraint continues into the present period, despite teams of women travelling to the North Pole and scaling mountains; there seems to still remain a public unease with women daring to travel into dangerous regions without males to protect them, which is witnessed in the often scathing media reports of women-only expeditions. As we mentioned in the introductory section to "Women and knowledge" above, women writers have developed a number of strategies to deal with these difficulties: one of them is an adoption of an impersonal scientific voice to describe landscapes as a means of authorising the narrative representation; another is making references to authorities on the subject; a third is a stern refusal to describe fear, sexual attack or danger.

Gender and the sublime

Whilst it is seen to be appropriate for women to be alone within the private sphere, when women are alone in the public sphere it can be seen as anomalous and it may

175

require some textual work or justification. Women travellers themselves, as well as their critics, could feel unease about such overt female singularity. Many women's travel accounts describe the sense of experiencing a new freedom, or conversely a terror, when they are by themselves in an otherwise unpeopled landscape. Generally, critics have argued that the sublime is a moment of confrontation between a solitary individual ego and a landscape where these problems of conflict and otherness are resolved. Yaeger terms this encounter "self-centred imperialism" and she states that the sublime is concerned with the attempt "in words and feelings [to] transcend the normative, the human" (Yaeger, 1989: 192). In this process of transcendence, the sublime subject is aggrandised and is ratified in its position of power. There are particular types of sublime experience which Yaeger suggests are prototypically masculinist: "Typically the male writing in the sublime mode will stage a moment of blockage which is followed by a moment of imagistic brilliance. That is, the mind fights back against the blocking source by representing its own inability to grasp the sublime object. This representation of inability becomes scriptive proof of the mind's percipience and stability of the mind's willed relation to a transcendental order, and thus of the mind's powerful univocity and its potential for mental domination of the other" (Yaeger, 1989: 202). Thus, the landscape is represented as Other and merely as a device whereby control and transcendence of the individual ego may be foregrounded. This psychoanalytic account of the sublime leads to a certain essentialism in relation to gender—it assumes that the sublime viewer is male. This spectatorial position in relation to an empty landscape recalls Mary Louise Pratt's work on colonial landscape, where the colonial male subject surveys the terrain often from a position of panorama (Pratt, 1992). She states that the land in colonial writing presents itself to the viewer, showing itself or unfolding beneath his gaze; the landscape is not seen to be one of human habitation or work, rather it is "emptied" by the colonising "improving" eye and "made meaningful only in terms of a capitalist future and of their potential for producing a marketable surplus" (Pratt, 1992: 61). The masculinity of this surveying "eye" is apparent when one considers that women are rarely classified as explorers, even when they have been involved in exploratory missions (see for example, Emily Creaghe [1883] 1998, May French-Sheldon [1892] 1999 and Olive Pink [1933] 1998).

Women travel writers often include scenes of panorama in their work, although occasionally there is a sense in which there is a textual unease in relation to this position of extreme power. Sometimes, women hedged these descriptions with ironising humour, deflating the pretensions to power and national pride which such descriptions generally contain within male-authored texts. In the case of Nina Mazuchelli, who describes sketching a mountain landscape late at night, rather than being awed by the magnificence of the sublime landscape, she portrays herself as terrified and forced to retreat back to her tent, frightened of the sight of her own shadow (Mazuchelli, 1876). Many women writers describe the sensations which they experience when alone, particularly in an alien environment, in ways which are similar to what might be classified as paranoia.

A British female traveller's relation to the sublime is thus necessarily different from a male's relation to this surveying imperial view, because of the socio-economic differences and differential access to the public sphere; however that is not to say that women travellers do not describe moments of sublime experience. As we suggest in the introductory section to "Women and knowledge" above, nineteenth-century female observers of dramatic or picturesque landscape frequently draw on the aesthetic vocabulary of the sublime in a way which combines a masculinist (in Yaeger's model) linguistic empowerment with a more "feminine" emotional response. Indeed, it could be argued that one of the first travellers to develop the notion of the sublime was Mary Wollstonecraft, an extract from whose work is included in this section. Consider this passage from Wollstonecraft's work where she describes her emotions when faced with an awe-inspiring vista:

> It is not the queen of the night alone who reigns here in all her splendour, though the sun, loitering just below the horizon, decks her with a golden tinge from his car, illuminating the cliffs that hide him; the heavens also, of a clear softened blue, throw her forward, and the evening star appears a lesser moon to the naked eye. The huge shadows of the rocks, fringed with firs, concentrating the views, without darkening them, excited that tender melancholy which, sublimating the imagination, exalts, rather than depresses the mind. (Wollstonecraft, [1796] 1987: 35)

Here, Wollstonecraft, as well as describing a scene, is simultaneously locating herself within a discourse of aesthetics, with her poetic metaphorical descriptions of the sun, the moon, the stars and the cliffs, and also positioning herself as a writer who is able to experience the excessive emotional response required of the sublime. This emotionalism necessary for an experience of the sublime could be seen to constitute a profoundly feminine response to landscape.

Furthermore, it might be argued that the conditions of representing travel abroad enabled women to adopt this seemingly very powerful position in relation to representing landscape. For example, Isabelle Eberhardt is able to represent herself travelling alone in disguise in Algeria and experiencing a kind of ecstacy which does not accord with the limitations imposed on Western middle-class women of the time; she states: "Oh, the long hours I spent in those woods so full of mystery and shadows, the sleepless nights gazing at a cosmos full of stars. I must have been headed for religious mysticism already at the time" (Eberhardt, [1902, 1905] 1987: 67).

As we mentioned earlier, the public sphere within Western cultures has been characterised as a sphere for men, where women on their own fear sexual attack. The private sphere is characterised as women's sphere and this colours women's experience of being in a natural environment differently from men's experience. As Hamner and Saunders state: "women's sense of security is profoundly shaped by our inability to secure an undisputed right to occupy that [public] space" (cited in Rose, 1993: 34), though it must be noted that their claims are applicable only to Western middle-class women.[2] The difference in the way that Western middle-class women and men see their position in relation to the site of the sublime is bound to have effects on the way that the sublime landscape is represented.

177

Space and knowledge/looking

Space is encoded and policed/regulated in different ways for women and men, and stereotypes of appropriate behaviour enforce these gendered divisions; however, it should be added that different groups of women have had different relations to space, and that working-class and upper-class British women in the periods we address have not experienced the same type of restrictions with regard to the public sphere as their middle-class counterparts. As we have already shown, too, middle-class women have tested out, challenged and transgressed the limits of these constraints. After all, the vast majority of women travellers were from the middle classes.

Rose also notes that, whilst women have tended to be represented as the space of the bodily, male observers of nature seem to do so not from a bodily space but from a seeing space. Landscape is a terrain mapped out from the limits of the human optical range, rather than being a "natural" geographical feature. This seeing position, as Rose goes on to show, is a space of power/knowledge, and it is more important in terms of the type of subject position that it maps out than for what is described (Rose, 1993).

Doreen Massey's work demonstrates the necessity of discussing women and men in space in materialist terms, for she states that "what is at issue is not social phenomena in space but both social phenomena and space as constituted out of social relations [. . . we therefore need to think of] the spatial [as] social relations 'stretched out'" (Massey, 1994: 2). This notion of space being imbricated with social relations is important in considering women in space, because it moves discussion away from simple notions of women as a group having a consistent unchanging relation to spatial frameworks, and also thus to aesthetic judgements and the sublime.

One's position in space necessarily maps out a position of knowledge when the landscape is described. Therefore a woman alone in a landscape will be writing herself and her subject position as much as she is producing knowledge about the country and the landscape. Her socio-economic position, and her relation to authority and knowledge will determine the type of landscape that she will produce in writing. Rose's work on the landscape has been very important in understanding women's different access to that position of intelligibility which is the viewer of landscape. Rose stresses that, when describing fieldworkers and the landscape, cultural geographers have begun to "problematise the term 'landscape' as a reference to relations between society and environment . . . and they have argued that it refers not only to the relationships between different objects caught in the fieldworker's gaze, but that it also implies a specific way of looking" (Rose, 1993: 87). This focus on a specific way of looking and a specific form of subjectivity determined by it is important in thinking about subjects describing themselves in relation to a landscape. Many cultures do not have a term for "landscape", that sense of a delimited terrain captured by a frame, and do not feel that this sense of distance involved in the viewing position pertains to them (Spain, 1992). Even though, as Haraway has argued, the particularities of our visual capabilities are presented as universal, necessitating certain ways of processing and interpreting visual stimuli, there are still marked cultural differences in relation to viewing landscapes (Haraway, 1988). Rose argues that the "domineering view of the single point of the omniscient observer of landscape" is one which is conventionally taken up by males and that women tend to see landscape in more relational ways; rather than seeking to subdue the landscape, in their writings they tend to see landscapes in relation to their domestic spaces and their networks of interaction. She describes the work of Pollock on women artists who abandon the conventional wide landscapes of male painters for more confined spatial representations; she states that they "(rearticulate) traditional space so that it ceases to function primarily as the space of sight for a mastering gaze, but becomes the locus of relationships" (Pollock, cited in Rose, 1993: 112). However, we would contest this view of women writers and artists representing landscape in a consistently different way to men. Sometimes, as we noted in the general Introduction above, when we focus on difference, we may tend to polarise positions where there is in fact common ground or similar strategies, and exclude consideration of other elements which do not fit within this scheme. What may be at issue here is other differences, for example, access to education and hence to discourses of aesthetics, science and so on, rather than the difference in description being due to gender (Spain, 1992). Although there may be a correlation between this access to discourse and gender, there will not be a complete fit. Thus, through an analysis of the socially constructed differences in middle-class women's and men's access to the public and private sphere, it is possible to map out the parameters for the negotiations which writers engage in when they produce a textual space for the representation of a landscape.

Challenges to spatial relations

Interestingly, it is women travellers themselves who most overtly seem to challenge the sense of restriction described here. By writing about themselves travelling alone, even when they describe their own sense of fear, or the problems they encountered, they seem to constitute a challenge to the perceived restriction of women to the private sphere. Many of the women travellers in the nineteenth century, even when they were opposed to suffrage for women, can be seen to be part of the New Woman philosophy, where gender and modernity unite in the figure of the young female walking in the city (Wilson, 1991). Thus, the accounts of women travelling from the eighteenth century to the present day constitute at one and the same time a reaffirmation of the stereotypical view that women should be restricted to the private sphere because of the perceived dangers in travelling, as well as a challenge to those norms, through the representation of women travelling alone without the aid of male companions.

Notes

1 Many of the discussions about spatial restriction are debated within the journal *Gender Place and Culture*, and an earlier version of some of this material appeared in an article by Mills entitled "Gender and colonial space" (1996).

2 In other cultures, particularly where women are the farmers and cultivators, the public sphere is viewed as women's terrain (Spain, 1992).

Celia Fiennes

The Illustrated Journeys of Celia Fiennes
(1698)

Thence I went to Kendall over steepe stony hills all like rocks to one Lady Middleton; and by some Gentlemen which were travelling that way that was their acquantaince had the advantage of going through her parke and saved the going round a bad stony passage; it was very pleasant under the shade of the tall trees; it was an old timber house [Leighton Hall] but the family being from home we had a free passage through on to the road againe much of which was stony and steep far worse than the Peake in Darbyshire; this Lady Middleton was a papist and I believe the Gentlemen that was travelling were too; in this park is the 3 Brother tree which a little from the root measures 13 yards circumference; thence to Kendall most of the way was in lanes when I was out of the stony hills, and then into inclosed lands; here you have very rich good land enclosed, little round green hills flourishing with corn and grass as green and fresh being in the prime season in July; there is not much woods but only the hedge rows round the grounds which looks very fine; in these Northern Countyes they have only the summer graine as barley oates peas beans and lentils noe wheate or rhye, for they are so cold and late in their yeare they cannot venture at that sort of tillage, so have none but what they are supply'd out of other countys adjacent; the land seems here in many places very fertile; they have much rhye in Lancashire Yorkshire and Stafford and Shropshire and so Herriford and Worcestershire which I found very troublesome in my journeys, for they would not own they had any such thing in their bread but it so disagrees with me as allwayes to make me sick, which I found by its effects when ever I met with any tho' I did not discern it by the taste; in Suffolke and Norfolke I also met with it—but in these parts its altogether the oatbread.

Kendall is a town built all of stone, one very broad streete in which is the Market Crosse, its a goode tradeing town mostly famed for the cottons; Kendall Cotton is used for blanckets and the Scotts use them for their plodds [plaids] and there is much made here and also linsiwoolseys and a great deale of leather tann'd here and all sorts of commodityes twice a weeke is the market furnished with all sorts of things.

The River Can [Kent] which gives name to the town is pretty large but full of rocks and stones that makes shelves and falls in the water, its stor'd with plenty of good fish and there are great falls of water partly naturall and added to by putting more stones in manner of wyers [weirs] at which they catch salmon when they leape with speares; the roareing of the water at these places sometymes does foretell wet weather, they do observe when the water roares most in the fall on the northside it will be faire, if on the southside of the town it will be wet; some of them are falls as high as a house—the same observation is at Lancaster at the wires [weirs] where they catch salmon, against storms or raines it will be turbulent and rore as may be heard into the town—there are 3 or 4 good houses in the town, the rest are like good traders houses very neate and tight, the streetes are all pitch'd which is extreame easy to be repair'd for the whole country is like one entire rock or pitching almost all the roads.

At the Kings Arms one Mrs. Rowlandson she does pott up the charr fish the best of any in the country, I was curious to have some and so bespoke some of her, and also was as curious to see the great water [Windermere] which is the only place that fish is to be found in, and so went from Kendall to Bondor [Bowness] 6 miles thro' narrow lanes, but the lands in the inclosures are rich; but here can be noe carriages but very narrow ones like little wheel-barrows that with a horse they convey their fewell and all things else; they also use horses on which they have a sort of panny- ers some close some open that they strew full of hay turff and lime and dung and every thing they would use, and the reason is plaine from the narrowness of the lanes: where is good lands they will loose as little as they can and where its hilly and stoney no other carriages can pass, so they use these horse carriages; abundance of horses I see all about Kendall streetes with their burdens.

Appleby 10 mile off is the shire town and is 7 miles to this great Lake Wiander- mer [Windermere] or great standing water, which is 10 mile long and near halfe a mile over in some places; it has many little hills or isles in it, one of a great bigness of 30 acres of ground on which is a house, the Gentleman that is Lord of the Manour lives in it Sir Christopher Phillips [Philipson], he has a great command of the water, and of the villages thereabout and many privileges, he makes a Major [Mayor] or Bailiff of the place during life; its but a small mean place, Mr. Majors was the best entertaining house where I was; the Isle did not looke to be so bigg at the shore but takeing boate I went on it and found it as large and very good barley and oates and grass; the water is very cleer and full of good fish, but the Charr fish being out of season could not easily be taken so I saw none alive, but of other fish I had a very good supper; the season of the Charrfish is between Michaelmas and Christmas, at that tyme I have had of them which they pott with sweete spices, they are as big as a small trout rather slenderer and the skinn full of spotts some redish, and part of the whole skinn and the finn and taile is red like the finns of a perch, and the inside flesh looks as red as any salmon; if they are in season their taste is very rich and fatt tho' not so strong or clogging as the lamprys are, but its as fatt and rich a food.

This great water seemes to flow and wave about with the wind or in one motion but it does not ebb and flow like the sea with the tyde, neither does it run so as to be perceivable tho' at the end of it a little rivulet trills from it into the sea, but it seemes to be a standing lake encompass'd with vast high hills that are perfect rocks and barren ground of a vast height from which many little springs out of the rock does bubble up and descend down and fall into this water; notwithstanding great raines the water does not seem much encreased, tho' it must be so, then it does draine off more at the end of the Lake; these hills which they call Furness Fells a long row continued some miles and some of them are call'd Donum Fells and soe from the places they adjoyne to are named, but they hold the whole length of the water; they have some parts of them that has wayes that they can by degrees in a compass ascend them and so they go onward in the countrys; they are ferried over the Lake when they go to market; on the other side over those fels there is a sort of stones like rubbish or broken pieces of stones which lies about a quarry that lies all in the bottom of the water; where its so shallow as at the shores it is and very cleer you see the bottom, between these stones are weeds which grows up that I had some taken up, just like sampyer [samphire] and I have a fancy its a sort of sampire that indeed is gather'd in the rocks by the sea and water, and this grows in the water but it resembles it in coullour figure and the taste not much unlike, it was somewhat waterish; there was also fine moss growing in the bottom of the water.

Here it was I saw the oat Clap bread made: they mix their flour with water so soft as to rowle it in their hands into a ball, and then they have a board made round and something hollow in the middle riseing by degrees all round to the edge a little higher, but so little as one would take it to be only a board warp'd, this is to cast out the cake thinn and so they clap it round and drive it to the edge in a due proportion till drove as thinn as a paper, and still they clap it and drive it round, and then they have a plaite of iron same size with their clap board and so shove off the cake on it and so set it on coales and bake it; when enough on one side they slide it off and put the other side; if their iron plaite is smooth and they take care their coales or embers are not too hot but just to make it looke yellow, it will bake and be as crisp and pleasant to eate as any thing you can imagine; but as we say of all sorts of bread there is a vast deale of difference in what is housewifely made and what is ill made, so this if its well mixed and rowled up and but a little flour on the outside which will drye on and make it mealy is a very good sort of food; this is the sort of bread they use in all these countrys, and in Scotland they breake into their milk or broth or else sup that up and bite of their bread between while, they spread butter on it and eate it with their meate; they have no other sort of bread unless at market towns and that is scarce to be had unless the market dayes, soe they make their cake and eate it presently for its not so good if 2 or 3 dayes old; it made me reflect on the description made in scripture of their kneeding cakes and bakeing them on the hearth when ever they had Company come to their houses, and I cannot but thinke it was after this maner they made their bread in the old tymes especially those Eastern Countryes where their bread might be soone dry'd and spoil'd.

Their little carts they use hereabout, the wheeles are fast'ned to the axletree and so turn altogether, they hold not above what our wheele barrows would carry at three or four tymes, which the girles and boys and women does go about with, drawn by one horse to carry any thing they want; here is a great deal of good grass and summer corn and pastures its rich land in the bottoms, as one may call them considering the vast hills above them on all sides, yet they contain a number of lesser hills one below another, so that tho' at one looke you think it but a little land every body has, yet it being so full of hills its many acres which if at length in a plain would extend a vast way; I was about a quarter of an hour in the boate before I reach'd the island which is in the midst of the water so by that you may guesse at the breadth of the water in the whole; they ferry man and horse over it, its sometymes perfectly calme.

Thence I rode almost all the waye in sight of this great water; some tymes I lost it by reason of the great hills interposeing and so a continu'd up hill and down hill and that pretty steep even when I was in that they called bottoms, which are very rich good grounds, and so I gained by degrees from lower to higher hills which I allwayes went up and down before I came to another hill; at last I attained to the side of one of these hills or fells of rocks which I passed on the side much about the middle; for looking down to the bottom it was at least a mile all full of those lesser hills and inclosures, so looking upward I was as farre from the top which was all rocks and something more barren tho' there was some trees and woods growing in the rocks and hanging over all down the brow of some of the hills; from these great fells there are severall springs out of the rock that trickle down their sides, and as they meete with stones and rocks in the way when something obstructs their passage and so they come with more violence that gives a pleaseing sound and murmuring noise; these descend by degrees, at last fall into the law grounds and fructifye it which makes the land soe fruit full in the valleys; and upon those very high fells or rocky hills its (tho') soe high and yet a moorish sort off ground whence they digg abundance of peat which they use for their fewell, being in many places a barren ground yielding noe wood, etc.; I rode in sight of this Winander Water up and down above 7 mile; afterwards as I was ascending another of those barren fells—which tho' I at last was not halfe way up, yet was an hour going it up and down, on the other side going only on the side of it about the middle of it, but it was of such a height as to shew one a great deale of the Country when it happens to be between those hills, else those interposeing hinders any sight but of the clouds—I see a good way behind me another of those waters or mers but not very bigge; these great hills are so full of loose stones and shelves of rocks that its very unsafe to ride them down.

There is good marble amongst those rocks: as I walked down at this place I was walled on both sides by those inaccessible high rocky barren hills which hangs over ones head in some places and appear very terrible; and from them springs many little currents of water from the sides and clefts which trickle down to some lower part where it runs swiftly over the stones and shelves in the way, which makes a pleasant rush and murmuring noise and like a snow ball is encreased by each spring trickling down on either side of those hills, and so descends into the bottoms which are a moorish ground in which in many places the waters stand, and so forme some of those Lakes as it did here, the confluence of all these little springs being gathered together in this Lake which was soe deep as the current of water that passed through it was scarce to be perceived till one came to the farther end, from whence it run a good little river and pretty quick, over which many bridges are laid.

Here I came to villages of sad little hutts made up of drye walls, only stones piled together and the roofs of same slatt; there seemed to be little or noe tunnells for their chimneys and have no morter or plaister within or without; for the most part I tooke them at first sight for a sort of houses or barns to fodder cattle in, not thinking them to be dwelling houses, they being scattering houses here one there another, in some places there may be 20 or 30 together, and the Churches the same; it must needs be very cold dwellings but it shews something of the lazyness of the people; indeed here and there there was a house plaister'd, but there is sad entertainment, that sort of clap bread and butter and cheese and a cup of beer all one can have, they are 8 mile from a market town and their miles are tedious to go both for illness of way and length of the miles.

They reckon it but 8 mile from the place I was at the night before but I was 3 or 4 hours at least going it; here I found a very good smith to shooe the horses, for these stony hills and wayes pulls off a shooe presently and wears them as thinn that it was a constant charge to shooe my horses every 2 or 3 days; but this smith did shooe them so well and so good shooes that they held some of the shooes 6 weeks; the stonyness of the wayes all here about teaches them the art off makeing good shooes and setting them on fast.

Here I cross'd one of the stone bridges that was pretty large which entred me into Cumberlandshire: this river together with the additional springs continually running into it all the way from those vaste precipices comes into a low place and form a broad water which is very cleer and reaches 7 mile in length, Ules water [Ullswater] its called; its full of such sort of stones and slatts in the bottom as the other, neer the brimm where its shallowe you see it cleer to the bottom; this is secured on each side by such formidable heights as those rocky fells in same manner as the other was; I rode the whole length of this water by its side sometyme a little higher upon the side of the hill and sometyme just by the shore and for 3 or 4 miles I rode through a fine forest or parke where was deer skipping about and haires, which by meanes of a good Greyhound I had a little Course, but we being strangers could not so fast pursue it in the grounds full of hillocks and furse and soe she escaped us.

There is exceeding good fish here and all sorts of provision at the market towns; their market town was Peroth [Penrith] a mile or two beyond this Ulls water; Tuesday is the market day which was the day I came thither its a long way for the market people to goe but they and their horses are used to it and go with much more facility than strangers; at the end of this Ulls water is a fine round hill look'd as green and full of wood, very pleasant with grass and corne very fruitefull, and hereabout we leave those desart and barren rocky hills, not that they are limitted to Westmorland only, for had I gone farther to the left hand on into Cumberland I should have found more such and they tell me farr worse for height and stony-nesse about White haven side and Cockermouth, so that tho' both the County's have very good land and fruitfull, so they equally partake of the bad, tho' indeed Westmorland takes it name from its abounding in moorish ground yet Cumberland has its share, and more of the hilly stony part; indeed I did observe those grounds were usually neighbours to each other, the rocks abounding in springs which distilling it self on lower ground if of a spungy soile made it marshy or lakes, and in many places very fruitfull in summer graine and grasse, but the northerly winds blow cold so long on them that they never attempt sowing their land with wheate or rhye.

The stones and slatt about Peroth [Penrith] look'd so red that at my entrance into the town thought its buildings were all of brick, but after found it to be the coullour of the stone which I saw in the Quarrys look very red, their slatt is the same which cover their houses; its a pretty large town a good market for cloth that they spinn in the country, hempe and also woollen; its a great market for all sorts of cattle meate corne etc.

Here are two rivers one called the Emount [Eamont] which parts Cumberland and Westmorland which bridge I should have passed over had I come the direct roade from Kendall to Peroth [Penrith], but strikeing off to Ambleside to Wiandermer I came another end of the town; in this river are greate falls of waters call'd cataracts by reason of the rock and shelves in it which makes a great noise, which is heard more against foul weather into the town tho' the bridge be halfe a mile out of the town; the other river is called Louder [Lowther] which gives name to Lord Landsdowns [Lonsdale] house call'd Louder-hall [Lowther Castle] which is four mile from Peroth; I went to it through fine woods, the front is just faceing the great road from Kendall and lookes very nobly, with severall rows of trees which leads to large iron gates, into the stable yard which is a fine building on the one side of the house very uniform, and just against it is such another row of buildings the other side of the house like two wings which is the offices; its built each like a fine house jutting out at each end and the middle is with pillars white and carvings like the entrance of a building, these are just equal and alike and encompass the two sides of the first court which enters with large iron gates and iron palasadoes in the breadth; there is 4 large squares of grass in which there is a large statue of stone in the midst of each and 4 little Cupids or little boys in each corner of the 4 squares; this is just the front of the house where you enter a porch with pillars of lime stone but the house is the red sort of stone of the country.

The staircase very well wanscoated and carv'd at the top; you are landed into a noble hall very lofty, the top and sides are exquisitely painted by the best hand in England [Antonio Verrio] which did the painting at Windsor; the top is the Gods and Goddesses that are sitting at some great feast and a great tribunal before them, each corner is the Seasons of the yeare with the variety of weather, raines and rainbows stormy winds sun shine snow and frost with multitudes of other fancyes and varietyes in painting, and looks very natural—it cost 500£ that roome alone; thence into a dineing room and drawing-roome well wanscoated of oake large pannells plaine no frettworks nor carvings or glass work only in chimney pieces; 3 handsome chambers, one scarlet cloth strip'd and very fashionably made up the hangings the same, another flower'd damaske lined with fine Indian embroidery, the third roome had a blew satten bed embroider'd, in this roome was very fine orris hangings in which was much silk and gold and silver; a little roome by in which was a green and white damaske canopy bed which was hung with some of the same hangings—being made for the Duke of Lortherdale [Lauderdale] and had his armes in many places, by his dying were sold to Lord Landsdon [Lonsdale], they containe a Scottish story and garb of the 4 quarters of the yeare; the chimney pieces are of a dark coulloured marble which is taken out of the ground just by, its well polish'd, there was some few white marble vein'd but that is not dug out of this country.

The house is a flatt rooffe and stands amidst a wood of rows of trees which with these statues and those in two gardens on each side (which for their walks and plantations is not finish'd but full of statues) which with the house is so well contrived to be seen at one view; the Lady Landsdown [Lonsdale] sent and treated me with a breakfast, cold things and sweetemeates all serv'd in plaite, but it was so early in the morning that she being indisposed was not up.

So I returned back to Peroth [Penrith] and came in sight of severall genteele seates, and came by a round green spott of a large circumfference which they keep cut round with a banke round it like a bench ['King Arthur's Table"]; its story is that it was the table a great Giant 6 yards tall used to dine at and there entertained another of nine yards tall which he afterwards killed; there is the length in the Church yard how farre he could leape a great many yards; there was also on the Church at Peroth a fine Clock which had severall motions, there was the starrs and signes there was the encrease and changes of the moone by a darke and golden side of a little globe.

A mile from Peroth in a low bottom a moorish place stands Great Mag and her Sisters, the story is that these soliciting her to an unlawfull love by an enchantment are turned with her into stone; the stone in the middle which is called Mag is much bigger and have some forme like a statue or figure of a body but the rest are but soe many craggy stones, but they affirme they cannot be counted twice alike as is the story of Stonidge [Stonehenge], but the number of these are not above 30; however what the first design of placeing them there either as a marke of that sort of moorish ground or what else, the thing is not so wonderfull as that of Stonidge.

The wayes from thence to Carlisle over much heath where they have many stone quarrys and cut much peate and turff, which is their chief fuel; its reckon'd but 16 mile from Peroth to Carlisle but they are pretty long, and I was a great while rideing it; you pass by the little hutts and hovels the poor live in like barnes some have them daub'd with mud-wall others drye walls.

Carlisle stands in view at least 4 mile distant; the town is walled in and all built of stone, the Cathedrall stands high and very eminent to be seen above the town; you enter over the bridge and double gates which are iron-grates and lined with a case of doores of thick timber; there are 3 gates to the town one called the English gate at which I entred, the other the Irish which leads on to White haven and Cokermouth, the other the Scottish gate through which I went into Scotland; the walls of the town and battlements and towers are in very good repair and looks well; the Cathedrall all built of stone which looked stately but nothing Curious; there was some few houses as the Deans and Treasurer and some of the Doctors houses walled in with little gardens their fronts looked gracefully, else I saw no house except the present Majors house of brick and stone, and one house which was the Chancellors built of stone very lofty 5 good sarshe [sash] windows in the front, and this within a stone wall'd garden well kept and iron gates to discover it to view with stone pillars; the streetes are very broad and handsome well pitch'd.

I walked round the walls and saw the river, which twists and turns it self round the grounds, called the Emount [Eamont] which at 3 or 4 miles off is flow'd by the sea; the other river is the Essex which is very broad and ebbs and flows about a mile or two off; there remaines only some of the walls and ruines of the Castle which does shew it to have been a very strong town formerly; the walls are of a prodigious thickness and vast great stones, its moated round and with draw bridges; there is a large Market place with a good Cross and Hall and is well supply'd as I am inform'd with provision at easye rates, but my Landlady notwithstanding ran me up the largest reckoning for allmost nothing; it was the dearest lodging I met with and she pretended she could get me nothing else, so for 2 joynts of mutton and a pinte of wine and bread and beer I had a 12 shilling reckoning; but since, I find tho' I was in the biggest house in town I was in the worst accomodation, and so found it, and a young giddy Landlady that could only dress fine and entertain the soldiers.

Mary Wollstonecraft

A Short Residence in Sweden, Norway and Denmark
(1796)

Tønsberg was formerly the residence of one of the little sovereigns of Norway; and on an adjacent mountain the vestiges of a fort remain which was battered down by the Swedes; the entrance of the bay lying close to it.

Here I have frequently strayed, sovereign of the waste, I seldom met any human creature; and sometimes, reclining on the mossy down, under the shelter of a rock, the prattling of the sea amongst the pebbles has lulled me to sleep—no fear of any rude satyr's approaching to interrupt my repose. Balmy were the slumbers, and soft the gales, that refreshed me, when I awoke to follow, with an eye vaguely curious, the white sails, as they turned the cliffs, or seemed to take shelter under the pines which covered the little islands that so gracefully rose to render the terrific ocean beautiful. The fishermen were calmly casting their nets; whilst the seagulls hovered over the unruffled deep. Every thing seemed to harmonize into tranquillity—even the mournful call of the bittern was in cadence with the tinkling bells on the necks of the cows, that, pacing slowly one after the other, along an inviting path in the vale below, were repairing to the cottages to be milked. With what ineffable pleasure have I not gazed—and gazed again, losing my breath through my eyes—my very soul diffused itself in the scene—and, seeming to become all senses, glided in the scarcely-agitated waves, melted in the freshening breeze, or, taking its flight with fairy wing, to the misty mountains which bounded the prospect, fancy tript over new lawns, more beautiful even than the lovely slopes on the winding shore before me.— I pause, again breathless, to trace, with renewed delight, sentiments which entranced me, when, turning my humid eyes from the expanse below to the vault above, my sight pierced the fleecy clouds that softened the azure brightness; and, imperceptibly recalling the reveries of childhood, I bowed before the awful throne of my Creator, whilst I rested on its footstool.

You have sometimes wondered, my dear friend, at the extreme affection of my nature—But such is the temperature of my soul—It is not the vivacity of youth, the hey-day of existence. For years have I endeavoured to calm an impetuous tide—labouring to make my feelings take an orderly course.—It was striving against the stream.—I must love and admire with warmth, or I sink into sadness. Tokens of love which I have received have rapt me in elysium—purifying the heart they enchanted.—My bosom still glows.—Do not saucily ask, repeating Sterne's question, "Maria, is it still so warm!" Sufficiently, O my God! has it been chilled by sorrow and unkindness—still nature will prevail—and if I blush at recollecting past enjoyment, it is the rosy hue of pleasure heightened by modesty; for the blush of modesty and shame are as distinct as the emotions by which they are produced.

I need scarcely inform you, after telling you of my walks, that my constitution has been renovated here; and that I have recovered my activity, even whilst attaining a little *embonpoint*. My imprudence last winter, and some untoward accidents just at the time I was weaning my child, had reduced me to a state of weakness which I never before experienced. A slow fever preyed on me every night, during my residence in Sweden, and after I arrived at Tønsberg. By chance I found a fine rivulet filtered through the rocks, and confined in a basin for the cattle. It tasted to me like a chalybeate; at any rate it was pure; and the good effect of the various waters which invalids are sent to drink, depends, I believe, more on the air, exercise and change of scene, than on their medicinal qualities. I therefore determined to turn my morning walks towards it, and seek for health from the nymph of the fountain; partaking of the beverage offered to the tenants of the shade.

Chance likewise led me to discover a new pleasure, equally beneficial to my health. I wished to avail myself of my vicinity to the sea, and bathe; but it was not possible near the town; there was no convenience. The young woman whom I mentioned to you, proposed rowing me across the water, amongst the rocks; but as she was pregnant, I insisted on taking one of the oars, and learning to row. It was not difficult; and I do not know a pleasanter exercise. I soon became expert, and my train of thinking kept time, as it were, with the oars, or I suffered the boat to be carried along by the current, indulging a pleasing forgetfulness, or fallacious hopes.—How fallacious! yet, without hope, what is to sustain life, but the fear of annihilation—the only thing of which I have ever felt a dread—I cannot bear to think of being no more—of losing myself—though existence is often but a painful consciousness of misery; nay, it appears to me impossible that I should cease to exist, or that this active, restless spirit, equally alive to joy and sorrow, should only be organized dust—ready to fly abroad the moment the spring snaps, or the spark goes out, which kept it together. Surely something resides in this heart that is not perishable–and life is more than a dream.

Sometimes, to take up my oar, once more, when the sea was calm, I was amused by disturbing the innumerable young star fish which floated just below the surface: I had never observed them before; for they have not a hard shell, like those which I have seen on the sea-shore. They look like thickened water, with a white edge; and four purple circles, of different forms, were in the middle, over an incredible number of fibres, or white lines. Touching them, the cloudy substance would turn or close, first on one side, then on the other, very gracefully; but when I took one of them up in the ladle with which I heaved the water out of the boat, it appeared only a colourless jelly.

I did not see any of the seals, numbers of which followed our boat when we landed in Sweden; for though I like to sport in the water, I should have had no desire to join in their gambols.

Enough, you will say, of inanimate nature, and of brutes, to use the lordly phrase of man; let me hear something of the inhabitants.

The gentleman with whom I had business, is the mayor of Tønsberg; he speaks English intelligibly; and, having a sound understanding, I was sorry that his numerous occupations prevented my gaining as much information from him as I could have drawn forth, had we frequently conversed. The people of the town, as far as I had an opportunity of knowing their sentiments, are extremely well satisfied with his manner of discharging his office. He has a degree of information and good sense which excites respect, whilst a chearfulness, almost amounting to gaiety, enables him to reconcile differences, and keep his neighbours in good humour.—"I lost my horse," said a woman to me; "but ever since, when I want to send to the mill, or go out, the mayor lends me one.—He scolds if I do not come for it."

A criminal was branded, during my stay here, for the third offence; but the relief he received made him declare that the judge was one of the best men in the world.

I sent this wretch a trifle, at different times, to take with him into slavery. As it was more than he expected, he wished very much to see me; and this wish brought to my remembrance an anecdote I heard when I was in Lisbon.

A wretch who had been imprisoned several years, during which period lamps had been put up, was at last condemned to a cruel death; yet, in his way to execution, he only wished for one night's respite, to see the city lighted.

Having dined in company at the mayor's, I was invited with his family to spend the day at one of the richest merchant's houses.—Though I could not speak Danish, I knew that I could see a great deal: yes, I am persuaded that I have formed a very just opinion of the character of the Norwegians, without being able to hold converse with them.

I had expected to meet some company; yet was a little disconcerted at being ushered into an apartment full of well-dressed people; and, glancing my eyes round, they rested on several very pretty faces. Rosy cheeks, sparkling eyes, and light brown or golden locks; for I never saw so much hair with a yellow cast; and, with their fine complexions, it looked very becoming.

These women seem a mixture of indolence and vivacity; they scarcely ever walk out, and were astonished that I should, for pleasure; yet they are immoderately fond of dancing. Unaffected in their manners, if they have no pretensions to elegance, simplicity often produces a gracefulness of deportment, when they are animated by a particular desire to please—which was the case at present. The solitariness of my situation, which they thought terrible, interested them very much in my favour. They gathered round me—sung to me—and one of the prettiest, to whom I gave my hand, with some degree of cordiality, to meet the glance of her eyes, kissed me very affectionately.

Ida Pfeiffer

Visit to the Holy Land, Egypt and Italy
(1852)

At length, towards noon, we approached the mountains of Judæa. Here we must bid farewell to the beautiful fruitful valley and to the charming road, and pursue our journey through a stony region, which we do not pass without difficulty.

At the entrance of the mountain-chain lies a miserable village; near this village is a well, and here we halted to refresh ourselves and water our poor horses. It was not without a great deal of trouble and some expense that we managed to obtain a little water; for all the camels, asses, goats, and sheep from far and wide were collected here, eagerly licking up every drop of the refreshing element they could secure. Little did I think that I should ever be glad to quench my thirst with so disgusting a beverage as the muddy, turbid, and lukewarm water they gave me from this well.

We once more filled our leathern bottles, and proceeded with fresh courage up the stony path, which quickly became so narrow, that without great difficulty and danger we could not pass the camels which we frequently met. Fortunately a few camels out of every herd are generally provided with bells, so that their approach is heard at some distance, and one can prepare for them accordingly.

The Bedouins and Arabs generally wear no garment but a shirt barely reaching to the knee. Their head is protected by a linen cloth, to which a thick rope would twice round the head gives a very good effect. A few have a striped jacket over their shirt, and the rich men or chiefs frequently wear turbans.

Our road now continues to wind upwards, through ravines between rocks and mountains, and over heaps of stones. Here and there single olive-trees are seen sprouting from the rocky clifts. Ugly as this tree is, it still forms a cheerful feature in the desert places where it grows. Now and then we climbed hills whence we had a distant view of the sea. These glimpses increase the awe which inspires the traveller when he considers on what ground he is wandering, and whither he is bending his steps. Every step we now take leads us past places of religious importance; every ruin, every fragment of a fortress or tower, above which the rocky walls rise like terraces, speaks of eventful times long gone by.

An uninterrupted ride of five hours over very bad roads, from the entrance of the mountain-range, added to the extreme heat and total want of proper refreshment, suddenly brought on such a violent giddiness that I could scarcely keep myself from falling off my horse. Although we had been on horseback for eleven hours since leaving Joppa, I was so much afraid that Mr. B. would consider me weak and ailing, and perhaps change his intention of accompanying me from Jerusalem back to Joppa, that I refrained from acquainting him with the condition in which I felt myself. I therefore dismounted (had I not done so, I should soon have fallen down), and walked with tottering steps beside my horse, until I felt so far recovered that I could mount once more. Mr. B. had determined to perform the distance from Joppa to Jerusalem (a sixteen hours' ride) at one stretch. He indeed asked me if I could bear so much fatigue; but I was unwilling to abuse his kindness, and therefore assured him that I could manage to ride on for five or six hours longer. Fortunately for my reputation, my companion was soon afterwards attacked with the same symptoms that troubled me so much; he now began to think that it might, after all, be advisable to rest for a few hours in the next village, especially as we could not hope in any case to reach the gates of Jerusalem before sundown. I felt silently thankful for this opportune occurrence, and left the question of going on or stopping altogether to the decision of my fellow-traveller, particularly as I knew the course he would choose. Thus I accomplished my object without being obliged to confess my weakness. In pursuance of this resolve, we stayed in the neighbouring village of "Kariet el Areb," the ancient Emmaus, where the risen Saviour met the disciples, and where we find a ruin of a Christian church in a tolerable state of preservation. The building is now used as a stable. Some years ago this was the haunt of a famous robber, who was scheikh of the place, and let no Frank pass before he had paid whatever tribute he chose to demand. Since the accession of Mehemet Ali these exactions have ceased both here and in Jerusalem, where money was demanded of the stranger for admission into the Church of the Holy Sepulchre and other sacred places. Even highway robberies, which were once on a time of daily occurrence among these mountains, are now rarely heard of.

We took possession of the entrance-hall of a mosque, near which a delicious spring sparkled forth from a grotto. Seldom has any thing strengthened and refreshed me so much as the water of this spring. I recovered completely from my indisposition, and was able to enjoy the beautiful evening.

As soon as the scheikh of the village heard that a party of Franks had arrived, he despatched four or five dishes of provisions to us. Of all these preparations we could only eat one—the butter-milk. The other dishes, a mixture of honey, cucumbers, hard-boiled eggs, onions, oil, olives, &c., we generously bestowed upon the dragoman and the muker, who caused them quickly to disappear. An hour afterwards the scheikh came in person to pay his respects. We reclined on the steps of the hall; and while the men smoked and drank coffee, a conversation of a very uninteresting kind was kept up, the dragoman acting as interpreter. At length the scheikh seemed seized with the idea that we might possibly be tired with our journey. He took his leave, and offered unasked to send us two men as sentries, which he did. Thus we could go to rest in perfect safety under the open sky in the midst of a Turkish village.

But before we retired to rest, my companion was seized with the rather original idea that we should pursue our journey at midnight. He asked me, indeed, if I was afraid, but at the same time observed, that it would be much safer for us to act upon his suggestion, as no one would suspect our departure by such a dangerous road at midnight. I certainly felt a little afraid, but my pride would not allow me to confess the truth; so our people received the order to be prepared to set out at midnight.

Thus we four persons, alone and totally unarmed, travelled at midnight through the wildest and most dangerous regions. Fortunately the bright moon looked smilingly down upon us, and illuminated our path so brightly, that the horses carried us with firm step over every obstruction. I was, I must confess, grievously frightened by the shadows! I saw living things moving to and fro—forms gigantic and forms dwarfish seemed sometimes approaching us, sometimes hiding behind masses of rock, or sinking back into nothingness. Lights and shadows, fears and anxiety, thus took alternate possession of my imagination.

A couple of miles from our starting-place we came upon a brook crossed by a narrow stone bridge. This brook is remarkable only as having been that from which David collected the five stones wherewith he slew the Philistine giant. At the season of my visit there was no water to be seen; the bed of the stream was completely dry.

About an hour's journey from Jerusalem the valley opens, and little orchards give indication of a more fertile country, as well as of the proximity of the Holy City. Silently and thoughtfully we approached our destination, straining our eyes to the utmost to pierce the jealous twilight that shrouded the distance from our gaze. From the next hill we hoped to behold our sacred goal; but "hope deferred" is often the lot of mortals. We had to ascend another height, and another; at length the Mount of Olives lay spread before us, and lastly JERUSALEM.

Isabella Bird

A Lady's Life in the Rocky Mountains
(1879)

Long's Peak, "the American Matterhorn," as some call it, was ascended five years ago for the first time. I thought I should like to attempt it, but up to Monday, when Evans left for Denver, cold water was thrown upon the project. It was too late in the season, the winds were likely to be strong, etc.; but just before leaving, Evans said that the weather was looking more settled, and if I did not get farther than the timber line it would be worth going. Soon after he left, "Mountain Jim" came in, and said he would go up as guide, and the two youths who rode here with me from Long-mount and I caught at the proposal. Mrs. Edwards at once baked bread for three days, steaks were cut from the steer which hangs up conveniently, and tea, sugar, and butter were benevolently added. Our picnic was not to be a luxurious or "well-found" one, for, in order to avoid the expense of a pack mule, we limited our luggage to what our saddle horses could carry. Behind my saddle I carried three pair of camping blankets and a quilt, which reached to my shoulders. My own boots were so much worn that it was painful to walk, even about the park, in them, so Evans had lent me a pair of his hunting boots, which hung to the horn of my saddle. The horses of the two young men were equally loaded, for we had to prepare for many degrees of frost. "Jim" was a shocking figure; he had on an old pair of high boots, with a baggy pair of old trousers made of deer hide, held on by an old scarf tucked into them; a leather shirt, with three or four ragged unbuttoned waistcoats over it; an old smashed wideawake, from under which his tawny, neglected ringlets hung; and with his one eye, his one long spur, his knife in his belt, his revolver in his waist-coat pocket, his saddle covered with an old beaver-skin, from which the paws hung down; his camping blankets behind him, his rifle laid across the saddle in front of him, and his axe, canteen, and other gear hanging to the horn, he was as awful looking a ruffian as one could see. By way of contrast he rode a small Arab mare, of exquisite beauty, skittish, high-spirited, gentle, but altogether too light for him, and he fretted her incessantly to make her display herself.

Heavily loaded as all our horses were, "Jim" started over the half-mile of level grass at a handgallop, and then throwing his mare on her haunches, pulled up along-side of me, and with a grace of manner which soon made me forget his appearance, entered into a conversation which lasted for more than three hours, in spite of the manifold checks of fording streams, single file, abrupt ascents and descents, and other incidents of mountain travel. The ride was one series of glories and surprises, of "park" and glade, of lake and stream, of mountains on mountains, culminating in the rent pinnacles of Long's Peak, which looked yet grander and ghastlier as we crossed an attendant mountain 11,000 feet high. The slanting sun added fresh beauty every hour. There were dark pines against a lemon sky, grey peaks reddening and etherealising, gorges of deep and infinite blue, floods of golden glory pouring through canyons of enormous depth, an atmosphere of absolute purity, an occasional foreground of cotton-wood and aspen flaunting in red and gold to intensify the blue gloom of the pines, the trickle and murmur of streams fringed with icicles, the strange *sough* of gusts moving among the pine tops—sights and sounds not of the lower earth, but of the solitary, beast-haunted, frozen upper altitudes. From the dry, buff grass of Estes Park we turned off up a trail on the side of a pine-hung gorge, up a steep pine-clothed hill, down to a small valley, rich in fine, sun-cured hay about eighteen inches high, and enclosed by high mountains whose deepest hollow contains a lily-covered lake, fitly named "The Lake of the Lilies." Ah, how magical its beauty was, as it slept in silence, while *there* the dark pines were mirrored motionless in its pale gold, and *here* the great white lily cups and dark green leaves rested on amethyst-coloured water!

From this we ascended into the purple gloom of great pine forests which clothe the skirts of the mountains up to a height of about 11,000 feet, and from their chill and solitary depths we had glimpses of golden atmosphere and rose-lit summits, not of "the land very far off," but of the land nearer now in all its grandeur, gaining in sublimity by nearness—glimpses, too, through a broken vista of purple gorges, of the illimitable Plains lying idealised in the late sunlight, their baked, brown expanse transfigured into the likeness of a sunset sea rolling infinitely in waves of misty gold.

We rode upwards through the gloom on a steep trail blazed through the forest, all my intellect concentrated on avoiding being dragged off my horse by impending branches, or having the blankets badly torn, as those of my companions were, by sharp dead limbs, between which there was hardly room to pass—the horses breathless, and requiring to stop every few yards, though their riders, except myself, were afoot. The gloom of the dense, ancient, silent forest is to me awe-inspiring. On such an evening it is soundless, except for the branches creaking in the soft wind, the frequent snap of decayed timber, and a murmur in the pine tops as of a not distant waterfall, all tending to produce *eeriness* and a sadness "hardly akin to pain." There no lumberer's axe has ever rung. The trees die when they have attained their prime, and stand there, dead and bare, till the fierce mountain winds lay them prostrate. The pines grew smaller and more sparse as we ascended, and the last stragglers wore a tortured, warring look. The timber line was passed, but yet a little higher a slope of mountain meadow dipped to the south-west towards a bright stream trickling under ice and icicles, and there a grove of the beautiful silver spruce marked our camping ground. The trees were in miniature, but so exquisitely arranged that one might well ask what artist's hand had planted them, scattering them here, clumping them there, and training their slim spires towards heaven. Hereafter, when I call up memories of the glorious, the view from this camping ground will come up. Looking east, gorges opened to the distant Plains, then fading into purple grey. Mountains with pine-clothed skirts rose in ranges, or, solitary, uplifted their grey summits, while close behind, but nearly 3000 feet above us, towered the bald white crest of Long's Peak, its huge precipices red with the light of a sun long lost to our eyes. Close to us, in the caverned side of the Peak, was snow that, owing to its position, is eternal. Soon the afterglow came on, and before it faded a big half-moon hung out of the heavens, shining through the silver blue foliage of the pines on the frigid background of snow, and turning the whole into fairyland. The "photo" which accompanies this letter is by a courageous Denver artist who attempted the ascent just before I arrived, but, after camping out at the timber line for a week, was foiled by the perpetual storms, and was driven down again, leaving some very valuable apparatus about 3000 feet from the summit.

Unsaddling and picketing the horses securely, making the beds of pine shoots, and dragging up logs for fuel, warmed us all. "Jim" built up a great fire, and before long we were all sitting round it at supper. It didn't matter much that we had to drink our tea out of the battered meat-tins in which it was boiled, and eat strips of beef reeking with pine smoke without plates or forks.

"Treat Jim as a gentleman and you'll find him one," I had been told; and though his manner was certainly bolder and freer than that of gentlemen generally, no imaginary fault could be found. He was very agreeable as a man of culture as well as a child of nature; the desperado was altogether out of sight. He was very courteous and even kind to me, which was fortunate, as the young men had little idea of showing even ordinary civilities. That night I made the acquaintance of his dog "Ring," said to be the best hunting-dog in Colorado, with the body and legs of a collie, but a head approaching that of a mastiff, a noble face with a wistful human expression, and the most truthful eyes I ever saw in an animal. His master loves him if he loves anything, but in his savage moods ill-treats him. "Ring's" devotion never swerves, and his truthful eyes are rarely taken off his master's face. He is almost human in his intelligence, and, unless he is told to do so, he never takes notice of any one but "Jim." In a tone as if speaking to a human being, his master, pointing to me, said, "Ring, go to that lady, and don't leave her again to-night." "Ring" at once came to me, looked into my face, laid his head on my shoulder, and then lay down beside me with his head on my lap, but never taking his eyes from "Jim's" face.

The long shadows of the pines lay upon the frosted grass, an aurora leaped fitfully, and the moon-light, though intensely bright, was pale beside the red, leaping flames of our pine logs and their red glow on our gear, ourselves, and Ring's truthful face. One of the young men sang a Latin student's song and two negro melodies; the other, "Sweet Spirit, hear my Prayer." "Jim" sang one of Moore's melodies in a singular falsetto, and all together sang "The Star-spangled Banner" and "The Red, White, and Blue." Then "Jim" recited a very clever poem of his own composition, and told some fearful Indian stories. A group of small silver spruces away from the fire was my sleeping-place. The artist who had been up there had so woven and interlaced their lower branches as to form a bower, affording at once shelter from the wind and a most agreeable privacy. It was thickly strewn with young pine shoots, and these, when covered with a blanket, with an inverted saddle for a pillow, made

195

a luxurious bed. The mercury at 9 P.M. was 12° below the freezing point. "Jim," after a last look at the horses, made a huge fire, and stretched himself out beside it, but "Ring" lay at my back to keep me warm. I could not sleep, but the night passed rapidly. I was anxious about the ascent, for gusts of ominous sound swept through the pines at intervals. Then wild animals howled, and "Ring" was perturbed in spirit about them. Then it was strange to see the notorious desperado, a red-handed man, sleeping as quietly as innocence sleeps. But, above all, it was exciting to lie there, with no better shelter than a bower of pines, on a mountain 11,000 feet high, in the very heart of the Rocky Range, under twelve degrees of frost, hearing sounds of wolves, with shivering stars looking through the fragrant canopy, with arrowy pines for bed-posts, and for a night lamp the red flames of a camp fire.

Day dawned long before the sun rose, pure and lemon-coloured. The rest were looking after the horses, when one of the students came running to tell me that I must come farther down the slope, for "Jim" said he had never seen such a sunrise. From the chill, grey Peak above, from the everlasting snows, from the silvered pines, down through mountain ranges with their depths of Tyrian purple, we looked to where the Plains lay cold, in blue grey, like a morning sea against a far horizon. Suddenly, as a dazzling streak at first, but enlarging rapidly into a dazzling sphere, the sun wheeled above the grey line, a light and glory as when it was first created. "Jim" involuntarily and reverently uncovered his head, and exclaimed, "I believe there is a God!" I felt as if, Parsee-like, I must worship. The grey of the Plains changed to purple, the sky was all one rose-red flush, on which vermilion cloud-streaks rested; the ghastly peaks gleamed like rubies, the earth and heavens were new-created. Surely "the Most High dwelleth not in temples made with hands!" For a full hour those Plains simulated the ocean, down to whose limitless expanse of purple, cliffs, rocks, and promontories swept down.

By seven we had finished breakfast, and passed into the ghastlier solitudes above, I riding as far as what, rightly or wrongly, are called the "Lava Beds," an expanse of large and small boulders, with snow in their crevices. It was very cold; some water which we crossed was frozen hard enough to bear the horse. "Jim" had advised me against taking any wraps, and my thin Hawaiian riding-dress, only fit for the tropics, was penetrated by the keen air. The rarefied atmosphere soon began to oppress our breathing, and I found that Evans's boots were so large that I had no foothold. Fortunately, before the real difficulty of the ascent began, we found, under a rock, a pair of small over-shoes, probably left by the Hayden exploring expedition, which just lasted for the day. As we were leaping from rock to rock, "Jim" said, "I was thinking in the night about your travelling alone, and wondering where you carried your Derringer, for I could see no signs of it." On my telling him that I travelled unarmed, he could hardly believe it, and adjured me to get a revolver at once.

On arriving at the "Notch" (a literal gate of rock), we found ourselves absolutely on the knife-like ridge or backbone of Long's Peak, only a few feet wide, covered with colossal boulders and fragments, and on the other side shelving in one precipitous, snow-patched sweep of 3000 feet to a picturesque hollow, containing a lake of pure green water. Other lakes, hidden among dense pine woods, were farther off, while close above us rose the Peak, which, for about 500 feet, is a smooth, gaunt, inaccessible-looking pile of granite. Passing through the "Notch," we looked along the nearly inaccessible side of the Peak, composed of boulders and *débris* of all shapes and sizes, through which appeared broad, smooth ribs of reddish-coloured granite, looking as if they upheld the towering rock-mass above. I usually dislike bird's-eye and panoramic views, but, though from a mountain, this was not one. Serrated ridges, not much lower than that on which we stood, rose, one beyond another, far as that pure atmosphere could carry the vision, broken into awful chasms deep with ice and snow, rising into pinnacles piercing the heavenly blue with their cold, barren grey, on, on for ever, till the most distant range upbore unsullied snow alone. There were fair lakes mirroring the dark pine woods, canyons dark and blue-black with unbroken expanses of pines, snow-slashed pinnacles, wintry heights frowning upon lovely parks, watered and wooded, lying in the lap of summer; North Park floating off into the blue distance, Middle Park closed till another season, the sunny slopes of Estes Park, and winding down among the mountains the snowy ridge of the Divide, whose bright waters seek both the Atlantic and Pacific Oceans. There, far below, links of diamonds showed where the Grand River takes its rise to seek the mysterious Colorado, with its still unsolved enigma, and lose itself in the waters of the Pacific; and nearer the snow-born Thompson bursts forth from the ice to begin its journey to the Gulf of Mexico. Nature, rioting in her grandest mood, exclaimed with voices of grandeur, solitude, sublimity, beauty, and infinity, "Lord, what is man, that Thou art mindful of him? or the son of man, that Thou visitest him?" Never-to-be-forgotten glories they were, burnt in upon my memory by six succeeding hours of terror. You know I have no head and no ankles, and never ought to dream of mountaineering; and had I known that the ascent was a real mountaineering feat I should not have felt the slightest ambition to perform it. As it is, I am only humiliated by my success, for "Jim" dragged me up, like a bale of goods, by sheer force of muscle. At the "Notch" the real business of the ascent began. Two thousand feet of solid rock towered above us, four thousand feet of broken rock shelved precipitously below; smooth granite ribs, with barely foothold, stood out here and there; melted snow, refrozen several times, presented a more serious obstacle; many of the rocks were loose, and tumbled down when touched. To me it was a time of extreme terror. I was roped to "Jim," but it was of no use, my feet were paralysed and slipped on the bare rock, and he said it was useless to try to go that way, and we retraced our steps. I wanted to return to the "Notch," knowing that my incompetence would detain the party, and one of the young men said almost plainly that a woman was a dangerous encumbrance, but the trapper replied shortly that if it were not to take a lady up he would not go up at all. He went on to explore, and reported that further progress on the correct line of ascent was blocked by ice; and then for two hours we descended, lowering ourselves by our hands from rock to rock along a boulder-strewn sweep of 4000 feet, patched with ice and snow, and perilous from rolling stones. My fatigue, giddiness, and pain from bruised ankles, and arms half pulled out of their sockets, were so great that I should never have gone half-way had not "Jim," *nolens volens*, dragged me along with a patience and skill, and withal a determination that

I should ascend the Peak, which never failed. After descending about 2000 feet to avoid the ice, we got into a deep ravine with inaccessible sides, partly filled with ice and snow and partly with large and small fragments of rock, which were constantly giving way, rendering the footing very insecure. That part to me was two hours of painful and unwilling submission to the inevitable; of trembling, slipping, straining, of smooth ice appearing when it was least expected, and of weak entreaties to be left behind while the others went on. "Jim" always said that there was no danger, that there was only a short bad bit ahead, and that I should go up even if he carried me!

Slipping, faltering, gasping from the exhausting toil in the rarefied air, with throbbing hearts and panting lungs, we reached the top of the gorge and squeezed ourselves between two gigantic fragments of rock by a passage called the "Dog's Lift," when I climbed on the shoulders of one man and then was hauled up. This introduced us by an abrupt turn round the south-west angle of the Peak to a narrow shelf of considerable length, rugged, uneven, and so overhung by the cliff in some places that it is necessary to crouch to pass at all. Above, the Peak looks nearly vertical for 400 feet; and below, the most tremendous precipice I have ever seen descends in one unbroken fall. This is usually considered the most dangerous part of the ascent, but it does not seem so to me, for such foothold as there is is secure, and one fancies that it is possible to hold on with the hands. But there, and on the final, and, to mythinking, the worst part of the climb, one slip, and a breathing, thinking, human being would lie 3000 feet below, a shapeless, bloody heap! "Ring" refused to traverse the Ledge, and remained at the "Lift" howling piteously.

From thence the view is more magnificent even than that from the "Notch." At the foot of the precipice below us lay a lovely lake, wood embosomed, from or near which the bright St. Vrain and other streams take their rise. I thought how their clear cold waters, growing turbid in the affluent flats, would heat under the tropic sun, and eventually form part of that great ocean river which renders our far-off islands habitable by impinging on their shores. Snowy ranges, one behind the other, extended to the distant horizon, folding in their wintry embrace the beauties of Middle Park. Pike's Peak, more than one hundred miles off, lifted that vast but shapeless summit which is the landmark of Southern Colorado. There were snow patches, snow slashes, snow abysses, snow forlorn and soiled-looking, snow pure and dazzling, snow glistening above the purple robe of pine worn by all the mountains; while away to the east, in limitless breadth, stretched the green-grey of the endless Plains. Giants everywhere reared their splintered crests. From thence, with a single sweep, the eye takes in a distance of 300 miles—that distance to the west, north, and south being made up of mountains ten, eleven, twelve, and thirteen thousand feet in height, dominated by Long's Peak, Gray's Peak, and Pike's Peak, all nearly the height of Mont Blanc! On the Plains we traced the rivers by their fringe of cotton-woods to the distant Platte, and between us and them lay glories of mountain, canyon, and lake, sleeping in depths of blue and purple most ravishing to the eye.

As we crept from the lodge round a horn of rock, I beheld what made me perfectly sick and dizzy to look at—the terminal Peak itself—a smooth, cracked face or wall of pink granite, as nearly perpendicular as anything could well be up which it was possible to climb, well deserving the name of the "American Matterhorn."[1]

Scaling, not climbing, is the correct term for this last ascent. It took one hour to accomplish 500 feet, pausing for breath every minute or two. The only foothold was in narrow cracks or on minute projections on the granite. To get a toe in these cracks, or here and there on a scarcely obvious projection, while crawling on hands and knees, all the while tortured with thirst and gasping and struggling for breath, this was the climb; but at last the Peak was won. A grand, well-defined mountain-top it is, a nearly level acre of boulders, with precipitous sides all round, the one we came up being the only accessible one.

Mary Kingsley

Travels in West Africa
(1897)

September 24th.—Lovely morning, the grey-white mist in the forest makes it like a dream of Fairyland, each moss-grown tree stem heavily gemmed with dewdrops. At 5.30 I stir the boys, for Sasu, the sergeant, says he must go back to his military duties. The men think we are all going back with him as he is our only guide, but I send three of them down with orders to go back to Victoria—two being of the original set I started with. They are surprised and disgusted at being sent home, but they have got "hot foot," and something wrong in the usual seat of African internal disturbances, their "tummicks," and I am not thinking of starting a sanatorium for abdominally-afflicted Africans in that crater plain above. Black boy is the other boy returned, I do not want another of his attacks.

They go, and this leaves me in the forest camp with Kefalla, Xenia, and Cook, and we start expecting the water sent for by Monrovia boy yesterday forenoon. There are an abominable lot of bees about; they do not give one a moment's peace, getting beneath the waterproof sheets over the bed, and pretending they can't get out and forthwith losing their tempers, which is imbecile, because the whole four sides of the affair are broad open.

---

[1] Let no practical mountaineer be allured by my description into the ascent of Long's Peak. Truly terrible as it was to me, to a member of the Alpine Club it would not be a feat worth performing.

The ground, bestrewn with leaves and dried wood, is a mass of large flies rather like our common house-fly, but both butterflies and beetles seem scarce; but I confess I do not feel up to hunting much after yesterday's work, and deem it advisable to rest.

My face and particularly my lips are a misery to me, having been blistered all over by yesterday's sun, and last night I inadvertently whipped the skin all off one cheek with the blanket, and it keeps on bleeding, and, horror of horrors, there is no tea until that water comes.

I wish I had got the mountaineering spirit, for then I could say, "I'll never come to this sort of place again, for you can get all you want in the Alps." I have been told this by my mountaineering friends—I have never been there—and that you can go and do all sorts of stupendous things all day, and come back in the evening to *table d'hôte* at an hotel; but as I have not got the mountaineering spirit, I suppose I shall come fooling into some such place as this as soon as I get the next chance.

About 8.30, to our delight, the gallant Monrovia boy comes through the bush with a demijohn of water, and I get my tea, and give the men the only half-pound of rice I have and a tin of meat, and they eat, become merry, and chat over their absent companions in a scornful, scandalous way. Who cares for hotels now? When one is in a delightful place like this, one must work, so off I go to the north into the forest, after giving the rest of the demijohn of water into the Monrovia boy's charge with strict orders it is not to be opened till my return. Quantities of beetles.

A little after two o'clock I return to camp, after having wandered about in the forest and found three very deep holes, down which I heaved rocks and in no case heard a splash. In one I did not hear the rocks strike, owing to the great depth. I hate holes, and especially do I hate these African ones, for I am frequently falling, more or less, into them, and they will be my end. So far I have never fallen down a West Coast native gold mine, but I know people who have; but all the other sorts I have tried, having pitched by day and night into those, from three to twelve feet deep, made by industrious indigenous ones, as Mrs. Gault calls them, digging out sand and earth to make the "swish" walls of their simple savage homes; and also into those from twenty to thirty feet deep with pointed stakes at the bottom, artfully disposed to impale the elephant and leopard of the South-West Coast. But my worst fall was into a disused Portuguese well of unknown depth at Cabinda. I "feel the place in frosty weather still," though I did not go down all the way, my descent being arrested by a collection of brushwood and rubbish, which had been cast into it, and which had hitched far down in the shaft. When I struck this subterranean wood raft, I thought—Saved! The next minute it struck me that raft was sinking, and so it was, slowly and jerkily, but sinking all the same. I clapper-clawed round in the stuffy dark for something at the side to hang on to, and got some tough bush rope, just as I was convinced that my fate was an inglorious and inverted case of Elijah, and I was being carried off, alive, to Shiöl.

The other demijohns of water have not arrived yet, and we are getting anxious again because the men's food has not come up, and they have been so exceedingly thirsty that they have drunk most of the water—not, however, since it has been in Monrovia's charge; but at 3.15 another boy comes through the bush with another demijohn of water. We receive him gladly, and ask him about the chop. He knows nothing about it. At 3.45 another boy comes through the bush with another demijohn of water; we receive him kindly; *he* does not know anything about the chop. At 4.10 another boy comes through the bush with another demijohn of water, and knowing nothing about the chop, we are civil to him, and that's all.

A terrific tornado which has been lurking growling about then sits down in the forest and bursts, wrapping us up in a lively kind of fog, with its thunder, lightning, and rain. It was impossible to hear, or make one's self heard at the distance of even a few paces, because of the shrill squeal of the wind, the roar of the thunder, and the rush of the rain on the trees round us. It was not like having a storm burst over you in the least; you felt you were in the middle of its engine-room when it had broken down badly. After half an hour or so the thunder seemed to lift itself off the ground, and the lightning came in sheets, instead of in great forks that flew like flights of spears among the forest trees. The thunder, however, had not settled things amicably with the mountain; it roared its rage at Mungo, and Mungo answered back, quivering with a rage as great, under our feet. One feels here as if one were constantly dropping, unasked and unregarded, among painful and violent discussions between the elemental powers of the universe. Mungo growls and swears in thunder at the sky, and sulks in white mist all the morning, and then the sky answers back, hurling down lightnings and rivers of water, with total disregard of Mungo's visitors. The way the water rushes down from the mountain wall through the watercourses in the jungle just above, and then at the edge of the forest spreads out into a sheet of water that is an inch deep, and that flies on past us in miniature cascades, trying the while to put out our fire, and so on, is—quite interesting. (I exhausted my vocabulary on those boys yesterday.)

As soon as we saw what we were in for, we had thrown dry wood on to the fire, and it blazed just as the rain came down, so with our assistance it fought a good fight with its fellow elements, spitting and hissing like a wild cat. It could have managed the water fairly well, but the wind came, very nearly putting an end to it by carrying away its protecting bough house, which settled on "Professor" Kefalla, who burst out in a lecture on the foolishness of mountaineering and the quantity of devils in this region. Just in the midst of these joys another boy came through the bush with another demijohn of water. We did not receive him even civilly; I burst out laughing, and the boys went off in a roar, and we shouted at him, "Where them chop?" "He live for come," said the boy, and we then gave him a hearty welcome and a tot of rum, and an hour afterwards two more boys appear, one carrying a sack of rice and beef for the men, and the other a box for me from Herr Liebert, containing a luxurious supply of biscuits, candles, tinned meats, and a bottle of wine and one of beer.

We are now all happy, though exceeding damp, and the boys sit round the fire, with their big iron pot full of beef and rice, busy cooking while they talk. Wonderful accounts of our prodigies of valour I hear given by Xenia, and terrible accounts of what they have lived through from the others, and the men who have brought up the demijohns and the chop recount the last news from Buea. James's wife has run away again.

I have taken possession of two demijohns of water and the rum demijohn, arranging them round the head of my bed. The worst of it is those tiresome bees, as soon as the rain is over, come in hundreds after the rum, and frighten me continually. The worthless wretches get intoxicated on what they can suck from round the cork, and then they stagger about on the ground buzzing malevolently. When the boys have had the chop and a good smoke, we turn to and make up the loads for tomorrow's start up the mountain, and then, after more hot tea, I turn in on my camp bed—listening to the soft sweet murmur of the trees and the pleasant, laughing chatter of the men.

September 25th.—Rolled off the bed twice last night into the bush. The rain has washed the ground away from under its off legs, so that it tilts; and there were quantities of large longicorn beetles about during the night—the sort with spiny backs; they kept on getting themselves hitched on to my blankets and when I wanted civilly to remove them they made a horrid fizzing noise and showed fight—cocking their horns in a defiant way. I awake finally about 5 a.m. soaked through to the skin. The waterproof sheet has had a label sewn to it, so is not waterproof, and it has been raining softly but amply for hours. I wish the camp bed had had a ticket sewn on, and nothing but my profound admiration for Kaiser Wilhelm, Emperor of Germany, its owner, prevents me from making holes in it, for it sags in the middle, and constitutes an excellent rain-water cistern. I have been saying things to it, during the night, about this habit, but the bed is so imbued with the military spirit that it says, "My orders are to be waterproof, and waterproof I'll be": so I decide to leave it behind, carefully drying it and protecting it as much as possible.

About seven we are off again, with Xenia, head man, cook, Monrovia boy and a labourer from Buea—the water-carriers have gone home after having had their morning chop.

We make for the face of the wall by a route to the left of that I took on Monday, and when we are clambering up it, some 600 feet above the hillocks, swish comes a terrific rain-storm at us accompanied by a squealing, bitter cold wind. We can hear the roar of the rain on the forest below, and hoping to get above it we keep on; hoping, however, is vain. The dense mist that comes with it prevents our seeing more than two yards in front, and we get too far to the left. I am behind the band to-day, severely bringing up the rear, and about 1 o'clock I hear shouts from the vanguard and when I get up to them I find them sitting on the edge of one of the clefts or scars in the mountain face.

I do not know how these quarry-like chasms have been formed. They both look alike from below—the mountain wall comes down vertically into them—and the bottom of this one slopes forward, so that if we had had the misfortune when a little lower down to have gone a little further to the left, we should have got on to the bottom of it, and should have found ourselves walled in on three sides, and had to retrace our steps; as it is we have just struck its right-hand edge. And fortunately, the mist, thick as it is, has not been sufficiently thick to lead the men to walk over it; for had they done so they would have got killed, as the cliff arches in under so that we look straight into the bottom of the scar some 200 or 300 feet below, when there is a split in the mist. The sides and bottom are made of, and strewn with, white, moss-grown masses of volcanic cinder rock, and sparsely shrubbed with gnarled trees which have evidently been under fire—one of my boys tells me from the burning of this face of the mountain by "the Major from Calabar" during the previous dry season.

We keep on up a steep grass-covered slope, and finally reach the top of the wall. The immense old crater floor before us is to-day the site of a seething storm, and the peak itself quite invisible. My boys are quite demoralised by the cold. I find most of them have sold the blankets I gave them out at Buana; and those who have not sold them have left them behind at Buea, from laziness perhaps, but more possibly from a confidence in their powers to prevent us getting so far.

I believe if I had collapsed too—the cold tempted me to do so as nothing else can—they would have lain down and died in the cold sleety rain.

I sight a clump of gnarled sparsely-foliaged trees bedraped heavily with lichen, growing in a hollow among the rocks; thither I urge the men for shelter and they go like storm-bewildered sheep. My bones are shaking in my skin and my teeth in my head, for after the experience I had had of the heat here on Monday I dared not clothe myself heavily.

The men stand helpless under the trees, and I hastily take the load of blankets Herr Liebert lent us off a boy's back and undo it, throwing one blanket round each man, and opening my umbrella and spreading it over the other blankets. Then I give them a tot of rum apiece, as they sit huddled in their blankets, and tear up a lot of the brittle, rotten wood from the trees and shrubs, getting horrid thorns into my hands the while, and set to work getting a fire with it and the driest of the moss from beneath the rocks. By the aid of it and Xenia, who soon revived, and a carefully scraped up candle and a box of matches, the fire soon blazes, Xenia holding a blanket to shelter it, while I, with a cutlass, chop stakes to fix the blankets on, so as to make a fire tent.

The other boys now revive, and I hustle them about to make more fires, no easy work in the drenching rain, but work that has got to be done. We soon get three well alight, and then I clutch a blanket—a wringing wet blanket, but a comfort—and wrapping myself round in it, issue orders for wood to be gathered and stored round each fire to dry, and then stand over cook while he makes the men's already cooked chop hot over our first fire, when this is done getting him to make me tea, or as it more truly should be called, soup, for it contains bits of rice and beef, and the general taste of the affair is wood smoke.

Kefalla by this time is in lecturing form again, so my mind is relieved about him, although he says, "Oh ma! It be cold, cold too much. Too much cold kill we black man, all same for one as too much sun kill you white man. Oh ma! . . . ," &c. I tell him they have only got themselves to blame; if they had come up with me on Monday we should have been hot enough, and missed this storm of rain.

When the boys have had their chop, and are curling themselves up comfortably round their now blazing fires, Xenia must needs start a theory that there is a better place than this to camp in; he saw it when he was with an unsuccessful expedition that got as far as this. Kefalla is fool enough to go off with him to find this place; but they soon return, chilled through again, and unsuccessful in their quest. I gather that they have been to find caves. I wish they had found caves, for I am not thinking of taking out a patent for our present camp site.

The bitter wind and swishing rain keep on. We are to a certain extent sheltered from the former, but the latter is of that insinuating sort that nothing but a granite wall would keep off.

Just at sundown, however, as is usual in this country, the rain ceases for a while, and I take this opportunity to get out my seaman's jersey, and retire up over the rocks to have my fight into it unobserved. It is a mighty fight to get that thing on, or off, at the best of times, but to-day it is worse than usual, because I have to get it on over my saturated cotton blouse, and verily at one time I fear I shall have to shout for assistance or be suffocated, so firmly does it get jammed over my head. But I fight my way unaided into it, and then turn to survey our position, and find I have been carrying on my battle on the brink of an abysmal hole whose mouth is concealed among the rocks and scraggly shrubs just above our camp. I heave rocks down it, as we in Fanland would offer rocks to an Ombwiri, and hear them go "knickity-knock, like a pebble in Carisbrook well." I think I detect a far away splash, but it was an awesome way down. This mountain seems set with these man-traps, and "some day some gentleman's nigger" will get killed down one.

The mist has now cleared away from the peak, but lies all over the lower world, and I take bearings of the three highest cones or peaks carefully. Then I go away over the rocky ground southwards, and as I stand looking round, the mist sea below is cleft in twain for a few minutes by some fierce down-draught of wind from the peak, and I get a strange, clear, sudden view right down to Ambas Bay. It is just like looking down from one world into another. I think how Odin hung and looked down into Nifelheim, and then of how hot, how deliciously hot, it was away down there, and then the mist closes over it. I shiver and go back to camp, for night is coming on, and I know my men will require intellectual support in the matter of procuring firewood.

The men are now quite happy; over each fire they have made a tent with four sticks with a blanket on, a blanket that is too wet to burn, though I have to make them brace the blankets to windward for fear of their scorching.

The wood from the shrubs here is of an aromatic and a resinous nature, which sounds nice, but it isn't; for the volumes of smoke it gives off when burning are suffocating, and the boys, who sit almost on the fire, are every few moments scrambling to their feet and going apart to cough out smoke, like so many novices in training for the profession of fire-eaters. However, they soon find that if they roll themselves in their blankets, and lie on the ground to windward they escape most of the smoke. They have divided up into three parties: Kefalla and Xenia, who have struck up a great friendship, take the lower, the most exposed fire. Head man, Cook, and Monrovia Boy have the upper fire, and the labourer has the middle one—he being an outcast for medical reasons. They are all steaming away and smoking comfortably.

I form the noble resolution to keep awake, and rouse up any gentleman who may catch on fire during the night, a catastrophe which is inevitable, and see to wood being put on the fires, so elaborately settle myself on my wooden chop-box, wherein I have got all the lucifers which are not in the soap-box. The very address on that chop-box, ought to keep its inside dry and up to duty, for it is "An den Hochwohlge-bornen Freiherrn von Stettin," &c. Owing to there not being a piece of ground the size of a sixpenny piece level in this place, the arrangement of my box camp takes time, but at last it is done to my complete satisfaction, close to a tree trunk, and I think, as I wrap myself up in my two wet blankets and lean against my tree, what a good thing it is to know how to make one's self comfortable in a place like this. This tree stem is perfection, just the right angle to be restful to one's back, and one can rely all the time on Nature hereabouts not to let one get thoroughly effete from luxurious comfort, so I lazily watch and listen to Xenia and Kefalla at their fire hard by.

They commence talking to each other on their different tribal societies; Kefalla is a Vey, Xenia a Liberian, so in the interests of science I give them two heads of tobacco to stimulate their conversation. They receive them with tragic grief, having no pipe, so in the interests of science I undo my blankets and give them two out of my portmanteau; then do myself up again and pretend to be asleep. I am rewarded by getting some interesting details, and form the opinion that both these worthies, in their pursuit of their particular ju-jus, have come into contact with white preju-dices, and are now fugitives from religious persecution. I also observe they have both their own ideas of happiness. Kefalla holds it lies in a warm shirt; Xenia that it abides in warm trousers; and every half-hour the former takes his shirt off, and holds it in the fire smoke, and then puts it hastily on; and Xenia, who is the one and only trouser wearer in our band, spends fifty per cent of the night on one leg struggling to get the other in or out of these garments, when they are either coming off to be warmed, or going on after warming. Those trousers of Xenia's have something wrong about them; I don't pretend to understand the garment, never having gone in for that sort of thing myself, but it is my belief he slings them too high, with those braces, which *more Alemanni* he wears. Anyhow, in season and out, they want taking off. Three mortal times to-day when on that wind- and rain-swept wall, the whole of us have been brought to a standstill by Xenia having to stand on one leg and do something to his peculiar vestments. It's a mercy he did not kill himself when he fell over while engaged in these operations among the rocks this afternoon—as it is, I see he has smashed the lantern glass again, so that I have to keep it under my blan-kets to prevent the candle getting blown out by this everlasting N.E. wind.

There seem but few insects here. I have only got two moths to-night—one pretty one with white wings with little red spots on, like an old-fashioned petticoat such as an early Victorian-age lady would have worn—the other a sweet thing in silver.

Then a horrid smell of burning negro interrupts my writing and I have to get up and hunt it down. After some trouble I find it is a spark in cook's hair, he sleeping the while sweetly. I rouse him, *via* his shins, and tell him to put himself out, and he is grateful.

My face is a misery to me, as soon as it dries it sets into a mask, and when I move it, it splits and bleeds.

(Later, *i.e.*, 2.15 A.M.). I have been asleep against that abominable vegetable of a tree. It had its trunk covered with a soft cushion of moss, and pretended to be a comfort—a right angle to lean against, and a softly padded protection to the spine from wind, and all that sort of thing; whereas the whole mortal time it was nothing in this wretched world but a water-pipe, to conduct an extra supply of water down my back. The water has simply streamed down it, and formed a nice little pool in a rocky hollow where I keep my feet, and I am chilled to the innermost bone, so have to scramble up and drag my box to the side of Kefalla and Xenia's fire, feeling sure I have contracted a fatal chill this time. I scrape the ashes out of the fire into a heap, and put my sodden boots into them, and they hiss merrily, and I resolve not to go to sleep again. 5 A.M.—Have been to sleep twice, and have fallen off my box bodily into the fire in my wet blankets, and should for sure have put it out like a bucket of cold water had not Xenia and Kefalla been roused up by the smother I occasioned and rescued me—or the fire. It is not raining now, but it is bitter cold and cook is getting my tea. I give the boys a lot of hot tea with a big handful of sugar in, and they then get their own food hot.

September 26th.—The weather is undecided and so am I, for I feel doubtful about going on in this weather, but I do not like to give up the peak after going through so much for it. The boys being dry and warm with the fires have forgotten their troubles. However, I settle in my mind to keep on, and ask for volunteers to come with me, and Bum, the head man, and Xenia announce their willingness. I put two tins of meat and a bottle of Herr Liebert's beer into the little wooden box, and insist on both men taking a blanket apiece, much to their disgust, and before six o'clock we are off over the crater plain. It is a broken bit of country with rock mounds sparsely overgrown with tufts of grass, and here and there are patches of boggy land, not real bog, but damp places where grow little clumps of rushes, and here and there among the rocks sorely-afflicted shrubs of broom, and the yellow-flowered shrub I have mentioned before, and quantities of very sticky heather, feeling when you catch hold of it as if it had been covered with syrup. One might fancy the entire race of shrubs was dying out; for one you see partially alive there are twenty skeletons which fall to pieces as you brush past them.

It is downhill the first part of the way, that is to say, the trend of the land is downhill, for be it down or up, the details of it are rugged mounds and masses of burnt-out lava rock. It is evil going, but perhaps not quite so evil as the lower hillocks of the great wall where the rocks are hidden beneath long slippery grass. We wind our way in between the mounds, or clamber over them, or scramble along their sides impartially. The general level is then flat, and then comes a rise towards the peak wall, so we steer N.N.E. until we strike the face of the peak, and then commence a stiff rough climb. We are all short of breath, but I do not think from the altitude; my shortness arises from a cold I have got, and my men's from too much breakfast, I fancy.

We keep as straight as we can, but get driven at an angle by the strange ribs of rock which come straight down. These are most tiresome to deal with, getting worse the higher we go, and so rotten and weather-eaten are they that they crumble into dust and fragments under our feet. Head man gets half a dozen falls, and when we are about three parts of the way up Xenia gives in. The cold and the climbing are too much for him, so I make him wrap himself up in his blanket, which he is glad enough of now, and shelter in a depression under one of the many rock ridges, and head man and I go on. When we are some 600 feet higher the iron-grey mist comes curling and waving round the rocks above us, like some savage monster defending them from intruders, and I again debate whether I was justified in risking the men, for it is a risk for them at this low temperature, with the evil weather I know, and they do not know, is coming on. But still we have food and blankets with us enough for them, and the camp in the plain below they can reach all right, if the worst comes to the worst; and for myself—well—that's my own affair, and no one will be a ha'porth the worse if I am dead in an hour. So I hitch myself on to the rocks, and take bearings, particularly bearings of Xenia's position, who, I should say, has got a tin of meat and a flask of rum with him, and then turn and face the threatening mist. It rises and falls, and sends out arm-like streams towards us, and then Bum, the head man, decides to fail for the third time to reach the peak, and I leave him wrapped in his blanket with the bag of provisions, and go on alone into the wild, grey, shifting, whirling mist above, and soon find myself at the head of a rock ridge in a narrowish depression, walled by massive black walls which show fitfully but firmly through the mist.

I can see three distinctly high cones before me, and then the mist, finding it cannot drive me back easily, proceeds to desperate methods, and lashes out with a burst of bitter wind, and a sheet of blinding, stinging rain. I make my way up through it towards a peak which I soon see through a tear in the mist is not the highest, so I angle off and go up the one to the left, and after a desperate fight reach the cairn—only, alas! to find a hurricane raging and a fog in full possession, and not a ten yards' view to be had in any direction. Near the cairn on the ground are several bottles, some of which the energetic German officers, I suppose, had emptied in honour of their achievement, an achievement I bow down before, for their pluck and strength had taken them here in a shorter time by far than mine. I do not meddle with anything, save to take a few specimens and to put a few more rocks on the cairn, and to put in among them my card, merely as a civility to Mungo, a civility his Majesty will soon turn into pulp. Not that it matters—what is done is done.

The weather grows worse every minute, and no sign of any clearing shows in the indigo sky or the wind-reft mist. The rain lashes so fiercely I cannot turn my face to it and breathe, the wind is all I can do to stand up against.

Verily I am no mountaineer, for there is in me no exultation, but only a deep disgust because the weather has robbed me of my main object in coming here, namely to get a good view and an idea of the way the unexplored mountain range behind Calabar trends.

No doubt had the weather been clear I should have been able to do this well, for the whole Omon range must be visible from this great summit of Cameroons, which rises at right angles to it. For when I was in Okyon close to this Rumby or Omon range, Mungo's great mass was perfectly visible looking seawards. My only consolation is that my failure to do this bit of work is not my own fault, save as regards my coming here at the wrong season, which matter was also beyond my control. Moreover there was just the chance, as this is the tornado season, and not the real wet, that I might have had a clear day on the peak. I took my chance and it failed, so there's nothing to complain about.

Comforting myself with these reflections, I start down to find Bum, and do so neatly, and then together we scramble down carefully among the rotten black rocks, intent on finding Xenia. The scene is very grand. At one minute we can see nothing save the black rocks and cinders under foot; the next the wind-torn mist separates now in one direction, now in another, showing us always the same wild scene of great black cliffs, rising in jagged peaks and walls around and above us. I think this walled cauldron we had just left is really the highest crater on Mungo.[1]

We soon become anxious about Xenia, for this is a fearfully easy place to lose a man in such weather, but just as we get below the thickest part of the pall of mist, I observe a doll-sized figure, standing on one leg taking on or off its trousers—our lost Xenia, beyond a shadow of a doubt, and we go down direct to him.

When we reach him we halt, and I give the two men one of the tins of meat, and take another and the bottle of beer myself, and then make a hasty sketch of the great crater plain below us. At the further edge of the plain a great white cloud is coming up from below, which argues badly for our trip down the great wall to the forest camp, which I am anxious to reach before nightfall after our experience of the accommodation afforded by our camp in the crater plain last night.

While I am sitting waiting for the men to finish their meal, I feel a chill at my back, as if some cold thing had settled there, and turning round, see the mist from

---

[1] Since my return to England I have read Sir Richard Burton's account of his first successful attempt to reach the summit of the Great Cameroons in 1862. His companions were Herr Mann, the botanist, and Señor Calvo. Herr Mann claimed to have ascended the summit a few days before the two others joined him, but Burton seems to doubt this. The account he himself gives of the summit is: "Victoria mountain now proved to be a shell of a huge double crater opening to the south-eastward, where a tremendous torrent of fire had broken down the weaker wall, the whole interior and its accessible breach now lay before me plunging down in vertical cliff. The depth of the bowl may be 360 feet. The total diameter of the two, which are separated by a rough partition of lava, 1000 feet. . . . Not a blade of grass, not a thread of moss, breaks the gloom of this Plutonic pit, which is as black as Erebus, except where the fire has painted it red or yellow." This ascent was made from the west face. I got into the "Plutonic pit" through the S.E. break in its wall, and was the first English person to reach it from the S.E., the third of my nation, all told, to ascend the peak, and the twenty-eighth ascender according to my well-informed German friends.

the summit above coming in a wall down towards us. These mists up here, as far as my experience goes, are always preceded by a strange breath of ice-cold air—not necessarily a wind.

Bum then draws my attention to a strange funnel-shaped thing coming down from the clouds to the north. A big waterspout, I presume: it seems to be moving rapidly N.E., and I profoundly hope it will hold that course, for we have quite as much as we can manage with the ordinary rain-water supply on this mountain, without having waterspouts to deal with.

We start off down the mountain as rapidly as we can. Xenia is very done up, and Head man comes perilously near breaking his neck by frequent falls among the rocks; my unlucky boots are cut through and through by the latter. When we get down towards the big crater plain, it is a race between us and the pursuing mist as to who shall reach the camp first, and the mist wins, but we have just time to make out the camp's exact position before it closes round us, so we reach it without any real difficulty. When we get there, about one o'clock, I find the men have kept the fires alight and Cook is asleep before one of them with another conflagration smoulder-ing in his hair. I get him to make me tea, while the others pack up as quickly as possible, and by two we are all off on our way down to the forest camp.

The boys are nervous in their way of going down over the mountain wall. The misadventures of Cook alone would fill volumes. Monrovia boy is out and away the best man at this work. Just as we reach the high jungle grass, down comes the rain and up comes the mist, and we have the worst time we have had during our whole trip, in our endeavours to find the hole in the forest that leads to our old camp.

Unfortunately, I must needs go in for acrobatic performances on the top of one of the highest, rockiest hillocks. Poising myself on one leg I take a rapid slide side-ways, ending in a very showy leap backwards which lands me on the top of the lantern I am carrying to-day, among miscellaneous rocks. There being fifteen feet or so of jungle grass above me, all the dash and beauty of my performance are as much thrown away as I am, for my boys are too busy on their own accounts in the mist to miss me. After resting some little time as I fell, and making and unmaking the idea in my mind that I am killed, I get up, clamber elaborately to the top of the next hillock, and shout for the boys, and "Ma," "ma," comes back from my flock from various points out of the fog. I find Bum and Monrovia boy, and learn that during my absence Xenia, who always fancies himself as a path-finder, has taken the lead, and gone off somewhere with the rest. We shout and the others answer, and we join them, and it soon becomes evident to the meanest intelligence that Xenia had better have spent his time attending to those things of his instead of going in for guiding, for we are now right off the track we made through the grass on our up journey, and we proceed to have a cheerful hour or so in the wet jungle, ploughing hither and thither, trying to find our way.

Isabelle Eberhardt

The Passionate Nomad
(1902)

Isabelle records her thoughts during her visit to her newly married brother Augustin in Sardinia.

Cagliari, 1 January 1900

I sit here all by myself, looking at the grey expanse of murmuring sea . . . I am utterly *alone* on earth, and always will be in this Universe so full of lures and disappointments . . . *alone*, turning my back on a world of dead hopes and memories.

The torments and confusion of the last six months have tempered my soul for good, and I can now face the worst of time, even death or destruction, without turning a hair. The knowledge I have acquired of the human heart is now so keen that I know the two months ahead will only bring me more sorrow, for I simply pay no attention to anything other than the dreams that make up my *true* personality. I seem to wear a mask that bespeaks someone cynical, dissipated . . . No one so far has ever managed to see through it and catch a glimpse of the sensitive soul which lives behind it.

No one has ever understood that even though I may seem to be driven by the senses alone, my heart is in fact a pure one filled with love and tenderness, and with boundless compassion for all who suffer injustice, all who are weak and oppressed . . . a heart both proud and unswerving in its commitment to Islam, a cause for which I long to give my life some day.

I shall dig in my heels and go on acting the lunatic in the intoxicating expanse of desert as I did last summer, or go on galloping through olive groves in the Tunisian Sahel, as I did in the autumn.

Those silent nights again, those lazy rides on horse-back through the salty plains of the Oued Righ's and the Oued Souf's white sands! That feeling, sad and blissful at once, that would fill my pariah's heart every time I struck camp surrounded by friends, among Spahis and nomads, none of whom ever considered me the despicable outcast I had so miserably become at the hands of fate.

Right now, I long for one thing only: to lead that life again in Africa . . . to sleep in the chilly silence of the night below stars that drop from great heights, with the sky's infinite expanse for a roof and the warm earth for a bed, in the knowledge that no one pines for me *anywhere on earth*, that there is no place where I am being missed or expected. To know that is to be free and unencumbered, a nomad in the great desert of life where I shall never be anything but an outsider. Such is the only form of bliss, however bitter, the Mektoub will ever grant me, but then happiness of the sort coveted by all of frantic humanity, will never be mine.

The light went out of my life when, two years ago, my white dove lay down to sleep in Bône's Cimetière des Croyants.

Now that Vava has returned to dust as well, and nothing is left of all that once seemed so solid and so permanent, now that all is gone, vanished, for all time and eternity! . . . and now that fate has so curiously, so mysteriously driven a wedge between myself and the only being who ever came close enough to my true nature to catch however pale a glimpse of it, Augustin . . .

And now that . . . Enough! I must put all those recent events to rest once and for all.

I am here out of friendship for the man Fate put across my path, just as I was in the midst of a crisis—᳁ *please Allah*, may it be the last one.

My feeling of friendship is all the stronger for it.

As a nomad who has no country besides Islam and neither family nor close friends, I shall wend my way through life until it is time for that everlasting sleep inside the grave . . .

MAHMOUD ESSADI

Cagliari, 7 January 1900
Impressions in a park, around 5 p.m.

A savage landscape, the jagged outlines of deeply gutted hills either reddish or grey in colour, cavalcades of maritime pines and Barbary fig trees. Greenery so lush it is almost out of place in the heart of winter. Salt lagoons with surfaces the colour of lead, dead and immobile like desert shotts.

And up there at the very top the town's silhouette straddles the steep hillside. Ancient ramparts and a square old tower, different levels of roofs, all cast in a pink hue against a sky of indigo.

Near the very top, barracks identical to the ones in Algeria, long and low in shape with red-tiled roofs and flaky, peeling walls. Dark old churches full of statues and mosaics, objects of great luxury in a country where poverty is the rule. Vaulted passageways that make for resounding footsteps and booming echoes. A maze of alleyways going up and going down, and intersected here and there by steps of grey stone; and because there is no traffic in a town located at this height, the tiny pointed paving stones are all covered with spindly grass of a yellowish-green hue.

Doors that lead to vast cellars below street level where whole poverty-stricken families live in age-old dankness.

Shops with small, coloured window displays; Oriental boutiques, narrow and full of smoke where one can hear the drawl of nasal voices . . .

Here and there a young man leans against a wall and makes signs to a girl bending over the railing of her balcony . . .

Peasants wearing headdresses that hang all the way down their black jackets pleated over their white calico trousers. Tanned and bearded figures with deep-set

211

eyes, heavy eyebrows and fierce, wary faces, a strange mixture of Greek mountain-dwellers and of tribesmen.

There is an Arab beauty about the women. The expression in their large languorous and melancholy jet-black eyes is resigned and sad like that of wary animals.

Beggars whine obsequiously in their incessant pursuit of the stranger everywhere he goes . . . Songs that sound infinitely sad, refrains that are curiously gripping, just like those heard in Africa, a place one cannot help but long for.

Cagliari, Thursday 18 January, 5.30 p.m.

Ever since I have been here, memories of *La Villa Neuve* haunt me more and more . . . good ones and bad ones alike . . . I say good ones, for now that all is dead and buried, I must not harbour any grudges against my poor hovel . . . I must not forget that it did shelter Mummy and her sweet kind heart, Vava and all his good intentions, none of which he ever carried out. Ever since I walked out of it, I have lived as if in a swift and dazzling reverie, moving through varied scenery under different names and guises.

I realise that the fairly restful winter I am spending here is but a breathing spell from the life that will be mine until the very end.

In a few days' time my aimless wanderings will take over again. Where? How? Only God can tell. I must not even speculate on that subject any longer, for just as I was about to stay on in Paris for months on end, I ended up in Cagliari of all places, an out-of-the-way spot if ever there was one.

Yet there is one thing to cheer me: the farther behind I leave the past, the closer I am to forging my own character. I am developing the most unflinching and invincible will, to say nothing of integrity, two traits I value more than any others and, alas, ones that are so hard to find in women.

That and the likely prospect of spending four months in the desert next spring make me feel confident of making a name for myself and, what's more, sooner or later fulfilling my life's goal.

I have given up the hope of ever having a corner on earth to call my own, a home, a family, peace or prosperity. I have donned the cloak of the rootless wanderer, one that can be a burden too at times. I have written off the thought of ever coming home to a happy family for rest and safety.

For the moment I have found a soothing enough temporary home here in Cagliari, and have the illusion of truly loving someone whose presence seems to have become a must . . . Yet that dream too will be short-lived, for I shall need to be alone again and do without the tranquil indolence of a shared existence once the moment will have come again for rough and risky travel.

That is what must be, and so it shall be. And in the gloom of that future existence I shall at least have one consolation, the thought that upon my return a friend, a living being may be happy to see me again. What is so terrible though, is the length of time spent apart to make for such reunions . . . And who knows, someone else may have taken my place by then. That is more than likely, given his ideas about women and marriage. It would be very strange indeed if he were never to meet a woman with whom to share those ideas which are so at odds with mine. I know that no such partner will appear while he is a vagabond outcast, unless he is prepared to make do with a wife somewhere who will quiver at the thought of him in danger, but only from a safe and comfortable distance.

But then he too, like Augustin, will yield to the lure of home and comfort once the present period of transition is behind him.

When that happens I will have no choice but to resume my journey, sad but certain of having nothing to look forward to but the empty hotel rooms, gourbis and tents that are the nomad's temporary shelter. ᴗ Mektoub!

The only thing to do is take things as they come and enjoy this heady interlude, for it will soon be over.

Cagliari, 29 January 1900

My brief interlude in this ancient Sardinian town has now come to an end.

Tomorrow at this time I shall be quite far from these Cagliari cliffs, on that leaden, grumbling, turbulent sea.

Last night Cagliari was booming with the echo of its rolling thunder . . . Today, the sea looks its most ominous; it has a dull shimmer.

I am full of the sorrow that goes with changes in surroundings, those successive stages of annihilation that slowly lead to the great and final void.

Isabelle travels to Paris and to Geneva in an attempt to sort out her inheritance.

Geneva, 27 May 1900, 9.30 p.m. [Sunday]

Back to this gloomy diary of mine in this evil city where I have suffered so much and have come close to perishing.

I have hardly been here a week and once again I feel as morbid and oppressed as I used to in the old days. All I want to do is get out for good.

I went to have a look at our poor house, with the sky low and sunless; the place was boarded up and mute, lost among the weeds.

I saw the road, white as ever, white like a silvery river heading for the Jura's great mountaintops between those tall velvet trees.

I saw the two graves in that faithless cemetery, set in a land of exile so very far away from that other sacred place devoted to eternal repose and everlasting silence . . .

I feel that I have now become a total stranger on this soil which I shall leave tomorrow and hope never to visit again.

(Recorded later)
Paris, April 1900

In the misty light of stars and streetlamps one night I saw the Montparnasse cemetery's white crosses outlined like so many ghosts against the velvety black of big trees, and it occurred to me that the powerful rumble of Paris could not disturb the slumber of all the strangers lying there . . .

[. . .]

Batna, Tuesday 26 March, 1 p.m.

Took Souf for a ride today to the foot of the mountain, let the horse roam freely about the meadow, and stretched out underneath a pine tree.

I daydreamed with my gaze upon the great valley, the blue mountains opposite and Batna in its slum-like setting. A sensuous delight at being out of doors in the sun, far from the grey walls of my dreary prison. Everything is turning green again, the trees are in bloom, the sky is blue and countless birds are singing.

Where is that long-past autumn day when, eyes closed and with a peaceful heart (so much for human nature's utter blindness!) I listened to the strong wind rustle through the tough djerids of Debila's palm trees! Where is that Oued Souf of ours, with its white dunes and gardens, and Salah ben Taliba's peaceful house, a stone's throw from the dunes of Sidi-Mestour and the silent necropolis that is the Ouled-Ahmed's final resting place! Where is the land of holy zawyias and marabouts' graves, the harsh, magnificent land that feeds the flames of faith and where we found such bliss? Where is all that, and will I ever see it again?

Over here, my poverty is total . . . No food, no money and no heat. Nothing!

The days all come and go, and blend into the past's black void; each new dawn brings us closer to the day of our deliverance, set for 20 February 1902, when real life will truly *begin* for the two of us at last.

Everything is in the hands of God, and nothing happens ◡ *against His will.*

Batna, Friday 12 April 1901, 5 p.m.

These days I go out every morning with my faithful Souf to spend a few hours of quiet in the open fields.

There I dismount and sit down by the edge of the road, near a field of colza, at the foot of the dark Ouled-Abdi, for a smoke and time to dream; I hold on to Souf's bridle while he greedily grazes on the green blades of grass he carefully picks out among the flowers.

In the distance to the north, the outlines of the dreary city full of barracks and administrative buildings. My back is turned toward it and my gaze is on the countryside in bloom.

I have already come to know this place quite well, and it gives me moments of serenity and bliss.

The other night I was lying next to Slimène on Khelifa's mat. Through the window I could see the blue sky, a few clouds gilded by the setting sun, and the tops of trees that are suddenly green again: all of a sudden, I was reminded of the past, in a flash so keen it left me in tears. The overall landscape is so similar here that memories of *La Villa Neuve* keep haunting me.

Dora Birtles

North-West by North
(1935)

The launch against which we were moored was on schedule to leave at seven o'clock, so perforce we were, for the first time, away early. The reefs were so numerous as to make night sailing dangerous, and from now on till Thursday Island we anchored each night. We were to try to make Snapper Island before sun-down, for we had been told of a deserted plantation there and we were in need of fruit and vegetables. Sven, who loved punctuality and an objective, and hated wait, wait, waiting around, roused me with a roll of drums in the voice, "Dona, we've got to make an early start". Bunks were for laggards and lovers. Grand to feel that there was a whole new day, begun well, fresh and white like a new page waiting to be written on.

He and I were beginning a new arrangement, a tentative agreement to share cook-days; he had difficulty in selecting menus, the problem of our likes and dislikes worried him, cooking was to him a fiddling business and he took it to seriously; as for me, frankly I didn't like washing greasy pots and pans soot-blackened from smoking primuses. And vegetables! Potatoes, of the earth earthy, stored in soil; and always onions to be peeled, strong brown onions; and some pumpkins we had bought because they were cheap—they were armoured in steel plate, not skin, and full of "bone". Two months' silent disciplining the soul by wiping pots and scrubbing floors had not thrust sainthood upon me. I was not going to thirst after sainthood any longer. Sven always did the pots and the floor better than anyone else; he believed in being "thorough" about everything, and we had all come to count on him doing them, with disastrous cumulative effects. I had a conscience about the pots I had left and I rather liked cooking, so he and I had struck the bargain. I was to plan, cook, serve and wipe up for two days, while he did the nasty work. The joint plan was not to interfere with watches.

It was a pleasant, warm, easy day's sailing. We spread the charts out on the deck-house and continued plotting Cook's route on our Admiralty charts, using the *Journal* as our authority. It was something I had been doing since Bribie Island, but the detailed nature of the bearings and courses had often puzzled me, and from being at hand with nautical whys and why nots Sven had now got involved with me in the text. There were discrepancies between the correct latitudes and longitudes and Cook's. The errors in longitude could be ascribed to the deficiencies in the chronometers and nautical tables of the eighteenth century. Flinders, thirty years after Cook, had suffered from similar inaccuracies and had had to re-check all his own positions owing to errors in the Greenwich tables which he used on his voyage of circumnavigation. He had re-identified the features of the eastern coast and had found that a reduction of twelve minutes in some parts of Cook's charts obtained a correction in the longitude of twenty and a half minutes west of Cape Gloucester, and that consequently his longitudes were at times as much as twenty and a half minutes greater than those of Cook.

Sven at first, because of these inaccuracies, was inclined to the attitude, "Is that the best your great navigator could do?" but gradually the magnitude of Cook's accomplishment stimulated him and he came to agree with the French navigators, Marion and Duclesmeur. The account of their voyage, though published in a war year between the two countries, yet pays this magnificent tribute to Cook's map: "Je l'ai trouvée d'une exactitude & d'un détail qui m'a étonné au-delà de toute expression. Je doute que les cartes de nos côtes de France soient dressées avec plus de précision."

We got absorbed in it during those weeks, changing Cook's West of Greenwich to our East of Greenwich, laying down forgotten courses, taking bearings, feeling changes in winds that had blown one hundred and sixty years before, experiencing the blankness, the reef-prickled dangers that had lain in the unknown seas ahead of him, wondering why he did this and guessing how he came to miss something else. Once we had him sailing on dry land; often we went wrong, then we would go back to the tightly-packed text, a sailorly text meant to be read by sailors and misinterpreted by landlubberly grammarians, as if a navigator, writing concisely, could be expected to have the long-winded inexact kind of precision lawyers achieve. Sven would h'm over the chart and then lay down a line to reconcile all the facts. Sometimes when we had shuffled through the brief strict phrases of those tantalizing sentences heaped like a pack of cards in sequence we found ourselves in doubt about time, for Cook's day began officially at noon, not midnight, a puzzling thing, two dates covering the same hours of daylight.

Interpreting charts was new to me, a fascinating work. Currents, shoals, the places of old wrecks—Maria, 1871, that had been a crew of adventurers on the way to New Guinea gold prospecting; the survivors had all been eaten when they had struggled to the mainland—anchorages, "foul ground", "the beacons are liable to be washed away", the dotted lines of famous voyages, and beyond them white spaces, unsounded waters. What a lot remained to be filled in! Some of the detail still depended on no more recent a survey than that of Flinders himself.

After all, sailors were a hurrying road-conscious crowd following the furrow-beaten track, this broad red-ink highway that some senior officer had laid down on the Company's charts and steamed over a dozen times or so, for our charts were not new. Henery had collected them from various sources, but we were new voyagers and the shortest distance between two points was not our method of travelling; fortunately the broad red line, even in glass chart-rooms on the Company's bridge, had been only an imaginative progress; by the very characteristic of sea the highway remained unruled, to be travelled afresh and strangely every time.

In the afternoon, content with the morning's work and with the onus of two cook-days upon me, I resolved to make pastry. Pastry, nothing less would satisfy me.

Why of all dishes pastry above a hissing primus at sea when there was surely no need to take trouble? Oh reason, not the need. The urge that tried to make a lyric poem one day turned to pastry the next with perhaps more success. When everyone had settled down to the afternoon coma of still going along and no change in the breeze, I scrubbed the top of the water tank and floured it. There were difficulties in the way of the project; to begin with I had never made pastry before, not real stock-in-trade pastry with flour and water and butter, only an easy imitation called rough puff with an egg. A succession of helps had all been, conveniently, expert pastry makers. It took cool hands M——, best of them, used to say. Well, cool hands in the tropics, the same hands that tended the primuses and the oven, would have to be dispensed with, that was all. So would butter, for we had none, but there was goat fat carefully melted down and saved. No flour dredger, no rolling pin, no recipe. Did one put baking powder in pastry? But there was no baking powder, so that problem was solved. Not a smooth bottle on board! All the bottles were printed in relief with the names of the manufacturers of their contents, "This bottle remains the property of . . ." The printing made a pattern on the pastry. One could at least eat the imprint of a threatening gentleman's inalienable right to a bottle; would he send divers down if one threw it overboard? Lastly the oven. I was fond of that oven though I had dratted it frequently. Had I not discovered it, a neglected and despised child on board, and coaxed it into producing the first damper? Like most delinquent children it was not really naughty, it only needed to be encouraged and understood.

There is a lot in the psychology of inanimate things. The fish lines for instance, they hadn't caught a fish until Ruth dyed them brown, and then they had responded to colour treatment like the lady in the advertisement for hair wash, "no admirers before, three caught already". Actually the oven was home-made, of galvanized iron, the size and shape of a biscuit tin, with a hole cut in the underside and meant to fit over the flame of the primus. There was a shelf one-third of the height of the oven above the hole. That was all, no packing, no flue, no browning shelf, just a thin metal box with a door that did not shut properly and a shelf that stood on two wobbling bands of metal. The whole oven too large to fit on the inner ring of the gimbal so that with every roll of the boat the oven and the pastry inside the oven rolled and pitched and tossed as well. Presumably the exercise made it lose weight, for it was unmistakably light. The material result of my effort was a jam tart, put aside and hidden till next day, a turnover and some Johnny slices with sugar and currants in them; but the satisfaction of the effort was much more, it lay in the achievement of making the oven bring forth pastry, of circumventing and overcoming its will to resistance, of climbing to a culinary civilization after days of low and monotonous living on onions and bully-beef and potatoes, hackneyed and faithful friends of the sea but stolid; beside them pastry was positively ethereal, an Ode to a Skylark in flour.

That day Joan had come upon the tin of dried pears, unseen since the day of their stowing in Brisbane. They were fine pears and had unexpectedly borne a harvest of fat succulent white grubs, big fellows that floated to the top of the bowl as the pears were washed before being spread out to dry in the sun and put back into the tin for future use. "Shall I save the grubs?" asked Ruth, emptying the bowl overboard. "You could make meat pies. . . ." I never made pastry again, this remained the culinary peak of the adventure, a gastronomic record best not re-attempted.

About four o'clock we came to Snapper Island, a large high island, densely wooded, with a rock-bound shore. It promised all sorts of things. We anchored in deep water close in, opposite the only strip of sand we could see, a length of twenty or thirty yards held between rocky arms that ran out and made a little lap of quiet water behind which the green bosom of the island rose steeply. To find the hidden paps of plenty we separated; if there were to be spoils we wanted to get them on board the same evening.

I chose the rocks to the north and clambered over them and along a windswept shore whose shelly surface was held together by trails of wild passion vines and another coarse binding vine, a "likely-looking herbage", that I thought resembled the seakale Cook frequently used in anti-scorbutic brews for his crew. I gathered a small quantity. A reef ran out on this side of the island, shallow and even more desolate in appearance than nature had made it because the stumps of what had once been a low jetty stood abandoned and decaying at its farther end.

The jetty had led to the plantation. I know these deserted plantations sound too good to be true and that possibly the reader like a sceptical mother when her son brings home "found" apples will query the "deserted", but deserted it assuredly was, unless the monstrous and gaily-coloured spiders that mounted guard over it and the battalions of big cockroaches that lurked under every piece of timber or iron could be said to own the plantation they infested.

As I came struggling through a crop of what had once been a legitimate, aristocratic and imported turnip family Joan came, a stumpy diminutive figure, through the wall of scrub on the south-eastern side of the hill. We met by some paw-paw trees in fruit. There was no need for words, a delectable specimen fell at the first shake of the tree and split open on the ground. We each took a large half and—what is a good word for the indrawn sucking, the guzzling that a melting, neither liquid nor solid paw-paw demands in order to be appreciated at its proper worth? Paw-paws are not fruit that carry and if picked when green they ripen unhappily, their dispositions not entirely soured but thwarted, not mellowed into the brave happiness congealed sunshine ought to have, for they are congealed sunshine, or rather sunshine that is just on the point of being frozen solid without turning cold in the process. There is a just time for the eating of paw-paw, it comes at the moment when the fruit tumbles off the tree because it can hang on no longer and the eaters stand beneath, hot, thirsty, empty-stomached and with the fulfilment of finding on them. If you add to this the circumstance that the paw-paw was a mammoth of its kind, had cost us nothing to procure and had evidently been waiting for us to arrive, you get what might be known as the orgasm of paw-paw eating, the apogee of the delight of tasting. We stood in the shade, the fruit a segment of light slung from ear to ear, a sunlit brightness that turned Joan's olive skin to the brass of an old and laughing idol and my redness to vermilion. We glistened with paw-paw juice, it dripped round us. Sven came along and then Henery; we all ate on but none was so good as the first.

With pieces of galvanized iron we dug up turnips and sweet potatoes, grubbing at the rich red earth and tearing at the vines that rioted on the ground, hacking down bunches of bananas and collecting as many paw-paws as we could, green ones to use as boiled vegetable, as well as those turning yellow. I had never seen such a choking profusion of growth; the tall walls of the jungle were advancing on the clearing with slow and menacing steps; the plants civilization had brought to the island were turning savage in their fight against the springing upthrust of native grasses and weeds and were developing strange habits, losing the thick roots for which they had originally been cultivated, growing to heights unforeseen in their domesticated lives in the effort to spread and spread and by extension to shut out every other striving form of life from the too-fertile, the rankly-suckling earth. On this island battle-front, rainy season after dry season, green blood was being shed, the soil was liquid with it and the air was liquid with the taint of it; our legs were stained with green, with yellow and purple splotches from unknown vegetable essences.

The man who had begun the battle, planting his forces against the established dominion of nature, had given up the struggle and left. His kitchen, separate from the hut, was in ruins, but the hut remained for a little longer, its walls neatly made of bundles of blady grass dried and wired together over a framework of wire netting; within it a bunk, a book on engineering, a paper-backed novel, *Henry of Navarre*, the fragments of a smashed violin, and some but not a disproportionate number of empty bottles. Things brought to the island for a purpose but not worth while taking away. What evidences of personality could one get from a book on engineering, an historical novel and an aspiration after music? Had he deliberately trampled on the violin? It looked like it. From the debris of one's own possessions what conclusions would change inheritors draw? Might they suppose more knowledge and skill than one had, credit one with a wider range of interests than one actually possessed? Make one not so human as one had been, so full of failings? The contents of the hut told nothing, the Man Who Had Gone Away remained an enigma.

At dusk we carried back to the anchorage the surplus booty that we could not pile in the dinghy. Sandflies bit our legs on the way, there was no shooing them off, the only protection would be to grow a pelt like the men whose hairy legs baffled them. English people loathe the Australian mosquitoes that pimple the smooth terrain of their complexions with huge and unsightly swellings and Australians have a tendency to be amused at it, but even we never got used to the sandflies that wielded a deadlier proboscis. They waged bitter war on us till the end of the trip. The insidious thing about them was that the stings did not begin to hurt till twenty-four hours afterwards. Till then one did not know how badly one had been bitten.

The sunset was lavish in colour, spectacular with reds, yellows and black, over-exuberant with splendour as the whole island was over-vital and struggling under its superabundant fertility like an unreproductive and unoccupied woman.

After supper and the stowing of the produce from the plantation I lay on the deckhouse to enjoy the late and feeble moonrise that turned Snapper Island into the humped outline of a camel resting; the still and coal-black surface of the sea reflected the diffused moonlight and filled the air with grey shapes that filched consciousness stealthily from me. I fell asleep in my clothes and was only roused when Ruth, who had been reading late and then leisurely preparing for bed, cried out in fright. As she had rolled up the canvas blind she had distinctly seen the rat in the pot shelf, a little place at the after end of the galley under the steering cockpit. Caught by the sudden illumination it had looked at her for an instant before hurdling the primuses and getting away into the food stowage space under the bilge bunk. A *big* rat. Ruth was impressive. We must have taken it on at Cairns. That morning we had found some gnawed pumpkin, now we were certain and the knowledge was not pleasant, even if the rat's arrival was an omen of good luck.

Wind again, at first light airs and then the south-east trade wind freshening. We had the squaresail up and that left all the deck house free for charts and books. Sven and I worked for three hours on the stretch between Sandy Cape and Cape Cleveland. He showed me how to use the sextant, but I got lost in a wilderness of tables in calculating my own observation and never found the correct answer. Instead of working it out I told them about grandfather's museum-pieces, a quadrant, too sacred for us ever to be allowed to touch, and an old-fashioned sextant with a double set of prisms and reflecting mirrors, a cumbersome thing of ebony wood, with chips of ivory inlaid to mark the degrees. He used to take it out on the veranda for the grandchildren's benefit and "shoot the sun from the quarter-deck".

A real old Sindbad he was: Welsh, religious, with a beard and a past so romantic as to be legendary; his father had "drunk away three ships, a clipper, a coaler and a barquentine"—for a long time I believed he swallowed them, masts and all—and so grandfather's mother had made him promise never, never to touch strong drink, and he never had, not once in ninety years. At the age of twelve, the ships being drunk and the drinker dead from the effects, grandfather was apprenticed to a friendly captain and shipped on an outward voyage round the Horn, but at Rio de Janeiro he had fallen down one of the hatches, broken a leg and been left behind in a Spanish Roman Catholic hospital where a German "sawbones" wanted to take the leg off but an American doctor saved it. "He's only a boy and doesn't want to take a peg-leg home to Wales." Nearly eighty years afterwards the "boy's" voice still trembled with gratitude to the American doctor. Five months he was in hospital and it was three years before he saw his mother again.

The yarns he used to tell us. How he was once on a ship carrying coal across the Indian Ocean and for three weeks they were on fire, and only managed to save the boat by beaching her on the coast of Java. How with three companions he had deserted a merchantman at Calcutta and taking the ship's boat had stolen away to join the Queen's forces and help against the Mutiny. They had got twenty-seven miles up the main stream and were caught, brought back and clapped in irons and then let off, ostensibly owing to the skipper's "sensibility of their patriotism" but actually because half his crew had already deserted and he had to have them to work the ship. How they had carried a cargo of cattle for the use of the troops in China and how a disease smote the cattle and they all swelled up, and though the skipper looked up a medical book and it said . . . there used to be gruesome and realistic details here . . . no one on board could find the right spot and they only saved six out of one hundred and fifty. How in the opium war the Chinese threw stink-pots on board . . . and what a wild place Hobart Town had been in the 'sixties. His milkman had been a "lag" sent over for rioting in the Liverpool troubles. How grannie had come over in the first free emigrant ship, and how he had met her and taken a coasting job and finally left the sea. A settled-down Sindbad of a Grandfather.

He used to take me down to the sailing ships that had Welsh captains and that were tied up at the Stockton wharves waiting their turns to go under the cranes and load coal for South America. In those days Newcastle harbour was so busy sailing ships had to wait three weeks for a berth in the Inner Basin. He had given me a bos'n's whistle with a thick yellow cord to put round my neck and I had a sailor collar with three lines of braid on it. In these interviews he used to get excited in Welsh and when I got bored and fidgeted he would tell me to go and look at Captain Davis' (or Williams' or Evans') pig, or chickens, and not to climb higher than the cross-trees. At one time his home was a regular port of call for Welsh sailor boys who came up to Sunday dinner and tea and had to pay for it afterwards by going to a service, a long Welsh service, and probably a lot of good advice on the way. A pious old Sindbad.

Saturday, July 9th. Joan's cook-day. She surprised and cheered us with a new dish, fried scones, fatty things dripping with golden syrup, sweet, delectable, very satisfy-ing after a morning spent in the south-easter. They were not so much an answer to the famous pastry as a sudden stimulation of her imagination by it. When had we had the same dish before? Because we had had it together and it had been new to me. Oh yes, years ago, when we were camping at Gerringong, Mildred had made them then. "Puff-de-loonies" she had called them, and we had all sung "Au clair de la lune" over and over again and she couldn't cook quickly enough to satisfy us. Joan would have forgotten those puff-de-loonies, and if they were recalled to her she would think it sentimental, or gluttonous. Only a glutton would remember such a long-ago meal. In any case I was sentimental and I had eaten far too many fried scones.

It was my watch in the afternoon. We were now near Endeavour Reef where Cook had been wrecked, and I had read and re-read the vivid account of those unhappy twenty-three hours when every man aboard had worked feverishly to lighten the ship and get her off. Now the reefs were beaconed and buoyed, but then the situation had been desperate, the nearest settlement in the Dutch East Indies, thousands of miles from help. The guns had gone overboard first, most properly, they could best be spared from a scientific expedition. But the other things that could so ill be spared? How to choose? Then when the ship was lightened the feverish work of pumping, the alarm when a new leadsman took over and swung in the water-filled hold and measured the leak as gaining, the relief when his mistake was noticed, the slow painfully careful work of fothering and warping, the joy when the ship came off and was still floating.

Prayerfully they had steered for Hope Islands. "I have named them Hope Islands because we were always in hopes of being able to reach those islands." Hope Islands! We passed close to them, any islands more hopeless I have yet to see. They were low and bare, waterless, shadeless, two sandy freckles on the sea's hot blue face. They looked as if a high tide would cover them. Hope Islands! But a "Merciful Providence" had sent the *Endeavour* creeping past them to the harbour of refuge the ship's boats had located on the little river where Cooktown now stands. Before they got to it a fresh gale had sprung up that prevented them making the anchorage for another thirty-six hours; the tiring, tireless reiteration of the pumps continued, while, mocking their labour, lay the distant and forbidding stretch of Weary Bay whose sombre blue shoreline we could see, the inhospitable façade of a great continent that held no easily-opened door to European explorers. After that had come the exact, the deliberate running-aground of the "cat-built" barque in the safety of Endeavour River.

Freya Stark

Baghdad Sketches
(1937)

"Would you like to visit my cousin, Shaikh Habib of the 'Azza?" said Nasir Effendi one day.

It is difficult to believe, when looking at Nasir's comfortable figure and city appearance, that he has anything so primitive as a Beduin cousin, but this is the manner of the East, where all holds together in the most intimate and unexpected way. I said I should be delighted, and, being still new to Baghdad and unaware of its peculiar attitude towards the female tourist, began to ask which of my English friends would like to join me.

This caused pain all round.

A document was handed to me,[1] printed for the guidance of ladies in Iraq and

---

[1] See page 226.

advising them, if they must wander, at least not to do so by themselves. "Ladies," it proceeded to say in language elegant but cautious, "are *deemed* to be accompanied when travelling with a European or American of the male sex."

This seemed to me an indelicate suggestion on the part of the British Civil Service with which it was unnecessary and hardly respectable to comply.

The next step, however, was even more crushing, "If you get into trouble by doing this sort of thing, no other woman will ever be allowed to do it afterwards," was one of those remarks which one can ponder over for hours without getting to the bottom of. An uncle of mine never allowed his hair to grow because he said that to keep it shaved prevented it from falling out: this was the same principle of prudence: but the sad moral came towards the end of his life, when he decided to give his locks their one fling, and nothing was left but baldness. I did not mention this instructive case to my friends.

The younger women were not unsympathetic: a gleam of adventure came into their eyes, which only made me unpopular with their husbands. A husband in an official position is like a Victorian débutante: a mere nothing blasts his career for ever. Apart from this, husbands in Services are expected to act as anchors when stray currents threaten to sweep their wives away, and the business of an anchor is, after all, to become unresponsive and spiky whenever one pulls at it. I began to feel like a Disturber of the Peace. This morbid nervousness about the doings of women when left to themselves could only be accounted for, I concluded, by the fact that Baghdad is near the site of the Garden of Eden: it must be a case of subconscious shock in the past. I began to feel like an anomaly: so many different people disapproved of me all at once, it might look as if I, and not they, were peculiar—which was absurd. I thought, rather bitterly, that if Paradise were run by the Colonial Office, there would be no chance of getting in at all, and felt thankful that in all probability it is not. I then went and told my woes to S., who instantly and gallantly said she would come, and would mention it to her husband—the most tolerant of anchors as a matter of fact—next morning at breakfast just before we started, when remonstrance would make him late for his office.

After this all sorts of risks and emotions might reasonably have been expected, but the rest of my diary is one continual anti-climax. Nothing showed the least sign of happening except the weather. We started off in the Solitude deplored in the printed definition, but otherwise and in our own minds rather tightly packed and crowded, what with Nasir, an Arab driver, a Jewish proprietor, and our food and bedding in a small but antique car. The Shaikh had gone ahead to prepare our reception.

We made north-east towards the Jebel Hamrin, through Ba'quba and Daltawa. The weather, as unencouraging as the remarks we left behind us, lay about in a thick white mist, most unusual and perverse. We took the desert with us, as it were, travelling in a small yellow patch surrounded by whiteness on all sides. The brambles were wet, the mist hung in festoons in the palm gardens of Daltawa, opening to show fronds here and there, high up as in cathedral aisles: the garden lanes between mud walls were silent: the gates, with wooden locks whose enormous bolts slide pegs into holes and are as clumsy and ingenious as any Eastern contrivance—were all fast closed: and near the village the mud became so bad that, after getting out of our car and watching its corkscrew wriggles, we insisted on having the chains put on.

After Daltawa the mist lifted; the desert appeared with sharp outlines under a watery sky. But the harm was done and every little hollow was a trap for motor cars. Our Arab drove slowly up and down the edge of the sticky streaks looking for a crossing place; he dashed at it full speed; there was a grinding noise in the middle; and after a quivering effort to grip earth that had the consistency of toothpaste, our car slid gently back while its wheels went round like fireworks, shooting water instead of sparks. Then we would get out and push, while the Arab driver used methods of persuasion with his gears: the Jewish proprietor was too well dressed to help us, but he stood in front and beckoned to our car with one finger, as if it were a baby.

We had just got out of our second ditch of this kind when we became aware of two Kurdish Members of Parliament, stuck in the mud more deeply than we had been, and in terror of their lives in the desert. Our united efforts had no effect at all on the magnificent saloon in which they travelled for their country's good, but as we were regretfully abandoning them, we saw help coming in the shape of three or four Beduin striding out of the mist towards us. We pointed them out, rejoicing, and apparently added the last strain to the already harassed feelings of the marooned politicians. "Do not leave us to the Beduin," they implored, as if it were a matter of certain death. We however, like greater powers before us, felt rather bored with the Safe-guarding of Minorities—and the Beduin looked very peaceful: we left in a pathetic silence, but enquired about the fate of the deserted ones on our way back next day and heard that they had been rescued in the most uneventful manner—another anti-climax.

The mist now rolled into clouds and fled, casting shadows under the sun, and the desert in the direction of Dali Abbas began to show cultivation and to become more solid underfoot: and when, long after our expected time, we reached the first cornland, a messenger from Shaikh Habib stood up to meet us, a dark-skinned, aquiline-faced, black-bearded figure dressed in white, whose fierce appearance would have made the Members of Parliament faint away altogether.

Crouching on the footboard, he guided us, with a sense denied to the town-bred driver, in and out of irrigation ditches to the mud village where the Shaikh and his people are leaving their nomad habits and settling on the land: they are in the early stages of the process and still look upon houses as scarcely more permanent than tents, things to be left and built up again somewhere else if for any reason, such as a dispute with the tax collector or difficulty over grazing or irrigation, the site becomes distasteful. Shaikh Habib was thinking of doing this soon, he explained, because of some business with rents. Followed by a little group of tribesmen, he took us round the village, on a mound whose gentle regular rise showed that it had probably been inhabited off and on since Babylonian days.

All here was a mixture of new things and very old. The Shaikh himself was such. Dressed in a yellow and black striped gown, or zibun, with a knife in his sash, and sleeves which ruffled over his hands, long and delicate as Van Dyck might have painted—a trait, by the way, often noticeable among the Beduin chiefs—he talked to us about the League of Nations, about his new school with French educational posters on its mud walls, and about raids in the neighbouring hills—a matter, he explained, of the past. His vegetable garden, with marigolds growing up among the cabbages, was a novelty to the tribe: but close by this sign of progress, in a room darkened so that her eyes might not be tired by the incessant turning, a young girl ground corn between two stones. The upper one had a hole into which a stick was thrust to make a handle to turn by. As she sat crooning an endless little song over that weary mill, one realized why this has ever been the labour of captives, a sad monotonous labour. How many mournful thoughts, how many dear and bitter memories, must have hovered over such grinding stones, from the days of Kassandra in the house of Agamemnon to those of our own women in Cawnpore.

We stood a while on the mound watching seven gazelles flashing away in the distance at great speed, their light hind-quarters making them visible in the sun. Then we turned out of the cold air into the Shaikh's hall and sat among the tribesmen in a half-circle round a fireplace piled high with sesame-plants and thorns, watching their faces in the flamelight and listening to the rebaba, the one-stringed ancestor of the fiddle, as it played one or other of their four modes of music, for love and war and tenderness and sorrow, as they say.

During the rising in 1920 Shaikh Habib sheltered a British officer and apparently acquired some useful knowledge, for before dinner was brought in, he got up with an air of secrecy and asked us to accompany him to our room; here, spread on a ledge which corresponded to a toilet table, we saw two glasses and four bottles: burgundy, whisky, brandy and crème de menthe, as far as I can remember. "I do not like to have them out in front of the tribesmen," said our host, "but I know this is what you are accustomed to." He prepared to stand by and watch us. We, however, assured him that the national standard is lower for women and, much touched by his thoughtfulness, returned to the hall to eat the most enormous and delicious dinner I can remember for a long time.

We went to call on the Shaikh's wife after dinner, and had an experience, for we saw real beauty—not the kind that depends for its charm on some combination or accident of light and expression, but beauty absolute in itself and satisfying. She was draped in black so that only her face showed—oval, delicately pointed at the chin, with eyebrows gently and regularly curved over her great eyes. The features were perfect; she was not dark-skinned, but very pale; and very shy, so that she would hardly speak; and in the dim room, in her black gown, with her quiet way and queenly loveliness, she might have been Proserpine imprisoned in the realms of night.

There was a prisoner in the room, as a matter of fact; but she, as is the contradictory way of things, did not look like one, and sat on the ground hung round with every conceivable bead and jewel. She was an Armenian bought by Shaikh Habib at the time of the massacres, and evidently happy in her master's home, where she had been brought up, and presented with a husband and with all the trinkets that adorned her. There are many of these Armenians among the tribes of Northern Syria

225

and Iraq, and they do not seem to be unkindly treated; but I remember one such among the Shammar who had not lost her sorrow through all these years, and would sit and weep day after day in her husband's tent (for she had been married to quite a well-to-do man among them); and when we stayed there she begged us for news of her people, of whom she had heard no word since the forced separation on the Nisibin road in her childhood.

This was the last of our stay with Shaikh Habib. We retired to rest with one of his men stretched across the outside of our threshold to guard us through the night, and next morning, reluctant but threatened by rain, and with the potential remarks of Authority loud in our consciences, returned by the Khalis canal to Baghdad.

Note

EUROPEAN AND AMERICAN LADIES IN IRAQ

REGULATIONS REGARDING RESIDENCE AND TRAVELLING.

An Administrative Order just issued states:

1.—GENERAL.

(i) The grant of visas to European and American ladies and ladies of similar national and social status for Iraq is subject to the following instructions defining procedure as regards residence and movements.

(ii) Ladies who do not comply with these instructions render themselves liable to the cancellation of their visas.

2.—RESIDENCE.

(i) Instructions may be issued from time to time specifying places at which European and American ladies and ladies of similar national and social status may reside without special permission.

(ii) From the date of coming into force of these instructions the cities of Baghdad, Basrah and Mosul are placed in this category but in respect of all other places a special "Residence Permit" must be obtained from the Minister of Interior.

3.—MOVEMENTS.

(i) *Definition.*—(*a*) By "local authority" is meant the Mutasarrif of the Liwa concerned, and in his absence the Commandant of Police.

(b) A lady is said to be "accompanied" when one European or American member of a similar national and social status of the male sex is travelling with her.

(ii) *Rules General.*—Ladies wishing to travel unaccompanied outside any of the cities referred to in para. 2 (ii) should (*a*) obtain the previous sanction of the local authority of the Liwas which they intend to visit; (*b*) arrange that all journeys by road are performed between sunrise and sunset and (*c*) keep to the main roads unless they have obtained the specific sanction of the local authority to do otherwise.

(iii) Ladies accompanied may travel on any of the main roads outside the cities referred to in para. (ii) without special permission with the exception of the special areas for which special rules are defined in para. 3 (iv), subject to the journey being performed between sunrise and sunset.

(iv) *Special Rules for Special Areas.*—

(a) Kerbala and Najaf.—

Ladies wishing to proceed accompanied or unaccompanied to the Kerbala Liwa (i.e. the Holy Cities of Kerbala or Najaf) must first obtain written permission from the Ministry of Interior. Applications can be made to the Assistant Director-General to the Ministry of Interior at the Serai, Baghdad.

(b) Arbil Liwa.—

Ladies, whether accompanied or unaccompanied, require special permission from the local authority for travel within the Liwa.

(c) Kirkuk Liwa.—

Ladies accompanied may travel without restriction on any of the car roads in the Liwa. If travelling unaccompanied they must first consult and get the permission of the local authority.

(d) Mosul Liwa.—

Ladies accompanied may visit Mosul town without special permission. They may enter the Mosul Liwa from Baghdad either via Baiji or via Guwair or Makhlat. Whether accompanied or unaccompanied they must obtain the previous permission of the local authority before visiting Tal Kaif, Tal Uskof, Al Qosh, Zakho, Ain Sifni, Shaikh Adi, Tal 'Afar, Sinjar, Hatra, Aqra, Amadia, and Ser Amadia. All journeys to Hatra must be made direct from Mosul. Two cars are necessary and a police escort must be taken. They must also obtain the permission of the local authority before proceeding by the transdesert routes from Mosul to Syria.

(e) Sulaimani Liwa.—

Ladies, whether accompanied or unaccompanied, proceeding to Sulaimani or Halabja, must ensure that the local authority is aware of their intention and the time of their departure. They must arrange beforehand for their accommodation in both places.

4.—CAMPING.

Ladies, whether accompanied or unaccompanied, should give notice to the local authority of their intention to camp out at night and should be guided by the advice given.

5.—ESCORTS.

Ladies are warned that in some cases the local authority require that a police escort should accompany them—such escort can be supplied at their expense.

6.—EXCEPTIONS.

These instructions do not apply to passengers travelling on the Kirkuk—Nisibin Railway Convoys, or by recognized cross-desert transport companies plying between Baghdad and Syria.

Minister of Interior.

NOTE.—For the convenience of travellers in Baghdad, applications under these rules may be made direct to the Assistant Director-General of the Ministry of Interior.

A letter to the Baghdad times

THE SOCIAL STATUS OF LADIES.

A PROBLEM FOR THE AUTHORITIES.

To the Editor.

Sir,—In your paper of Oct. 18th you give a detailed though possibly not a comprehensive list (for that would be beyond any human ingenuity) of things that Ladies in Iraq are not supposed to do.

As an earnest and interested enquirer, may I ask for a few further details?

What, exactly, is meant by a "Similar Social Status"?

It is quite difficult enough, in these days, to define a "Lady," but when she has to have a Similar Social Status as well, it becomes impossible without the help of some lucid official definition.

It is rather important, for I gather from the above-mentioned document that if she is neither a Lady, nor possessed of any Social Status in particular, the authorities do not really mind what becomes of her, and she may pic-nic off the main road without notifying the Ministry of Interior.

I take it that before accepting any invitation that may be made, she must also be very careful to look into the adequate Social Status of the European or American who is to accompany her. This is always judicious, especially when travelling abroad—and cannot be too carefully recommended. But a few hints as to how to decide on such a matter at short notice, would be very useful. Socks and ties and an Oxford manner are apt to be misleading, and a short test that could be applied rapidly whenever any excursion or expedition is under discussion, appears to be highly advisable.

As to main roads—they are not always recognizable in this country. They suddenly turn into a flat desert and one finds that one is off them. Under such circumstances, is a real lady, with Social Status and all, liable to have her visa cancelled?

Yours,

ENQUIRER.

Mildred Cable and Francesca French

The Gobi Desert
(1942)

I saw no change in the lake among the dunes, for there was nothing there to fix the passage of time, and the Abbot and his assistants followed such an even tenor of life that days, months and years slipped by unnoticed, marked only by the monotonous procession of the seasons. My two companions and I were the only guests at the rest-house, and the Abbot understood at once that we had come for quiet after the long pilgrimage, and gave us our choice of the rooms. "You can rest here," he said, "visitors are few these days, for all are busy in the fields and no one will disturb you."

That evening I walked round the margin of the lake. It was full moon and the place had that intense quality of stillness which is peculiar to moonlit nights. The clear-cut ridge of the high dune, reflected in the water, divided its surface transversely, leaving half of it dim and showing the remainder bright with a silvered reflection. Where the pavilion steps dipped to the water's edge there was a faint sound of lapping wavelets, and here I sat for long, stilling my heart to a calm which would be in accord with the outer quiet.

The daylight hours at Crescent Lake, though not quite so silent as the night, were no less tranquil, for the blue heavens above, the reflecting lake below, the encircling sand-hills, the quiet rest-house, and complete absence of news from the outer world, combined to create an atmosphere where solitude brought thought to fruition, and in which it was possible to review the events of the past years. The simplicity of the guest-house did not supply a chair, so I scooped out the sand to make a restful seat for myself and reclined on its soft, yet resisting surface.

I thought myself back to those days so long past when, turning away from the ordinary conditions of busy life in a Chinese city, I had set myself to learn the habits of those who dwell in deserts. Released from a whole round of trivial activities which were an inevitable part of normal life, I immediately came into a new environment. No neighbours would now be concerned about me, none of my friends would even know where I was, and henceforth my place would be with a moving caravan. In that hour I felt as detached as an early mariner must have felt when his small sailing-vessel lifted anchor and set off alone across the boundless ocean. My course would now lie over a sea of sand, and as the seafaring man stands at the prow of his vessel and looks across the trackless waste of waters, so I stood on a small desert eminence and looked over the boundless plain.

My first feeling had been a sense of liberation which was intoxicating. I threw up my arms as if to take flight, saying: "I have the freedom of the spaces and I can go anywhere"; but even as I looked, my eye caught the faint trace of a scarcely perceptible line leading across the waste and I realised that this was the desert foot-track, a path trodden out through the ages by countless wayfarers. The dust-storm might cover it over for a time, but its ancient foundation would slowly and surely re-emerge. As I looked at the path I became conscious that never before had my feet been held to so narrow a way.

Between the high banks of the old cart-road on the other side of Kiayükwan I was safely enclosed, and the age-abiding ruts of the highway made it impossible for me to lose my direction. But on this foot-track I was free and uncontrolled; yet it was a matter of life and death to leave the faint path so lightly traced by the feet of those who had been treading it for generations. It needed great care to keep to that one line, so illusive that at a distance I questioned if it were a road at all, and only as I followed it step by step was I aware that there was something different on that one line from the surrounding sandy space, something which showed that others had walked there before me. Many had left it, and their bleaching bones witnessed to their folly. I saw that the desert is not a trackless waste but a wilderness with a path through it, and that where the traveller finds no sign of a track he has missed the way and the only hope of life for him is to retrace the line of his own footsteps until he rediscovers the path at the point where he stepped aside from it.

Just because I had the whole desert spaces to myself, and there was no compulsion to keep me in the straight and narrow way, the greater was the need for vigilance. To keep my feet to so exacting a path while my eyes were sweeping such limitless horizons, this was discipline. I was free to enjoy the spaces and the liberty, everything was mine, but enjoyment was only possible so long as my feet kept steadfastly to the one track. If I once left it, confusion and anxiety, leading to terror, would be my fate. Was this what Christ meant, I wondered, when He spoke those severe words: "Narrow is the way which leadeth unto life"? If so, then I began to see that the acceptance of a severe rule of life is an integral part of the absolute freedom which is theirs whom He makes free.

Another form of discipline also met me. In the old days of easy travel, how often I broke the stage at the half-way house. "Unhitch the beasts, we will go no farther today," was a common order; but on these great journeys, being committed to my stage, I must make it through heat, cold or blizzard, from early dawn till dark or even through the night. There could be no turning back, nor was any provision made for the procrastinating, the slack, the feeble or the purposeless traveller.

As time went on the charm of wide plains, the sweep of distant horizons, the austerity of silence and solitude, increasingly attracted me. Long uneventful stages were not now something to be endured as a necessary means of reaching a goal beyond the tedious waste, but were desirable in themselves, and I ceased to crave for rapid transit which would obliterate the spaces by mechanical means, for these very spaces now meant so much to me that I valued them intensely for their own sake. Night travel, which had been rather terrifying at first, became a spiritual and mental refreshment. For the first time in life I was in a position to "consider the heavens" from the hour when the too dazzling sun sank below the horizon until it reappeared to blind me once more with the confusing glitter of the mirage.

Desert dwellers have keener sight than other men, for looking out over wide spaces has adjusted their eyes to vastness, and I also learnt to turn my eyes from the too constant study of the minute to the observation of the immense. I had read about planets, stars and constellations, but now, as I considered them, I realised how little the books had profited me. My caravan guide taught me how to set a course by looking at one constellation, to check the progress of the night by observing the shifting position of others, to recognise the succession of morning and evening stars, and to observe the seasons by the place of Orion in the heavens. The quiet, forceful, regular progress of these mighty spheres indicated control, order and discipline. To me they spoke of the control of an ordered life and the obedience of a rectified mind which enables man, even in a world of chaos, to follow a God-appointed path with a precision and dignity which nothing can destroy.

My guide also taught me another lesson, and that was how to walk by starlight. At first I stumbled and hurt my feet among the stones, but I saw that he walked as quickly, as securely and as freely by night as by day. Then I realised that he had used his daylight powers of sense to train the more subtle instinct which served him in the dark, and gradually I too learnt the art of training and then trusting my instincts until I also felt secure in the clear darkness, which is the only darkness that the desert knows. I remembered a wise word spoken by an old prophet concerning a man who was faithful and obedient yet who walked in darkness and had no light. Surely, like the desert wayfarer who walks securely by starlight, that man had learnt obedience and quick response in days of normal experience, and when dark hours came he walked confidently, his heart stayed upon God and relying on the certainties which he had proved in the hour of clear vision.

I recalled my early fears when the uncanny loneliness of the night made me shudder as I realised the utter isolation of our solitary way. We had embarked on an enterprise of which our most experienced Chinese friends spoke only in terms of warning; the natural shrinking from such loneliness, however, soon became a thing of the past, and those particular fears ceased for ever directly I realised that they were but the mock armaments of a foe with no power really to hurt, but who, as master in the region of fear, tries to dominate through frightening suggestions.

If, as those soldier-boys at Kiayükwan had so confidently declared, the Gobi is the haunt of demons, then the night should have been the time when their presence was most real, yet in fact it was more by day than by night that the word *kwei* (demon) was on the driver's lips, and most often it was the desert dust-spout which provoked it. However breezeless the day, somewhere on the horizon a slender spiral of sand would rise, move, circle, walk across the plain, leave the earth and vanish in the sky. Sometimes the whole desert floor was alive with them. At a distance they seemed insignificant, but close at hand they were fearful in their cyclonic force. Travellers call them dust-spouts from their likeness to an ocean water-spout, but the desert dweller, certain that these waterless places are peopled by *kwei*, calls them dust-demons. The pillar of sand gives the impression of an invisible being daintily folding a garment of dust round its unseen form. Some whirl from left to right, and some from right to left. "This one is the male and that one the female *kwei*," said the men; "you can distinguish them by the way they fold the dust cloak around them, right to left or left to right; see how they come in pairs."

The couple came gliding across the plain in our direction, then suddenly turned aside, passing quite close, yet enveloped in such a narrow whirlwind that the curtains of the cart scarcely moved, though we saw sand and stones lifted high from the ground. A laden camel can scarcely resist the full force of a dust-spout, and when I was caught in the fringe of one, it nearly swept me off my feet.

The scientific mind of the Westerner studies the phenomenon with a view to understanding the atmospheric conditions which cause it, but the oasis man who lives and dies among desert scenes believes that waterless places are peopled by spirits who desire to be reclothed with flesh. "The best for the demon," they say, "is when a living human will let himself be possessed, but, failing this, the *kwei* uses the dust from which flesh is made as cover for its nakedness."

The spirit which agitates the long night hours uses fear as its weapon, but the demon of noon is the demon of discouragement. When the chill of night is dispelled by the sun's rays the heat quickly grows in intensity until the midday hour brings unutterable weariness to every member of the caravan. The landscape itself seems to take on a metallic and inimical aspect, and every hill and boulder is rimmed with a yellow aura which gives a hard and repellent outline to the unfriendly scene. The expectant joyousness of the morning start has faded away, pleasant anticipation of the journey's end is still too far ahead to be any consolation, and although half the stage is accomplished yet there is as much still to cover as lies behind, so the half-way line brings no sense of exhilaration. This is the moment when the noonday demon has power to transmute physical exhaustion into such weariness of spirit as drains all joy from service, leaving only stern duty to issue orders. Inertia invades beasts as well as men, and it is useless to urge flagging powers to greater effort. This, however, is no new difficulty to the caravan *bash*, and experience has taught him how to meet it. A halt must be called and a pause allowed in which to release tension and recover poise. In the desert there can be no rest without escape from the direct rays of the sun, the glare and the scorching heat, therefore some shade must be secured. The shadow of a rock is best, but where there is no rock there may be a man-built landmark made of desert clay, which throws reliable shade. Sometimes there was only the plain and its uncompromising nakedness, then the desert guide taught me how to use the shadow of my own cart and seek refuge between its high wheels. A brief period of rest for man and beast sent the caravan on its way renewed in strength and courage. The noonday demon had been overcome by recognising the noontide right to relax.

The still days when dust-demons walk abroad are good for caravans on the march, but sooner or later the time comes when the camels, alert as a barometer to atmospheric changes, show signs of uneasiness and become restive. The driver knows the indications and scans the horizon for signs of the coming storm, then moves among his animals, tightening ropes and securing packs. Before long there is a distant roar, and a cloud like rolling smoke with a livid edge advances and invades the sky, blotting out sun and daylight; then suddenly the sand-storm breaks on the caravan. No progress is possible and human beings shelter behind a barrage of kneeling camels from the flying stones and choking sand. When such a blinding storm is in progress there is no indication by which to find the way, and the only safe course is to stay still until it has exhausted itself by the surcharge of its own violence. It is a stirring of earth's surface which blots out the light of day, robs the atmosphere of its purity, blurs the outline of tracks and landmarks and takes all sense of direction from men, making them helpless to use even their natural powers of orientation. It cannot be overcome by resistance, and those who dissipate energy in fighting it will inevitably be exhausted by its fury. The camel-driver is too wise to waste strength in fight and, following the instinct of the camel that kneels in order to offer less resistance, he learns to shelter till the terrible blast passes over. Such a storm will not last many hours, and as soon as it has spent itself the sun reappears in a serene sky, the violently disturbed sand and stones sink to their own place, and the caravan can continue its journey.

Had I been without an experienced guide I should certainly have been deceived when I first heard that strange illusory voice calling for help, of which so many travellers have spoken.

"Halt," I said, "there is someone calling!"

"There is no one calling," said the *bash*, "and there is no reason to halt."

"Cannot you hear?" I persisted. "Someone is calling from among the dunes."

"Never listen to those voices," he replied. "It is not a man's cry, and those who follow it may never come back to the caravan. We must push on." He urged the beasts forward and refused to listen. As he trudged ahead he spoke again: "Those voices are heard all over Gobi, but are worse in the Desert of Lob. One night when I was travelling there I got separated from my caravan. I heard a shout and the sound of camel-bells which I tried to overtake for hours. Then the moon rose and I saw there were no recent tracks of camels, so I halted, and turned back, but something held me and the voice still called. At last, with a great effort I retraced my steps to where I could see the tracks of our camels leading off in another direction. It was a strange experience, but as soon as I was on the right road those devilish voices ceased, and by midday I caught up with the caravan once more. They nearly had me that time, as they have had many others."

"What then," I asked, "are those strange voices which I heard?"

"The people of Lob call them *Azghun*," he replied, "and say that it is a *kwei* which lives among the sand-hillocks and sometimes takes the form of a black eagle. If travellers listen, it leads them away to waterless places where they perish."

Dust-demons, phantom voices with their insistence, always trying to turn travellers out of the way—it sounded so fantastic that at first I was inclined to dismiss it all with an incredulous smile, but something in the subconscious arrested me, and I repeated aloud those words: "When an evil spirit has left a man it roams about in the desert, seeking rest." I had to acknowledge that they were spoken by the only One Who really knows, so I thought on those words and kept silence.

It seemed as though the pastime of those demons was to make sport of the few lonely human beings who ventured into the desert, by encircling them with every manner of deception.

By night, lights which were like flames from a camp-fire played on the horizon, but no one has ever located them or come any nearer by following them. Watching my two companions walking ahead of the caravan one day, I was amazed to see four people where I had believed there were only two. My eyes saw something which my reason refused to accept. I overtook them and there were but two: I dropped back, and again there were four. Thus do the refractions of desert light shake confidence in the powers of discernment and call for a new standard of discrimination in which things seen with mortal eye are not to be relied upon, whereas the things which are relied on may be contrary to the evidence of the senses.

Mirage is the desert traveller's constant companion and his perpetual torment. As

233

soon as the sun is high above the horizon, the sand begins to glitter like water and appears to move like wavelets, while the clumps of camel-thorn look like tall bushes or stunted trees, and seem to be set by the edge of a lake. All through the day this illusion persists, and not until near sunset does the mirage vanish, the sand cease to glitter, and the landscape show itself for what it really is, a dull grey surface. Even the old traveller must never reckon himself free from the snare of illusion. On one occasion we were to spend a night in a Qazaq tent, but it was autumn, and the coarse desert-grass grew rank and hid the encampment. In the late afternoon the carter gave the cry: "*Dao-liao!*" (We have arrived), and, sure enough, there were the tents, the herds and the pasturing flocks. A man hurried on to prospect, and we urged our tired beasts to further effort. In an hour's time the tents, herds and pastures, though still there, were no nearer, and when darkness fell the voice of our man was heard shouting: "We are lost! I cannot find any *yurts*. We must stay here till morning." In the straight clear light of dawn we saw the plain in its true aspect; there were no tents, no cattle and no water in sight. Not till the following sunset did we reach the encampment.

How terrible if in this realm of illusion where that which seemed real was not true, and where true things appeared false, I were left to find my way without a guide. Never could I hope to disentangle the web of deception, and free both mind and sense from its impalpable net. In the desert I learnt to detect some of the illusions which constantly surround me on the greater journey of life, and to depend for direction on the wisdom of Him Who is my unerring guide.

Dervla Murphy

Full Tilt
(1965)

GILGIT, 4 June
Never, *never* again will I allow myself to be persuaded to leave Mother Earth, and bounce in a nightmarish way through the Himalayas. If I have to stay here in Gilgit until August, waiting for the pass to open, I am *not* going back in that unspeakable little plane over that monstrous route to Pindi. I had expected the flight to be fairly blood-curdling but it was beyond my worst imaginings.

I got to the airport at 1.30 p.m. and after the six-mile cycle run out from the city I needed to drink every drop in my six-pint water-bottle. Today was the hottest yet, with the sky an ugly colourless arc and the sun fiendishly scourging the city and its surrounding dust-suffocated plain.

There were only two other passengers waiting on the verandah—a couple of young men from Karachi named Mukhtar and Rifat, who thought the combination of a woman and a bicycle flying to Gilgit was the weirdest thing that had ever happened.

"But *why* are you going?" asked Mukhtar.

"To get away from all this," I replied, watching the sweat trickle briskly down my arms and cascading off at the elbows onto my already saturated shorts.

They both considered this reply very witty indeed and chuckled with delight. Mukhtar said provokingly, "You don't like our weather?"

I diverted a torrent of sweat from my eyes and answered savagely, "I *hate* your weather," adding, "but it's the only thing in Pakistan I don't like, and no country can be perfect."

Rifat then ordered a round of Coca-Colas and remarked, in a friendly, reproving voice, "You must know that Gilgit is a very interesting and historical place—it should be taken seriously."

"Yes," I agreed wearily, "once upon a time I had lots of positively erudite reasons for wanting to visit Gilgit, but now I can only think of one moronic reason."

Rifat sighed, "I'm afraid you'll be disappointed," he said, "because Gilgit itself is quite hot." (He was right, as I now know.)

At 2 p.m. a few figures moved lethargically across the tarmac, towards our plane, pushing a hand-cart loaded with supplies for Gilgit—plus Roz. By 2.20 p.m. I was inside the little Dakota which had been standing exposed to the sun for hours, and was so hot inside that I would have fainted if I hadn't been too afraid. Somehow it seemed even more likely that I'd be killed if I was not fully conscious when hurtling through the Himalayas in a contraption like this. As I tied my safety belt, one of the crew handed me a newspaper to distract me from my worries. On the front page I read "Twenty-three killed in Indian Himalayan Air-crash".

We took off punctually at 2.30 p.m., when the heat was rising up so frenziedly from the plain that we fell, rather than bumped, in and out of air-pockets, until I didn't know whether my tummy was in my head or my head in my tummy—but I thought I knew that the next time we fell, we'd fall all the way. Yet at that point I almost longed for the crash; at least my tummy would then remain *in situ*, or, if it didn't, the matter would be of no importance to me.

Soon the plain was left behind and we passed over the terrain I had cycled through on the Azad Kashmir detour. Then this region of brown, rounded foothills and deep green valleys was replaced by a landscape of naked rock peaks, giant glaciers and vast sweeps of loose shale. We were flying so low that it was, in a sense, the next best thing to trekking through this area, which even the hardiest tribes have never attempted to inhabit and which has been trodden by no more than a few of the bravest traders and mountaineers. Yet only in one sense was it the next best thing;

when we passed the 26,000-foot Nanga Parbat, whose triple peak dominated the thousands of snow mountains which stretched to the horizon in every direction, I suddenly became acutely aware that this was the wrong approach to a noble range. One should *win* the privilege of looking down on such a scene, and because I had done nothing to earn a glimpse of these remote beauties I felt that I was cheating and that this nasty, noisy little impertinence, mechanically transporting me, was an insult to the mountains. You will probably accuse me of a tiresome outburst of romanticism—but I'm not sure you'll be right. The more I see of unmechanized places and people the more convinced I become that machines have done incalculable damage by unbalancing the relationship between Man and Nature. The mere fact that we think and talk as we do about Nature is symptomatic. For us to refer to Nature as a separate entity—something we admire or avoid or study or paint—shows how far we've removed ourselves from it. Marco Polo saw it as the background to human adventures and endeavours—a healthy reaction possible only when our lives are basically in harmony with it. (Granted that Roz is a machine and that to be logical I should have walked or ridden from Ireland, but at least one exerts oneself cycling and the speed is not too outrageous and one is constantly exposed to the elements.) I suppose all our scientific advances are a wonderful boost for the superior intellect of the human race but what those advances are doing to us seems to me quite literally tragic. After all, only a handful of people are concerned in the excitement and stimulation of discovering and developing, while millions lead feebler and more synthetic lives because of the achievements of that handful. When Sterne toured France and Italy he needed more guts and initiative than the contemporary traveller needs to tour the five continents; people now use less than half their potential forces because "Progress" has deprived them of the incentive to live fully. All this has been brought to the surface of my mind by the general attitude to my conception of travelling, which I once took for granted as normal behaviour but which strikes most people as wild eccentricity, merely because it involves a certain amount of what is now regarded as hardship but was to all our ancestors a feature of everyday life—using physical energy to get from point A to point B. I don't know what the end result of all this "progress" will be—something pretty dire, I should think. We remain *part of Nature*, however startling our scientific advances, and the more successfully we forget or ignore this fact, the less we can be proud of being men.

During the last fifteen minutes of the flight, however, I had no time for such quasi-philosophical speculations, for by then we had left behind the prosaic world of passenger transport and had entered the sphere of aerial acrobatics. Here the mountains are far too high for a Dakota to fly over them, so we were confined to a rock-strewn gorge which in my opinion is far too narrow for a Dakota to fly *through*. It is said that at this point even hardened air-travellers begin to think of alternative routes back to Pindi. The sensation of looking out to see rough rock-walls apparently within one and a quarter inches of the wing-tips is not a pleasant one. I am assured that there are twenty yards to spare on either side, but I stick to it that from the passenger's point of view this is, morally speaking, one and a quarter inches!

When we came out over the valley we descended so abruptly that I got an excruciating pain in my right ear—it was so severe that I could think of nothing else and forgot to be afraid of the landing, which usually reduces me to a bundle of craven terror. Before I'd even registered the touch-down, Roz and I were being hurled out with the rest of the cargo and I found myself in the charge of a young lieutenant of the Gilgit Scouts who had been sent with a jeep to meet me. Ten minutes later I was being welcomed to the headquarters of the Scouts by Colonel Shah, who obviously thought he had a lunatic on his hands and immediately began to dissuade me from attempting to cross the Babusar Pass with Roz. But fortunately he is a perceptive man and he soon realized that every time he uttered "impossible" my perverse determination hardened. So we changed the subject and discussed the Gilgit Agency from more impersonal angles.

My host told me that the first jeepable track from the Kagan Valley to Chilas was constructed about four years ago and is now frequently used during those three summer months when the Babusar Pass remains open. The arrival of the first jeep in Chilas was an historic occasion. Everyone turned out to see it and with characteristic thoughtfulness the peasants provided a large meal of freshly-cut grass for this strange new animal. They were then quite convinced that a jeep is the offspring of two of those curious creatures so often seen in the sky over the valleys and they assumed that it would be able to fly when mature. This, of course, is not an original story—all over the world primitive peoples react thus on first meeting machines. Nor, to my mind, is it a funny story, though it is so often told as a joke at the expense of "ignorant peasants".

Colonel Shah went on to inform me proudly that work is now in progress on an all-weather jeep road, which, within a few years, will greatly improve communications with the rest of Pakistan—always referred to as "down-country" by the English-speaking residents of Gilgit. You can imagine how unenthusiastically I received this information. Granted something must be done to improve this area's economy—after even a few hours here I can see that for myself—but as usual I fear that the disimprovements will outweigh the improvements when the Twentieth Century comes bustling along the New Road. If only someone could think of a way to utilize Gilgit's natural resources—chiefly a superabundance of fruit—without destroying her individuality! After all, this region has only recently become impoverished and forgotten. Before international tensions made their terrible impact on the ordinary man's life Gilgit Town was an important trade centre on the Sinkiang—India route and was a thriving market for the sale and exchange of Central Asian, Chinese and Indian wares—a sad contrast to its present importance as a Military Centre.

It was very pleasant sitting on the smooth lawn of the officers' mess beneath plane trees so tall and graceful that it was impossible to associate them with their sooty London cousins. An orderly served us with frequent orange drinks to which everyone automatically added quantities of salt, because it *is* hot here, with an average June temperature of 94° in the shade—which I'd consider hellish if I hadn't come direct from Pindi. Behind us, almost overhanging the mess buildings, rose a 9,000-foot mountain wall of stark, grey rock which was repeated on the other side of the narrow valley; it's this confinement which keeps the temperature so high despite an altitude of nearly 5,000 feet. Down the valley snow-capped peaks of over 20,000 feet were sharply beautiful against the gentle evening sky and as the setting sun caught the valley walls they changed colour so that their pink and violet glow seemed to illuminate the whole scene.

While we were having dinner on the verandah a full moon rose and by the time the meal was over the valley looked so very lovely that I took myself off for a walk—to the unspoken disapproval of all those present! Having descended steeply for about half a mile my path turned west along the valley floor, leaving the shuttered stalls of the bazaar behind. Tall mulberry and apricot trees laid intricate shadows on the sandy path and the silence was broken only by the snow-enraged Gilgit River. The sky was a strange royal-blue with all but the brightest stars quenched, while on either side the mountains were transformed into silver barricades, as their quartz surfaces reflected the moonlight. I walked for over an hour and that walk alone made the horrors of the flight here seem well worth while.

My bed for tonight is a charpoy under a plane tree and I've written this by moonlight-cum-cycle-lamplight. Yesterday, as you may have noticed, there was no entry. I should have gone out to watch the Muharram procession at 10 a.m. but I simply hadn't the guts to leave my air-conditioned room—even within it I hadn't the energy to put pen to paper. However, atonement has now been made at the expense of my eye-sight.

GILGIT, 5 June

1 set out at 6 a.m. to climb the mountain directly overlooking Gilgit Town from the south. The path went through a tiny farming hamlet which, if Gilgit were a city, might be described as its suburb, and filthy pot-bellied children collected in groups to stare at me. The Gilgitis are white-skinned (or would be if they washed themselves) though they are of different origins, none of which has been definitely established. Probably some have Pathan ancestors, as Afghan raiders periodically crossed the border in the past, and Afghan traders still bring their camel-caravans over the Babusar Pass during the summer months. A tradition which, as far as I am aware, has no supporting evidence, claims that the valleys were first populated by a detachment of Alexander's army which went astray in the course of his Indian campaign. Despite the lack of evidence there is, of course, nothing inherently ridiculous about this legend, and it is pleasingly romantic. Another theory refers to Arab ancestry—doubtless a lost detachment of the Arab army which invaded Afghanistan in the 9th century—but this theory is supported only by the fact that the Gilgitis carry all loads on their backs, not on their heads as in the neighbouring countries, and such tenuous support invites disagreement more than does the lack of any support for the Alexandrian theory.

I was told yesterday evening that many mutually incomprehensible languages are spoken throughout the Gilgit Agency, and most of them are unwritten. The majority of the people understand neither Pushto nor Urdu, and are of course illiterate, though every village of any size now has its school. However, throughout rural

Pakistan the standard of intelligence of the average village school-teacher is incredibly low and the children's help is needed by their farming parents—a combination of circumstances which makes it extremely difficult to cope with rural illiteracy. Many Western observers find this quite shocking, yet I must admit that it leaves me undisturbed; we have yet to prove that universal literacy as we know it advances the mass of the people in any worth-while direction.

Walking slowly upwards through the hamlet and across the fertile strip of land at the base of the mountain I was again reminded of the Aran Islands. Here too the fields are "made" and enclosed within high stone walls, grassy lane-ways run between the walls, little donkeys carry big loads, the sense of remoteness is strong and the tiny cottages are built of stone—though instead of thatch they have flat stone and mud roofs, laid on wooden beams. At one stage the similarity was so great that if I lowered my eyes from the mountains I could almost hear the music of the Atlantic on the shores of Inishere.

Less than two miles from Gilgit the cultivated land ends abruptly and the steepening slope is covered with large loose stones. Now all around me were jagged brown-grey rocks, and stretches of barren scree, and devastated dry water courses, revealing the savage velocity of melted snows. The only vegetation was a splendid shrub, about five feet high, which at intervals flared up spectacularly in the midst of a wide desolation of grey stones and was so laden with deep pink flowers that from a distance it looked like some mysterious bonfire burning untended.

It was quite a stiff climb to the top and at times I had to go very cautiously indeed. Once I was so "trapped" that the only way up was through a waterfall, where the secure stones offered safer hand- and foot-holds than the loose scree on either side. It was a "thin" waterfall, yet the power of even that comparatively low volume of water astonished me. (By this time the sun was so hot that my clothes were dry in half an hour.)

Just before this I found the corpse of a young man—dead eight or ten days I should think. His skull had been bashed in so I've officially "forgotten" the discovery as I wish to remain on good terms with *all* the local factions while trekking here. My nose led me to the poor devil, who was pushed into a crevice between two big boulders. I notice that rifles are not carried in this part of the Agency but they evidently manage to liquidate each other without them. After investigating I was quite glad to immerse myself in the waterfall!

From the summit I had a magnificent view of a tumult of rough white peaks in every direction—including Nanga Parbat again, triumphantly conspicuous above the rest. On the way down I saw a couple of cave-man types, with long, tangled hair and beards, carrying ice from the glaciers to Gilgit Town. By following them my return route was shorter—but much more hair-raising—and I got back at 5.20 p.m. utterly exhausted and ravenously hungry.

After a nameless but very satisfying meal I went for a stroll around the town. In some stalls of the bazaar goods from downcountry—films, biscuits, toothpaste and the like—are on sale, but they all look excessively fly-blown and cost the earth because of air-freight charges. The townspeople strike me as a surly lot—not impolite or in any way unpleasant, but lacking the frank friendliness which so impressed me in Afghanistan and Pakistan proper. In fact, from the human society point of view it's rather like being back in Persia, except that these people are more uncouth than the Persians—and by uncouth I don't mean spitting on the street or squatting in public, but something deeper inside that governs a man's attitude to others. The actual town has nothing to distinguish it and but for its surroundings would be slightly depressing. Now (10 p.m.) I'm going to bed early in preparation for tomorrow's trek up the valley.

GULAPUR, 6 June

My "military advisers" had laughed at the idea of anyone cycling up the valley, but I couldn't bear the thought of abandoning Roz now so we left Gilgit at 4.45 a.m., soon after sunrise, to attempt the first stage of the trek together, and for a few miles it was possible to cycle—though at little more than walking pace, over a track covered with several inches of sand.

Already, taking advantage of the morning coolness, peasants were harvesting barley, reaping and binding by hand with leisurely movements. The women wear gay, ankle-length petticoats of imported cotton, but the men have homespun trousers and jackets, again recalling the Aran Islands. Gilgit's entire population is Muslim—different sects predominating in different regions—but the turban is here replaced by a soft cloth cap, turned up around the edges, which gives the men an oddly European appearance.

Today's landscape was a series of dramatic contrasts. The valley floor around Gilgit Town showed the fragrant abundance of early summer—fields of trembling, silver-green wheat and richly golden barley, bushes of unfamiliar, lovely blossoms and, most beautiful of all, a rock-plant with tiny, golden-pink flowers, growing so lavishly in the crevices of the walls that it was like a sunset cloud draped over the grey stones. Then the valley narrowed to exclude the early sun until there was room only for the river between the opposing precipices and we were alone in a barren, rough, shadowy world, where nothing moved but the brown flood-waters.

Next the track soared upwards, overhanging the river-bed, and it became so rocky underfoot that I was often carrying, rather than pushing, Roz. At one stage I couldn't get her up an impossibly steep gradient with kit "on board", so I unloaded, carried Roz up, slithered down to retrieve the kit and, as I dragged myself up for the second time, admitted defeat. By now Roz has gallantly carried me through quite a variety of improbable terrains, but clearly she can *not* carry me through the Karakoram Mountains—nor can I carry her through them. . . .

After some miles of this dare-devil upward spiralling the track wriggled around a jutting thousand-foot cliff and I saw, far below, on the other side of the river, a fertile semicircle of land, hidden and tranquil at the base of a snow-capped mountain. A few of the hamlet's farmhouses were visible between willow, plane, sinjit and mulberry trees, growing tall and strong among neat little patches of corn and shimmering young meadows. Sunlight was brilliant on the dark green waters and white foam of a nullah leaping down the mountainside to join the mud-stained river, and through the still, clear air I could hear the faint shouts of men directing the donkeys which were walking round and round on mud threshing-floors.

After this the track descended to river level, before again climbing steeply, and it was almost as difficult to manœuvre Roz down such a gradient as it had been to haul her up. My wrists ached from the strain of holding the brakes while I stumbled against rocks and slipped on the deep sand: I wished then that I'd had the good sense to heed my "military advisers".

Beyond the next pass the mountains receded slightly on our left and for a few miles I was able to cycle across the boulder-strewn moor, though a surface littered with sharp flints kept my speed down. Then, at 10 a.m., trees ahead showed that we were approaching the first hamlet on this side of the river, where the reaction to my appearance was rather disconcerting. Only a few old people and children were about, and the children, after one horrified look, either screamed loudly and buried their faces in their elders' laps, or bounded over the low walls and vanished. The adults, though more restrained, looked no less alarmed, and obviously didn't wish to improve the acquaintance, so I realized that apart from the physical difficulties of cycling here an approach on wheels is psychologically unsound.

Soon after mid-day I met the problem of finding shade—something uncommonly scarce at noon on a bare mountainside. It wouldn't have been too difficult to find a patch for myself but here again poor Roz complicated things as it was unthinkable that she should be left exposed to such a ferocious sun. So for her sake I had to walk further than was prudent, until an overhanging rock offered protection to us both.

Having slept soundly for two hours I woke to find it even hotter than before, though fortunately the track was now partly in shadow. Today's highest pass lay immediately ahead and to prepare for it I had a swim—one of the coldest of my life—at a spot where high, projecting rocks gave protection from the current and where there was a nice little "strand" of soft silver sand between the water and the track.

From the top of this pass I could see the orchards and fields of another village about eight miles up the valley. The descent here was more gradual than most and we free-wheeled slowly down—if "free-wheeled" is the *mot juste* for zig-zagging between boulders! Then, when the track ran level with the river, there was no space left for zig-zagging so Roz and I again exchanged rôles. Near the village a man came riding towards us—the first person we'd met since leaving Gilgit.

Colonel Shah had given me a map which shows that this village is twenty-one miles from Gilgit Town and as I reckon that I cycled no more than one-third of the way it's obvious that the time has come to be disloyal to Roz and temporarily acquire a more adaptable mount.

The food situation here is very grim—an acute scarcity of flour and no tea, sugar or salt left after the winter. Most people are living on goats' milk, eggs and mulberries—not my favourite diet when served simultaneously but this evening I was too starved to fuss. I wolfed five eggs and about two pounds of white mulberries—but stuck at the milk. This is odd as I've so often taken it in my stride before: yet

I suppose five eggs do make an insecure foundation for goats' milk, which so undeniably tastes exactly as a billy-goat smells! Of course, in a few weeks' time, when the maize harvest has been saved and ground, there will be no shortage of flour and by then too the camel-caravans will have crossed the Babusar Pass with this year's supply of tea, sugar, salt and cotton.

I find that the people here are much easier to get on with than the folk of Gilgit Town—who make me wonder if they have not already lost something through their comparatively close contacts with down-country. This village has one tiny shop, in which a tubercular-looking young man sits on the floor chatting with a few friends and surrounded by almost empty shelves: after eight long months of commercial isolation only a half-bale of cotton and a few boot-laces and pocket-combs remain of the winter's stock. Yet to my surprise cigarettes are available, at 6*d.* for twenty, and I'm told that these are flown up regularly, though few other goods are imported by plane—air-freight charges would put them beyond the reach of most Gilgitis. But again I'm experiencing the dignified generosity of the very poor: when I produced money for forty cigarettes the young man looked quite hurt and firmly refused to accept it.

My arrival here caused no less of a sensation than in that other hamlet down the valley. However, this community is better prepared to meet an invasion by bicycle, as some of the older men have served in the Indian Army under the British and two have even been to Italy, so the peculiarities of European women are vaguely comprehended.

The village has a school as well as a shop and within minutes of my arrival the young teacher came hurrying to the rescue. He speaks Urdu, which is of no assistance whatever, and a very few words of English, which is of the greatest assistance. Supplementing these few words with scores of complicated signs, I explained my position and was assured that a suitable horse will be awaiting me at dawn tomorrow and that Roz will be respectfully cherished until I rejoin her.

I'm often astounded by the complicated explanations, discussions and arrangements which can be conducted through signs, even without a single mutually comprehensible word. Admittedly the usefulness of signs varies according to the intelligence of the local population; I found the superbly quick-witted Afghans the easiest of all in this respect. A language barrier does inevitably impede the collection of concrete information and the exchange of ideas, but it really is surprisingly flimsy when one wishes to arrange practical details and in unsophisticated societies it ceases to count where personal relationships are concerned. What can be an embarrassment when visiting Europeans, to whom elaborate signs may seem undignified, actually helps to overcome shyness and awe in primitive homes. When you ask for fried eggs by making noises like a hen after laying, followed by noises like something sizzling in fat, the whole household is convulsed with laughter and not only are fried eggs served, but you are unanimously elected as one of the family.

A local detail which absolutely astounds me is that the women knit heavy unbleached woollen sweaters for their menfolk *on an Aran pattern*. It's unmistakable—and they certainly didn't get it from women's magazines!

During the summer, in river-level villages, every one here sleeps out of doors—either on the flat roofs of their little houses, or in their compounds, if they have them, or simply in village streets or in orchards; my bed for tonight is a charpoy under an apricot tree in the teacher's compound.

Robyn Davidson

Tracks (Australia)
(1982)

As I left the settlement, alone, I was aware only of a flatness, a lack of substance in everything. My steps felt achingly slow, small and leaden. They led me nowhere. Step after step after step, the interminable walking dragged out, pulling my thoughts downward into spirals. The country seemed alien, faded, muted, the silence hostile, overwhelming.

I was twenty miles out, tired and thirsty. I drank some beer. I was about to turn off and make camp when through the beer-hazed afternoon heat came striding three large strong male camels in full season.

Panic and shake. Panic and shake. They attack and kill, remember. Remember now, one—tie up Bub securely, two—whoosh him down, three—take rifle from scabbard, four—load rifle, five—cock, aim and fire rifle. They were just thirty yards away and one was spurting a cylindrical arch of red blood. He didn't seem to notice it. They all came forward again.

I was scared deep in my bones. First, I could not believe it was happening, then I believed it was never going to stop. My ears thumped, cold sweat stuck to the hollow of my back. My vision was distorted by fear. Then I was past it, not thinking any more, just doing it.

Zzzzt. This time just behind his head and he turned and ambled away. Zzzt. Near the heart again, he slumped down but just sat there. Zzzt. In the head, dead. The other two trundled off into the scrub. Shake and sweat, shake and sweat. You've won for now.

I unsaddled the camels and hobbled them close, glancing around constantly. It was getting dark. They came back. Braver now, I shot one, but only wounded it. Night came too quickly.

The fire flickered on white moonstruck sand, the sky was black onyx. The rumbling sound of bulls circled the camp very close until I fell asleep. In the moonlight, I woke up and maybe twenty yards away was a beast standing in full profile. I loved it and didn't want to harm it. It was beautiful, proud. Not interested in me at all. I slept again, drifting off to the sound of bells on camels, peacefully chewing their cud.

Came dawn, I was already stalking, gun loaded and ready. They were both still there. I had to kill the wounded one. I tried to. Another cylinder of blood and he ran away nipping at his wound. I could not follow, I had my own survival to think of. There he was, the last young bull, a beautiful thing, a moonlight camel. I made a decision. This one of the three would be allowed to live until he did something direct to jeopardize my safety. Happy decision. "Yes, maybe he'll tag along right to Carnarvon. And I'll call him Aldebaran and isn't he magnificent, Diggity, what a match for Dookie. I don't have to kill him at all." I snuck around to catch the camels. He watched me. Now, last camel to catch, Bub. Off he galloped in his hobbles, the new bull pacing lazily beside him. I couldn't catch him with the other bull so close. I tried for an hour, I was exhausted, I wanted to kill Bubby, to dismember him, rip his balls out, but they'd already gone. I took the rifle and walked to within thirty feet of the now excited and burbling young bull. I put a slug right where I knew it would kill him. It did not, and he bit and roared at his wound. He didn't understand this pain, I was crying. I fired again into his head and he sat down, gurgling through his own blood. I walked up to his head, we stared at one another—he knew then. He looked at me, I shot him in the brain, point blank.

Bubby was puzzled. He walked up to the carcass and drank some blood. It was all over his nose, like clown's lipstick, and he threw his lips around. He allowed himself to be caught, I didn't hit him. I walked on.

I entered a new time, space, dimension. A thousand years fitted into a day and aeons into each step. The desert oaks sighed and bent down to me, as if trying to grab at me. Sandhills came and sandhills went. Hills rose up and hills slipped away. Clouds rolled in and clouds rolled out and always the road, always the road, always the road, always the road.

So tired, I slept in the creek and thought of nothing but failure. I could not even light a fire. I wanted to hide in the dark. I thought it was surely longer than two days, I had walked so far. But time was different here, it was stretched by step after step and in each step a century of circular thought. I didn't want to think like this, was ashamed of my thoughts but I could not stop them. The moon, cold marble and cruel, pushed down on me, sucked at me, I could not hide from it, even in dream.

And the next day and the next day too, the road and the sandhills and the cold wind sucked at my thoughts and nothing happened but walking.

The country was dry. How could the camels be so thirsty and thin. At night, they came into camp and tried to knock over the water drums. I hadn't enough to spare, I rationed them. The map said "rockhole". Thank god. I turned off the track somewhere in that haze of elastic time and walked in. More sandhills, then a stretch of gibberflat, wide and dry and desolate with one dead bird, and two empty holes. Some string somewhere inside me was starting to unravel. An important string, the one that held down panic. I walked on. That night I camped in those sandhills . . .

The sky was leaden and thick. All day it had been grey, smooth, translucent, like the belly of a frog. Spots of rain pattered on me but not enough to lay the dust. The sky was washing me out, emptying me. I was cold as I hunched over my meagre fire. And somewhere, between frozen sandhills, in a haunted and forgotten desert, where time is always measured by the interminable roll of constellations, or the chill call of a crow waking, I lay down on my dirty bundle of blankets. The frost clung like brittle cobwebs to the black bushes around me, while the sky turned thick with glitter. It was very still. I slept. The hour before the sun spills thin blood colour on the sand, I woke suddenly, and tried to gather myself from a dream I could not remember. I was split. I woke into limbo and could not find myself. There were no reference points, nothing to keep the world controlled and bound together. There was nothing but chaos and the voices.

The strong one, the hating one, the powerful one was mocking me, laughing at me.

"You've gone too far this time. I've got you now and I hate you. You're disgusting, aren't you. You're nothing. And I have you now, I knew it would come, sooner or later. There's no use fighting me you know, there's no one to help you. I've got you. I've got you."

Another voice was calm and warm. She commanded me to lie down and be calm. She instructed me to not let go, not give in. She reassured me that I would find myself again if I could just hold on, be quiet and lie down.

The third voice was screaming.

Diggity woke me at dawn. I was some distance from camp, cramped, and cold to my bones. The sky was cold, pale blue and pitiless, like an Austrian psychopath's eyes. I walked out into the time warp again. I was only half there, like an automaton. I knew what I had to do. "You must do this, this will keep you alive. Remember." I walked out into that evil whispering sea. Like an animal, I sensed a menace, everything was quite still, but threatening, icy, beneath the sun's heat. I felt it watching me, following me, waiting for me.

I tried to conquer the presence with my own voice. It croaked out into the silence and was swallowed by it. "All we have to do," it said, "is reach Mount Fanny, and there is certain to be water there. Just one step and another, that's all I have to do, I must not panic." I could see what had to be Mount Fanny in the hot blue distance, and I wanted to be there, protected by those rocks, more than anything I'd ever wanted. I knew I was being unreasonable. There was more than enough water to get by on to Wingelinna. But the camels, I'd been so sure they'd do a week comfortably. I hadn't planned on the sudden dryness—the lack of green feed. "But there'll be water there, of course there will. Haven't they told me so? What if there's not? What if the mill's run dry? What if I miss it? What if this thin little piece of string that keeps me tied to my camels breaks? What then?" Walk walk walk, sandhills for ever, they all looked the same. I walked as if on a treadmill—no progress, no change.

The hill came closer so slowly. "How long is it now? A day? This is the longest day. Careful. Remember, it's just a day. Hold on, mustn't let go. Maybe a car will come. No cars. What if there's no water, what will I do? Must stop this. Must stop. Just keep walking. Just one step at a time, that's all it takes." And on and on and on went that dialogue in my head. Over and over and round and round.

Late in the afternoon—long creeping shadows. The hill was close. "Please please let me be there before night. Please don't let me be here in the dark. It will engulf me."

It must be over the next sandhill surely. No, then the next one. OK, all right, the next, no the next, no the next. Please god, am I mad. The hill is there, I can almost touch it. I started to yell. I started to shout stupidly at the dunes. Diggity licked my hand and whined but I could not stop. I had been doing this for ever. I walked in slow motion. Everything was slowing down.

And then, over the last sandhill, I was out of the dunes. I crouched on the rocks, weeping, feeling their substance with my hands. I climbed steadily, up the rocky escarpment, away from that terrible ocean of sand. The rocks were heavy and dark and strong. They rose up like an island. I crawled over this giant spine, where it emerged from the waves, in a fuzz of green. I looked back to the immensity of where I had been. Already the memory was receding—the time, the aching time of it. Already, I had forgotten most of the days. They had sunk away from memory, leaving only a few peaks that I could recall. I was safe.

"The mill will be easy to find. Or the rockhole, it doesn't matter. There will be water here somewhere, Everything will be OK." Panic melted and I laughed at myself for being so absurd, an effect of emotional and physical exhaustion, that was all it was. I was all right. I was going to be all right. The threads bound together and I touched Diggity. "Diggity's here, it's OK. It's too dark to find the mill tonight, Dig, but there's a green patch of roly-poly here, that will make them happy, eh, little one? We'll find the mill tomorrow, the birds and tracks will lead us to it. And I'll give the camels a big drink, but right now I'll make a roaring fire and have some tea and feed you, my little friend."

I slept deeply and dreamlessly, woke early and rose as easily and cleanly as an eagle leaving its nest. There was no trace of the previous day's fatigue, or the previous night's enemy. My mind was rinsed clean and sparkling and light. Everything around me was bursting with life and vibrance. The colours danced and glistened in the crisp dawn light. Early morning birds, hundreds of them. My spirits high, I packed up quickly, expertly even, like a precision machine. I felt bigger somehow, expanded. I walked a hundred yards around the corner, and there was the mill. The camels drank, Diggity drank and I had a freezing invigorating bath.

About half a mile from the mill, I walked slap bang into a herd of forty camels. The gun came out smoothly and quietly. I had watched them descend like quiet ghosts, from their drinking spot high up in the hills. I looked at them, and they looked at me, sharing the same path. I knew I wouldn't have to shoot this time, but play it safe, that's the rules of this particular game. I smiled at them. They were more beautiful than I could describe. The big boss bull kept them slightly ahead, and glanced back constantly, to size up the situation. They stopped, I stopped—impasse. I shouted, hooted and laughed at them. They looked faintly quizzical. I waved my arms in the direction of the big bull and said, "Shoo . . ." in a loud and authoritative shout. He looked infinitely bored. I fired some shot-gun pellets into the air and he recognized that sound. He rounded up his family, nipping at their heels, and they gathered momentum, until forty beautiful wild free camels were bucking and galloping down the valley into an echo and a vortex of dust, and then they were gone. I was remembering exactly who I was now.

That night, I was about to turn in when I heard cars purr in the distance. Such a foreign, incongruous sound. I didn't need them any more, didn't want them. They would be an intrusion. I was even slightly afraid of them, because I knew I was still half crazy. "Yea or nay for human company tonight, Dig? Well let's let the fire do the talking. But will I make sense to them? What if they ask me questions? What will I say? Best thing is just to smile a lot and keep the trap shut, eh, little dog, what you reckon?" I fossicked around in my head, trying to find the pleasantries of conversation that had been blasted into fragments by the previous week's experience. I muttered them to Diggity. "Oh god, they've seen the fire, here they come." I checked myself nervously for signs of dementia.

Aborigines. Warm, friendly, laughing, excited, tired Pitjantjara Aborigines, returning to Wingelinna and Pipalyatjara after a land rights meeting in Warburton. No fear there, they were comfortable with silence. No need to pretend anything. Billies of tea all round. Some sat by the fire and chatted, others drove on home.

The last car, a clapped-out ancient Holden, chug-a-chugged in. One young driver, and three old men. They decided to stay for the night. I shared my tea and blankets. Two of the old men were quiet and smiling. I sat by them in silence, letting their strength seep in. One I especially liked. A dwarfish man with dancing hands, straight back, and on his feet, one huge Adidas and one tiny woman's shoe. He handed me the best bit of his part-cooked rabbit, dripping grease and blood, fur singed and stinking. I ate it gratefully. I remembered that I had not eaten properly for the past few days.

The one I didn't like so well was the voluble one who could speak a little English and knew all about camels and probably everything else in the world as well. He was loud, egotistical, not composed like the others.

Early in the morning, I boiled the billy and started to pack up. I talked to my companions a little. They decided that one of them should accompany me to Pipalyatjara, two days' walk away, to look after me. I was sure it was going to be the talkative one, the one who spoke English, and my heart sank.

But as I was about to walk off with the camels, who should join me but—the little man. "Mr Eddie," he said, and pointed to himself. I pointed to myself and said "Robyn", which I suppose he thought meant "rabbit", since that is the Pitjantjara word for it. It seemed appropriate enough. And then we began to laugh.

[. . .]

A few days later. Well, a few days ago in your time that is. In my time, I could just as well say I wrote that tomorrow or a thousand years ago. Time ain't the same out here you know. Maybe I've gone through a black hole. But let's not get involved in time concepts—I could really lose the thread doing that.

Today was a wham-bammer of a day—still is in fact. Although now as I stare out at the glinting gibbers and dead trees . . . but let me begin at the beginning.

Today began like most others except there were clouds in the sky. Two in fact, just pinkly peeping over the northern horizon. Rain, I think, was the first thing I thought as the first light slithered under my eyelids and blankets. The clouds evaporated in seconds though, and the next thing I thought was, "I can't hear my camel bells." You're right, mountain-man, the camels had evaporated also. Well, two had anyway, and the other one, I was soon to discover, didn't evaporate because he couldn't walk.

A very wise friend in Alice once said to me, "When things go wrong on the track, rather than panic, boil the billy, sit down and think clearly."

So I boiled the billy and I sat down and I went through the salient points with Diggity.

1 We are 100 miles from anything.
2 We have lost two camels.
3 We have one camel who has a hole in his foot so big you could curl up and go to sleep in it.
4 We have enough water for six days.
5 My busted hip is still intolerably painful.
6 This is a god-awful place to spend the rest of our lives, which according to my mathematical calculations will be about a week.

So, having tidied all that up, I panicked. Many hours later, I found my lost beasties and brought them back to the fold. They were chastened. That only left the problem of the cripple. Now, Dookie is normally a quiet, reserved, dependable kind of fella. But when he has a hole in his foot, he changes into a raging demon. Well, he struck, he kicked, he twisted, he snarled, he vomited, he rolled, he gawped and he gurgled, and finally I had to truss him up like a turkey to get at his foot, which sounds easy on paper but I swear I lost a gallon of sweat in that struggle. And remember how I was saying before (salient point 5 I think) about my poor old hip, the poor old hip that's dislocated in about 7 places, well, isn't it always the way, *that* was the hip Dookie got with his front leg. But, to cut a long grumble short, I got him down, I tied him up, and I gouged four sandhills and six boulders out of that hole in his foot, and I packed it with cotton wool and terramycin, and I covered it with a patch, and I kissed it all better and at last we got under way.

Sweet holy Jesus, mountain-man, there's a herd of camels coming into my camp RIGHT NOW. As I write. There's absolutely nothing I can do, so I'm writing to still my panic. Why oh why does this happen to me. Looks OK, no bulls with this lot thank heavens. But I have my rifle loaded just in case. You know, the rifle that doesn't work. Well you never know, miracles can happen. Now, where was I. Got to write because I'm feeling desperate. OK, left camp about midday and then I came to the most beautiful place I've ever seen—Mungilli claypan.

Let me try to describe it to you. You come down an incline and suddenly you're in another country. There is shade everywhere and the sand is soft salmon pink. Giant ghost gums glisten and sway and there are birds tweeting and warbling. On the right, like a tidal estuary that hasn't seen the sea in aeons, is the claypan. It's empty and flat and rimming it all round are low swells of dunes and trees and red-berried salt-bushes. Some of the trees have smooth pink trunks, like shot silk, which glow crimson in the evening sun, and their leaves are deep deep shining green. Now, I know most people would drive through that three miles of heaven and not even gasp, let alone pull out the prayer mat, but it sent ripples to the pit of my stomach. I wish I could explain it to you. What a piece of country—so moving, so subtly powerful. Didn't stop long though. Dookie's foot-hole was growing in my consciousness like a triffid in the tropics.

So now I am here, one ear cocked for the burbling of bull camels (where there are mums there are usually dads, unfortunately).

Funny thing about this trip you know. One day it has me flying through the clouds in ecstasy (although, having been to the clouds, I can honestly say they're a nice place to visit but I wouldn't want to live there, the cost of living's too high) and the next day . . .

Now, as I stare out at the glinting gibbers and dead trees, if you want me to be perfectly truthful, mountain-man, and this is just between you and me, and I wouldn't want it getting around, I'm just a weensy bit tired of this adventure. In fact, to be quite honest, fantasies are beginning to worm their way between the spinifex clumps, skeletons and rocks—fantasies pertaining to where I'd like to be right now.

Somewhere where cool clover comes almost to your crutch, where there are no tidal waves, tai-funs, stray meteors, camels, nasty night noises, blaring, thrumming, cancer-producing sun, no heat shimmer and raw rocks, no spinifex, no flies, somewhere where there's lots of avocados, water, friendly people who bring cups of tea in the morning, pineapples, swaying palms, sea breezes, puffy little clouds and mirrored streamlets. A silk farm perhaps, where you can just sit and listen to the worms spinning money for you as you lazily build wind-chimes for select friends and when you get tired of that you can stroll down to your own huge bath in a little shoji house in your garden and eat frosty pink water-melon cut into exquisite shapes while a six-foot, slim slave slides ice-cubes down your back and . . .

Sorry, sorry Stevie, I was getting carried away.

But you know what I mean.

Christ, right now I'd give anything for a friendly face. Even an unfriendly face. Even a human noise would be nice. Yes, even the resonating base blart of a human fart from behind that dead salt-bush over there would do. I must be crazy, I'm sitting here wondering if I'll ever get out of this alive, wondering if I'll ever see Sydney neon and venom again, writing like crazy to people who only exist in the warped recesses of my memory, who could be all dead, and all I can do is laugh and crack pooh jokes. If I do depart this world out here, let it be known that I went out grinning will you, and loving it. LOVING IT.

4

Adventure and gender

The role of the adventure hero

Gender roles for the British within the colonial context seemed to be excessively polarised, so that masculinity within Africa and India was constructed out of an exaggerated form of the masculine features which were valued within Britain. Character traits such as strength and fortitude in the face of adversity were deemed important as one of the ways of making clear demarcations between white masculinity and "native" males. Manliness seemed to become one of the most dominant features of national identity within the colonial period. But as Stoler and Cooper have argued, perhaps this very excessiveness of stereotypical masculinity is a result of the attempt to assert difference, the separateness and stability of identities in the face of the impossibility of maintaining such clear distinctions (Stoler and Cooper, 1997: 7).

As Graeme Dawson and others have shown, within fictional texts the adventure hero narratorial position within the imperial context is one which is generally reserved for male characters (Bristow, 1991; Dawson, 1994; Phillips, 1997). Female figures within fictional narratives are generally portrayed as passive or are represented symbolically. Novelists such as Rider Haggard (1885) and R.M. Ballantyne (1861), but also travel writers such as John Hanning Speke (1863) and Richard Burton (1894), mapped out the characteristics of this adventure hero role. The following qualities seem to be important: the risking of one's life to perform heroic deeds of national significance, the outwitting of enemies, and the overcoming of physical difficulties and obstacles. Quick-wittedness and an ability to assess difficult situations without reference to authority figures serve to display the ideal form of masculinity for the imperial context. Although very little colonial activity was enacted within the wilderness, the desert or the jungle, the idealised and stereotypical form of colonial masculinity found within adventure novels and travel narratives was constructed against this backdrop. This had the benefit of not only being outside the sphere of colonial authority but also outside the domestic sphere and the values associated with domesticity. Dawson asserts that this leads to a rejection of female "interiority" and that instead novelists focus on "adventure scenarios of male camaraderie, rivalry and contest" where actions rather than thought or consideration are considered to be the true test of "character" (Dawson, 1994: 63–64). It also leads to a rejection of the "home" environment, that is, Britain, such that Britain itself becomes feminised. Consider, for example, this quotation from a Canadian travel book, *By Track and Trail*, by Roper:

> I am determined not to go back to England, to be a drudge in an office, in a bank or something of that sort, the very thought of which disgusts me. Just think of what most of those fellows are at home: they spend one half of their lives at a desk, the other half fadding about their dress and appearance. Why, they are mostly as soft as girls, and know nothing but about dancing, and theatres, and music-hall-singers." (Roper, 1891, cited in Phillips, 1997: 55)

Staying in Britain, in contrast to adventure in Canada, is seen as emasculating.

This rejection of the domestic was important not only in the exploration of Africa, but also in the expansion by white people in Canada and America. Annette Kolodny notes that white male settlers often seemed to be pursuing a fantasy of themselves as "solitary Indian-like hunters of the deep wood" (Kolodny, 1984: 5), whilst at the same time restricting their wives to the domestic sphere; one Wisconsin farmer in 1869 notes: "We could roam and fish or hunt as we pleased, amid the freshness and beauties of nature. As for our wives, . . . from all these bright and to us fascinating scenes and pastimes, they were excluded. They were shut up with the children in log cabins" (cited in Kolodny, 1984: 9).

This role described in this way in novels and travel narratives by men clearly does not determine the way that British men and women behaved within the colonies. However, at least within writing, the role is open to men in a way which is more problematic for middle-class women writers within the nineteenth century, because of stereotypes of feminine frailty and because women would seem to be undermining their gender identity if they described themselves using these stereotypes of masculinity. Furthermore, this stereotypical masculinity is not restricted to the imperial setting, because it is clearly drawn upon by many men and, as we will show, by some women, when writing about non-imperial contexts. Even today, there are many narratives which draw on this adventure hero role, despite its association with colonial supremacy.

The role of adventurer hero seems within the colonial period to be closely allied to the construction of a national subject position. This national subject position is one which is based on the notion of exclusion just as much as it is based on qualities intrinsic to masculinity. Thus, the adventure hero is defined by what it is not: not British female, not male "native", and not British male from any class other than the middle class. Let us consider each of these exclusions in turn. As we noted above, the adventure hero is tested in the world outside the domestic sphere and the qualities which are valued are those which are the antithesis of the stereotypical feminine qualities associated with the "Angel in the House" (Armstrong and Tennenhouse, 1987). Whilst the adventurer is clearly battling for the civilisation of the non-British world, and Christian values are the ones which he is fighting to impose on the "natives", the religious values which are espoused are not those associated with the feminine, but are a more "muscular" kind which interpreted privation and the overcoming of pain as an aesthetic and thoroughly masculine endeavour (Phillips, 1997).

As well as excluding all that is feminine or female, this hero position is also founded on the exclusion of certain stereotypical qualities which are presumed to be characteristics of the "native". As Mrinalini Sinha has shown, this type of masculinist position is constructed in stark contrast to models of "native" subjectivity, such as the Bengali "babu" figure, the scribe who works within the British administration in India, who is seen to epitomise all that is effeminate and weak (Sinha, 1995). The "babu" is presented in many British accounts as a pale imitation of Western masculinity and values, but is seen to be deficient because of stereotypical failings such as perceived dishonesty, laziness and cowardice.

In addition to being defined in relation to other nations, this narrative and national subject position consolidated itself within the nineteenth century partly as an attempt to set the ruling male apart from males of other classes within Britain. The British middle-class male, who within the nineteenth century constituted the majority of the colonisers, was intent on setting himself apart from the lower ranks and from the aristocracy, and he attempted to do this through stressing physical differences. The effeteness of the aristocracy and the physical debility of the working classes are often referred to by colonists, and the importance of physical prowess is stressed, so that they demonstrate themselves to be, in Haggard's terms, "the blood and sinew of the race" battling against nature and the elements, in stark contrast to the "puny pigmies growing from towns or town bred parents" (Haggard cited in Low, 1993: 189). Furthermore, the development of a sporting culture for boys within public schools and for middle-class men as part of a national culture was also intrinsic to the evolution of a particular form of colonial masculinity. R.M. Ballantyne argues in *The Gorilla Hunters* that boys need to take risks and extend themselves physically in order to reach the ideal of masculinity:

> "Boys ought to practise leaping off heights into deep water. They ought never to hesitate to cross a stream on a narrow unsafe plank for fear of a ducking. They ought never to decline to climb up a tree to pull off fruit, merely because there is a possibility of their falling off and breaking their necks. I firmly believe that boys were intended to encounter all kinds of risks in order to prepare them to meet and grapple with the risks and dangers incident to man's career with cool, cautious self-possession, a self-possession founded on experimental knowledge of the character and powers of their own spirits and muscles." (Ballantyne, 1861, cited in Phillips, 1997: 59)

A further example from Garnet Wolsley makes it clear that this risk-taking is an essential part of the construction of a national male identity: "It is the nature of the Anglo-Saxon race to love those manly sports which entail violent exercise, with more or less danger to limb if not life . . . This craving for the constant practice and employment of our muscles is in our blood, and the result is the development of bodily strength unknown in most nations and unsurpassed by any other breed of men" (Garnet Wolsley, 1888, cited in Low, 1993: 190). This sense that national identity is constructed from risking one's life and constantly extending one's physical capabilities plays a large role in male travel accounts. This could not be further from the type of education and advice meted out to young women of the period, which often stressed the importance of their not exerting themselves; instead, stress is laid on taking care of their appearance (Armstrong and Tennenhouse, 1987). Even when more forward-looking commentators recognised the importance for women of cultivating a degree of bodily health, they continued to point out that the feminine image of modesty and self-control should never be at risk. In her treatise, *Womankind*, for instance, Charlotte Yonge, while approving of physical exercise for women, insists that there must be "no usurpation of manhood" in any such activity (Yonge, [1879] 1889: 103). As Iris Marion Young has documented, this focus on appearance and the constraint around movement has had an inhibiting effect on women, leading to a sense of being positioned and restricted rather than being in control of one's own movements (Young, 1989).

The adventurer role is thus difficult for women writers to adopt because of its association with national masculine subjectivities and this sometimes results in fissures within women's writing when elements of this stereotype are included in texts. Occasionally, women adopt these narrative positions only to mock them or to subvert them, and sometimes they are adopted with self-deprecating humour—the fact that it is difficult to adopt this position becomes a source of humour at the narrator's expense. Youngs (1997) has argued that this self-deprecating strategy could in fact be read as paradoxically self-assertive in that it is positioning the narrator in a superior and knowing position in relation to the discourse. However, it seems that it is possible within women's travel writing to include accounts of accidents and incompetence without the use of humour. One of the narrative events which occurs with surprising regularity in women's travel accounts is the description of accidents and setbacks. Accidents are extremely frequent within men's narratives, since they are often employed as incidents where the central character can display his strength and quickwittedness; however, within women's accounts, accidents sometimes are represented without the narrator being shown in a position of power. Instead, the narrator is sometimes shown to be a figure of ridicule. In Mary Kingsley's travel writing there are frequent references to her comic appearance when she falls through the roof of a hut, or falls from a boat. These accounts are often followed by descriptions of laughter that this occasions in the "natives". Isabella Bird Bishop, like Kingsley, carried out feats which could be considered "manly" in their demanding physicality and enterprise, as well as self-confidence. For example, when she is trying to reach Estes Park in the company of a shiftless settler and his wife, in desperation after endless mishaps, she tells them that "I had had much experience of travelling, and would take control of the party" (Bird, [1879] 1982: 71). But at other times she counters this proto-masculine assertiveness by confessions of her inability to manage without the help of a man. This is revealed in her description of the ascent of Long's Peak with "Jim" and two youths: Bird stresses continually that she would never have achieved the climb had Jim not been there to assist her; and after they have finally reached the summit, she adds in a self-deprecating footnote, "Let no practical mountaineer be allured by my description of Long's Peak. Truly terrible as it was to me, to a member [presumably male] of the Alpine Club it would not be a feat worth performing" (Bird, [1879] 1982: 113) (see pp. 193–9). Even for twentieth-century women, this is a strategy which is often employed; in the text included within this section by Ysenda Maxtone Graham, she asserts repeatedly that she was unable to navigate without the help of her male companion and that when he is injured she finds it almost impossible to find her way through the desert to get help. She constantly draws attention to her own incompetence. It is clear that the complexity of certain types of self-deprecation must be acknowledged, but for women travel writers it seems that it is possible to present the self in ways which are not necessarily available to male writers.

Some women writers, however, find no difficulty in adopting these masculine roles and simply construct narrative figures which accord with all the stereotypes of the adventure hero. Alexandra David-Neel, for example, in the extract included in

255

this section, represents herself in complete control of the situations and portrays her companion as in need of her physical aid when he is injured. She portrays herself as pitting herself against the indigenous people of Tibet and fooling them by wearing a disguise. And Mary Kingsley, while sometimes presenting herself as a figure of fun, at other times casts herself in a male role, able to take charge and stronger and braver than the "boys" who are supposed to be her guides. May French-Sheldon also describes great difficulties only to demonstrate that she has the strength of will to overcome them. Other women travellers, though not attempting to negate the weakness or vulnerability attached to their gender, refused to act in ways that were expected of them as women. Both Margaret Brooke ([1913] 1986) and Frances Cobbe (1894), for example, describe their sense of achievement in refusing to capitulate to female fears and in proving that they are able to defend themselves against possible danger. Many of the writers included here also stress the fact that because they were women many people doubted their ability to travel through dangerous regions and to overcome the difficulties that they did.

However, for other women writers, in order to minimise the risks of representing themselves in this masculinist way, some of them portrayed themselves in fairly stereotypical feminine roles. It is evident that one of the roles is that of the incorporated wife who takes her identity and perhaps her definition from the identity of the male to whom she is married (Callan and Ardener, 1984). Women travellers sometimes adopt this position, stressing their dependence on male figures and cataloguing the problems which beset them in travelling: Catherine Traill ([1846] 1989) and Susanna Moodie ([1852] 1986) stress the problems they endured as settlers' wives when their husbands were away. The doctor/nurse and missionary figures are frequently adopted, as these are legitimised roles which allow a certain amount of power without jeopardising gender roles. These roles are available to women who cannot for one reason or another adopt the adventure hero position, or who do not wish to adopt it consistently. That is not to say that the only roles available to females within the imperial context are those of passive femininity. The imperial context seems to empower British women and to enable them to perform tasks which would have been difficult for them within the home context. For example, women involved in the settlement of America and Canada, including Traill and Moodie, frequently displayed qualities of endurance and bravery in the face of very difficult physical conditions—qualities which might be characterised as masculine (see for example the Donner Party letters in this section). Interestingly, the representation of their experiences in this respect shows how it is possible to hold two narrative positions simultaneously—reliant wife and competent individual. However, as Anne Butler argues, in her discussion of the letters of the women who travelled on the Western Trails in America, even though the actions might have been similar, the interpretation given them is often different:

> Although husbands and wives spoke the same language, used the same vocabulary, they did not necessarily share parallel responses to the surrounding new worlds. Their personal goals diverged; their personal fears differed. For men, the economic prize at the

end of the trip diminished the dangers of the road. For women, the overland trip, with its many hazards, intensified ordinary concerns about family safety and survival. (Butler, 1983)

Thus, making global statements about the personae that women adopted in their travel writing is fraught with difficulty; it is clear however that there was a range of different narrative positions within which women could negotiate a subject position to represent themselves.

Disguise

One of the interesting features of colonial masculinity in particular is the way that it often operates through the taking of a disguise. This may seem paradoxical, that in order to assert one's superiority over another nation one must take on their clothing and culture so thoroughly that you can pass as a "native" yourself. It is interesting that although the effeminate "native" male is often a measure against which the masculine British man can assert his own strength and endurance, other indigenous male figures often form the basis of their disguises. As Low asserts, in the context of Africa it is precisely because the British colonial male is pitted against strong warriors who are portrayed as warlike and well-drilled as soldiers that his own position of superior strength is confirmed (Low, 1993). For example, Richard Burton disguised himself as a Moslem in order to reach Mecca, and there is a mythology of male colonial officials disguising themselves as Pathan tribesmen, which often surfaces in fictional texts such as Paul Scott's *The Raj Quartet*, and many others. Thus, indigenous males are not only represented as passive and feminised; it is clear that the "natives" who are considered to be war-like, brave and resisting British rule are those whom the British male will attempt to disguise himself as. Some women travellers also disguised themselves in order to reach territories which were forbidden to Westerners. However, the disguise itself does not seem so intrinsically wedded to the construction of particular forms of gender identity for women. This may be partly to do with the fact that women in other cultures may be restricted in their movements and, for a woman traveller, there may be little to gain from adopting a disguise. Alexandra David-Neel's disguise as an old Tibetan woman does not seem to be the same as the colonial move to simultaneously set oneself apart and inhabit certain types of indigenous desired gendered identities, although for David-Neel, it is clear that disguise involves attempting to deceive the very people for whom she professes such sympathy. In the section on harems, we have also shown how women often took on native dress as an act of reciprocity or at least of cultural curiosity.

In narrative terms, the adoption of a disguise is one which puts the narrator in a position of some power, and there is a great deal of play around the suspense of being discovered. On a continuous basis, the narrator must prove his or her quick-wittedness in fooling others and reaching the goal before being discovered. Thus, a disguise is a strategy which involves adopting a fairly authoritative position, and because of women's position, it may be one which for some women is difficult to adopt.

Danger and dangerous landscapes

An important feature of the adventurer hero is that he puts himself in potentially dangerous positions but overcomes those difficulties. An essential part of femininity is the avoidance of danger. Thus, for women to adopt the role of the adventure hero by describing the dangers that they have overcome is to undermine their own claims to femininity.

For male adventurers there is a sense in which they have to describe privations and difficulties. They travel without the comforts of civilisation, and often describe pitting themselves against inhospitable environments. Often, they describe the sense of "roughing" it in the wilderness in positive terms, endorsing it as character-building, as Robert Ballantyne writes in a letter of 1856:

> "Roughing it" I certainly have been, inasmuch as I have been living on rough fare, associating with rough men, and sleeping on rough beds under the starry sky; but I assure you, that all this is not half so rough upon the constitution as what they call leading an easy life, which is simply a life that makes a poor fellow stagnant, body and spirit . . . I am thriving on it, growing like a young walrus; eating like a Canadian voyageur and sleeping like a top. (Ballantyne, cited in Phillips, 1997: 57)

This type of character-building activity is however not available to those women who wish to appear to be feminine. In this context, the title of Susanna Moodie's book, *Roughing it in the Bush* ([1852] 1986), has an ironic gender resonance.

For British women, certain landscapes, as well as particular situations, are considered to be dangerous and off-limits; for example, whereas it is considered relatively normal for an explorer such as Ranulph Fiennes to cross the Antarctic, and be hailed as a hero, for an all-female exploratory team to undertake the same journey was subjected to ridicule in the media, as if their presence was anomalous. Similarly the female mountain climber, Alison Hargreaves, who died whilst climbing, was reviled for having risked her life because of her responsibilities to her children. Susie Rijnhart's account of her trip to Tibet where her husband and child both die, an extract from which is included in this section, is often described in terms of tragedy and as if Rijnhart herself is in some ways guilty of their deaths (Rijnhart, 1901). Flora Tristan is considered exceptional in describing war in South America and putting herself at risk (an example of her writing is also included here). Simply venturing into uninhabited territories is considered dangerous for females, but mountains and deserts are two environments which are considered by Western societies to be alien to females. Norwood and Monk state of the New World wildernesses that

> It has been a world of men exploring unknown continents, subduing wildernesses and savage tribes, felling forests, butchering buffaloes, trailing millions of longhorned cattle . . . digging gold out of mountains, and pumping oil out of hot earth beneath the plains. It has been a world in which men expected, fought for and took riches beyond computation—a world, indeed, if not of men without women, then of men into whose imaginings woman has hardly entered. (Norwood and Monk, 1987: 5)

Wilderness areas, mountains and the outback regions, have all been portrayed as areas which are antithetical to women. Writers such as Robyn Davidson and Sara Wheeler, extracts from whose work is included in this book, both find it necessary to establish their place as women within these environments. It was a long time before women were allowed to join mountaineering clubs, and also before they were allowed to wear "rational" dress, so that they could climb safely. At the same time, however, to climb a mountain was, for exceptional women such as many of these travellers were and are, a physical goal which they were determined to achieve, perhaps because of their own society's strictures against female undertaking in this area. In extracts both in this section and in "Women and space", women travellers depict their unwavering intent to achieve feats hitherto reserved for male endeavour. For Isabella Bird ([1879] 1983) and Mary Kingsley ([1897] 1982), the challenge of ascent was irresistible and the sense of triumph paramount. In recording how she was "tormented by the desire" to climb the Sasso di Ronch, in the Italian Dolomites, Amelia Edwards also notes the amazed observation of the local people that no women had ever gone up there before (Edwards, [1873] 1986: 181).

In several of the accounts of women travelling through deserts the sheer physical difficulty of the travel is described in great detail. Because of the difference of women's bodies and the sense that menstruation can only be dealt with adequately within settled areas, separation from towns and cities is seen to constitute a problem (Davidson, 1982). The fear of attack when travelling outside settled communities is often drawn attention to in accounts, such as that by May French-Sheldon, ([1892] 1999). When women did assert that they had travelled in dangerous countries, their role as "feminine" was often in conflict with the type of actions which they described. Thus if a woman travelled in a particularly dangerous environment which was difficult physically, it is likely that her claim to having travelled there would be questioned (David-Neel, 1927).

Within the role of adventure hero, there is a specific role which is open to very few, that is, the explorer. As Neil Whitehead has shown, the figure of the man who sets out to "discover" a new country or region is fraught with difficulties (Whitehead, 1996). In some senses, this figure, in the very process of seemingly discovering a region, necessarily has to negate the presence of the indigenous people amongst whom he is travelling, whilst at the same time relying on these people for his survival and for his sources of information. The role of explorer has generally been reserved for males and there have been very few women who have been classified as explorers. As Miller states: "Underlying all the great sagas of exploration was an understanding that the impulse to roam and explore was masculine. The necessary complement to this understanding was the assumption that all women, because of their child-bearing ability, are creatures close to nature, and therefore content to remain enclosed within domestic life" (Miller, 1976: 13). We would argue that rather than assuming that there is a biological distinction between women and men which leads to women not being classified as explorers, it is simply the case that it was more difficult to adopt the roles necessary for this position. Boisseau's analysis of May French-Sheldon shows the way that in *Sultan to Sultan* ([1892] 1999), Sheldon was forced to adopt certain theatrical strategies in order to claim explorer status for herself and in order to be allowed to be a member of the Royal Geographical Society (Boisseau, 1999).

Thus, women travellers have had to negotiate with certain discursive structures in order to represent their travels. The type of narratorial position has been determined by textual histories which privilege the adventure hero over other narrative positions. This is not to assert that women have been restricted in the way that they have represented themselves, for it is clear that perhaps there are more restrictions involved in the adventure hero role itself. Because of the difficulty of adopting this role unproblematically, perhaps women writers have been freed to explore other narrative positions and roles.

Anna Maria Falconbridge

Narrative of Two Voyages to the River Sierra Leone
(1791)

BANCE ISLAND, *Feb.* 10, 1791

My dear Friend,

We sailed the very day I wrote you from Portsmouth, and our passage was unusually quick, being only eighteen days from thence to this place.

The novelty of a ship ploughing the trackless ocean, in a few days became quite familiar to me; there was such a sameness in every thing (for some birds were all we saw the whole way) that I found the voyage tiresome, notwithstanding the shortness of it.

You will readily believe my heart was gladdened at the sight of the mountains of Sierra Leone, which was the land we first made.

Those mountains appear to rise gradually from the sea to a stupendous height, richly wooded and beautifully ornamented by the hand of nature, with a variety of delightful prospects.

I was vastly pleased while sailing up the river, for the rapidity of the ship through the water afforded a course of new scenery almost every moment, till we cast anchor here: Now and then I saw the glimpse of a native town, but from the distance and new objects hastily catching my eye, was not able to form a judgment or idea of any of them; but this will be no loss, as I may have frequent opportunities of visiting some of them hereafter.

As soon as our anchor was dropped, Captain Mc Lean saluted Bance Island with seven guns, which not being returned I enquired the cause, and was told that the last time the Duke of Buccleugh came out, she, as is customary, saluted, and on the fort returning the compliment, a wad was drove by the force of the sea breeze upon the roof of one of the houses (which was then of thatch) set fire to the building, and consumed not only the house but goods to a large amount.

When the ceremony of saluting was over, Captain Mc Lean and Mr. W. Falconbridge went on shore; but it being late in the evening, I continued on board 'till next day.

Here we met the Lapwing cutter. She sailed some time before us from Europe, and had been arrived two or three weeks.

The master of her, and several of the people to whose assistance Mr. Falconbridge is come, and who had taken refuge here, came to visit us.

They represented their suffering to have been very great; that they had been treacherously dealt with by one *King* Jemmy, who had drove them away from the ground they occupied, burnt their houses, and otherwise devested them of every comfort and necessary of life; they also threw out some reflections against the Agent of this island; said he had sold several of their fellow sufferers to a Frenchman, who had taken them to the West Indies.

Mr. Falconbridge, however, was not the least inclined to give entire confidence to what they told us; but prudently suspended his opinion until he had made further enquiries.

Those visitors being gone, we retired to bed—I cannot say to rest; the heat was so excessive that I scarcely slept at all.

The following day we received a polite invitation to dine on shore, which I did not object to, although harassed for want of sleep the night before.

At dinner the conversation turned upon the slave trade: Mr. Falconbridge, zealous for the cause in which he is engaged, strenuously opposed every argument his opponents advanced in favour of the *abominable* trade: the glass went briskly round, and the gentlemen growing warm, I retired immediately as the cloath was removed.

The people on the island crowded to see me; they gazed with apparent astonishment—I suppose at my dress, for white women could not be a novelty to them, as there were several among the unhappy people sent out here by government, one of whom is now upon the island.

Seeing so many of my own sex, though of different complexions from myself, attired in their native garbs, was a scene equally new to me, and my delicacy, I confess, was not a little hurt at times.

Many among them appeared of superior rank, at least I concluded so from the preferable way in which they were clad; nor was I wrong in my conjecture, for upon enquiring who they were, was informed one was the *woman* or *mistress* of Mr. ———, another of Mr. B———, and so on: I then understood that every gentleman on the island had his *lady*.

While I was thus entertaining myself with my new acquaintances, two or three of the gentlemen left their wine and joined me; among them was Mr. B——, the agent; he in a very friendly manner begged I would take a bed on shore.

I thanked him, and said, if agreeable to Mr. Falconbridge, I would have no objection: however, Falconbridge objected, and gave me for reason that he had been unhandsomely treated, and was determined to go on board the Lapwing, for he would not subject himself to any obligation to men possessing such *diabolical* sentiments.

It was not proper for me to contradict him at this moment, as the heat of argument and the influence of an over portion of wine had *quickened* and *disconcerted* his temper; I therefore submitted without making any objection to come on board this tub of a vessel, which in point of size and cleanliness, comes nigher a hog-trough than any thing else you can imagine.

Though I resolved to remonstrate the first seasonable opportunity, and to point out the likelihood of endangering my health, should he persist to keep me in so confined a place.

This remonstrance I made the next morning, after passing a night of torment, but to no purpose; the only consolation I got was,—as soon as the settlers could be collected, he would have a house built on shore, where they were to be fixed.

I honestly own my original resolutions of firmness was now warped at what I foresaw I was doomed to suffer, by being imprisoned, for God knows how long, in a place so disgusting as this was, in my opinion, at that time.

Conceive yourself pent up in a floating cage, without room either to walk about, stand erect, or even to lay at length; exposed to the inclemency of the weather, having your eyes and ears momently offended by acts of indecency, and language too horrible to relate—add to this a complication of filth, the stench from which was continually assailing your nose, and then you will have a faint notion of the Lapwing Cutter.

However, upon collecting myself, and recollecting there was no remedy but to make the best of my situation, I begged the master (who slept upon deck in consequence of my coming on board) to have the cabin thoroughly cleaned and washed with vinegar; intreated Falconbridge to let me go on shore while it was doing, and hinted at the indecencies I saw and heard, and was promised they would be prevented in future.

With these assurances I went on shore, not a little elated at the reprieve I was to enjoy for a few hours.

The gentlemen received me with every mark of attention and civility; indeed, I must be wanting in sensibility, if my heart did not warm with gratitude to Messrs. Ballingall and Tilly, for their kindnesses to me: the latter gentleman I am informed will succeed to the agency of the island; he is a genteel young man, and I am told, very deservedly, a favourite with his employers.

Mr. Falconbridge this day sent a message to Elliotte Griffiths, the secretary of Naimbana, who is the King of Sierra Leone, acquainting him with the purport of his mission, and begging to know when he may be honored with an audience of *his Majesty*.

In the evening he received an answer, of which the following is a copy:

R O B A N A T O W N.

King Naimbana's compliments to Mr. Falconbridge, and will be glad to see him to-morrow.

(Signed)

A.E. G R I F F I T H S, S E C.

Such an immediate answer from a *King*, I considered a favorable omen, and a mark of condescension in his Majesty, but the result you shall hear by and by; in the mean while, I must tell you what passed the remainder of the day at Bance Island, and give, as far as my ideas will allow me, a description of this factory.

We sat down to dinner with the same party as the first day, consisting of about fifteen in number; this necessary ceremony ended, and towards the cool of the afternoon, I proposed walking for a while: Mr. Tilly and a Mr. Barber offered to accompany and show me the island, which not being objected to, we set out.

Adam's Town was the first place they took me to; it is so called from a native of that name, who has the management of all the gramattos, or free black servants, but under the control of the Agent.

The whole town consists of a street with about twenty-five houses on each side:— on the right of all is Adam's house.

This building does not differ from the rest, except in size, being much more spacious than any other, and being barracaded with a mud wall;—all of them are composed of thatch, wood, and clay, something resembling our poor cottages, in many parts of England.

I went into several of them—saw nothing that did not discover the occupiers to be very clean and neat; in some was a block or two of wood, which served for chairs,—a few wooden bowls or trenchers, and perhaps a pewter bason and an iron pot, compleated the whole of their furniture.

In every house I was accosted by whoever we found at home, in the Timmany language *Currea Yaa*, which signifies——How do you do, mother?—the most respectful way they can address any person.

Leaving the town, we proceeded first to the burying ground for Europeans, and then to that for the blacks;—the only distinction between them was a few orange trees, that shaded two gravestones at the former,—one in memory of a Mr. Knight, who had died here after residing fifteen years as Agent;—the other on the supposed grave of a Captain Tittle, who was murdered by one Signior Domingo, a native chief, for (as Domingo asserts) being the cause of his son's death.

The circumstance leading to the murder, and of the murder itself, has been represented to me nearly in the following words:

"One day while the son of Domingo was employed by Captain Tittle, as a gramatto, or pull away boy,[1] Tittle's hat by accident blew overboard, and he insisted that the boy should jump into the water and swim after it, as the only means of saving his hat.

"The boy obstinately refused, saying, he could not swim, and he should either be drowned, or the sharks would catch him; upon which Tittle pushed him into the water, and the poor boy was lost; but whether devoured by sharks, or suffocated by water, is immaterial, he was never heard of, or seen after.

"The father, though sorely grieved for his son's death, was willing to consider it as accidental, and requested Tittle would supply him with a small quantity of rum to make a cry or lamentation in their country custom.

"The Captain, by promise, acquiesced to the demand, and sent him a cask; but, instead of Spirit, filled with emptyings from the *tubs* of his slaves.

"As soon as Domingo discovered this insult and imposition, he informed Tittle he must either submit to the decision of a Palaver, or he would put him to death if ever an opportunity offered; but Tittle laughed at these threats, and disregarded them, vauntingly threw himself into the way of Domingo—while the trick played upon him, and the loss of his son were fresh in his memory.

"The African, however, instead of being daunted at the sight of this headstrong man, soon convinced him he was serious: he had Tittle seized, and after confining him some time in irons, without food, ordered him to be broken to death, which was executed under the inspection of the injured father, and to the great joy and satisfaction of a multitude of spectators."

Not a sentence or hint of the affair is mentioned on the tombstone; the reason assigned for the omission, was a wish to obliterate the melancholy catastrophe, and a fear lest the record might be the means of kindling animosities at a future day.

Now, although I cannot without horror contemplate on the untimely end of this man, yet he assuredly in some degree merited it, if the account I have heard, and just now related to you, be true, which I have no reason to question; for he who unprovoked can wantonly rob a fellow creature of his life, deserves not life himself!

From the catacombs which lay at the south east end, we walked to the opposite point of the island; it is no great distance, for the whole island is very little more than a fourth of a mile in length, and scarcely a mile and a half in circumference.

Several rocks lay at a small distance from the shore at this end; they are by the natives called the Devil's Rocks,—from a superstitious opinion, that the *old Gentleman* resides either there or in the neighbourhood.

Sammo, King of the Bulloms, comes to this place once a year to make a sacrifice and peace-offering to his Infernal Majesty.

From this King Messrs. Andersons hold all their possessions here, and I understand they pay him an annual tribute—but to what amount I cannot say.

The King comes in person to receive his dues, which are paid him in his canoe, for he never ventures to put his foot on shore, as his *Gree Greemen* or fortune-tellers have persuaded him the island will sink under him, if ever he lands.

---

[1] African term for an Oar-man.

I am told at one time he suffered himself to be dragged up to the Factory House in his boat, but no argument was strong enough to seduce him to disembark, for he did not consider he incurred the penalty his prophets denounced while he continued in his canoe; though he could not avoid shewing evident tokens of uneasiness, till he was safe afloat again.

We now returned to the Factory, or as it is otherwise called Bance Island House.

This building at a distance has a respectable and formidable appearance; nor is it much less so upon a nearer investigation: I suppose it is about one hundred feet in length, and thirty in breadth, and contains nine rooms, on one floor, under which are commodious large cellars and store rooms; to the right is the kitchen, forge, &c. and to the left other necessary buildings, all of country stone, and surrounded with a prodigious thick lofty wall.

There was formerly a fortification in front of those houses, which was destroyed by a French frigate during the last war; at present several pieces of cannon are planted in the same place, but without embrasures or breast-work; behind the great house is the slave yard, and houses for accommodating the slaves.

Delicacy, perhaps, prevented the gentlemen from taking me to see them; but the room where we dined looks directly into the yard.

Involuntarily I strolled to one of the windows a little before dinner, without the smallest suspicion of what I was to see;—judge then what my astonishment and feelings were, at the sight of between two and three hundred wretched victims, chained and parcelled out in circles, just satisfying the cravings of nature from a trough of rice placed in the centre of each circle.

Offended modesty rebuked me with a blush for not hurrying my eyes from such disgusting scenes; but whether fascinated by female curiosity, or whatever else, I could not withdraw myself for several minutes—while I remarked some whose hair was withering with age, reluctantly tasting their food—and others thoughtless from youth, greedily devouring all before them; be assured I avoided the prospects from this side of the house ever after.

Having prolonged the time till nine at night, we returned to our floating prison, and what with the assiduity of the master in removing many inconveniencies, my mind being more at ease, want of rest for two nights, and somewhat fatigued with the exercise of the day, I thank God, slept charmingly, and the next morning we set sail for Robana, where we arrived about ten o'clock: I think it is called nine miles from Bance Island.

We went on shore, and rather caught his *Majesty* by surprise, for he was quite in *dishabille*; and at our approach retired in great haste.

I observed a person pass me in a loose white frock and trowsers, *whom I would not have suspected for a King!* if he had not been pointed out to me.

Mr. Elliotte and the *Queen* met us; and after introducing her Majesty and himself, we were then conducted to her house.

She behaved with much indifference,—told me, in broken English, the *King* would come presently,—he was gone to *pegininee* woman house to dress himself.

After setting nigh half an hour, Naimbana made his appearance, and received us with seeming good will: he was dressed in a purple embroidered coat, white sattin waistcoat and breeches, *thread stockings*, and his left side emblazoned with a flaming star; his legs to be sure were *harliquined*, by a number of holes in the stockings, through which his black skin appeared.

Compliments ended, Mr. Falconbridge acquainted him with his errand, by a repetition of what he wrote the day before: and complained much of King Jemmy's injustice, in driving the settlers away, and burning their town.

The King answered through Elliotte, (for he speaks but little English) that Jemmy was partly right—the people had brought it on themselves; they had taken part with some Americans, with whom Jemmy had a dispute, and through that means drew the ill will of this man upon them, who had behaved, considering their conduct, as well as they merited; for he gave them three days notice before he burned their town, that they might remove themselves and all their effects away; that he (Naimbana) could not prudently re-establish them, except by consent of all the Chiefs—for which purpose he must call a court or palaver; but it would be seven or eight days before they could be collected; however he would send a summons to the different parties directly, and give Falconbridge timely advice when they were to meet.

Falconbridge perceived clearly nothing was to be effected without a palaver, and unless the King's interest was secured his views would be frustrated, and his endeavours ineffectual; but how this was to be done, or what expedient to adopt, he was at a loss for.

He considered it impolitic to purchase his patronage by heavy presents, least the other great men might expect the same; and he had it not in his power to purchase them all in the same way, as the scanty cargo of the Lapwing would not admit of it.

At length, trusting that the praise-worthy purposes he was aiming at insured him the assistance of the King of Kings he resolved to try what good words would do.

Having prefaced his arguments with a small donation of rum, wine, cheese, and a gold laced hat, (which Naimbana seemed much pleased with) Falconbridge began, by explaining what advantages would accrue to his *Majesty*, and to all the inhabitants round about, by such an establishment as the St. George's Bay Company were desirous of making;——the good they wished to do—*their disinterestedness in point of obtaining wealth*, and concluded by expostulating on the injustice and imposition of dispossessing the late settlers of the grounds and houses they occupied, which had been honestly and honorably purchased by Captain Thompson of the Navy, in the name of our gracious Sovereign, his Britannic Majesty.

That it was unusual for Englishmen to forego fulfilling any engagements they made; and they held in detestation every person so disposed.

He then entreated the King would use all his might to prevent any unfavourable prejudices which a refusal to reinstate the Settlers, or to confirm the bargain made with Captain Thompson, might operate against him in the minds of his good friends the King of England and the St. George's Bay Company.

The King said he liked the English in preference to all white men, tho' he considered every white man as a *rogue*, and consequently saw them with a jealous eye;

yet, he believed the English were by far the honestest, and for that reason, notwithstanding he had received more favors from the French than the English, he liked the latter much best.

He was decidedly of opinion, that all contracts or agreements between man and man however disadvantageous to either party should be binding; but observed, he was *hastily drawn in* to dispose of land to Captain Thompson, *which in fact he had not a right to sell*, because says he, "this is a great country, and belongs to many people—where I live belongs to myself—and I can live where I like; nay, can appropriate any unhabited land within my dominions to what use I please; but it is necessary for me to obtain the consent of my people, or rather the head man of every town, before I sell any land to a white man, or allow strangers to come and live among us."

"*I should have done this you will say at first*—Granted—but as I disobliged my subjects by suffering your people to take possession of the land without their approbation, from which cause I was not able to protect them, unless I hazarded civil commotions in my country; and as they have been *turned away*—it is best now—they should be replaced by the unanimous voice of all interested.

"I am bound from what I have heretofore done, to give my utmost support; and if my people do not acquiesce, it shall not be my fault."

Here Falconbridge, interrupting the King, said—"The King of the English will not blame your people, but load yourself with the stigma; it is King *Naimbana* who is ostensible to King *George*—and I hope King, you will not fall out with your good friend."

This being explained by *Mr. Secretary Elliotte*, his Majesty was some moments silent—when clasping Falconbridge in his arms, told him—"*I believe you and King George* are my good friends—do not fear, have a good heart, I will do as much as I can for you."

They then shook hands heartily, and Naimbana retired, I suppose to his *Pegininee woman's house*, but presently returned dressed in a suit of black velvet, except the stockings, which were the same as before.

I often had an inclination to offer my services to close the holes: but was fearful least my needle might blunder into his *Majesty's* leg, and start the blood, for drawing the blood of an African King, I am informed, whether occasioned by accident or otherwise, is punished with death [. . .]

Flora Tristan

Peregrinations of a Pariah (South America)
(1833–4)

We left Santa-Catalina on Tuesday 1 April: my aunt, worried about her husband and her household and unable to curb her impatience, was anxious to return home. Besides, everybody said that San-Roman, alarmed at the size and impressive appearance of Nieto's forces, would not dare to advance any further, but would remain at Cangallo until Gamarra had sent him reinforcements from Cuzco. The general shared the opinion of the populace and, still worrying lest Orbegoso should arrive, he chafed at the slow progress of the enemy but took no measures to make ready for him; the monk, in his broadsheet, was already singing songs of victory, while the wits of Arequipa were composing ballads in honour of Nieto, Carillo and Morant and lamenting the fall of San-Roman, all this in a farcical and exaggerated style which reminded me of the Paris street singers after the July Days of 1830.

That same Tuesday, a feast-day, the troops were paid, and in order to ingratiate himself with the soldiers Nieto gave them leave to enjoy themselves, a favour of which they took the fullest advantage. They went off to the taverns to drink *chicha*, sang all the songs I have mentioned above at the tops of their voices, and spent the whole night in drunkenness and disorder. They were doing no more than follow the example of their leaders, who for their part had gathered together to drink and gamble. They were so sure that San-Roman would not dare to advance before he had received reinforcements that they made no preparations and took no precautions; the same negligence prevailed at the outposts. On Wednesday 2 April, while the defenders of the fatherland were still sleeping off the wine of the previous night, it was suddenly learned that the enemy was approaching, and everybody climbed onto the housetops. It was two o'clock in the afternoon; the sun was burning and a dry wind made the heat even more intolerable as it swept across the roofs of the houses blowing dust into the faces of the watchers. Only a person of my intrepid nature could have borne to remain there long. My uncle called from the patio that I would be blinded by the sun, that I was waiting in vain, that San-Roman would not come that day, but I took no heed of his advice. I had settled myself on top of the wall; I had taken a big red umbrella to protect me from the sun, and, armed with a telescope made by Chevallier, I felt very comfortable. As I contemplated the valley and the volcano I let my mind wander and forgot all about San-Roman until I was suddenly reminded of the reason for our being there by a negro who called out to me: "Here they come, madame!" I heard my uncle coming up; and training my telescope in the direction the man was pointing, I clearly saw, high on the mountain next to the volcano, two black lines, fine as a thread, winding their way through the desert in a series of unbroken curves, like flocks of migrating birds.

At sight of the enemy the whole town uttered a cry of joy. Conditions under Nieto and the monk had become so intolerable that people were willing to pay any price to escape from them. There was great rejoicing in Nieto's camp as well; officers and men resumed their drinking and songs of victory, celebrating the funeral of all those they were going to *crush* and *annihilate*. Towards three o'clock Althaus came galloping into the courtyard, and as he saw that we were all on the roof, he called to me urgently to come down. I did so, promising my uncle to tell him if there was any news.

"Ah! cousin," cried Althaus, "never have I been in such a critical situation; no doubt about it, they are all mad out there. Would you imagine it, all those wretches are drunk; not one officer is in any state to give an order, and not one soldier is capable of loading his gun. If San-Roman has a good spy, we are lost; in two hours he will be master of the town."

I went up and told my uncle the ominous news. "I was expecting this," he said. "These men are totally incompetent; their cause will be lost, and perhaps it will not be a bad thing for the country."

San-Roman's little army took nearly two hours to come down the mountain. It took up its position to the left of the volcano on the hill called *La Pacheta*, which dominated Nieto's defences, and was in fact the position Althaus had predicted the enemy would occupy. San-Roman extended his lines to give an illusion of greater numbers, but it was perfectly plain that they were only two deep. He drew up in a square the whole of his cavalry, which amounted to only seventy-eight men: in short, he did all an able tactician could do to make out that he had four times as many troops. The *rabonas* lit a multitude of fires on top of the hill and spread out their gear with so much noise that they could be heard shouting from the bottom of the valley.

But once in view, the two armies were afraid of one another, each being convinced of the superiority of the other. If San-Roman's display of military skill made Nieto fear that his elegant Immortals would be no match for the seasoned troops of his adversary, San-Roman, for his part, perceiving the great numerical superiority of Nieto's forces, began to fear he had been rash, and this made him lose his head. Although a good soldier, San-Roman was no wiser or less presumptuous than Nieto; from the reports of his spies, he thought he was marching towards an easy victory; he even believed it could be won without a fight. Several of his officers told me later that when they left Cangallo in the morning they were all so confident of entering Arequipa the same evening that they had no thought of anything but their personal appearance, so that they would be ready to visit the ladies as soon as they arrived. The soldiers, just as confident, had thrown away what remained of their food, overturned the cooking-pots, and cried: "Here's to the soup at the barracks in Arequipa!"

However, in spite of all their efforts to make it appear that they were busy cooking, the *rabonas* had nothing, not even a cob of maize, to offer their companions, and to crown their misfortunes, they had camped in a place where there was not a drop of water. When San-Roman realised his predicament he gave himself up to despair and wept like a child, as we heard later, but fortunately for his cause he had three young officers, Lieutenants Torres, Montaya and Quirroga, who took command, restored the morale of the soldiers, calmed the rebellious murmuring of the *rabonas*, and set an example of the resourcefulness which every soldier in such circumstances ought to possess by cutting down with their sabres the prickly pears which grow abundantly in the mountains, and chewing them to quench their thirst, after which they distributed them to the soldiers and the *rabonas*, who all accepted them meekly and fed upon them without daring to utter a word of objection. But the officers knew very well that this measure could not keep their men satisfied for more than a few hours, and they decided to risk battle, preferring to die by the sword rather than of thirst. Lieutenant Quirroga asked his soldiers whether they wished to retire without a fight, to flee ignominiously in full view of the enemy and return to Cangallo, thereby exposing themselves to the risk of dying of hunger and thirst in the desert like mules; or whether they wished to make Nieto's braggarts, who were incapable of standing up to them despite their superior numbers, feel the strength of their arms; and the soldiers, who in any other circumstances would have turned tail and fled at the mere sight of such a large force opposing them, acclaimed this warlike speech and demanded battle.

It was nearly seven o'clock in the evening; I had just returned to my post on the roof. Both camps were quiet, and considering how late it was, we assumed that the battle would not take place until dawn next day. Suddenly I saw a figure which I took to be a standard-bearer detach itself from San-Roman's square, immediately followed by the whole of his cavalry; and at the same time Nieto's dragoons, led by Colonel Carillo, advanced to meet them. The two troops galloped furiously to the charge, and when they came within range, there was an exchange of musket fire, followed by another; the battle had begun. I was now aware of a great commotion in both camps, but the smoke became so thick that it hid the scene of carnage from our view. Then night fell, and we remained in complete ignorance of all that passed.

Towards nine o'clock a man arriving from the battle-field passed by the street of Santo-Domingo; we stopped him and he told us that all was lost, that Nieto had sent him to bid his wife retire immediately to the convent of Santa-Rosa. He added that there was frightful disorder among our troops; that Colonel Morant's artillery had fired on our dragoons, taking them for the enemy, and that a great number had been killed. The news spread through the town and everybody was in the grip of panic; all those who had thought they could stay in their homes, terrified at their own courage, now hastened to leave them. They were rushing about like madmen, loaded with their silver dishes and chamber pots of the same metal; one woman clutching a casket of jewels, another a *brasero*, while negresses and *sambas* carried off piles of their mistresses' gowns and carpets. It was probably the first time these black and white countenances had openly expressed all the vileness of their souls. The Indian threatened, the white cringed, the slave refused to obey, his master dared not strike him. Calm amid the chaos, I contemplated with a disgust I could not repress this panorama of all the worst passions of our nature. I spoke to my *samba* just as I always did, and this girl, who was drunk with joy, obeyed me because she saw that I was not afraid. My aunt and I had no wish to enter any more convents, so my cousins went off alone with their children. The tumult of the dreadful scene I have just described was followed by the silence of the desert; in less than an hour the entire population was crammed into the convents, monasteries and churches. I am sure there were not twenty houses still inhabited.

Our house had become the general meeting-place, first because of the security offered by its proximity to the church of Santo-Domingo, and next because it was hoped that Althaus would manage to get news through to Don Pio. We were all gathered in my uncle's study, an immense vaulted room giving onto the street; there was no light, so as not to attract the attention of passers-by, only the glow of the cigars which that evening were never extinguished. It was a scene worthy of Rembrandt's brush. Through the thick haze of smoke which filled the room one could make out the broad and stupid faces of four Dominican monks with their long white habits, heavy rosaries with black beads, and clumsy shoes with silver buckles, with one hand shaking the ash from their cigar, the other toying with their scourge. My aunt was sitting in a corner of one of the sofas, her hands clasped, praying for the dead on both sides. As for my uncle, he came and went from one end of the room to the other, talking and gesticulating in an animated manner. I was sitting on the window-sill wrapped in my cloak, enjoying the double spectacle offered by the study and the street. That night was an education for me. Peruvian society has a character all its own; its taste for the exaggerated and the miraculous is extraordinary. I could not say how many frightening stories I heard that night, embroidered with every kind of falsehood and related with a dignity and aplomb which amazed me, though from the calm indifference with which they were received it was plain that not one of the listeners believed a word of them.

But the story-telling was abandoned each time any news, whether true or false, arrived from the camp. If a wounded soldier, dragging himself off to the hospital, reported that the Arequipans had lost the battle, there immediately arose throughout the room a chorus of recrimination against that *coward*, that *scoundrel*, that *imbecile* Nieto, and loud praise for the *worthy*, the *brave*, the *glorious* San-Roman. The good monks of Santo-Domingo addressed to heaven their heartfelt supplications that the dog Nieto should be killed, and began to plan the brilliant reception they would give the illustrious San-Roman. A quarter of an hour later another soldier happened to pass by shouting, "Long live General Nieto! Victory is ours! San-Roman is crushed!" Then there was wild applause: the good fathers clapped their hands and cried, "Oh, the brave general! What courage! What talent! May that wretched Indian, that *sambo* San-Roman be damned!" My uncle was afraid of being compromised by these impertinent chatterboxes, as ludicrous as they were contemptible; but in vain did he employ all his eloquence to silence them, for it is in the nature of people here to be just as pitiless in their abuse as they are extravagant in their praise.

Towards one o'clock in the morning Althaus sent one of his aides to tell us that there had been no action since eight the previous evening, that the enemy, intimidated by their numbers, had not dared venture at night into unknown territory, that because of Morant's fatal mistake we had already lost thirty or forty men, including one officer, and that an alarming disorder reigned in our camp. My cousin sent me a pencilled note in which he said he considered the battle as lost.

At about two o'clock, feeling very tired, I retired to my room, but as at this stage I was anxious not to miss anything, I begged my aunt to wake me as soon as it began to grow light.

At four in the morning I was on top of the roof: as the sun rose I admired the magnificent spectacle which the domes and towers of the numerous convents and churches presented to my view. The mass of human beings gathered there formed one single whole. There were men, women and children of every hue from black to white, all dressed according to their rank in the various costumes of their respective races, yet at that moment all were equal, because the same thought was in every mind. From all those thousands of breasts arose one single heart-rending cry which moved me to tears. There was no need for me to turn my head towards the battlefield, I could tell that the fighting had begun. That great cry of grief was followed by a deathly silence: the tense attitude of the watchers showed how concentrated their attention was. Suddenly a second cry went up, and from its tone and the gesture which accompanied it I was reassured as to the fate of the combatants. I turned and saw signs of great activity in both camps. I begged my uncle to lend me his telescope, and then I saw officers hurrying from one camp to the other firing pistol-shots in the air, then General Nieto, followed by his officers, went to meet a group of officers from the enemy camp. I saw the two sides mingle in mutual embraces, and this convinced us that San-Roman had just surrendered and that everything would now be settled.

As we were wondering what was happening, Althaus entered the courtyard at full gallop shouting at the top of his voice: "Ho, you up there, come down quickly, I have important news for you!" I was first down the ladder and reached the courtyard before any of the others. I fell upon his neck and embraced him tenderly for the first time; he was not wounded, but, good God! what a state he was in! Always so immaculate before, he was now covered with mud, dust and blood. His features were unrecognisable; his eyes, red and puffy, were starting out of his head; his nose and lips were swollen; his skin was broken and bruised, his hands were black with gunpowder and his voice so hoarse that what he said was almost unintelligible.

"Ah! cousin," I said, my heart wrung, "I did not need to see you in this state to make me loathe war; after what I saw yesterday I think there is no punishment too cruel for the men who cause it."

"Florita, I'm no match for you today, I can't speak; but for pity's sake don't dignify by the name of *war* a farcical shambles in which not one of those greenhorns knew how to aim a gun. Just look at me! Anyone would think I was a burglar! And to put me in an even better humour, my dear wife has hidden everything away down to my last shirt!"

Althaus made the best of things, gulped down four or five cups of tea, ate a dozen slices of bread, and then began to smoke, managing at the same time to grumble about his wife, laugh and joke as usual, and tell us everything that had happened since the previous evening.

"Yesterday," he said, "the engagement was only a *skirmish*, but what inextricable confusion it caused! Luckily the Gamarrists took fright and withdrew. It took me all night to restore a bit of order on our side. This morning we were occupying the battlefield and expecting the enemy to attack at any moment with all the advantage of his position, when instead of that we saw him send somebody to parley who demanded to speak to the general in the name of San-Roman. Nieto, forgetting his dignity and not stopping to think, was all for accepting the invitation there and then; the monk was against it, and the others too. To cut the discussion short, I said: "As chief of staff, it's up to me to go," and without waiting for a reply I galloped off towards the messenger, but he announced that San-Roman wished to speak to the general in person, so as this was all I could get out of him, I went back to the general and said: "If you want my opinion, the only conversation you'll have with him will be bullets: they're always understood." The idiot took no notice of my advice, he wanted to do the generous thing, see his old comrade, his brothers-in-arms from Cuzco; the monk ground his teeth, foamed with rage, but there was nothing for it but to yield to the man he had been hoping to use for his own ends. Nieto shut him up with these words: "Senor Valdivia, *I* am the only leader here." The furious *padre* gave him a look which said: "If ever I get my hands on you, I'll squeeze the life out of you." All the same, not wanting to throw in his hand, he resigned himself to following the tender-hearted Nieto. At this very moment, together with two journalists, Quiros and Ros, they are in conference with the enemy; but as for me, now that I've eaten and cleaned myself up a little, I'm going back to the camp, where I propose to sleep until someone comes and tells me whether we are to fight or kiss and make friends."

The news Althaus gave us spread rapidly through the town and into all the convents. People thought that the interview between the two leaders would bring peace; this hope alone was enough to make everybody happy. The Arequipans are essentially indolent: the cruel agitation they had suffered during the past day and night had quite exhausted them, and they eagerly seized upon the opportunity to recuperate. I was certainly feeling tired myself; I went to bed after giving my *samba* orders not to wake me until the enemy was actually in the courtyard. It was now Thursday 3 April.

Towards six in the evening I was still fast asleep when Emmanuel and my uncle entered.

"Well?" my uncle asked him. "What news do you bring us?"

"Nothing positive; the general stayed with San-Roman from five in the morning until three this afternoon, but on his return he said nothing about this long conference except that he thought that everything would be settled. We knew from what one of the aides told us that the meeting of the two leaders was very touching; they both shed floods of tears over the misfortunes of the country and the loss of the officer Montenegro; they stood over his body and swore by his memory an oath of *union* and *fraternity*. The whole day was spent in exchanging flowery speeches. The Gamarrists are playing the innocent, they are gentle as lambs; while Nieto, more soft-hearted than ever, has allowed San-Roman to send his men and horses to water at the spring of Agua-Salada; he has even sent them food and is treating them like brothers."

Emmanuel persuaded me to visit the camp; my uncle was very willing to accompany me, and off we went. I found the little taverns and Menao's house almost completely destroyed, and the camp in the greatest disorder. From the look of it you would have thought it had been taken by the enemy; the fields of maize were ruined, the poor peasants had been forced to flee, and their cabins were full of the *rabonas*. At headquarters the handsome officers, usually so elegant, were dirty, with red eyes and hoarse voices; most of them were sleeping on the ground like the soldiers. The quarters of the *rabonas* had suffered most: in the confusion Morant's artillery had scored a hit and wrought havoc there. Three of the women had been killed and seven or eight seriously wounded. I did not see the general or Valdivia; they were sleeping.

On our return my uncle said to me: "Florita, I do not like the look of this. I know the Gamarrists, and they are not the sort to give up. San-Roman has some good men on his side; Nieto is no match for them in finesse. If I am not mistaken there is a trap hidden beneath this show of cordiality."

The next day Nieto went to see San-Roman again and sent him wine, meat and bread for his troops. People were expecting the general to issue a proclamation informing the army and the townsfolk about the result of these meetings, but two o'clock came, and still no proclamation appeared. Then voices were raised against this man who had been appointed supreme head of the department by popular acclaim, who for three months had done as he pleased with the fortune, life and liberty of its inhabitants, and who had repaid their trust by giving himself the airs of a president, or rather a *dictator*.

This conduct raised the exasperation against Nieto to its highest pitch: the entire population of thirty thousand souls, forced to abandon their normal routine to cower in monasteries and churches, was impatient to know how things stood. The small number of people remaining in their homes, as we had done, were extremely uncomfortable, as everything was hidden away in the convents: there was no linen, cutlery, chairs, or even beds. But if we suffered from all these privations, the thousands of poor wretches crammed into the convents suffered very much more, for they were short of clothes and had no means of preparing food. Men, women, children and slaves were compelled to live together in very little space, so their situation was appalling.

Apart from these material sufferings, the people experienced real moral anguish because they did not know which of the two rival candidates they ought to support. As they could not predict which would be victorious they were forced to wait; and to wait without being able to speak was a cruel punishment for this talkative people.

Towards three o'clock the rumour ran through the town that everything was settled, as San-Roman had recognised Orbegoso as the legitimate president and fraternised with his former comrades from Arequipa; and that his entry was deferred until the following Sunday so that he could, as an act of thanksgiving, attend high mass. The people were overcome with joy at the news, but alas! their joy was short-lived. At five o'clock an aid-de-camp came from Althaus to inform us that negotiations had broken down and that he himself would come that evening to give us an account of the whole affair. When the people heard what had happened they were too frightened to protest, but fell into a kind of stupor.

We were gathered in my uncle's study, not knowing, after so many contradictory reports, how things were going to turn out, when the unfortunate general happened to pass by, followed by the monk and several others. I went to the window and said to him: "General, would you be good enough to tell us if there is really going to be a battle?"

"Yes, mademoiselle, tomorrow at daybreak, that is definite." Struck by the tone of his voice, I began to pity him, and while he was talking to my uncle I examined him closely. Everything about him betrayed moral anguish pushed to its limits: his haggard eyes, the veins of his forehead stretched taut like cords, his distorted features, his tense muscles, all showed plainly enough that the poor distracted general had just been victim of a shameful deception. He could hardly stay in the saddle, great drops of sweat ran down his temples, his hands gripped the reins of his horse convulsively; I truly believed he was mad. . . . The monk was gloomy but impassive; I could not bear to meet his glance, it froze me. They stopped for only a few minutes; as they moved off, my uncle said to me: "But Florita, the poor general is ill; he will never be able to command tomorrow."

"Uncle, the battle is *lost*; that man is out of his mind, his limbs refuse to function. It is absolutely necessary to replace him, otherwise tomorrow he will commit every folly imaginable."

Then, yielding to the impulse of my heart, I begged my uncle to go and find the prefect, the mayor, the military commanders, make them realise the critical position Nieto had put them in and compel them to take action to relieve Nieto of his command and appoint another general in his place.

My uncle looked at me in alarm and demanded whether I had gone mad in my turn, asking him to *compromise himself* by an act of this nature. And it is men like him who want to be in a republic! As we were talking, Althaus arrived.

"Florita is right," he said. "Your duty, Don Pio, is to assemble the chief citizens of the town immediately so that Nieto is relieved of his command this very evening. Nieto is not a wicked man, but his weakness and sentimentality have done more harm than downright wickedness could ever do. Today he sees the full extent of his blunders and his feeble mind is so appalled that he has lost his reason."

My uncle did not dare say another word. Still haunted by the fear of being compromised, he feigned illness and went to bed.

Althaus told me that the whole army was disgusted with the general and there was talk in the camp of stripping him of his epaulettes.

"In a word, this is what happened: San-Roman had no provisions. He talked Nieto into giving him some by promising to recognise Orbegoso, and our general was simple enough to trust a promise dictated by sheer necessity. At last he came back; we were all exceedingly impatient after so long a wait. Morant asked him: "Are we definitely going to fight, General? And must we prepare for this evening?" "For tomorrow, monsieur, at sunrise." He brought with him three of San-Roman's officers; he has had them placed under arrest, and, just think of it, tonight he wants to have them shot. I tell you again, the man is mad. It is vital to replace him, but the choice of another leader is a very embarrassing matter; how are we to set about it? You see how it is: all these citizens who ought to be dying for the fatherland hide in the convents; your uncle goes off to bed; the Goyeneches, the Gamios, etc. are content just to weep and wail. Well, I ask you, what the devil can you do with such a bunch of wet hens? I am quite certain we shall lose the battle, and I'm thoroughly annoyed about it, because I detest that Gamarra!"

Althaus clasped my hand and assured me he would come to no harm: "Don't worry about me," he said, "the Peruvians know how to run away but not how to kill"; and he returned to the camp.

I was awakened before daybreak by an old *chacarero* Althaus had sent to tell us that San-Roman, profiting from the darkness of the night, had withdrawn towards Cangallo and that Nieto had set off in pursuit with the whole of the army, followed even by the *rabonas*.

When daylight appeared I climbed up to the roof and saw no trace of either camp on the plain, so at last they had gone to do battle.

Once again the domes of convents and churches were thick with people, but they no longer formed the single entity whose silence had so impressed me two days before; now a confused and muffled murmur arose from these huge masses and the continual movement which agitated them was like the tumult of the waves in an angry sea.

At nine o'clock there came the sound of artillery, and firing continued with frightening rapidity. Then there was deepest silence among the people, the silence of the condemned man in the presence of the scaffold. At the end of half an hour we noticed a cloud of smoke rising behind the mountain; as the village of Cangallo lay at its foot we assumed that this was where the fighting was taking place. Towards eleven o'clock a number of soldiers appeared on the flat summit: hardly another half-hour had elapsed before they had disappeared behind the mountain and only a handful remained, some on foot, the others on horseback. With the help of old Hurtado's excellent telescope I saw perfectly clearly that several of them were wounded: one was sitting binding up his arm with his handkerchief, another was bandaging his head, yet another was lying across his horse; all were making their way down the difficult narrow mountain path.

At about half-past twelve the Arequipans finally realised the full extent of the disaster. We had before our eyes the spectacle of an army in flight, as magnificent in its way as a tempest and just as terrifying! I had witnessed the July Revolution of 1830, but then I was exalted by the heroism of the people and I had no thought of the danger; in Arequipa I saw only the misfortunes which threatened the town.

Tamsen E. Donner

"The Donner Party Letters"
(1846)

Independence Mo. May 11th 1846.

My Dear Sister[1]

I commenced writing to you some months ago but the letter was laid aside to be finished the next day & was never touched. A nice sheet of pink letter paper was taken out & has got so much soiled that it cannot be written upon & now in the midst of preparation for starting across the mountains I am seated on the grass in the midst of the tent to say a few words to my dearest & only sister. One would suppose that I loved her but little or I should have not neglected her so long. But I have heard from you by Mr Greenleaf & every month have intended to write. My three daughters are round me one at my side trying to sew Georgeanna fixing herself up in old indiarubber cap & Eliza Poor knocking on my paper & asking me ever so many questions. They often talk to me of Aunty Poor. I can give you no idea of the hurry of the place at this time. It is supposed there will be 7000 waggons start from this place this season We go to California, to the bay of San Francisco. It is a four months trip. We have three waggons furnished with food & clothing &c. drawn by three yoke of oxen each. We take cows along & milk them & have some butter though not as much as we would like. I am willing to go & have no doubt it will be an advantage to our children & to us. I came here last evening & start tomorrow morning on the long journey. Wm's family was well when I left Springfield a month ago. He will write to you soon as he finds another home He says he has received no answer to his two last letters, is about to start to Wisconsin as he considers Illinois unhealthy.

---

[1] This letter from Mrs. George Tamsen Donner to her sister, Eliza Poor, is located in the Huntington Library, San Marino, Calif.

Farewell, my sister, you shall hear from
me as soon as I have an opportunity,
Love to Mr. Poor, the children & all friends.
Farewell

T.E. Donner

FROM THE CALIFORNIA COMPANY

The following letter is from Mrs. George Donner, (one of the emigrants from this County, now on the way to California,) to a friend in this city: It is dated—

NEAR THE JUNCTION OF THE
NORTH AND SOUTH PLATTE,
June 16th, 1846

My Old Friend:—We are now on the Platte, 200 miles from Fort Laramie. Our journey so far, has been pleasant. The water for a part of the way has been indifferent—but at no time have our cattle suffered for it. Wood is now very scarce, but "*Buffalo chips*" are excellent—they kindle quick and retain heat surprisingly. We had this evening Buffalo steaks broiled upon them that had the same flavor they would have had on hickory coals.

We feel no fear of Indians. Our cattle graze quietly around our encampment unmolested.—Two or three men will go hunting twenty miles out from camp:—and last night two of our men laid out in the wilderness rather than tire their horses after a hard chase. Indeed if I do not experience something far worse than I yet have done, I shall say that trouble is all in getting started.

Our wagons have not needed much repair; but I cannot yet tell in what respect they could be improved. Certain it is they cannot be too strong. Our preparation for the journey, in some respects, might have been bettered. Bread has been the principal article of food in our camp. We laid in 150 lbs. of flour and 75 lbs. of meat for each individual and I fear bread will be scarce. Meat is abundant. Rice and beans are good articles on the road—corn-meal, too, is acceptable. Linsey dresses are the most suitable for children. Indeed if I had one it would be comfortable. There is so cool a breeze at all times in the prairie that the sun does not feel as hot as one could suppose.

We are now 450 miles from Independence.—Our route at first was rough and through a timbered country which appeared to be fertile. After striking the prairie we found a first rate road; and the only difficulty we had has been crossing creeks. In that, however, there has been no danger. I never could have believed we could have travelled so far with so little difficulty. The prairie between the Blue and Platte rivers is abundant beyond description. Never have I seen so varied a country—so suitable for cultivation. Every thing was new and pleasing. The Indians frequently come to see us and the chiefs of a tribe breakfasted at our tent this morning.—All are so friendly that I cannot help feeling sympathy and friendship for them. But on one sheet what can I say?

Since we have been on the Platte we have had the river on one side, and the ever varying mounds on the other—and have travelled through the Bottom lands from one to two miles wide with little or no timber. The soil is sandy, and last year on account of one dry season, the emigrants found grass here scarce. Our cattle are in good order, and where proper care has been taken none has been lost. Our milch cows have been of great service—indeed, they have been of more advantage than our meat. We have plenty of butter and milk.

We are commanded by Capt. Russel—an amiable man. George Donner is himself yet. He crows in the morning, and shouts out, "Chain up, boys!—chain up!" with as much authority as though he was "something in particular."—John Denton is still with us—we find him a useful man in camp. Hiram Miller and Noah James are in good health and doing well. We have of the best of people in our company, and some, too, that are not so good.

Buffalo show themselves frequently. We have found the wild tulip, the primrose, the lupine, the ear-drop, the larkspur, and creeping holyhock, and a beautiful flower resembling the bloom of the beach tree, but in bunches as big as a small sugar-leaf, and of every variety of shade to red and green. I botanize and read some, but cook a "heap" more.

There are 420 wagons, as far as we have heard, on the road between here and Oregon and California.

Give our love to all enquiring friends—God bless them. Yours truly,

Mrs. George Donner.[1]

Independence rock July [th]12 1846[2]

My Dear Couzin I take this opper tuny to Write to you to let you know that I am Well at present and hope that you are well. We have all had good helth—We came to the blue—the Water was so hye we had to stay there 4 days—in the mean time gramma died. she be came spechless the day before she died. We buried her verry decent We made a nete coffin and buried her under a tree we had a head stone and had her name cutonit, and the date and yere verry nice, and at the head of the grave was a tree we cut some letters on it the young men soded it all ofer and put Flores on it We miss her verry much evry time we come in the wagon we look up at the bed for her We have came throw several tribs of indians the Caw Indians the saw the shawnees, at the caw viliage paw counted 20050 Indians We diden see no Indians from the time we left the cow viliage till we come to fort Laramy the Caw Indians are gong to War With the crows we hav to pas throw ther fiting grounds the sowe Indians are the pretest drest Indians thare is Paw goes a bufalo hunting most every day and kils 2 or 3 buffalo every day paw shot a elk som of our compan saw a grisly bear We have the thermometer 102°—average for the last 6 days We selabrated the 4 of July on plat at bever criek several of the Gentemen in Springfield gave paw a botel of licker and said it shoulden be opend tell the 4 day of July and paw as to look to the east and drink it and thay was to look to the West an drink it at 12

---

[1] From *The Sangamo Journal*, Springfield, Ill., July 23, 1846.
[2] The following two letters are from Virginia Reed, and are in the Southwest Museum, Los Angeles, Calif.

oclock paw treted the company and we all had some leminade. maw and pau is well
and sends there best love to you all. I send my best love to you all We hav hard from
uncle cad severe times he went to california and now is gone to oregon he is well. I
am a going to send this letter by a man coming from oregon by his self he is going
to take his family to oregon We are all doing Well and in hye sperits so I must close
yur letter. You are for ever my affectionate couzen

Virginia E.B. Reed

Napa Vallie
California
May 16th 1847

My Dear Cousan
I take this oppertunity to write to you to let you now that we are all Well at presant
and hope this letter may find you all well to My dear Cousan I am a going to Write
to you about our trubels geting to Callifornia; We had good luck til we come to big
Sandy thare we lost our best yoak of oxons we come to Brigers Fort & we lost another
ox we sold some of our provisions & baut a yoak of Cows & oxen & they pursuaded
us to take Hastings cut of over the salt plain thay said it saved 3 Hondred miles, we
went that road & we had to go through a long drive of 40 miles With out water or
grass Hastings said it was 40 but i think it was 80 miles We traveld a day and night
& a nother day and at noon pa went on to see if he coud find Water, he had not
bin gone long till some of the oxen give out and we had to leve the Wagons and
take the oxen on to water one of the men staid with us and others went on with the
cattel to water pa was a coming back to us with Water and met the men & thay was
about 10 miles from water pa said thay git to water that night, and the next day to
bring the cattel back for the wagons any [and] bring some Water pa got to us about
noon the man that was with us took the horse and went on to water We wated thare
thought Thay would come we wated till night and We thought we start and walk
to Mr doners wagons that night we took what little water we had and some bread
and started pa caried Thomos and all the rest of us walk we got to Donner and thay
were all a sleep so we laid down on the ground we spred one shawl down we laid
doun on it and spred another over us and then put the dogs on top it was the couldes
night you most ever saw the wind blew and if it haden bin for the dogs we would
have Frosen as soon as it was day we went to Miss Donners she said we could not
walk to the Water and if we staid we could ride in thare wagons to the spring so pa
went on to the water to see why thay did not bring the cattel when he got thare
thare was but one ox and cow thare none of the rest had got to water Mr Donner
come out that night with his cattel and braught his Wagons and all of us in we staid
thare a week and Hunted for our cattel and could not find them so some of the
companie took thare oxons and went out and brout in one wagon and cashed the
other tow and a grate manie things all but what we could put in one Wagon we had
to divied our propessions out to them to get them to carie them We got three yoak
with our oxe & cow so we [went] on that way a while and we got out of provisions
and pa had to go on to callifornia for provisions we could not get along that way,

in 2 or 3 days after pa left we had to cash our wagon and take Mr. graves wagon and cash some more of our things well we went on that way a while and then we had to get Mr Eddies Wagon we went on that way awhile and then we had to cash all our our close except a change or 2 and put them in Mr Brins Wagon and Thomos & James rode the 2 horses and the rest of us had to walk, we went on that way a Whild and we come to a nother long drive of 40 miles and then we went with Mr Donner

We had to Walk all the time we was a travling up the truckee river we met that and 2 Indians that we had sent out for propessions to Suter Fort thay had met pa, not fur from Suters Fort he looked very bad he had not ate but 3 times in 7 days and thes days with out any thing his horse was not abel to carrie him thay give him a horse and he went on so we cashed some more of our things all but what we could pack on one mule and we started Martha and James road behind the two Indians it was a raing then in the Vallies and snowing on the montains so we went on that way 3 or 4 days tell we come to the big mountain or the Callifornia Mountain the snow then was about 3 feet deep thare was some wagons thare thay said thay had atempted to cross and could not, well we thought we would try it so we started and thay started again with thare wagons the snow was then way to the muels side the farther we went up the deeper the snow got so the wagons could not go so thay packed thare oxons and started with us carring a child a piece and driving the oxons in snow up to thare wast the mule Martha and the Indian was on was the best one so thay went and broak the road and that indian was the Pilot so we went on that way 2 miles and the mules kept faling down in the snow head formost and the Indian said he could not find the road we stoped and let the Indian and man go on to hunt the road thay went on and found the road to the top of the mountain and come back and said they thought we could git over if it did not snow any more well the Woman were all so tirder caring there Children that thay could not go over that night so we made a fire and got something to eat & ma spred down a bufalorobe & we all laid down on it & spred something over us & ma sit up by the fire & it snowed one foot on top of the bed so we got up in the morning & the snow was so deep we could not go over & we had to go back to the cabin & build more cabins & stay thare all Winter without Pa we had not the first thing to eat Ma maid arrangements for some cattel giving 2 for 1 in callifornia we seldom thot of bread for we had not had any since [blot, words not readable] & the cattel was so poor thay could note hadley git up when thay laid down we stoped thare the 4th of November & staid till March and what we had to eat i cant hardley tell you & we had that man & Indians to feed well thay started over a foot and had to come back so thay made snow shoes and started again & it come on a storme & thay had to come back it would snow 10 days before it would stop thay wated tell it stoped & started again I was a goeing with them & I took sick & could not go—thare was 15 started & thare was 7 got throw 5 Weman & 2 men it come a storme and thay lost the road & got out of provisions & the ones that got throwe had to eat them that Died not long after thay started we got out of provisions & had to put Martha at one cabin James at another Thomas at another & Ma & Elizea & Milt Eliot & I dried up what littel meat we had and started to see if we could get across & had to leve the childrin o Mary you may think that hard to leve theme with strangers & did not now wether we would see them again or not we could hardle get a way from them but we told theme we would bring them Bread & then thay was willing to stay we went & was out 5 days in the mountains Elie giv out & had to go back we went on a day longer we had to lay by a day & make snow shows & we went on a while and coud not find the road & we had to turn back I could go on verry well while i thout we wer giting along but as soone as we had to turn back i coud hadley git along but we got to the cabins that night I froze one of my feet verry bad & that same night thare was the worst storme we had that winter & if we had not come back that night we would never got back we had nothing to eat but ox hides o Mary I would cry and wish I had what you all wasted Eliza had to go to Mr Graves cabin & we staid at Mr Breen thay had meat all the time & we had to kill littel cash the dog & eat him we ate his head and feet & hide & evry thing about him o my Dear Cousin you dont now what trubel is yet a many a time we had on the last thing a cooking and did not now wher the next would come from but there was awl wais some way provided

there was 15 in the cabon we was in and half of us had to lay a bed all the time thare was 10 starved to death there we was hadley abel to walk we lived on litle cash a week and after Mr Breen would cook his meat we would take the bones and boil them 3 or 4 days at a time ma went down to the other caben and got half a hide carried it in snow up to her wast

it snowed and would cover the cabin all over so we could not git out for 2 or 3 days we would have to cut pieces of the loges in sied to make a fire with I coud hardly eat the hides and had not eat anything 3 days Pa stated out to us with providions and then came a storme and he could not go he cash his provision and went back on the other side of the bay to get compana of men and the San Wakien got so hye he could not crose well thay Made up a Compana at Suters Fort and sent out we had not ate any thing for 3 days & we had onely a half a hide and we was out on top of the cabin and we seen them a coming

O my Dear Cousin you dont now how glad i was, we run and met them one of them we knew we had traveled with them on the road thay staid thare 3 days to recruet a little so we could go thare was 20 started all of us started and went a piece and Martha and Thomas giv out & so the men had to take them back ma and Eliza James & I come on and o Mary that was the hades thing yet to come on and liev them thar did not now but what thay would starve to Death Martha said well ma if you never see me again do the best you can the men said thay could hadly stand it it maid them all cry but they said it was better for all of us to go on for if we was to go back we would eat that much more from them thay give them a littel meat and flore and took them back and we come on we went over great hye mountain as strait as stair steps in snow up to our knees litle James walk the hole way over all the mountain in snow up to his waist he said every step he took he was a gitting nigher Pa and something to eat the Bears took the provision the men had cashed and we had but very little to eat when we had traveld 5 days travel we met Pa with 13 men going to the cabins o Mary you do not nou how glad we was to see him we had not seen him for months we thought we woul never see him again he heard we was coming and he made some seet cakes to give us he said he would see Martha and Thomas the next day he went to tow days what took us 5 days some of the compana was eating from them that Died but Thomas & Martha had not ate any Pa and the men started with 12 people Hiram O Miller CarriedThomas and Pa caried Martha and thay wer caught in [unreadable word] and thay had to stop Two days it stormed so thay could not go and the Bears took their provision and thay weer 4 days without anything Pa and Hiram and all the men started one of Donner boys Pa a carring Martha Hiram caring Thomas and the snow was up to thare wast and it a snowing so thay could hadley see the way they raped the chidlren up and never took them out for 4 days & thay had nothing to eat in all that time Thomas asked for somthing to eat once those that thay brought from the cabins some of them was not able to come and som would not come Thare was 3 died and the rest eat them thay was 10 days without any thing to eat but the Dead Pa braught Thom and pady on to where we was none of the men was abel to go there feet was froze very bad so they was a nother Compana went and braught them all in thay are all in from the Mountains now but five they was men went out after them and was caught in a storm and had to come back thare is another compana gone thare was half got through that was stoped thare sent to their relief thare was but families got that all of them got we was one

O Mary I have not wrote you half of the truble we have had but I hav Wrote you anuf to let you now that you dont now whattruble is but thank the Good god we have all got throw and the onely family that did not eat human flesh we have left every thing but i dont cair for that we have got through but Dont let this letter dishaten anybody and never take no cutofs and hury along as fast as you can

My Dear Cousin

We are all very well pleased with Callifornia partucularly with the climate let it be ever so hot a day thare is all wais cool nights it is a beautiful Country it is mostley in vallies it aut to be a beautiful Country to pay us for our trubel geting there it is the greatest place for catle and horses you ever saw it would Just suit Charley for he could ride down 3 or 4 horses a day and he could lern to be Bocarro that one who lases cattel the spanards and Indians are the best riders i ever say thay have a spanish sadel and woden sturups and great big spurs the wheel of them is 5 inches in diameter and thay could not manage the Callifornia horses witout the spurs, thay wont go atol if they cant hear the spurs rattle they have littel bells to them to make them rattle thay blindfold the horses and then sadel them and git on them and then take the blindfole of and let run and if thay cant sit on thay tie themselves on and let them run as fast as they can and go out to a band of bullluck and throw the reatter on a wild bullluck and but it around the horn of his sadel and he can hold it as long as he wants

a nother Indian throws his reatter on its feet and throws them and when thay git take the reatter of of them they are very dangerous they will run after you then hook there horses and run after any person thay see thay ride from 80 to 100 miles a day & have some of the spanard have from 6 to 7000 head of horses and from 15 to 16000 head Cattel we are all verry fleshey Ma waies 10040 pon and still a gaing I weigh 80 tel Henriet if she wants to get Married for to come to Callifornia she can get a spanyard any time that Eliza is a going to marrie a a spanyard by the name of Armeho and Eliza weighs 10070 We have not saw uncle Cadon yet but we have had 2 letters from him he is well and is a coming here as soon as he can Mary take this letter to uncle Gurshon and to all tha i know to all of our neighbors and tell Dochter Meniel and every girl i know and let them read it Mary kiss little Sue and Maryann for me and give my best love to all i know to uncle James and Lida and all the rest of the famila and to uncle Gurshon aunt Percilla and all the Children and to all of our neighbors and to all she knows so no more at present

  pa is yerbayan [Yerba Buena]

My Dear casons
Virginia Elizabeth B Reed

Emily Lowe

Unprotected Females in Norway
(1857)

The boat was ordered to be ready very early in the morning, and after a solid breakfast of meat, &c., fit for any country; we embarked on the lovely lake opposite the house, and the rowers darted across in half an hour to the ferry-banks on the other side. Here was a picturesque farm, standing in very rich land, with no one about; but whose yielding doors admitted us into a large room, out of boxes round the sides of which simultaneously sprang several figures robed in white. This to eyes just come from the sun's glare had rather a ghostly effect, the spirits tripping about, not in the least regarding us mortals, till at length they assumed the appearance of damsels, and proffered porridge. In the mean time we had peeped into the next room—same apparitions; these were the farmers themselves, so we beat a hasty retreat, having had peeping enough, but could not, like Fatima, let the key drop, as such an instrument seemed unknown, and the tale of Bluebeard can never have made one in the Norwegian nursery collection. Fancy a nation that has not heard of Bluebeard!

When the toilette had occupied the usual Norwegian five minutes, the question of a horse was propounded; the nearest was seven miles off. No one liked to set out for it before breakfast, which did not seem unreasonable; but it would be better for future travellers to send word from Green some hours before coming themselves. As there was no very comfortable place to wait in, we had to take up our quarters in a cart, and sketch; the rooms with the shelves requiring some airing, though the occupants were going to overlook that precaution entirely and sit down to eat without it. On my opening a window, the Kone looked surprised, did not shut it again, but lighted a fine fir fire as a preventive to chills, on a warm summer day!

In two hours two horses came, were put into two little cars, and accompanied by two full-grown schoolboys, we set off into the forest. I say schoolboys, for nothing else has such very short waists; and the most dreadful hobbledehoy never had such desperate trousers, drawn up quite under the arms, while a stiff cap and long tassel gave a faint idea of a caricatured chorister. They were capital fellows, and let us drive fast to make up for lost time. The road was hilly, but very good; the trees shed a sweet cooling shade, while the more distant ones were veiled in that soft blue which throws a lovely mystery over forest depths—air which can be seen. We were truly sorry to part with the schoolboys, who were not troublesome, and be consigned to the care of an old lady at Sigdahl, whose horses were also seven miles off. A schoolmaster lived near, and while some one went the fourteen miles' walk for the animals, we tried to get information out of him, as he spoke (he said) German and French, besides Norske. He probably was not in practice, or had forgotten them, being obliged to return to the latter after various incursions upon the former. The young ladies, his daughters, apparently understood nothing, as most incomprehensible giggles from a distant corner were all we could elicit. However, the father said, in referring to the roads we were inquiring about, that the Bishop had once come that way, and vowed he would never do it again; so we may conclude the Norwegian lords spiritual like things as easy as our own: there must be something soft in the episcopal bench all over the world, which makes everything feel hard after it. After this we beat a retreat amid offers of wine and beer, but I must say the volleys of giggles were beginning to take some effect upon us; I never had the courage to face that artillery, it makes one nervous, and would have spilt the wine. Porridge in quiet for me, against a whole banquet with giggle sauce! These were the only Norwegians I ever saw that way inclined.

A victim had arrived at the farm with his horses, but only one lady's saddle, of course secured for my mother. We had entered the third phase of the journey—the forest. Hurrah for the three glories of Norwegian travel! The fjord! the fjeld! the forest! Wild Graces of Scandinavia—vast, rugged, grand, as befits a stern northern Queen of beauty! The ponies long to gallop beneath the shade—one spring—they start. Now the *non-talk-aboutables* proved their usefulness: bagging all my clothes in their ample folds, I at once mounted *à la Zouave*, and can assure every one for a long journey this attitude has double comforts; while mamma sat twisted sideways on a saddle which would not keep its balance, I was easy and independent, with a foot in each stirrup; besides the scarlet having the most beautiful effect through the green trees. We got on magnificently till our guide suddenly pulled up at a farm in an opening of the forest, and proposed our dismounting; what was it for? Oh, he did not know the way any further. "Well, but you should have said so before,—you cannot deposit us here:" and we put in such a strong light the impossibility of remaining in the midst of a lone wood, and making a future home of the secluded farm, that, after deep consultations with the proprietors on whose hands he wished to leave us, it was concluded he should try another farm across the wood, where two horses were kept by a very sharp fellow who knew everything. So resignedly penetrating deeper into the piny arches, a rising piece of ground showed at length the welcome sight of two horses ploughing with a jaunty boy, who instantly entered into the exchange plan with alacrity, as if it were the most capital fun. Requesting us to sit on the grass while the horses rested a little, he put on all his best, and reappeared quite a respectable young man. These doings had taken up time; the afternoon was pretty well on before we re-started; it would have been better to have stayed overnight at the jolly ploughboy's. The traveller must be prepared for these surprises in unfrequented parts, and never try to persuade an unwilling man to continue, as we did; it would have been most dangerous had he consented, which the nature of the road afterwards proved.

Duskiness soon came on; the twilight feebly penetrating the thick woods, and the hearty laughs of our guide were the only cheering sounds. He was in the highest spirits; my costume and attitude excited his warmest admiration. He was under the impression they were the last English fashion; and that great nation, which he knew swayed the world from somewhere, seemed to rise in his imagination in still more mysterious grandeur, and a stray cigar or two given him completed the illusion. What would one think of two French ladies, or two of any other nation, penetrating into the wildest recesses of Norway, and finding out new roads for the natives? Who but English could do it? Madame Ida Pfeiffer has been rather active, but she confesses to being skinny and wiry, and was able to wriggle about unmolested; the English or Americans are rarely of that make, and so generally blooming and attractive, that it must be a certain inborn right of conquest which makes them nearly always the first to penetrate into the arcana of countries triumphantly.

At length no light, even grey, was left. Dismounting for a variety, we found it impossible to walk, as the forest was full of small pools of water, into which we went splashing every moment, and had to remount, and continue for two hours in utter darkness, save when a friendly spark flew from the cigar. There had been no path the whole time, the horses going confidently on through the thickest glades, and the lively man making little excursions on each side to reconnoitre, though he could see nothing; his cheerful holloa and our response uniting us again; but as the forest became thicker and thicker, it was with great difficulty we kept our heads on our shoulders, the branches of the fir-trees continually trying to catch them. One, more dexterous than the rest, hooked my mother Absalom-like, the pony coolly continuing from under her; and it was only by hearing the most frightful screams we were aware of her suspended state, and after groping about to find and bring her to *terra firma*, discovered the bonnet had obligingly played the part of hair, and remained aloft. I must say ten hours were quite enough of this, the time appearing doubled. Thick darkness in a forest really makes itself felt, and it was like striking a light when, some cots appearing, the guide whispered the electric word, "Kaffee."

The way in which he set about getting it was amusing, walking into the open doors, and waking up the slumberers without the least compunction. They seemed to have lain down in their clothes, after merely slipping off a jacket; some were asleep in the barn on hay, with no door at all: each and every one got up in the most cheerful manner to attend upon us, and lighted a large fire; while the women prepared the green coffee for roasting, then ground and warmed it, placed a large can full before us, with rich cream, and three highly-prized lumps of barley-sugar. Our guide made use of his in a novel manner, putting it in his mouth, taking a suck, then out again, and drinking a mouthful of coffee after, repeating the same till his cup was empty. We noticed others doing this also, and found it the general way of sweetening in these parts, when they indulge in such a luxury. Much refreshed, we were casting our eyes around for the best means of turning the form into a comfortable bed, when our guide pressed us to continue on, saying the worst was over, and it would be dividing the journey much better. A hint of our objections to another "Absalom" accident was met by the assurance that the moon had now risen, and would protect us; also the host intended to supply a fresh horse, and send his son, thus making double escort. Our deep confidence in the people made us assent to their plans for us; for who could resist the charm of seeing a whole house-hold rise from their sleep in deep midnight to make coffee, not only without murmuring, but with cheerful alacrity, as if hospitality were their nature at all times—(is not this the real thing?)—while a youth proposed himself turning out with his horse on an expedition which must keep him up all night? Such rare generosity would brace one against any fatigue.

The moon did now and then faintly gleam through the trees with a ghastly effect, hardly better than nothing, and it was but lagging work altogether, when we were startled by our jovial guide saying, "You had better make haste, for this wood swarms with bears and wolves;" and though they were not likely to make an attack, the announcement gave one a very creepy feeling, and to each large stump a horrid Bruin look, whilst the jovial fellow kept bouncing suddenly out in front of the horses, and startling them with growls! We were heartily glad to see something like four walls within which we could retreat again. After some knocking at the door, a fine old man came out, and then hurried up his wife, who, just as our worthy companion had said, provided us directly with one of the nicest rooms and downiest of beds; and I think we never put our heads under the clothes with such a feeling of relief, able at last to chuckle over the bears and wolves.

Susie Rijnhart

With the Tibetans in Tent and Temple
(1901)

Following the occidental road from the Ts'aidam we had ascended many passes, and though some of them were over 16,000 feet above the sea, on none of them did we find old snow, and hence the snow-line in that region cannot be lower than about 17,500 feet. Wild animals abounded in many localities, yak sometimes being visible from very near. One fine day we surprised a number of the latter which, on seeing us, dashed across a large stream, their huge tails high in the air, the spray from their headlong rush into the water rising in clouds, presenting a magnificent sight. Wild mules had been seen in large numbers, especially after we crossed the Mur-ussu river, while bears and antelopes were everyday sights. On August the twenty-first, after we had been ascending for several days, we found ourselves traveling directly south, following up to its source a beautiful stream full of stones, probably one of the Murussu high waters. In front of us were the Dang La mountais, snow-clad and sunkissed, towering in their majesty, and, to us tenfold more interesting because immediately beyond them lay the Lhasa district of Tibet, in which the glad tidings of the gospel were unknown, and in which the Dalai Lama exercises supreme power, temporal and spiritual, over the people. Moreover, as we hoped to obtain permission to reside in that district as long as we did not attempt to enter the Capital, it seemed that our journeyings for the present were almost at an end. This hope, added to the fact that our darling's eight teeth, which had been struggling to get through, were now shining white above the gums, revived our spirits and we all sang for very joy, picking bouquets of bright pink leguminous flowers as we went along.

The morning of the darkest day in our history arose, bright, cheery, and full of promise, bearing no omen of the cloud that was about to fall upon us. Our breakfast was thoroughly enjoyed, Charlie ate more heartily than he had done for some days, and we resumed our journey full of hope. Riding along we talked of the future, its plans, its work, and its unknown successes and failures, of the possibility of going to the Indian border when our stay in the interior was over, and then of going home to America and Holland before we returned to Tankar, or the interior of Tibet again. Fondly our imagination followed the career of our little son; in a moment years were added to his stature and the infant had grown to the frolicking boy full of life and vigor, athirst for knowledge and worthy of the very best instruction we could give him. With what deliberation we decided to give his education our personal supervision, and what books we would procure for him—the very best and most scientific in English, French and German. "He must have a happy childhood," said his father. "He shall have all the blocks, trains, rocking-horses and other things that boys in the homeland have, so that when he shall have grown up he may not feel that because he was a missionary's son, he had missed the joys that brighten other boys' lives." How the tones of his baby voice rang out as we rode onward! I can still hear him shouting lustily at the horses in imitation of his father and Rahim.

Suddenly a herd of yak on the river bank near us tempted Rahim away to try a shot, but the animals, scenting danger, rushed off into the hills to our right; then across the river we saw other yak, apparently some isolated ones, coming towards us, but on closer examination we found they were tame yak driven by four mounted men accompanied by a big, white dog. The men evidently belonged to the locality, and we expected they would come to exchange with us ordinary civilities, but to our surprise when they saw us they quickly crossed our path, and studiously evading us, disappeared in the hills. This strange conduct on their part aroused in our minds suspicions as to their intentions. Carefully we selected a camping-place hidden by little hills; the river flowed in front and the pasture was good.

Though baby's voice had been heard just a few moments previous, Mr. Rijnhart said he had fallen asleep; so, as usual, Rahim dismounted and took him from his father's arms in order that he might not be disturbed until the tent was pitched and his food prepared. I had also dismounted and spread on the ground the comforter and pillow I carried on my saddle. Rahim very tenderly laid our lovely boy down, and, while I knelt ready to cover him comfortably, his appearance attracted my attention. I went to move him, and found that he was unconscious. A great fear chilled me and I called out to Mr. Rijnhart that I felt anxious for baby, and asked him to quickly get me the hypodermic syringe. Rahim asked me what was the matter, and on my reply a look of pain crossed his face, as he hastened to help my husband procure the hypodermic. In the meantime I loosened baby's garments, chafed his wrists, performed artificial respiration, though feeling almost sure that nothing would avail, but praying to Him who holds all life in His hands, to let us have our darling child. Did He not know how we loved him and could it be possible that the very joy of our life, the only human thing that made life and labor sweet amid the desolation and isolation of Tibet—could it be possible that even this—the child of our love should be snatched from us in that dreary mountain country—by the cold chill hand of Death? What availed our efforts to restore him? What availed our questionings? The blow had already fallen, and we realized that we clasped in our arms only the casket which had held our precious jewel; the jewel itself had been taken for a brighter setting in a brighter world; the little flower blooming on the bleak and barren Dang La had been plucked and transplanted on the Mountains Delectable to bask and bloom forever in the sunshine of God's love. But oh! what a void in our hearts! How empty and desolate our tent, which in the meantime had been pitched and sorrowfully entered! Poor Rahim, who had so dearly loved the child, broke out in loud lamentations, wailing as only orientals can, but with real sorrow, for his life had become so entwined with the child's that he felt the snapping of the heart-strings. And what of the father, now bereft of his only son, his only child, which just a few moments before he had clasped warm to his bosom, knowing not how faint the little heart-beat was growing? We tried to think of it euphemistically, we lifted our hearts in prayer, we tried to be submissive, but it was all so real—the one fact stared us in the face; it was written on the rocks; it reverberated through the mountain silence: Little Charlie was dead.

As I sat in the tent clasping the fair form of my darling, Mr. Rijnhart tenderly reminded me that the Tibetans do not bury their dead, but simply throw the body devoid of clothing out upon the hillside to be devoured by the beasts of the field and the fowls of the air. If the men whom so recently we had seen and whose actions were so suspicious, should come to rob us, they would, he feared, dispose of our darling's body as was their custom, and that would be to us a still greater trial than the loss of our goods; and so, reluctantly and tenderly he suggested, to avoid such a calamity, that our precious little boy should have a Christian sepulture on that very day. Kneeling together we prayed that God who loved us and whose children we were, would make us strong and brave. Our drug box, emptied of its contents, and lined with towels, served as a coffin, which I myself prepared, while Mr. Rijnhart and Rahim went to dig the grave. With hands whose every touch throbbed with tenderness I robed baby in white Japanese flannel, and laid him on his side in the coffin, where he looked so pure and calm as if he were in a sweet and restful sleep. In his hand was placed a little bunch of wild asters and blue poppies which Rahim gathered from the mountain side, and as the afternoon wore away he seemed to grow more beautiful and precious; but night was coming on and dangers threatened, and the last wrench must come. Many of his little belongings were put into the coffin, accompanied by our names written on a piece of linen and on cards. Then there was the agony of the last look. Our only child, who had brought such joy to our home, and who had done so much by his bright ways to make friends for us among the natives—to leave his body in such a cold, bleak place seemed more than we could endure. As the three of us stood over the grave, the little box was lowered. Mr. Rijnhart conducted the burial service in the native tongue, so that Rahim might understand, and the cold earth of Tibet, the great forbidden land, closed over the body of the first Christian child committed to its bosom—little Charles Carson Rijnhart, aged one year, one month and twenty-two days. Mr. Rijnhart and Rahim rolled a large boulder over the grave to keep wild animals from digging it up, and obliterated as well as possible all traces of a recent burial. There was another reason for this. The natives often bury goods when their transport animals break down, and robbers search for booty wherever they find the surface of the ground disturbed. If such should discover our little grave we knew they would disturb it, and in their disappointment desecrate it with wanton indifference. When the funeral was over we went to the tent, but could we eat food? could we drink tea? could we close our ears to the frenzied mourning of Rahim? We could only say, "Lord we are stricken with grief, we cannot see why this should be, but help us to say 'Thy will be done.'" Less than a month afterward we realized that the All Loving had dealt very kindly with us in taking our little darling when we were comfortable, when we had plenty of food for him, a tent to sleep in and horses to ride on; for later we found ourselves with barely enough common food to exist on for a few days, while we traveled on foot, Mr. Rijnhart carrying on his back a heavy load.

When night came on the sky was unusually dark. What more fitting than a nocturnal storm after the inward tumult of the day? The thunder rolled, the lightning flashed, while from the sable clouds in torrents fell the rain, which as the winds grew colder, was congealed into snow. We could not sleep. We could only think of our precious one and be thankful that the body from which the vital spark had fled, had no power to feel the chill of the mountain blast. The little fellow's bed had always been made of blankets and furs, while every precaution had been taken to exclude any draft from his corner, and now what need had we to be careful? No need, for he slept not with us, but in another world, free from all care, and future sorrowing. Dear child, now, as then, it is still well with thee. On arising the following morning how I missed him, for there was no little boy to dress, no one to joyously relish his food, watching the spoon go backwards and forwards for every fresh spoonful. When the time came for departure we took a sorrowful farewell of the little grave with its protecting boulder of strength. It seemed impossible to tear ourselves away, knowing that every step took us further from the spot that held our most precious treasure, with the conviction that we should probably never return there again. Before leaving we covenanted that by God's help we would seek to be instrumental in sending out another missionary to Tibet, in the name of our little boy. Mr. Rijnhart, instead of mounting first and having Baby handed to him as was his custom, tenderly placed me in the saddle, and all three of us sobbing, we tore ourselves away. Following the stream we saw some bears with their cubs digging for roots—and again we felt thankful for the strong boulder over the little grave. If Mr. Rijnhart could speak, he would wish to say some word in tribute to his little son, but since his voice is silent, what more fitting than to close this chapter by a quotation from his diary, dated August 23, the day of our departure, from this, to us, the most sacred spot in Tibet? It reads thus: "To-day we started with broken hearts, leaving the body of our precious one behind in regions of eternal snow, where the mother of the Yangtse Kiang flows tranquilly past. His grave is on the western bank of one of the southern branches of the Mur-ussu, at the foot of the Dang La mountains, a little over two hours north of the mineral springs of the Dang La, and about ten hours' travel from the nearest *kopa* encampment in the Lhasa district under Nagch'uk'a."

Margaret Brooke

My Life in Sarawak
(1913)

Shortly after this incident, Tunku Ismael came to me one morning with a grave face and said, "Rajah Ranee, you are under my care, you go out for long walks all round the settlement, and seem to have no idea of danger, or that there might be bad spirits about. Sunok is exceedingly old, and if anything should happen to you during your long walks, what could I do to protect you?" I inquired what danger there was, for I knew of none. "Oh yes," he said, "there are many dangers. There are people we call *Peniamuns* who dress in black, cover their faces with black cloth, and sit in trees waiting to pounce on passers-by. Now, Rajah Ranee, should one of these *Peniamuns* get hold of you, we could never get you back again, so will you kindly walk up and down the terrace of the Fort, and not go any farther, for the *Peniamuns* are a real danger." I listened politely to Tunku Ismael, but continued to take my customary walks down to the Bazaar, across a plank of wood thrown over a ditch, separating the Chinese Bazaar from the Malay settlement, along the row of Malay houses, where the women and children were always on the look-out for me, and then home by the more lonely orchards and sugar plantations, so feared by Tunku Ismael.

One morning, I saw through the lattice-work of the Fort a flotilla of some fifteen war-boats coming up the river. I hastily sent for Tunku Ismael to inquire what these boats were. Tunku Ismael could not quite make them out, because, he said, they looked like war-boats. We watched the boats as they were paddled past the Fort, anchoring along the banks near the Bazaar, and we stepped outside to see what was happening. We saw a group of Kayans from the boats, carrying spears and swords, rushing up to the Fort, headed by a small man recognized by Tunku Ismael as being a chief named Tama Paran, who did not bear a very good character in the Rejang district. This chief came up to me, brandishing his spear, and carrying a basket which, he said, the tribe had made for me. I asked him where they had come from, and tried to look very stern. "We hear the Rajah has gone on the war-path, and we have come to accompany him," said Tama Paran. "But," I replied: "the Rajah has been gone on the war-path this last month, and you do not know exactly where he has gone. You cannot accompany him now to the scene of action." "Yes," he said; 'we are going on to-morrow, because we wish to fight for the Rajah." I realized that this was a serious state of things. If I allowed this force to go after the Rajah, with no responsible European or Malay leader to keep it in check, the Kayans might attack some unprotected village up the higher reaches of the Batang Lupar River, take some heads, and pretend it was done on the Rajah's behalf. I said to the chief, "You must not move from here until the Rajah comes back, unless you return to your village."

The man did not look pleased. He could not wait in Simanggang, he said, neither could he return home, but at any rate he consented to remain at Simanggang that evening. Tunku Ismael and I, with Sunok present, then held a council of war. We agreed it would never do to allow these Kayans to follow the Rajah, as they would probably endanger the safety of the country up river and frighten its inhabitants. We could see the fleet from the Fort, anchored near the Bazaar, and the Tunku estimated that the force numbered some six hundred men. He owned it would be somewhat difficult to keep them in order if the Rajah's return was long delayed, but, at the same time, we intended to do our best.

Tunku Ismael warned me not to walk out that evening along the Bazaar, because he feared that these Kayans, not being accustomed to white Ranees, might be disagreeable. I also felt a little apprehensive as to what my reception would be, but after thinking the matter well over, I came to the conclusion that if I did not take my usual walk, the women and children of the settlement would feel nervous, for, after all, it was unlikely the Kayans would do me any harm, for fear of the consequences when the Rajah returned. I therefore sallied forth that evening feeling a bit nervous, accompanied by the trembling octogenarian, Sunok, and the small dog Fury. I went along the Bazaar, and found the Chinamen standing outside their shops, who told me, in Malay, as I passed, that they wished very much those men would go away. The Kayans were cooking their rice, and were not at all friendly. They made no attempt to shake hands with me, and say "How do you do," as they would have done under ordinary circumstances. They looked rather impertinently, I thought, at my humble procession. When I reached the end of the Bazaar and was about to cross the narrow plank of wood leading to the Malay settlement, I saw a big burly Kayan standing the other side of the plank with his legs straddled, almost daring me to pass. His arms and legs were tattooed, his ears were ornamented with wild boar's tusks, his hair hung over his neck, cut square in the front, and he wore a little straw crown and a waist-cloth of bark. I got within two feet of the man, who gave a not very pleasant smile as Fury barked loudly. There he stood motionless. I turned to Sunok. "Remove that man," I said, but Sunok weakly replied: "He is too strong, I can't!" The situation was ludicrous. Had I turned back, it would have shown fear on my part, so I asked the man, in Malay, to get out of my way, but he remained as though he had not heard me. There was nothing left for me but to press forward. I walked slowly across the plank until my chin (I was taller than the Kayan) nearly touched his forehead. Still he did not move, so I stood as immovable as he, and waited. After a few seconds the man skulked off, and I went on my way. The Malay women had witnessed this incident from their gardens, and they rushed up to me saying: "Do take care, Rajah Ranee, and do not go out by yourself like this. The Kayans are a terrible people, and might cut off all our heads before we know where we are." I laughed lightly, although feeling somewhat upset, and finished my evening walk.

The next day, two or three Kayan chiefs came and asked for a sum of money which they knew was kept at the Fort, in order, as they said, that they might buy provisions and follow the Rajah. I again told them they were not to follow the Rajah and that I should not give them any money. Every day the chiefs came on the same errand, requesting money and permission to move. Personally, I was surprised they did not move, because nothing I could do would have prevented them. Tunku Ismael said they feared me, and he was sure the course we were taking was the only one to prevent disturbances in the country.

These Kayans were a great nuisance in Simanggang. They went about flourishing their spears and swords, frightening the shop-keepers and agriculturists into providing them with food. Indeed, the situation was daily becoming more alarming, and the interviews between the intruders and myself became more and more stormy, until one afternoon, when they had been in the neighbourhood for ten or twelve days, they became almost unmanageable. "We must have money," they said, "and we must follow the Rajah, and we do not care what anyone says." Tunku Ismael and I hardly knew what to do, when a bright thought struck me. I knew these people liked long speeches, discussions, councils of war, etc., and attached great importance to dreams; so putting on a very grave expression, I said, "Tama Paran and you all who are his followers, listen to my words. You are not to go up river, and you are not to have money, because the Rajah would not wish it. But as I see there is a strong will among you to do what you should not do, at any rate, stay here over to-morrow; for to-morrow is a particular date I have fixed within myself, having last night had a dream. To-morrow I will tell you about that dream, and I will make you understand my reasons for wishing you to do as I tell you." "And if we go to-day, what will you do?" inquired Tama Paran. I pointed to the guns—with, I hope, a magnificent gesture. "If you disobey my orders, the medicine from those guns will swamp every boat of yours in the river." With those words, I got up and dismissed them, after they had promised to come and hear my speech the next day. Tunku Ismael gently remarked: "But we do not know how to fire the guns." "No," I said; "that does not matter; they think we know, and after all that is the chief thing!"

That evening I went for my walk unmolested, and retired to bed earlier than usual. I felt anxious. I should have been so disgusted had the Kayans gone away, in spite of my orders to the contrary. I should have lost prestige with the women and even the children of Simanggang, so that I think had I seen any signs of their boats leaving the place, I should somehow have found means to fire the guns into their midst. All that night I could not sleep. I was wondering what on earth I could say to the intruders to make them realize the force of my arguments.

The question, however, settled itself. The very next morning I heard the yells of victorious Dyaks in the distance, then their paddles, and I knew all would be safe because the Rajah was returning. The Rajah soon sent the Kayans back to their homes, and, when all was said and done, I had quite enjoyed the novel experience.

Alexandra David-Neel

My Journey to Lhasa
(1927)

Before the day has dawned I nudge Yongden quietly to awaken him. We must complete our toilet before the light permits the others to notice too many details about us. For me, this consists first in darkening my face with the black I procure by rubbing the bottom of our only saucepan with my hand. This precaution prevents my too fair skin from astonishing the natives. Then, beneath our robes we must arrange the belts containing our gold and silver, our maps, thermometer, miniature compasses, watches, and other objects which must on no account be perceived.

We have scarcely finished when the mistress appears. She calls her daughters and the servant; the fire is rekindled, the saucepan containing the remains of last night's soup placed on the brazier, and a few moments later we are invited to hold out our bowls for its distribution. The bowls were not washed last night; it is not the custom amongst Thibetan villagers. Each one possesses a special bowl which he never lends. He licks it carefully after every meal and that is the cleansing process. Poor me! I lack practice in the art of licking my bowl; it is still smeared over with a layer of soup and of tea which has frozen during the night. But protesting nerves must be subdued and the rising gorge swallowed, for the success of my journey depends upon it. Let us shut our eyes and drink off our soup though it is even more nauseating than last night's, because of the water added to make it go further.

Our packages are soon tied up. No present is forthcoming, and I regard with a look of amusement the discomfited countenance of my lama who has poured forth so many blessings, chants, and official ministrations of all kinds. It is useless to delay any longer. The whole family comes for one more blessing by the imposition of hands, and I can guess that Yongden would willingly administer a sound cuffing to the old miser upon whose shock of hair he lays his hands.

We go down the ladder again, pass in front of the horses which eye us curiously, the goats whose odd and diabolical gaze seems to jeer at the crestfallen lama, and the ever placid cows. Once outside, we walk for a while in silence. Then, out of sight and earshot, Yongden turns suddenly and, having made some cabalistic signs in the direction of our host, he bursts forth:

"Oh, you rogue, you base deceiver, in whose service I toiled a whole day long! . . . Telling me to go down the ladder again to bless his pigs, forsooth! I take back all my blessings, unworthy old miser! May the wool never grow on your sheep's back, your cattle prove barren, and your fruit trees be blighted!"

His comical indignation, which was only half feigned, amused me very much. For, after all, my companion was a real lama, and he had been cheated of dues that were justly his. But he himself could not long withstand the funny side of the adventure, and we both burst out laughing in the face of the wintry Salween, which seemed to be singing as it wended its way over its pebbly bed: "That's the way things are done in the fine country of Thibet, my adventurous little strangers; you will see many more such!"

That very day, after having again crossed a pass, we reached the vicinity of the dreaded Ubes. We delayed our walk through the village until dusk, and then, leaving behind a group of houses in one of which we supposed that the Big Man was sleeping, we allowed ourselves a short rest in a narrow crevice of the hill, the dry bed of a summer stream.

At dawn the first rays of light revealed a decorated building which was doubtlessly the present abode of the official. As it was still early, we were lucky enough to meet no one in the vicinity.

We made great haste, and when the sun rose we had already put about two miles between us and the dangerous spot. We joyfully congratulated each other on our escape.

In the middle of the afternoon, while we were still in this gay mood, we were told that the *pönpo* had moved three days ago from Ubes to another village situated farther on.

We tramped on again at night till we had passed the place. Perfectly convinced, this time, that our troubles were over we slept happily in a chaos of rocks and thorns. The following morning, after ten minutes' walk, we reached a large house sheltered in a recess of the mountain. About thirty good horses were tethered outside. Country people were already crowding in, bringing grain, grass, butter, meat, and so forth.

This was the place where the official had actually put up! A stalwart head servant supervised the entrance of the things brought by the villagers. He stopped Yongden, and after a talk which appeared to me endless, he ordered a man to give us a meal of tea and *tsampa*. We could not refuse this kind offer. Beggars like us could but rejoice at this piece of good luck. We made a pretense of it, seated on the steps of the kitchen, smiling, laughing, and joking with the attendants of the gentleman, but all the while we felt rather inclined to take to our heels!

The thing which proved most tiresome, and even at times became excessively difficult in the life I was now leading, was the part that I was always obliged to play in order to preserve my incognito. In a country where everything is done in public, down to the most intimate personal acts, I was forced to affect peculiar local customs which embarrassed me terribly. Happily, our way lay at times through large tracts of uninhabited land, and the greater freedom which I enjoyed there somewhat relieved my painful nervous tension. There, especially, I was able to avoid the indescribable soups which the kindly but poverty-stricken fellows, our hosts, bestowed upon us, and which we had to swallow down with a smile, for fear of suspicious comments. Once only did I depart from my accustomed attitude of the beggar to whom everything tastes good, but that day! . . .

We have arrived toward nightfall in a little village. It was very cold and the stark surroundings afforded no shelter. We had already been refused hospitality at several houses, when a woman opened her door to us—the rickety door of an exceedingly miserable dwelling. We entered; a fire burned on the hearth, and in this frosty weather this in itself afforded comfort. The husband of the woman came back shortly afterwards, bringing out some handfuls of *tsampa* from the bottom of a beggar's wallet, and we realised that no supper could be expected from people who had nothing to eat themselves. After a few words of praise for the generosity of an imaginary chief who has given him a rupee, Yongden declares that he will buy some meat, if there is any to be had in the village.

"I know of a good place," said our host at once, scenting a windfall. From the corner where I was crouching, I insisted that it should be of good quality. Most Thibetans eat without any repugnance the putrefied flesh of animals which have died of disease.

"Do not bring back the flesh of an animal which has died, nor a piece which is decayed," I said.

"No, no," said the man. "I know what I am about. You shall have something good."

About ten minutes passed. The village is not large, and the peasant soon returned.

"There," he said, triumphantly, drawing a large parcel of some kind from beneath his sheepskin robe.

What can this be? . . . The room is lighted only by the embers of the fire, and I cannot clearly distinguish anything. . . . The man seems to be opening something, probably a cloth which he has wrapped round his purchase.

Ugh! . . . A most fearsome odour suddenly fills the room, the smell of a charnelhouse. It is sickening.

"Oh," says Yongden, in a voice that trembles slightly, concealing the nausea that he is obliged to repress. "Oh, it is a stomach!"

I understand now. The Thibetans, when they kill a beast, have a horrible habit of enclosing in the stomach, the kidneys, heart, liver, and entrails of the animal. They then sew up this kind of bag, and its contents go on decaying inside for days, weeks, and even longer.

"Yes, it is a stomach," repeats its purchaser, whose voice also trembles somewhat, but with joy, seeing the mass of foodstuff falling out of the now opened bag. "It is full," he exclaims, "quite full! Oh, what a lot!"

He has placed the horror on the floor, is plunging his hands into it, taking out the gelatinous entrails. Three children who were asleep on a heap of tatters have awakened, and are now squatting in front of their father, watching him eagerly with covetous eyes.

"Yes . . . yes, a stomach!" repeats Yongden, in consternation.

"Here, mother, here is a saucepan," says the woman, kindly, addressing me: "You can prepare your supper."

What! Am I to handle this filth? I whisper hastily to my son, "Tell them that I am ill."

"It always seems your turn to be ill when something unpleasant befalls us,"

Yongden growls, under his breath. But the boy is resourceful; he has already regained his self-possession.

"The old mother is ill," he announces. "Why do you not make the *tupa* [thick soup] yourselves? I want everybody to have a share."

The two peasants do not wait to be invited a second time, and the youngsters, realizing that a feast is in course of preparation, stay quietly by the fire, having no desire to go to sleep again. The mother takes up a chopper and a rustic chopping-block made out of a log, on which she cuts the carrion into small pieces. From time to time one of these drops upon the floor, and then the children fall upon it like young puppies and devour it raw.

Now this foul soup is boiling, and a little barley meal is added. Finally the supper is ready.

"Take some, mother; it will do you good," say the husband and wife. I confine myself to groaning, in the corner where I have stretched myself.

"Let her sleep," says Yongden.

He cannot himself be excused. *Arjopas* who spend a rupee on meat and do not touch it do not exist. To-morrow the whole village would be talking about it. He has to swallow down a full bowl of the evil-smelling liquid, but beyond that he cannot go, and he declares that he, too, is not feeling very well. I do not wonder at it. The others feast long and gluttonously upon the broth, smacking their lips in silence, overcome with joy at this unexpected *bonne bouche*, and I am overtaken by sleep whilst the family is still masticating noisily.

We travelled across more hills and more valleys; we passed by more *gompas*. We sat with more peasants, and met two *pönpos* on the road, one of whom bestowed on us most useful presents of food. Thus we progressed in the direction of the Sepo Khang *la*.

At the foot of the pass one of those mysterious and inexplicable incidents was to befall us, such as sometimes bewilder the traveller in Thibet. A long tramp had brought us to a gorge in which a clear stream flowed toward the invisible Salween, which we were again approaching for the last time.

It was scarcely noon, and we felt reluctant to waste a whole afternoon in a village house when we could still have gone on for several hours. We had been informed that it was impossible to cross the range in one day, even if we started before dawn, so that we were bound in any case to spend the night on the hills. We therefore thought it wiser to continue on our way, and if the cold prevented us from camping, we could walk on through the night, as we had often done. But before starting on this long tramp I wished to eat a good meal. Water was now at our feet, and we could not guess when we should again run across a stream. Yongden gladly agreed to make a halt, and as soon as we had reached the bank we put our loads on the shingle, and my companion began to light a fire with the few twigs that I had gathered under some trees which grew at the end of the fields.

A little boy whom I had noticed on the other side of the river then crossed the bridge and ran toward Yongden. He bowed down three times before him as

Thibetans do in their greetings to great lamas. We were most astonished. What could have made that child give such a deep token of reverence to a mere beggar pilgrim. Without giving us time to put any question, the boy addressed Yongden.

"My grandfather, who is very ill," he said, "has told us all, this morning, that a lama coming down that hill, was to make tea in the dry part of the river bed and that he wanted to see him. Since the sun has risen my brother and I have watched in turn at the bridge to invite the lama to our house. Now that you have come, please follow me."

"It is not my son whom your grandfather expects," I told the boy. "We are people from a far-off country. He does not know us."

"He said the lama *who would make tea on the stones*," insisted the child; and as we did not comply with his request he crossed the river again and disappeared between the fences of the fields.

We had just begun to drink our tea when the boy reappeared, accompanied by a young *trapa*.

"Lama," the latter said to Yongden, "be kind enough to come to see my father. He is very ill and says that he is about to die. He only waits for a lama who will arrive to-day and who is the one and only person who can direct him to a happy place of rebirth in the next world. He told us all this morning that you would come down that hill and make tea, here on the stones, near the river. All has happened as he said. Now please be kind to us and come."

Neither Yongden nor I knew what to think about this queer affair. We persisted in believing that the sufferer meant some lama whom he knew and had some reason to expect on this road. Nevertheless, seeing the *trapa* weeping, I advised my companion to pay a visit to the sick villager. So he promised to go as soon as we had finished our meal.

The boy and the young *trapa*—his uncle, I understood—went to report our answer to the farmer. But presently I saw another boy seated near the bridge observing us. These people were certainly afraid that Yongden would fail to keep his promise, and therefore kept him in sight. No escape was possible, and why indeed should Yongden have disappointed an old invalid? The latter would evidently see that my son was not the one he expected, and all would end with no more than ten minutes' delay.

All the family had assembled at the door of the farm. They greeted Yongden with the greatest respect. My companion was then led into the room, and while he went toward the cushions on which the farmer lay I remained near the threshold with the women of the house.

The old man did not really appear as one who is near death. His voice was firm and his intelligent eyes showed that his mental faculties were in no way dimmed. He wished to rise and bow down to my son, but the latter prevented him from moving out of his blankets, saying that sick people need only *mean* the respectful salute.

"Lama," the farmer said, "I have been longing for your coming, but I knew that you were to come and I waited for you, to die. You are my true *tsawai lama*;[1] no one but you alone can lead me to the 'Land of Bliss.' Have compassion on me, bless me, do not refuse me your help."

What the old man wished was for Yongden to utter for his benefit the mystic words called *Powa* which are pronounced at the deathbed of a lay lamaist or of any monk who is not an initiate, when the latter is quite beyond all hope of recovery.

As I have said, the old Thibetan did not seem to be near to death, and for religious reasons whose explanations would be out of place here, my companion hesitated to yield to his wishes. He tried in vain to hearten the sick man, assuring him that he would not die, and offering to recite the spells which "mend" life and give it new strength. This the farmer, however, obstinately refused, maintaining that he knew his hour to be at hand and had only awaited the spiritual aid of his lama to take his departure.

He then began to weep and order those present to entreat the lama on his behalf. The family did so, sobbing and weeping, with repeated prostrations, until, overpowered, Yongden finally gave in. Then, deep moved he recited the ritual words which loosen the ties of the "*namshés*",[2] and lead them safely through the labyrinthine paths of the other worlds.

When we left him the old farmer's face expressed a perfect serenity, a complete detachment from all earthly concerns, having, it seemed, entered the true Blissful Paradise which, being nowhere and everywhere, lies in the mind of each one of us.

I shall not venture to offer any explanation of this peculiar incident. I have related the fact thinking that it might interest those who pursue psychic researches, but I would feel exceedingly sorry if my account provoked commentaries disrespectful to the memory of the departed Thibetan. Death and the dying are never to be made a subject of raillery.

Those who had told us that the road across the Sepo Khang hills was a long one, were certainly right. We walked on from the dawn, meeting nobody and mistaking our way on several occasions at the intersection of trails leading to *dokpas'* summer camps. At dusk we were still far from the pass. A blizzard then rose, as we climbed a steep and waterless slope. There was no camping-place in the vicinity, and we had almost decided to retrace our steps and shelter ourselves much lower down at a place where we had seen some empty huts, when we heard the tinkling of horses' bells and three men appeared on the way up like ourselves. They were traders, and told us that a little farther along on the road there was a farm wherein we could get shelter.

It was pitch dark when we arrived. I understood from the large stables, that the place was a kind of inn for the use of travellers crossing the pass at a season when camping in the open is rather dangerous. We were admitted to the kitchen with the

---

[1] Either the head lama of the sect to which one belongs, or the head lama of the monastery of which one is either a benefactor, a monk, or a serf. But in this case it means a spiritual father and guide with whom one has been connected in that way for several lives.

[2] *Namshés*: consciousness, which is multiple. Not in any case to be translated by *soul*.

merchants who fed us with soup, tea, *tsampa* and dried fruits. These men belonged to a village in the same neighbourhood as the sick farmer. Passing there in the morning, they had heard all about Yongden, and brought us the sad news that at dawn, when we ourselves had left the village, the old man had smiled and died. The traders had been deeply impressed by the account of their friend's last hours. The thoughts of all being turned toward religion, they begged Yongden to preach them a sermon, which he did.

The kitchen, the only living room of the farm, was very small, and with the blazing fire that burned quite near us, we were half roasted. Then, when the time came to sleep, we understood that the owner and his wife wished to remain alone. The traders went down the ladder to the stable, where they slept near their beasts. As for us, we were told to accommodate ourselves on the flat roof. What a change from that ovenlike kitchen to the cold air of a frosty night, with a blizzard raging, at fifteen or sixteen thousand feet above sea level! It was not the first time that I had experienced this kind of hospitality. More than once villagers had invited us, treated us to a good supper, and then sent us on the roof or into the courtyard. Nobody apparently thought much of it in Thibet!

But that night I lacked the courage to lie down in the open air, and I begged permission (which was granted) to sleep next the kitchen in a shelter shut in on three sides.

The next day we crossed the pass and descended to the Sepo monastery, beautifully situated in a lonely spot with an extended view in front of it. The traders were on horseback, and had reached the *gompa* long before us. They had stayed there for a while and had told the lamas about Yongden, so that when he arrived, meaning to purchase some food, he was cordially welcomed and invited to remain a few days to discuss matters concerning the Buddhist doctrine with some of the monastery's learned inmates. As for myself, I could also get lodging in a guest house. But as I had not accompanied my adopted son to the monastery, and had continued my way, I was already out of sight amongst the hills, so Yongden declined the kind invitation. I regretted it afterwards; but as my rôle of a lay woman would very likely have kept me away from the place where the *literati* of the monastery would hold their meetings with Yongden, I consoled myself with no great difficulty.

A little later in the evening, we met a woman going to the *gompa* who told us that we could find a shelter in a partly ruined house that was easily seen from the road. The country was once more a complete desert, and we could not hope to reach the lower valley on the same day. It proved more and more true that the crossing of the Sepo Khang *la* was a long one. We walked about an hour longer without discovering the house, but at last reached it when it was nearly dark.

It had been a really large and well-built farm with a good number of stables, sheds, storerooms, servants' quarters, and a pretty apartment upstairs for the owners. Everything was now in a dilapidated condition, but with a little work it would have been quite possible to make the necessary repairs, for no essential parts of the building were ruined.

We had nearly finished our meal when the woman who had told us about that house arrived with a young boy, her son. She was the owner of the farm and had left it, though there were good fields around it, after a terrible drama.

A few years before, a gang of robbers from the Po country had attacked this isolated farm and there had been a terrific struggle. Four of the masters, the woman's husband, her two brothers, another relative, and a few servants had been killed, while others were wounded. The robbers also had left several dead on the ground. Since then the unhappy housewife and her family lived in the village near the monastery. The fear that a similar outrage would happen again, naturally kept her away from her farm, which gradually fell into ruins.

But another and still stronger fear prevented her from returning to her former house. The farm was believed to be haunted by evil spirits. The violent death of so many men had attracted them, and, with the ghosts of the murderers and their victims, they roamed about the buildings. For this reason the woman had come back from the *gompa* to ask the lama to spend the night in her house, to exorcise it.

She could have requested the services of the lamas of Sepo, and most likely some of them had already performed the required rites on her behalf; but, as I have already mentioned, "Red Cap" lamas are deemed more powerful exorcists than their colleagues of the yellow sect. Moreover, Yongden, for obvious reasons, had a real success as a lama "Holder of the Secret Spells." Had he established himself somewhere, clients would have flocked to his residence. But he hated that kind of trade; he had seen it from too near.

Nevertheless, kindness compelled him to comply with the wishes of the woman. He told her that if she wished to cultivate her property again, she could do so without fear of any denizen of another world, but that serious precautions were to be taken against robbers.

The following day we arrived in the Dainshin province, and here again, as along the Salween, I was the guest of many. I never regretted my roundabout tour in that country. It is out of the way of the great trade routes, and absolutely unknown to foreigners. Yet it is a well-cultivated area. Large and prosperous monasteries are seen in several places, the villages seem to be well built, and the people are agreeable. I saw some interesting soda fields from which Thibetans get the stuff they mix with their tea when boiling it.

Once we passed a rich traveller on the road, carrying presents to a *gompa*. He gave us two rupees each, without our asking for money. We were naturally most astonished at this unexpected windfall.

We did not always take our disguise as beggars very seriously. Once in the heart of Thibet, we preferred to save time by purchasing our supplies. Nevertheless, unsolicited alms came our way several times. Never in my life have I made so economical a journey. We used to laugh as we tramped along the road, recalling all the stories we had read of travellers who started out with many camels laden with heavy and expensive stores and luggage only to meet with failure more or less near their goal.

I could have done the whole journey without any money in my pocket, but as we were extravagant beggars, indulging in molasses cakes, dried fruits, the best tea, and plenty of butter, we succeeded in spending one hundred rupees in our four months' journey from Yunnan to Lhasa. One need not be rolling in riches to travel in the blessed lands of Asia!

Ysenda Maxtone Graham

"Through a barren land"
(1996)

I fell in love with America, as many well-brought-up English girls do, in my mid-twenties. Through my American cousins, the hyphenated Maxtone-Grahams, I met a delightful man of my age called William Petty, who, three days after I met him, began to show me the America he knew and loved. We started, safely enough, with the Staten Island Ferry, and, a year or so later, graduated to the Grand Canyon in all its ruggedness. There we had a proper life-threatening adventure.

The "John and Mary" I am writing to are my cousins in New York, John and Mary Maxtone-Graham; John is the writer on ocean liners. I needed to set down the story in order to preserve the small but horrifying details, which might otherwise be lost in a fog of vague memories. I happened to write it as a letter, and in fact the letter form helped. You can't be too pseudy or purple in a letter—it won't wash, and your cousins will fall asleep. The thought that they would read it, hand-written, over tea in their Manhattan drawing room kept my lyrical urges in check. I managed not to mention God or Eternity once.

Dear John and Mary,
I am writing to tell you what happened in the Grand Canyon, as you asked me to. Before I start, I beg you not to think of Bill Petty as the baddy in the story, the man who took Ysenda down the Grand Canyon and had no idea how to get her out again. He had planned the journey carefully, and had followed our difficult trail, "Tonto East," two years before, in August. He knew exactly how far we had to walk each day, where we could look for shade and water, and how to find routes when they were not clear. His rucksack was twice as heavy as mine, and he was endlessly optimistic, saying things like, "I think our camping ground's just round the corner. Not far now."

And please don't think we shouldn't have gone down the Grand Canyon at all, knowing how hot it was going to be. We were looking forward to it. If you have been sitting in a magazine office in London for months, putting hyphens between "twentieth" and "century" (if it is adjectival), and dreaming of the somethingth wonder of the world which is a mile deep and teaches you all about Time, when you actually arrive at the South Rim you are bursting to go down. Bill had got us reservations on this particular back-country trail, and had booked a table for dinner at the bottom of the Grand Canyon at five o'clock on Thursday evening. We confirmed it when we arrived at the Grand Canyon Village: "Two steak dinners," the piece of paper said. It was heartening. Today was Monday: this time in three days, I thought, we will have joined the main trail and will be having our "steak dinner," surrounded by jolly Germans again.

I will tell you what we had done the day or two before, because it is part of the story. Bill and I converged in his parents' family kitchen in Denver in the middle of the night of the 1st July. I had flown from London and Bill had driven from his brother's wedding in Nebraska. I arrived first, and there was no one at home except a poodle. I looked through the brochures on the kitchen table about the Grand Canyon. They were riveting. Descriptions of beauty beyond your wildest dreams—of the drama of mesas, the shock of the gorge, the timelessness of creeks—were interspersed with small warning paragraphs in italics:

> *Body, 26, female, found under a rock in Grapevine Creek. Full canteen lying next to her. The victim had obviously tried to call for help but . . .*

Bill arrived and we listened to William Byrd on CD.

The next morning, feeling light-headed as you do on the first day of a hot holiday, we put our stuff into Bill's father's beautiful old Mercedes sports car and drove off, southwards. Very soon, we realised two things: first, that the car wasn't air-conditioned, and second, that the sun bore down on one in a monstrous way. All we could do was cower beneath it. Opening the windows didn't help. We decided to take the roof off—better a scorching breeze, we thought, than no breeze at all—so we covered ourselves in sun block factor 30 and drove along like merry people do in old films, shouting above the noise. It was great fun, but at the border of New Mexico, while ringing up my sister to ask how to find her house in Santa Fe, I had to rush into the oily garage and sit down. A few seconds later I fell off the chair, crashing my head on to the floor, and came round with the shock of it, saying "Where am I?" Bill nursed me with an ice-pack.

So we had a glimpse of the sun's power before going down the Grand Canyon. Arriving at Santa Fe was bliss. Livia had made a picnic to take to the opera; we sat under the poplars in the early evening, watching the sun disappear.

On Grand Canyon day, we left Santa Fe at dawn and drove all day through the bleached landscape of New Mexico and Arizona. We drove straight to the back-country office to confirm our reservations on the Tonto trail.

"No one's been on your trail for a month now," the ranger-in-uniform said.

"Is there any water in Cottonwood Creek?" Bill asked.

"It's pretty dry down there. There was a trickle three or four weeks ago. It's probably dried up by now. Take a lot of water."

I sat sullenly in the back of the office, letting the coolness of the room seep into my hot body, while Bill and the ranger talked deeply and slowly about possible water sources.

"We don't have a checking service any more," the ranger said. "You'd better tell a member of your family when to start worrying."

If it had been me talking to the ranger, I would have made high-pitched exclamations such as "Gosh. How frightening. I suppose we'd better." But Bill just stood still, hiding whatever reaction he might be having. "OK," he said, occasionally.

To the Grand Canyon General Store next. It is fun being in America because you take a trolley rather than a basket. Basking, again, in the coolness of the huge aisles, we wandered up and down, picking things off shelves and crossing them off our list: iodine pills, snake-bite kit, first-aid kit, canteens, nuts, beef jerky, freeze-dried vegetables (Bill insisted that these would be useful), torches, batteries, zip-lock bags, pink energy-giving powder to put in our water, and Power Bars with zestful zig-zags on the wrappers.

Then, supper. We went to the Bright Angel Lodge and drank two jugs of iced water. We had soup, roast beef, and apple crumble—nursery food—to set us up. We felt we were beginning to procrastinate, so we paid the bill and drove, via a tap where we collected four gallons of water, to Grandview Point, twelve smooth miles away. In a frenzy of concentration, we pared down our luggage and put it into rucksacks. Mine was small, Bill's was manly. He carried the tent with its nine metal poles; I carried the mats. He carried a huge and potentially leaky water container, as well as his own gallon canteen; I carried my canteen and one of those pretty Spanish water pouches which you squeeze and which stink of fresh leather. We were in a car park. Everyone else was about to go home.

"Let's split out of here," Bill said.

"Yes, let's. How d'you put this thing on? Can you help me?"

My role as weed had started. We took our first step downwards. There it was, the Grand Canyon itself, pinkish and impossible to understand. An eagle was flying over it. We were full of descending energy and had no qualms at all.

It was a stony and rough path, and quite steep. The weight of rucksack bore down on us from behind and we had to use our hands to hold us back. It was seven o'clock and we knew we had to walk for three hours to get to the Horseshoe Mesa, our first camp ground.

"I love the Grand Canyon. I want to *be* the Grand Canyon," I said. It sounds a pretentious remark now, but it did mean something then. Perhaps being in a place like that makes one speak like a hippy.

We had brought twice as much water as we expected to. So when we started sucking on the leather pouch, we felt we were making no impression at all on our supply. But two slightly serious things happened now: first, we passed three people who were coming in the opposite direction. The difference between their mood and ours was sinister. We were in a skipping, light-hearted mood, tripping from stone to stone and agreeing about things. These people, though blond and sporty, were hanging their heads and not smiling at all—not even to be polite to us. They looked exhausted.

"We're out of water," they said. "Can you lend us some?"

"We can't give you much, because this might have to last us for days, but you can have a gulp each."

They fell on the Spanish leather pouch, and each went into a momentary state of bliss, instantly cut short.

"How much further is it to the top?"

"About an hour."

"An *hour*! We thought we were nearly there. I can't go on for another hour."

"It's really not very far," Bill said. "The water will help you."

"Thanks very much. Bye."

They stomped on upwards and we skipped on downwards. The second serious thing was that it grew dark. You always hope that twilight will last for ever, but it doesn't. We wondered whether to pitch our tent there, or to try to get our torches working and walk on in the dark. Bill decided on the torches. We rummaged for them in our side-pockets. We had to find the batteries as well. Bill sat on a rock and got out the quarter-dollar coin he had brought to undo the screw of the torch, but it didn't fit. This mattered terribly; a small thing like a coin not fitting into a screw does matter in a place like this, I realised. But Bill didn't curse or panic; he just felt about patiently for a spoon. The end of the spoon worked. It was too dark to read the "positive" and "negative" signs, but he got it right, and with the light of the first torch assembled the second.

On we walked, feeling proud with our beams of light showing us the way. We arrived at the Horseshoe Mesa at ten, and found a group of people there, chatting and rustling their sleeping bags.

"Is there any water down in Cottonwood Creek?" Bill asked.

"There's tadpole water, so we drank that. It's disgusting!"

Bill set up our tent—the tent he had been setting up since he was seven; a sturdy, trusty tent which does not need to be attached to the ground. We put on our smart flannel pyjamas (we had brought them instead of blankets), brushed our teeth and got inside.

"We got here!" Bill said. "We now know two things: we can walk in the dark, and there's water in Cottonwood. Those people are so ignorant. They came down with two quarts of water each. And they don't seem to realise that tadpole water is what you always drink down here. Look at the Milky Way. Have you ever seen it before?"

We used our trousers for pillows. In the middle of the night I woke up shivering but hot. I put Bill's pyjama top, which he had taken off, over my shoulders and went back to sleep, shuddering slightly.

We woke to the sound of people leaving. It was half-past five. I got out of the tent and talked to a girl in shorts.

"I don't advise going down there," she said.

"Why not?"

"It's very hot, and very dry."

"But we've got lots of water, and we can walk in the dark."

At six o'clock we started walking down the dusty, slippery path to Cottonwood Creek. The expression "route-finding ability" was at the front of my mind, "route" pronounced as "rout" is in England. Our hikers' guide said that you needed it for this path. Bill had it, thank goodness. I just followed. We passed yucca plants, dead-looking and solitary, sticking out of the ground and taller than anything else.

"That's a barrel cactus," Bill said. "If you are dying of thirst you can take all the prickles off and find water inside." The poor cactus was guarding its water, hugging its prickles so that thirsty animals wouldn't try to tear it apart.

"Look. D'you see down there, the pale green trees? They're cottonwoods. That's where we're spending the day." It was before eight o'clock when we reached the creek but the heat was already unbearable. We sat on a rock and shared a Power Bar. Bill said we should walk up the creek to find water; we *could* make do with tadpole water, of course, but it would be better to go further up and find fresh spring water which had not had time to be bred in. So we left our rucksacks and started scrambling through the confusing, choked creek, hoping that water might appear, but it didn't. I grew cross and demoralized.

"Let's just have tadpole water," I said. "Come on. Please. Tadpole water's fine. You said so last night."

"You wait here and I'll go further up on my own."

I waited.

"Ysenda! Found some!"

It was true. He was standing on a blanket of bright green grass, and the weight of his body was forming a small lake of water.

"Desert water," he said. "Let's have a drinking party."

We took gulp after gulp of our clean tap water, so that we could have an empty canteen to fill with desert water.

Until this moment I had never been at all interested in a zip-lock bag. But when Bill pulled one out of his pocket, tore a hole in one corner, put his hand inside, pressed it into the grass, watched it fill up with pink water (the colour of the water at the dentist's when the man says, "Have a good rinse now. It's all over") and let the water trickle into the canteen, I suddenly took notice of one. It was not a thankless task, this water-collecting. The canteen filled fairly quickly. I had a few goes of pressing with the zip-lock bag, but was not as good as it as Bill. We took uneven turns.

We walked victoriously back to our rucksacks and carried them to a hiding-place for the day.

"When are we going to stop?" I asked Bill.

"Very soon. There's a bit more shade further on."

We tried lying under some squat, dark trees, but they weren't shady enough: shafts of sunlight forced their way through the dense branches. So we took our mats, a book, some beef jerky and nuts, and our water, to a great slab of shade among some

Indian ruins. It was becoming absurdly hot—so hot that we couldn't move. We lay in our slab of shade, unable to talk, eat or think "How pretty this is." I tried to read the beginning of *Huckleberry Finn* but was too jealous of the characters because they were not in the Grand Canyon. My one thought was "If only it were this time tomorrow. By this time tomorrow I will be so much happier. But it isn't. It's still this time today."

Bill had warned me that our walk to Grapevine Creek this evening was the hardest part of our journey, and would take a long time. We knew that this meant leaving at five. Between noon and two o'clock the heat was at its height; I know now that it was 125 degrees. But by five o'clock it didn't seem much cooler. We trudged back to our rucksacks and forced ourselves to roll up our mats. We searched for the vital iodine pills in endless side-pockets before finding them. I started to cry with the heat.

"I hate the Grand Canyon's guts," I said.

"Oh, Ysenda, I'm terribly sorry. It's all been a great mistake. I should never have brought you."

"No, it's all right. I love it really. But if only it were this time tomorrow, Bill."

Once we had started walking, it wasn't as bad as all that. Every step brought us nearer to our steak dinner. This walk was not steep, so we made good progress and could walk almost at a normal pace. We wound our way through miniature orchards of cactus plants, and every now and then came across a small heap of three stones, which meant that a human being had been here before. We drank as we walked. Bill drank much more than me, but he was a big man. We longed for the shady sides of creeks.

We had still not seen the geological reason for the Grand Canyon. But now we saw it, and for the first time I made touristy remarks: "Golly. The actual Colorado River! But it's green. You said it was hot-chocolate-coloured. Shall we take a photograph?"

As it grew darker, the canyons towards Grapevine Creek grew strangely threatening. I had never seen an evil landscape before. Until now, the place had merely seemed indifferent to us; now it seemed to be against us. We couldn't understand it, but we both felt it. We kept not being nearly there. Our destination was a small, round camp ground at the end of a creek: Bill began to take on the shape of one of those statues of the Virgin and Child made of an ivory tusk, which curves inwards. On our right was a drop-off which it was better not to think about. Its sides were horribly smooth.

"Think of Frodo Baggins, Ysenda. *He* went through much worse things than this."

"But he was fictional," I said, grumpily.

Just before needing to use a torch, we arrived, and dropped on to the ground. It was comforting to be surrounded by a circle of stones laid by a human being.

"Let's sleep under the stars," I said. I couldn't bear the idea of sorting out the metal poles.

"I'd feel happier in a tent," Bill said. "You never know what animals might come."

So we put it up, in silence, much too hot to think of eating and too worried to brush our teeth. We wanted to keep a gallon of water each for the next day. But our thirst was great.

I got inside the tent. Bill was lying on his back, thinking hard and staring at the ceiling.

"This is the plan," he said. "We'll wake up at four. We'll look for water in the creek, and if we don't find any in a half-hour we'll go back to Cottonwood."

"Back to Cottonwood! No, we simply can't go back to Cottonwood. We've just come all the way from there. We're on our way to the bottom. I'm not going back."

"But we need water, Ysenda. We know we can find it at Cottonwood."

"You just drink too much."

"We'll go back the way we came, back up to Horseshoe Mesa and Grandview Point. It's the sensible plan."

So our longed-for arrival at the bottom, our easy descent on the last morning, and our steak dinner, were not going to take place after all. Instead, we would have to climb out the difficult way—the way we knew all too well, having come down it.

"Also," Bill said, "there's no proper shade to hide in tomorrow if we carry on going down. We know there's shade in Cottonwood. We'll spend all day there, and climb out in the evening. Now drink: drink as much as you like."

The night was like a night in hell. A vicious, fiery wind blew hard at us, and it was so hot that you had to lie on your side in order to sweat as little as possible. We had no difficulty in waking at four. Bill folded up the tent and went to look for water. I felt for our bags of nuts and dried fruit, and found that they had tooth-marks in them: a desert rat or ringtail cat had come in the night and eaten everything except for the beef jerky and a few nuts. It had tried to force its way into the freeze-dried vegetables, but had not managed.

Bill came back, without water, so we put our rucksacks on and walked back the way we had come last night, treading on our old foot-prints. Stomping English hymns such as "Onward, Christian soldiers" and "Guide me, O, thou great Redeemer, pilgrim through this barren land" helped me along: I marched in rhythm. By eight o'clock we were approaching our dear Cottonwood Creek. It was almost homely compared with Grapevine.

We had memorized where our spring was by looking hard at a large, round rock above it. But it was much harder to find than we expected. It was getting absurdly hot again, and I couldn't believe we were scrambling about, not finding our spring.

"Let's leave our rucksacks and come back for them when we've found it. Take the beef jerky and nuts, and the canteens."

A few minutes later, we found our darling spring. We took our shirts off, trod them into the wet grass, and put them on again. It was delicious. Our minds were at rest. We lay down, snuggled up as close as possible to the bamboo copse, and fell asleep.

We spent the whole day by the spring, drinking all the water we already had: we had left the iodine pills in our rucksacks and couldn't contemplate going to collect them. The heat above the creek was deadly and it would have exhausted us to walk in it even for a minute. Bill had been sick as soon as we arrived at Cottonwood, but he didn't mind. He just kept drinking. The water was hot and disgusting, of course, tasting of a mixture of earth, leather or plastic (depending on the canteen), pink powder and iodine pills. But I loved it. A yard or so above us, a black and white snake writhed about in a bamboo tree, showing off. We didn't have the energy to worry about it. "It's not poisonous," Bill said. "It's not a rattlesnake, and rattlesnakes are the only poisonous snakes in the Grand Canyon."

Time passed peacefully and slowly. We looked at our little world of spring, grass, bamboo trees and zip-lock bag and felt satisfied and happy. The sun passed over us and we had to move to the other side of the bamboo copse. While Bill slept, I beat a bamboo tree with a twig, in order to frighten off the snakes. "The sun shines bright on my old Kentucky home," I tapped, because my choir had sung it a few weeks ago at a concert in Cambridgeshire.

At five o'clock we decided it was just about cool enough to start the hard work of filling a canteen with spring water. Bill pressed his fingers into the grass and discovered to his horror that it had dried up.

"It can't have," I said. "It's a spring."

But it had. If Bill pressed with all his might, he could form a tiny, dark-brown pool of thick mud.

"This isn't funny," I said.

"No, it's not funny."

"It's the most stupid thing we've ever done."

"We'll have to make do with drinking mud. Muddy water's better than no water."

So Bill started pressing. It was a cruel task, especially since we could remember how easy it had been yesterday, and how we had squandered water today, dipping our shirts into it. Bill yanked clods of mud out of the ground and squeezed them as hard as he could, so that drips would trickle into the bag. He shook with the effort, and needed to drink almost as much water as he was collecting. In an hour or so, with a few gestures of demoralized help from me, he had put two inches of mud into our transparent canteen. It settled, leaving a thick residue. We poured the top layer of brown liquid into our own canteens and went back to our rucksacks to find the iodine pills.

We decided (after wondering whether we ought to stay here till morning in the hope that the spring would fill up again—but what if it didn't?) to leave at eight, which would give us half an hour of day-light to find our way back to the trail. At eight o'clock it was still sweltering; but my spirits were high because I so desperately wanted to get out, and now we were on our way OUT of this terrifying place. We started climbing up the steep, parched path towards the Horseshoe Mesa. We used a code—"Mmm?" "Mmm," meaning, "Are you all right?" "Yes," in order to save energy. We took tiny sips of water. Bill took his shirt off, and advised me to: "It's so much cooler," he said. So I did; and walked on in a Marks & Spencer's bra which had become pink with days of Grand Canyon grime.

After two hours of dogged climbing, Bill said, "OK, we're going to abandon our rucksacks."

"What? Leave them here?"

"I don't mind if I never see mine again."

So we left them, taking only our bag of passports, tickets and money, and one or two sentimental things such as *The Grand Canyon Songbook*, a book I had made for Bill which contained psalms, chants, Bach chorales and the words of "Sumer is icumen in."

Our burden was lightened, and we felt better. And much sooner than we expected, we saw the wooden signpost which meant we were at the Horseshoe Mesa, where we had spent our first night. It was ten o'clock at night, and there was no one at the camp ground. "Only three or four hours to go," I thought.

Then Bill was sick again. The water he had been drinking all day had not been going into his system at all, just sitting there, uselessly.

"But I feel a whole man again now," he said. "Let's go on."

So we did. The joy of being on the home stretch was so great that I could have skipped, even in my state of thirst. I just prayed that Bill would be all right, and he seemed to be at the moment. He told me there was a bottle of sparkling cranberry juice in the car on the rim of the Canyon.

My torch went out. Bill tried to mend it, taking it apart and wiggling a small piece of wire.

"It's broken," he said.

"I'll just have to walk close behind you, and use the light of yours."

That worked all right. But our minute-long rests became two-minute ones, then five-minute ones. Bill was not feeling at all well. Soon he lay down on the path, so dehydrated that he couldn't move.

"We'll lie here for ten minutes," he said, "and if I'm not better by then, will you go to the rim on your own and bring me down the bottle of sparkling cranberry juice?"

"Oh, Bill, please be well enough. I couldn't go up there on my own. Just be well enough for three more hours."

"Ysenda," he said, ten minutes later, "I've stopped sweating. Will you pour some of that mud over me?"

I rubbed the brown gunge from Cottonwood Creek, the smell of which was what Bill's body was revolting against, on to his tummy and his forehead.

"Do you think you could go to the top alone, Ysenda, and find a ranger to come and rescue me?"

"No. I really couldn't. I don't know how to find the path. I'd get lost."

"But I might die. If you're as dehydrated as I am you really can die."

"OK, then." I grabbed the torch, the car keys, the spoon to open the torch with, some more batteries and a 20-dollar note. I felt furious rather than pitying. This reversal of roles was absurd. In five minutes I was lost. I had gone off the path and scrambled up a bank of stones which led to nowhere. Then I thought, "Of course. This is a nightmare. I'm going to wake up in bed in London."

I found my way back to Bill. "I got lost," I said. "Please can I stay here with you? I'd rather die with you than die alone."

So we lay there, looking up at the indifferent stars.

"Ysenda," Bill said. "I really *might* die, you know. Will you try going to the top again? The way to find the path is to shine the torch on to the ground in front and look for old footprints."

"All right. I'll go. Bye."

The footprint method worked. I leaped from stone to stone in a kind of frenzy, taking tiny sips from the muddy dregs of my water. That walk has contracted in my memory so that I can't describe how long or far it was; all I can remember are moments of it: sitting, panting on a stone, looking into the dark wastes and think-ing of Bill lying there; tipping my head back to take sips from the bottom of the canteen, and only then seeing the rim which was still far above me; worrying that if and when I reached the car, I wouldn't be able to start it (it had been difficult recently) or actually drive it, never having driven an automatic car. And where would I drive to? I had no idea what time it was. The walk went on and on and didn't change character for two or three hours; every steep, dry footstep just led to another one. My lips tasted as salty as crisps. Every now and then I allowed a minute drop of water to escape on to the outside of my mouth rather than be swallowed. All I thought about was sparkling cranberry juice. It seemed impossible to believe that a world existed where you could come across a whole bottle of liquid.

When I pointed my torch at a wooden step for the first time, I was encouraged: I remembered from our journey down that some of the steps in the first half-hour were wooden and level. Then (oh the joy of it) I saw a wooden signpost: "To go beyond this point you must make a reservation at the back-country office." So now I really was within lazy-tourist walking distance of the car park.

Then—the beloved wall. I have never been so excited to see a wall before. There I was, on the Tarmac, shining my torch round the empty parking lots. The beam shone onto something which looked like a useful map but it turned out to be one of those pretty National Park weatherproof signs which told me all about the inter-esting trees which grow near Grandview Point.

I looked for the car and couldn't find it immediately. Then I did. I ran towards it and opened the boot. I knew exactly where the bottle was. Like a drunkard, I tore off the gold wrapper, prized open the lid and took gulp after gulp of strange fizzy juice. Then I put one of Bill's shirts on, and got into the driving seat. The car started. I worked out what "P", "R" and "D" must mean, and in a minute was driving along the deserted road. No one passed me. I drove for twelve miles, into the village, and swung into a petrol station but it was closed, so I swung out again. Then I saw a light on in what looked like a hotel reception room. I parked the car and ran in.

There was a large woman behind the desk.

"Hello. I've just come out of the Grand Canyon and I've left my friend down there, who's dying. Can you send someone to rescue him?"

"Yes, Ma'am."

She rang the Park Ranger service. For an hour a man asked me questions: when did I leave Mr. Petty? What colour was he? "Mudcoloured." What had he been drinking? "Mud." Where was he exactly? How did you spell Ysenda? I answered every question as promptly and desperately as someone in an oral exam.

"Stay by the phone," the man said. So I collapsed into a chair in the lounge, having gone to the car to collect a jersey: suddenly I felt rather cold. I went to the ladies' "restroom" and saw my reflection for the first time for days: apart from having white, dried-out lips and the old bruises from fainting, I looked fine. I splashed my face with tap water.

The telephone rang again. This time it was the young ranger who was going down to find Bill. It was four in the morning. I told him I would be in the Yavapai Lodge (that was the hotel) until Bill came to find me. Then I sat on the chair again and a night-time ash-tray cleaner came to talk to me and brought me some cold coffee. At five o'clock I started to cry.

"Is there a room here?" I asked the woman behind the desk.

"No, Ma'am. We're all booked up."

"I've got a sleeping bag. Could I possibly sleep on the floor somewhere?"

She put me behind the Grand Canyon Flights and Tours desk. With my bottle beside me, like a tramp, I got inside and shuddered to think what might happen. For the first time I realised that Bill's dead body might be hauled out of the Grand Canyon; that I would tell his parents the story and we would stand round a coffin at a quiet funeral in Denver, with an electronic organ playing slow, vibrating chords. The terrible sadness of it overwhelmed me and I turned away from the Flights and Tours desk towards the skirting board.

When I woke up the room was loud with bustle. People were checking in and checking out. The large woman was standing over me.

"Your friend's doing fine," she said. "The ranger's with him now and they'll be hiking out later this morning."

I spent the morning in the cafeteria and the lounge, drinking and dozing. I worked my way through glass after glass of iced orange juice, basking in relief and watching American families having breakfast. On my chair in the lounge I felt like an exhibit: there should have been a notice beside me saying, "This sleeping girl has just been down the Grand Canyon and has not seen a human being (except her companion, who nearly died last night) or a running tap for days. Notice her pinkish shoes and sore lips. Don't let this happen to you. Take a flight or tour."

In the middle of the morning I drifted across the road to the general store to buy a new hat (the old one was in the abandoned rucksack) and two litres of water. At lunch-time I went back to the cafeteria and ate a plate of tomatoes. I wished Bill would come in.

Then he did. I turned and saw a dazed, muddy figure walking towards me.

"You're alive," I said.

"Have you got us a room?"

"Yes. let's go there now."

We drove: it was in a motel-ish wing.

"Let's have baths."

The inside of the bath was brown and encrusted; I had always longed to need to wash as badly as medieval people must have, just to see what it was like.

We didn't stop smiling for two days. Bill told me his story: he had lain on the path, not sleeping but obsessed with sparkling cranberry juice. Dawn broke at five o'clock and he began to worry, because the monster sun would come and kill him. He thought I might not have got to the top. At half-past five he decided he had better pull himself upwards as a last gesture. He felt his heart might burst, so weak and dehydrated was he. He was worried for me; and says now that he frankly was resigned to die. But he heaved himself upwards at a snail's pace, as the air grew hotter. Then he heard a voice.

"William?"

It was Barry the ranger. Bill says he couldn't believe how quickly he was brought back from death's door to the jolly world of American chat about this and that. Barry had a huge rucksack and gave Bill three litres of water, very slowly. He told him he had lost half his body fluid. By the time he was ready to walk, it was too hot to climb out, so Bill had the choice of waiting till evening, or ordering a helicopter to come and collect him from the Horseshoe Mesa, the nearest flat place. He chose the helicopter.

He loved his helicopter ride and promised to take me on one the next day. We spent two nights in the Grand Canyon village, convalescing—drinking, sleeping, having scrambled eggs and bacon for breakfast and writing letters. We drove everywhere and arranged for our rucksacks to be collected by a young ranger who was saving up for a truck. We stood on the rim in the evening, gazing at our desert.

We had our helicopter ride, "a complete sight and sound experience," with headphones and the *Water Music* playing. I loved it. But I turned round and saw Bill quietly being sick into the bag provided.

Love from Ysenda.

Sara Wheeler

Terra Incognita: Travels in Antarctica
(1997)

. . . people are trying to fathom themselves in this antarctic context, to imagine their coordinates, how they are fixed in time and space. (Barry Lopez, Crary Lab dedication talk, McMurdo, 1991)

A Frenchman appeared in my office shortly after I returned to McMurdo: someone had told him I spoke French. He was an ice-corer en route to Vostok, the Russian base in the empty heart of East Antarctica. Vostok was a potent name in the history of the continent. There they had recorded the coldest temperature in the world, minus 129.3 degrees Fahrenheit, which is minus 89.2 Celsius. The annual mean temperature at Vostok was minus 55 Celsius—five degrees colder than at the South Pole. They had also drilled deeper than anyone else, so they had the world's oldest ice. The harsh conditions at the base had earned it a reputation as a gulag of the south. The French corer knew it well.

"It's not unusual to wake up to fist fights outside the bedroom door," he said airily. And to think that in the sixties, at the height of the Cold War, the Soviets used Vostok as a behavioural testbed for the Salyut space programme.

I had read a book by the geophysicist who was station chief at Vostok in 1959. Despite dabs of Russian colour, such as frequent references to cabbage pie and the October Revolution, the text was painfully guarded. Besides the temperature, they had to cope with the problems of living at an altitude of 4,000 metres, and Viktor Ignatov, the author of the book, reports grimly that potatoes boiled at 88 degrees Celsius and took three hours to cook. Being so high and so remote, Vostok cannot be adequately supplied by air, and therefore each summer a convoy of Kherkovchenka tractors heavily laden with food, fuel and other essential goods sets out from Mirny, the Russian station on the east coast. I once saw a film of this traverse, shot in the late sixties. The Amsterdam Film Museum found the spools languishing in their dungeons, restored them, put them on video and sent me a copy. It told a story of polished Ilyushins, white huskies, a solitary grave (well-tended), grubby calendars with days crossed-off and men sunbathing in pneumatic bathing trunks on the deck of a vast icebreaker and polishing stiff lace-up shoes when they saw land. It ended with a little girl's face, eyes tightly closed and thin arms clutching her weeping father's neck. The sombre military music played over the footage of the traverse itself made it seem as if they were marching across the steppe into the Siberian permafrost to defend the motherland against a marauding barbarian horde. When the tractors arrived at Vostok it was to bearhugs and a tray of vodka. The fact that I couldn't understand a word of the narration only made the film seem more exotic.

The Frenchman eventually left for Vostok, and on the same day Seismic Man and his group finally took off for their deep-field destination. They had been delayed by both weather and planes for two weeks, and some of them had checked in for their flight fifteen times. Most of them hadn't known each other before they came south, and during the fraught waiting period they had knitted together as a team. I was terribly jealous of that, especially as I had got to know them as they lounged over the sofas on the top floor of the Crary and wandered the corridors like nomads. I was sorry to see them go, though they had invited me out to their camp, an invitation which wouldn't, in theory, be difficult to take up as their project was being supported with a large number of fixed-wing resupply flights. They called me Woo after my W-002 label, and as we waved goodbye they shouted that when I arrived they would have a Welcome Woo party on the West Antarctic ice sheet.

It was seven o'clock on Saturday night, and I felt depressed. I sat in my office, listening to people next door arguing about fish bait. When this group were out of their office, which was most of the time, they put a sign on their door saying "Gone fishin'". Going fishing involved drilling holes in the sea ice and hauling up primeval creatures which survived the depths of the Southern Ocean by producing their own anti-freeze. The project leader was an Antarctic soldier who first came to the ice the year I was born. His name was Art DeVries, and he appeared in my doorway brandishing a small, dead fish.

"Come fishing tonight!" he said imperiously. I kept a set of cold-weather clothes under my desk, so I put them all on and walked out of the door. A tracked vehicle with DR COOL stencilled on the fender was warming up outside, and various members of the team were fiddling with equipment in the back. Art had a knack of assembling a disparate bunch of research scientists and graduate students, from ex-janitors to an antifreeze specialist he had met at an airport. They were all good fun, and they all smelt of fish.

We drove to a small wooden fish hut on the sea ice in which a battery-operated winch positioned over a hole in the floor was lowering bait 1,500 feet into the spectral depths of the Sound. The bait consisted of fish brought in from New Zealand. Much winching later, the fish which emerged weighed 125 pounds and looked as ancient as the slime from which we all crawled.

"*Dissostichus mawsoni*—Antarctic cod to you," said Art as he heaved it off the scales. "Phenomenally small brain."

"Can you eat them?" I asked.

"Sure you can. Sashimi cut from the cheeks is kind of nice. But it's the antifreeze everyone's after. Aircraft manufacturers want it to develop a product to prevent airplane wings from freezing."

When a row of specimens were lying on the floor, the biologists started arguing again, this time about which to keep, talking about "nice shaped throats" as if they were judging a beauty contest. Most of their fish were named after explorers: *mawsoni, bernacchii, borchgrevinki*. Art had his own—a deep-water bottom dweller called *Paraliparis devriesi*. The Channichthyidae "ice fish" which live in slightly warmer Antarctic waters have no haemoglobin at all, and their blood is white.

The Chapel of the Snows was a pink and confectionary-blue Alpine chalet with a stained-glass penguin at the end looking out over the Transantarctic mountains. It was serviced by a Catholic priest and a protestant minister, and on Sunday morning I went to mass. The priest called us the Frozen Chosen. It was after this service that I met Ann Hawthorne, a photographer in her early forties who was over six feet tall with salt-and-pepper hair down to her waist. She came from North Carolina and spoke in a beguiling southern drawl. Ann was also on the Artists' and Writers' Program, and we saw a good deal of one another while we were at McMurdo. She had first come south to take pictures ten years previously, and on that trip she had fallen in love with a pilot and subsequently married him. It hadn't worked out as planned, and I got the feeling that she was back laying ghosts to rest. Ann had an eye for a party, and if we had spent any more time together than we did, we would have got into trouble.

"Hey, I've borrowed a tracked vehicle," she said to me triumphantly one morning. "I figured we could go to Cape Evans for the day and hang out in Scott's hut. It's about twelve miles along the coast. What d'you say, babe?"

"Can we drive over the sea ice, then?"

"Sure we can."

"What happens if it gets thin?"

"We fall in. But that won't happen, because every so often we get out of the vehicle and drill the ice to test its thickness. It it's thinner than thirty inches, we turn back. Trust me."

Cape Evans was the site of Scott's main hut on the *Terra Nova* expedition. It had almost pushed the smaller one I had visited on Hut Point out of the history books. Hut Point was not intended as a permanent "home" and was never used as such. The Cape Evans hut, on the other hand, erected in January 1911, was occupied continuously for two years. In 1915 one of Shackleton's sledge parties from the ill-fated *Aurora* arrived, and they also lived in it intermittently for a couple of years. Preserved by the cold, and recently by the efforts of the New Zealand Antarctic Heritage Trust, it stands on its lonely cape, intact, like some icy Valhalla of the south.

Scott named the cape after Lieutenant Teddy Evans, later Admiral Sir Edward, who went on four Antarctic expeditions. He returned home sick in 1911 after almost dying of scurvy and exhaustion on the 750-mile march back to the hut from the top of the Beardmore Glacier. Two years later he went back to Antarctica in command of the *Terra Nova* to pick up Scott and the other men who had remained on the ice. As the ship sailed up to the hut, the officers' dining table was laid for a banquet. Evans, pacing the deck, was worried about the Northern Party. Then he spotted Campbell on shore. They had made it!

"Is everyone all right?" he yelled across the pack ice.

Campbell hesitated. "The polar party have perished," he shouted back.

Every death is the first death, and so it seemed, at that moment, to Teddy Evans.

For generations, the myth that had been created obscured the fact that Scott was a human being. Just as the image of the band on the *Titanic* playing "Nearer My God to Thee" is cemented on to the British national consciousness, along with tuxedoed gentlemen standing to attention as water rises over the razor creases of their trousers, so Scott has been institutionalised as a national icon, and for many years criticising him was a heretical act. Yet he wasn't universally popular in Antarctica. Among the four he took on the last haul to the Pole, Titus Oates wrote home to his mother "I dislike Scott intensely." At times, Scott's leadership was questionable. When everything—food, tents, fuel and depots—was arranged for four-man units, at the eleventh hour he decided that five were to go to the Pole. The perfect hero of the great English myth never existed, just as our national emblems, the lion and the unicorn, never roamed the South Downs.

All the same, there is much that is heroic about Scott. His expeditions still constitute landmarks in polar travel. As a man, rather than a Navy captain, Scott was much more than a wooden product of his background. Like all the best people, he was beset by doubt. "I shall never fit in my round hole," he wrote to his wife Kathleen, and on another occasion, "I'm obsessed with the view of life as a struggle for existence." He was a good writer, especially towards the end of his journey. "Will you grow to think me only fitted for the outer courtyard of your heart?" he asked Kathleen. The Antarctic possessed a virginity in his mind that provided an alternative to the spoiled and messy world, and he wrote in his diary about "the terrible vulgarizing which Shackleton has introduced to the Southern field of enterprise, hitherto so clean and wholesome".

Through his writings, Scott elevated the status of the struggle. It was no longer man against nature, it was man against himself. The diaries reveal a sense of apotheosis: the terrible journey back from the Pole was a moral drama about the attainment of self-knowledge. Scott went to the mountaintop, there on the blanched wasteland. He failed to return from the last journey, but in that failure he found a far more precious success. Defeat on this earthly plane was transfigured. The journey becomes a quest for self-fulfilment, and Scott's triumph is presented as the conquering of the self.

Similarly, after George Mallory and Sandy Irvine disappeared into the mists of Everest twelve years after Scott perished, everyone quickly forgot what had actually happened and glorified the climbers' transcendental achievements. At their memorial service in St Paul's Cathedral, the Bishop of Chester used a quotation from the Psalms to establish a connection between Mallory and Irvine's climb and the spiritual journey upwards, referring to it "as the ascent by which the kingly spirit goes up to the house of the Lord". So it was, too, that out of the tent on the polar plateau rose the myth of the saintly hero.

By nimble sleight of hand in their portrayal of Scott, the mythmakers reversed the David and Goliath roles of Norway and Britain. Scott was the gentlemanly amateur who played the game and didn't rely on dogs. Amundsen, on the other hand, was a technological professional who cheated by using dogs. Frank Debenham, Scott's geologist on the *Terra Nova* expedition, wrote in his book *Antarctica: the Story of a Continent*, published in 1959, that both Scott and Shackleton deployed techniques which were slower, more laborious, and failed, but that to criticise them for doing it their way instead of Amundsen's "is rather like comparing the man who prefers to row a boat across a bay with the man who hoists up a sail to help himself'. Scott's advocates made a virtue of the fact that he had hauled to the Pole without dogs or ponies, and they still do, but this is disingenuous. He had been perfectly prepared to use caterpillar motor-sledges and took three south on the *Terra Nova* (these were a failure). Furthermore, as Debenham himself wrote, "The fact of the matter is that neither Scott nor Shackleton, the two great exponents of manhauling, understood the management of sledge dogs."

As he lay dying, Scott somehow found the rhetorical language to invest the whole ghastly business with the currency of nobility. This is his greatest achievement, and with it he paved the way for the making of the legend. "Had we lived," he wrote famously, "I should have had a tale to tell of the hardihood, endurance, and courage of my companions which would have stirred the heart of every Englishman." He even had the presence of mind to recognise the emotive value of altering "To My Wife" on Kathleen's envelope to "To My Widow". In a few pages he scorched himself into the national consciousness. By the time the letters and diary reached home the spiritual and the national coalesced perfectly. *The Times* said of Scott's last venture, "The real value of the expedition was spiritual, and therefore in the truest sense national . . . proof that we are capable of maintaining an Empire." King George expressed the hope that every British boy could see photographs of the expedition, "for it will help promote the spirit of adventure that make the empire". On the wilder shores of journalism Scott actually became the nation: "Like Captain Scott," proclaimed *World's Work*, "we are journeying in a cold world towards nothing that we know." True enough.

Scott touched the imagination of the country and exemplified not just England but a strain of Edwardian manhood. Later, Apsley Cherry-Garrard, who was there, wrote of Scott and his dead men, "What they did has become part of the history of England, perhaps of the human race, as much as Columbus or the Elizabethans, David, Hector or Ulysses. They are an epic." In the Great War, Scott became a handy placebo for the soldiers floundering in muddy trenches. Over 100,000 officers and men in France alone saw expedition photographer Herbert Ponting's moving-picture film, and in his book *The Great White South*, Ponting quotes from the following letter despatched by a Forces chaplain ministering to the frontline troops.

> I cannot tell you what a tremendous delight your films are to thousands of our troops. The splendid story of Captain Scott is just the thing to cheer and encourage them out here . . . The thrilling story of Oates' self-sacrifice, to try and give his friends a chance of "getting through", is one that appeals to so many at the present time. The intensity of its appeal is realised by the subdued hush and quiet that pervades the massed audience of troops while it is being told. We all feel we have inherited from Oates and his comrades a legacy and heritage of inestimable value in seeing through our present work. We all thank you with very grateful hearts.

When Kathleen Scott died scores of crumpled letters from the front lines were found among her papers, the senders all telling her they could never have faced the dangers and hardships of the war had they not learned to do so from her dead husband's teaching. With Scott, they believed they could rise above it.

Would Scott have become the myth that he is had he lived? I doubt it. The most powerful hero is the dead hero, the one who never loses his teeth. Like Peter Pan, he must never grow old. It is central to the myth of Mallory and Irvine that they died on Everest. Lytton Strachey, who was passionate about Mallory and his Dionysian good looks, perceptively noted before the 1924 expedition even sailed from Birkenhead that the legend of Mallory would only survive if the climber died young. "If he were to live," Strachey wrote, "he'll be an unrecognisable middle-aged mediocrity, probably wearing glasses and a timber toe." Instead, Mallory became Sir Galahad, like Scott before him.

Though it is tempting to indulge the cliché that a national preference for dead heroes is peculiarly British, an examination of, say, Russian polar literature also reveals a large cast of heroic dead. Like most clichés, however, this one is woven with a thread of truth, and Scott would probably have had to stagger back to the hut to cut much ice with North Americans.

When Tryggve Gran, one of Scott's men, emerged from the tent on the plateau after he had seen the three frozen bodies which had lain there through the long polar night, he said that he envied them. "They died having done something great," he wrote. "How hard death must be having done nothing."[1]

The ice was more than four feet thick wherever we drilled it, and an hour after we set out for Cape Evans, around Big Razorback island, we lay down among the Weddell seals.

"Listen to that," said Ann. It was a faint scraping sound, like hard cheese on a grater.

"The pups are weaned," she announced. "It's their teeth raking against the edge of the ice holes."

Adult Weddells weigh up to 1,000 pounds and are able to live further south than any other seals because they can maintain an open hole in the ice with their teeth. Ann went off to photograph them doing it, and I pressed my ear to the ice and heard the adults underneath calling their ancient song, ululant and ineffably sad.

Later, I recognised the gabled ridged roof and weatherboard cladding of the hut in the distance. It was a prefabricated hut, made in England and shipped south in pieces. I once saw a picture of it taken when it was first erected, not at the foot of a smoking Mount Erebus but in a grimy urban street in Poplar in London's East End. The men had stitched quilts with pockets of seaweed to use as insulation between the walls.

When I pushed open the wooden door I smelt my grandmother's house when I was a child—coal dust and burnt coal—and it was chilly, as it used to be at six o'clock in the morning when I followed my grandfather downstairs to scrape out the grate. The Belmont Stearine candles Scott's men had brought were neatly stacked near the door, and the boxes said, "made expressly for hot climates", which some people would say summed up their preparations. The wrappers bore the picture of a West Indian preparing something delicious on a fire under a palm tree. It was the familiarity of the surroundings which struck my English sensibility—blue-and-orange Huntley and Palmer biscuit boxes, green-and-gold tins of Lyle's golden syrup, blue Cerberos salt tubes and the shape of the label on Heinz tomato ketchup bottles. Atora, Lea and Perrins, Fry's, Rising Sun Yeast ("certain to rise"), Gillards *Real* Turtle Soup— the brand names cemented in our social history. I still lived with many of these prod-

---

[1] The importance of Scott's death was brilliantly illustrated in a seven-part Central Television series, *The Last Place on Earth* (screened on PBS in the States), based on Roland Huntford's book. Amundsen, back in Norway after his great triumph, is soaping himself in the bath. His brother and confidant appears in the doorway to tell him that Scott died on the journey back from the Pole. "So he has won," says the actor playing Amundsen quietly.

ucts, and the continuum they provided intensified the hut experience. I remembered a very long novel by an American woman called Elizabeth Arthur who had spent some time on the ice. Describing the profoundly moving experience of visiting the hut, she talked about a "Hunter" and Palmer biscuit box. To an English sensibility this sounds as odd as "Heinzer" baked beans.

A single beam of sunlight fell on the bunk in Scott's quarters, the small space immortalised by Ponting and described by Teddy Evans as the "Holy of Holies". On the desk, someone—a good artist—had drawn a tiny bird in violet ink on the crisp ivory page of a pocket notebook. Unlike Shackleton, Scott separated the quarters of men and officers, and the difference is often deployed to illustrate their contrasting styles of leadership. Wayland Young, Baron Kennet of the Dene and Kathleen Scott's son by her second marriage, has set out a convincing defence of Scott's decision. As far as the state of class divisions in the Navy was concerned, Young wrote that it was "unchanged for 1,000 years, so to complain about it now is no more interesting or original than to complain about it in the army of Wellington, Marlborough, Henry V or Alfred the Great".

They were extremely resourceful. Clissold, the cook, rigged up a device whereby a small metal disc was placed on top of rising dough, and when it reached the right height it came into contact with another piece of metal, and an electrical circuit rang a bell next to his bunk. The battered books included Kipling (of course), and a tiny edition of *The Merry Wives of Windsor* held together with string, in the fly of which a spidery hand had inscribed Milton's "When will the ship be here/Come sing to me." There is something disingenuous about Scott's hut, however, just as there is about the myth. The mummified penguin lying open-beaked and akimbo next to a copy of the *Illustrated London News* had been placed there by the New Zealand Antarctic Heritage people, and Ponting's photographs show that Scott's desk is not the original (the replacement was brought over from the Cape Royds hut). The historic huts were often plundered in the early days. Richard Pape visited Cape Evans in 1959 with one of the American Operation Deep Freezes under Admiral Dufek. In his very bad book, *Poles Apart*, he records quite candidly that he pocketed "a glass inkwell on which 'R.F. Scott' had been painted, also a bottle of Indian ink marked 'Wilson'".

Still, I saw them everywhere. A gap in a row of cuphooks, the dented rubber of a Wellington boot tossed aside, a carefully rerolled bandage, the whiff of Ponting's developing fluid in his tiny darkroom, a half-spent candle in a chipped candlestick— perhaps it was the whistling of the wind, but I swear I could have turned round and seen them tramping back, spent dogs at their heels.

Later, the public manipulated the myth according to its own needs and ends. A crackpot society called the Alliance of Honour, founded in 1903 and devoted to purity, had spawned flourishing branches in 67 countries by the 1930s. The Alliance was vigorously opposed to masturbation, and the following quotation is culled from its voluminous literature: "We may safely assert that among the heroes of that dreadful journey from the South Pole there were no victims of the vice which the Alliance seeks to combat."

Secondhand bookshops are rife with musty first editions of the diaries inscribed in a Sunday School teacher's best copperplate, rewarding a child for good attendance. I found a 1941 bus ticket pressed inside one of them. It was a tough time to be living in London, and perhaps the diaries helped. During the Second World War the calls of the legend were legion, and they were often voiced by cranks. In 1941 Kathleen received a letter from a woman in New York who said she had borne Scott's illegitimate child when she was fifteen. A handwritten note on the envelope said, "The lady is now dead."

A few years after the war crocodiles of schoolchildren marched through provincial towns and into cavernous cinemas to watch *Scott of the Antarctic.* John Mills had already played countless war heroes, so he was a prepacked role model. By the mid-fifties, however, liberals at least were suspicious of the myth and had lost faith in the concept of England. In Peter Vansittart's recent book of social and cultural commentary, *In the Fifties,* he recalls a game he devised during that period to test the objectivity of his intellectual chums. He would read out a passage from Scott's diaries, including "We are showing that Englishmen can still die with a bold spirit, fighting it out to the end . . ." Assuming that Vansittart was being ironic, the audience tittered. Later he amended the reading to make it sound as if it had come from the Warsaw Ghetto in 1944, or from Mao Tsetung, and on those occasions his friends applauded respectfully.

Shibboleths were mocked. Scott became a cliché. In the Monty Python television sketch "Scott of the Sahara", the captain fights a 25-foot electric penguin. Similarly, Scott appears as an astronaut in Tom Stoppard's play *Jumpers,* written in 1972. The first Englishman to reach the moon, Scott's triumph is overshadowed by the plight of his only colleague Astronaut Oates. Scott kicks Oates to the ground at the foot of the spacecraft ladder and pulls it in behind him with the words, "I am going up now, I may be some time."

Historical revisionism is as unavoidable as the grave: it pursues leading figures of any age long after their work on earth is done. In the 1970s, when imperialism was widely reviled, Roland Huntford published his joint biography *Scott and Amundsen* (called *The Last Place on Earth* in the States), a passionate book which sought to demolish the Scott myth, suggesting not only that Scott was mortal, but that he was an unpleasant character and a poor leader. According to Huntford, he used science only as an excuse to participate in the race, unlike Amundsen "who did not stoop to use science as an agent of prestige". Nobody had criticised Scott before, and Huntford did so comprehensively. Many felt inclined to agree with him, while the keepers of the flame would have had him sent to the Tower. The book whipped up a blizzard of angry protests, vitriolic reviews and a furious exchange of correspondence and "statements" in national newspapers, including lengthy debate provoked by Huntford's assertion that Kathleen Scott had sex with Nansen while her husband was slogging up a glacier and was worried about becoming pregnant. The central argument was over how she recorded the arrival of her periods in her diary. How disappointing it had to come to that.

Wayland Young wrote an article refuting Huntford's criticism of Scott for *Encounter* magazine in May 1980. He demonstrates the weakness of portions of Huntford's scholarship. Others had pressed Huntford on the same points raised by Young, and in October 1979 the biographer was obliged to admit on national television that his description of Scott staring at Oates in the tent at the end to try to force him to his death was based on *intuition*. In short, he got carried away by his own argument. Prejudice is not necessarily fatal in a biography, however, and Huntford's book is intelligent, gripping, full of insight and elegantly written. I enjoyed it as much as any polar book I have read, and a good deal more than most of them. It is a pity that Huntford was quite so obsessed with the destruction of the legend, for if he had reined in his prejudices he could have produced a masterpiece.

A similar controversy raged in the Norwegian press after a book was published portraying Amundsen as a bounder and Scott a man worthy of beatification. Kåre Holt's *The Race*, published in English in 1974, was admittedly a novel; it was nonetheless a useful counterweight to Huntford's book. Bob Headland, archivist at the Scott Polar Research Institute, told me that he likes to keep the two volumes next to one another on the shelf, "preferably with a layer of asbestos between them".

"The Scandinavians", Huntford told me when I met him at Wolfson College in Cambridge for lunch in a dining hall smelling of boiled cauliflower, "by and large set out from a country at ease with itself. They have no need for an ego boost. They are not play-acting. The Norwegian will always look for a glimpse of the sun, because he actually wants to be happy.' Self-delusion, he said, was the besetting sin of the British. "Scott and Amundsen inhabited totally different mental words," he added, leaning across the table conspiratorially. "You mustn't be deluded by the fact that they were contemporaries. The Scandinavians live in a landscape which has enormous natural power, so that when they go to the polar regions it's sort of an extension of what they are."

Huntford lived in Scandinavia for many years ("mainly because I like skiing"). He writes exceptionally well about polar scenery; so well that it is hard to imagine him not hankering to go south himself. When I put this to him, he prevaricated.

"No," he said eventually. "These are landscapes of the mind, you see."

He had referred obliquely to a note written by Bowers on the back of one of Wilson's last letters; it apparently indicated that Bowers died last, but Huntford said the envelope had been suppressed by the people at Scott Polar Research Institute in order to maintain Scott's preeminence. When I asked them, they denied it. Who cares? I wanted to know about the power of the human spirit to transcend mortality, and what one human heart can learn from another, not whose aorta packed up first.

At McMurdo the project leaders were giving a series of weekly science lectures. An eminent geologist among them had developed theories on the prehistoric supercontinents in which Antarctica was attached to South America. His name was Ian Dalziel, and I found him nursing a whiskey in the Corner Bar.

323

"I used to be a respected geologist," he said, "but now I move continents around like armchairs." His wife called it playing God. He was Scottish, had defected, but still displayed the characteristic dry wit of the Scots. He had an easy manner which was self-assured without being confident, and he was a repository of stories. He could remember the geologist who used live baby penguins as toilet paper and reported that it was important to keep the beaks out of the way.

As nature's satire on humanity, it was part of the penguin job description to provide mirth for the colonising hordes. Stories from the days before anyone had heard of environmental awareness were legion. Officers would paint bowties on penguin breasts and set the birds loose in the messroom, navy construction workers flung them down seal holes "to watch them shoot up", and the 1956 Personnel Manual for Williams Field Air Operating Facility on Ross Island laid out procedures for obtaining a stuffed penguin. Now, abusing a penguin carried a stiffer fine than molesting a person.

I found myself reading a good deal about deserts while I was in the south, and at that time I was engrossed in Thesiger's *Arabian Sands*. Like Antarctica, the heart of the desert was a blank in time, devoid of human history. Both places could be perceived as a gigantic reflection of all you had known of emptiness and loss, if you were minded to internalise the landscape in that way. I felt the reverse. Even sitting in a base which resembled a small Alaskan mining town, I had similar intimations about the cold southern desert to those which Thesiger had in the hot sands of Arabia. "Here in the desert", he wrote, "I had found all that I had asked; I knew that I should never find it again."

I finished the book in my office late one night, and the light from the Anglepoise lamp spilled into the dark corridor. Hans, a Danish fish biologist on Art's project, came in and installed himself on the spare chair. We must have been the only people in the building, and it was as silent as a mausoleum. He made small talk for a few minutes, but he was fidgeting, as if he were trying to release an object that had got stuck between the layers of his garments. When he started saying what he had come to say all along, it spewed out like a torrent of coins from a slot machine.

He had fallen in love five weeks before coming south.

"Britta is fifteen years younger than I, but one day after I met her, I was in love," he said in his musical Danish accent. "The next five weeks were like rushing towards a waterfall, becoming faster all the time. I find a branch to cling to and everything would be OK for a while, but then I would be swept away again. Then comes the day when no branches are left."

He wrote every day, and once a week he sent a present, too, a commitment which must have tested his imagination as there weren't any shops except the navy store, and that offered a limited range of out-of-date film, tampax and Y-fronts.

"I am an all or nothing man," he said seriously, zipping himself into his vermilion parka and setting off to write another instalment.

Bibliography

Primary texts

Anon. (1855) *The Englishwoman in Russia; Impressions of the Society and Manners of the Russians at Home. By a Lady Ten Years Resident in That Country*, John Murray, London, pp. 14–18

Baillie, M. (1819) *First Impressions on a Tour Upon the Continent in the Summer of 1818, Through Parts of France, Italy, Switzerland, the Borders of Germany, and a Part of French Flanders*, John Murray, London, pp. 110–112, 203–206, 222–225

Barker, M.A. ([1870] 1984) *Station Life in New Zealand*, Virago, London, pp. 40–45, 68–71

Bird, I. ([1879] 1982) *A Lady's Life in the Rocky Mountains*, Virago, London, pp. 98–113

Birtles, D. ([1935] 1985) *North-West by North*, Virago, London, pp. 177–188

Blessington, M. (1839–40) *The Idler in Italy*, 3 vols, Colburn, London

Bodichon, B.L.S. (1972) *An American Diary 1857–8*, ed. J.W. Reed, Routledge and Kegan Paul, London

Brooke, M. ([1913] 1986) *My Life in Sarawak*, Oxford University Press, Singapore, pp. 18–29, 61–62; 122–128

Bunbury, S. (1857) *Russia After the War: The Narrative of a Visit to that Country in 1856*, 2 vols, Hurst and Blackett, London

Burton, R. ([1894] 1987) *First Footsteps in East Africa, or an Exploration of Harar*, Dover, New York

Butler, E. (1903) *Letters from the Holy Land*, A. & C. Black, London

Cable, M. and French, F. (1927) *Through Jade Gate and Central Asia*, Wyman and Sons, London

Cable, M. and French, F. ([1942] 1943) *The Gobi Desert*, Hodder and Stoughton, London, pp. 288–295

Carey, W. (1902) *Travel and Adventure in Tibet, Including the Diary of Miss Annie R. Taylor's Remarkable Journey from Tau-Chau to Ta-Chien-Lu*, London, Hodder and Stoughton

Cobbe, F.P. (1894) *The Life of Frances Power Cobbe: By Herself*, 2 vols, Bentley, London

Creaghe, E. ([1883] 1998) "Unpublished letters", Mitchell Library, New South Wales, extract in Flannery, T. ed. *The Explorers*, Text Publishing, Melbourne, Australia

David-Neel, A. ([1927] 1983) *My Journey to Lhasa*, Virago, London, pp. 103–116

Davidson, R. (1982) *Tracks*, Paladin, London, pp. 150–157, 198–201

Donner, T. ([1846] 1995) "The Donner Party Letters", pp. 68–82, in Holmes, K. ed. *Covered Wagon Women: Diaries and Letters from the Western Trails, 1840–1849*, University of Nebraska, Lincoln and London, pp. 69–82

Dowie, M. (1891) *A Girl in the Karpathians*, George Philip and Son, London

Duncan, M. (1852) *America as I Found it*, J. Nisbet and Co., London

Eberhardt, I. ([1902, 1905] 1987) *The Passionate Nomad: The Diary of Isabelle Eberhardt*, Virago, London, pp. 1–6, 42–43

Eden, E. ([1930] 1983) *Up the Country: Letters from India*, Virago, London

Bibliography

Edwards, A. ([1888] 1997) *A Thousand Miles Up The Nile*, Parkway, London, pp. 13–17, 185–191

Edwards, A. ([1873] 1986) *Untrodden Peaks and Unfrequented Valleys*, Virago, London

Edwards, M.B. (1888) *Through Spain to the Sahara*, Hurst and Blackett, London

Elwood, Mrs A.C. (1830) *Narrative of a Journey Overland from England by the Continent of Europe, Egypt and the Red Sea to India*, Henry Colburn and Richard Bentley, London, pp. 334–340; 383–395

Eyre, M. (1865) *Over the Pyrenees into Spain*, Richard Bentley, London

Falconbridge, A.M. ([1791] 1967) *Narrative of Two Voyages to the River Sierra Leone*, Frank Cass, London, pp. 18–39

Fiennes, C. ([1698] 1982) *The Illustrated Journeys of Celia Fiennes*, ed. Morris. C., Macdonald Webb and Bower, London, pp. 165–172

Finch, M. ([1853] 1969) *An Englishwoman's Experience in America*, Negro Universities Press, New York

Gordon, L.D. ([1875, 1902] 1983) *Letters from Egypt*, Virago, London, pp. 99–103, 111–112, 141–142

Graham, Y. Maxtone ([1994] 1996) "Through a Barren Land", pp. 71–88, in Govier, K. ed. *Without a Guide: Contemporary Women's Travel Adventures*, Pandora, London, pp. 71–88

Grey, Mrs W. (1869) *Journal of a Visit to Egypt, Constantinople, the Crimea, Greece etc*, Smith, Elder, London

Haggard, R.H. (1885) *King Solomon's Mines*, Dent, London

Hall, M. (1931) *The Aristocratic Journey, Being the Outspoken Letters of Mrs Basil Hall Written During a Fourteen Months' Sojourn in America 1827–1828* ed. Una Pope-Hennessy, G.P. Putnam's Sons, New York and London

Hornby, E.B. (1863) *Constantinople During the Crimean War*, Bentley, London, pp. 234–254

Houston, M. (1844) *Texas and the Gulf of Mexico: or, Yachting in the New World*, 2 vols, Murray, London

Houston, M. (1850) *Hesperos: or, Travels in the West*, 2 vols, Parker, London

Jameson, A. ([1838] 1990) *Winter Studies and Summer Rambles in Canada*, McClelland and Stuart, Toronto, pp. 454–455; 57–63, 202–205; 380–383, 386–387, 436, 500–501

[Jameson, A.] (1915) *Anna Jameson: Letters and Friendships (1812–1860)*, ed. Mrs Steuart Erskine, T. Fisher Unwin, London

Kemble, F. (1847) *A Year of Consolation*, 2 vols, Moxon, London

Kemble, F. (1835) *Journal*, 2 vols, Murray, London, pp. 285–287

Kemble, F. ([1863] 1961) *Journal of a Residence on a Georgian Plantation*, Cape, London, pp. 40–41, 66–70, 93–94, 127–128, 132–133, 219–220, 254–256

Kemble, F. (1878) *Records of a Girlhood*, 3 vols, Bentley, London, pp. 308, 309–314

Kemble, F. (1882) *Records of Later Life*, 3 vols, Bentley, London

Kingsley, M. ([1897] 1982) *Travels in West Africa*, Virago, London, pp. 581–597

Lott, E. (1865) *The Governess in Egypt: Harem Life in Egypt and Constantinople*, 2 vols, Bentley, London, pp. 24–36, 300–307

Lowe, E. (1857) *Unprotected Females in Norway; or, The Pleasant Way of Travelling There, Passing through Denmark and Sweden*, Routledge, London, pp. 221–231

Maillart, E.K. ([1947] 1986) *The Cruel Way*, Virago, London, pp. 23–34

Martin, S. (1828) *Narrative of a Three Years' Residence in Italy 1819–1822*, John Murray, London

Martineau, H. (1837) *Society in America*, 2 vols, Saunders and Otley, London

Martineau, H. (1838) *Retrospect of Western Travel*, 2 vols, Saunders and Otley, London

Martineau, H. (1848) *Eastern Life, Present' and Past*, 3 vols, Moxon, London, pp. 147–167

Martineau, H. ([1878] 1983) *Autobiography*, 2 vols, Virago, London

Mazuchelli, N. (1876) *The Indian Alps and How We Crossed Them: Being a Narrative of Two Year's Residence in the Eastern Himalayas and a Two Month Tour of the Interior by a Lady Pioneer*, Longmans, Green and Co., London

Meredith, Mrs C. (1844) *Notes and Sketches of New South Wales, During a Residence in that Colony from 1839 to 1844*, John Murray, London, pp. 36, 91–95

Millett, Mrs E. (1872) *An Australian Parsonage; or, the Settler and the Savage in Western Australia*, Stanford, London, pp. 138–145

Montagu, M.W. ([1718] 1993) *Turkish Embassy Letters*, ed. Desai, A., Pickering, London, pp. 57–60, 69–72, 86–91, 118–119

Moodie, S. ([1852] 1986) *Roughing it in the Bush, or, Life in Canada*, Virago, London, pp. 270–274

Murphy, D. (1965) *Full Tilt: Ireland to India with a Bicycle*, John Murray, London, pp. 141–153

Murray, A. ([1856] 1969) *Letters from the United States, Cuba and Canada*, Negro Universities Press, New York, pp. 202–203, 250–253; 197–200, 268–271

North, M. (1892) *Recollections of a Happy Life*, 2 vols, Macmillan, London

North, M. (1893) *Some Further Recollections of a Happy Life*, Macmillan, London, pp. 29–32, 82–89, 101–102, 305–307

Osborne, E. (1876) *Twelve Months in Southern Europe*, Chapman and Hall, London

Parks, F. ([1850] 2000) *Wanderings of a Pilgrim in Search of the Picturesque*, ed. Ghose, I. and Mills, S., Manchester University Press, Manchester

Pfeiffer, I. (1852) *Visit to the Holy Land, Egypt and Italy*, Chapman and Hall, London, pp. 105–108

Pfeiffer, I. (1850) *A Woman's Journey Round the World*, Office of the National Illustrated Library, London

Pink, O. ([1933] 1998) "Personal papers", University of Sydney Archives, extracts in Flannery T. ed. *The Explorers*, Text Publishing, Melbourne, Australia

Rijnhart, S. (1901) *With the Tibetans in Tent and Temple: Narrative of Four Years' Residence on the Tibetan Border and of a Journey into the Far Interior*, Oliphant, Anderson and Ferrier, London, pp. 245–258

Rogers, M. (1862) *Domestic Life in Palestine*, Bell and Daldy, London

Sewell, E.M. (1862) *Impressions of Rome, Florence, and Turin*, Longman, London, pp. 38–49

Sheldon, M.F. ([1892] 1999) *Sultan to Sultan: Adventures among the Masai and other Tribes of East Africa*, Saxon, London, ed. Boisseau, T.J., Manchester University Press, Manchester

Shelley, M. (1844) *Rambles in Germany and Italy in 1840, 1842 and 1843*, 2 vols, Moxon, London, pp. 49–52, 18–21

Soltera, M. (1884) *A Lady's Ride Across Spanish Honduras*, Blackwood, London

Speke, J.H. (1863) *Journal of the Discovery of the Source of the Nile*, Dover, New York, 1996

St Maur, Mrs A. (1890) *Impressions of a Tenderfoot during a journey in search of sport in the Far West*, John Murray, London, pp. 111–117

Stark, F. ([1937] 1946) *Baghdad Sketches*, John Murray, London, pp. 40–47

Traill, C.P. ([1846] 1989) *The Backwoods of Canada*, McClelland and Stuart, Toronto, pp. 136–137, 173–175

Tristan, F. ([1833–4] 1986) *Peregrinations of a Pariah*, Virago, London, pp. 205–220

Trollope, A. ([1862] 1987) *North America*, 2 vols, Alan Sutton, Gloucester

Bibliography

Trollope, F. ([1832] 1984) *Domestic Manners of the Americans*, Oxford University Press, Oxford, pp. 248–244, 208–211

Trollope, F. ([1836] 1985) *Paris and the Parisians*, Sutton, Gloucester, pp. 68–72

Trollope, F. (1842) *A Visit to Italy*, 2 vols, Bentley, London

Trotter, I. (1859) *First Impressions of the New World on Two Travellers from the Old in the Autumn of 1858*, Longman, London

Wheeler, S. (1997) *Terra Incognita: Travels in Antarctica*, Verso, London, pp. 47–61

Wollstonecraft, M. ([1796] 1987) *A Short Residence in Sweden, Norway and Denmark*, Penguin, Harmondsworth, pp. 110–113

Wright, F. ([1821] 1963) *Views of Society and Manners in America*, ed. Baker, P.A., Harvard University Press, Cambridge, Massachusetts

Critical and theoretical texts

Adams, P. (1983) *Travel Literature and the Evolution of the Novel*, University Press of Kentucky, Lexington

Adams, P. (1962) *Travellers and Travel Liars*, University of California Press, Berkeley

Allen, A. (1980) *Travelling Ladies: Victorian Adventuresses*, Jupiter, London

Armstrong, N. and Tennenhouse, L. eds. (1987) *The Ideology of Conduct: Essays in Literature and the History of Sexuality*, Methuen, London

Ballantyne, R.M. (1861) *The Golden Dream or Adventures in the Far West*, John F. Shaw, London

Barr, P. (1985) *A Curious Life for a Lady: The Story of Isabella Bird, Traveller Extraordinary*, Penguin, Harmondsworth

Batten, C. (1978) *Pleasurable Instruction: Form and Convention in Eigtheenth Century Travel Literature*, University of California Press, Berkeley

Bermingham, A. (1994) "The picturesque and ready-to-wear femininity", pp. 81–119, in Copley, S. and Garside, P. eds. *The Politics of the Picturesque*, Cambridge University Press, Cambridge

Bergvall, V., Bing, J. and Freed, A. eds. (1996) *Rethinking Language and Gender Research: Theory and Practice*, Longman, London and New York

Bhabha, H. (1994) *The Location of Culture*, Routledge, London

Birkett, D. (1992) "The 'white woman's burden' in the 'white man's grave': the introduction of British nurses in colonial West Africa", pp. 177–190, in Chaudhuri, N. and Strobel, M. eds. *Western Women and Imperialism: Complicity and Resistance*, Indiana University Press, Bloomington

Birkett, D. (1989) *Spinsters Abroad: Victorian Lady Explorers*, Oxford University Press, Oxford

Birkett, D. and Wheeler, S. eds. (1998) *Amazonian: The Penguin Book of Women's New Travel Writing*, Penguin, Harmondsworth

Black, J. (1985) *The British and the Grand Tour*, Croom Helm, London

Blake, S. (1992) "A woman's trek: what difference does gender make?", pp. 19–34, in Chaudhuri, N. and Strobel, M. eds. *Western Women and Imperialism: Complicity and Resistance*, Indiana University Press, Bloomington

Blunt A. (1994) *Travel, Gender and Imperialism: Mary Kingsley and West Africa*, Guilford, New York

Blunt, A. (1994) "Mapping authorship and authority: reading Mary Kingsley's landscape descriptions", pp. 51–73, in Blunt, A. and Rose, G. eds. *Writing Women and Space: Colonial and Postcolonial Geographies*, Guilford, New York

Blunt, A. and Rose, G. (1994) "Introduction: women's colonial and postcolonial geographies", pp. 1–29, in Blunt, A. and Rose, G. eds. *Writing Women and Space: Colonial and Postcolonial Geographies*, Guilford, New York

Bohls, E. (1995) *Women Travel Writers and the Language of Aesthetics 1716–1818*, Cambridge University Press, Cambridge

Boisseau, T.J. ed. (1999) "Introduction", *Sultan to Sultan Adventures among the Masai and other Tribes of East Africa by M. French-Sheldon*, Manchester University Press, Manchester

Bristow, J. (1991) *Empire Boys: Adventure's in a Man's World*, Harper and Collins, London

Burton, A. (1992) "The white woman's burden: British feminists and 'the Indian woman' 1865–1915," pp. 137–157, in Chaudhuri, N. and Strobel, M. eds. *Western Women and Imperialism: Complicity and Resistance*, Indiana University Press, Bloomington

Butler, A. (1983) "Introduction", pp. 1–8, in Holmes, K. ed. *Covered Wagon Women: Diaries and Letters from the Western Trails, 1840–1849*, Bison/University of Nebraska Press, Lincoln and London

Butler, J. (1990) *Gender Trouble: Feminism and the Subversion of Identity*, Routledge, London

Buzard, J. (1993) *The Beaten Track: European Tourism, Literature, and the Ways to "Culture" 1800–1918*, Oxford University Press, New York

Callan H. and Ardener, S. eds. (1984) *The Incorporated Wife*, Croom Helm, London

Callaway, H. and Helly, D. (1992) "Crusader for empire: Flora Shaw, Lady Lugard," pp. 79–97, in Chaudhuri, N. and Strobel, M. eds. (1992) *Western Women and Imperialism: Complicity and Resistance*, Indiana University Press, Bloomington

Chard, C. (1999) *Pleasure and Guilt on the Grand Tour: Travel Writing and Imaginative Geography*, Manchester University Press, Manchester

Chaudhuri, N. and Strobel, M. eds. (1992) *Western Women and Imperialism*, Indiana University Press, Bloomington

Comaroff, J. (1997) "The empire's old clothes: fashioning the colonial subject", pp. 400–418, in Lamphere, L., Ragone, H. and Zavella, P. eds. *Situated Lives: Gender and Culture in Everyday Life*, Routledge, London

Darian Smith, K., Gunner, L. and Nuttall, S. eds. (1996) *Text, Theory, Space: Land Literature and History in South Africa and Australia*, Routledge, London

Davidson, L.C. (1889) *Hints to Lady Travellers at Home and Abroad*, Iliffe and Son, London

Davies, K. (1985) *Women Explorers*, Macmillan Educational, Basingstoke

Dawson, G. (1994) *Soldier Heroes: British Adventure, Empire amd the Imagining of Masculinities*, Routledge, London

Foster, S. (1990) *Across New Worlds: Nineteenth Century Women Travellers and their Writings*, Harvester Wheatsheaf, Hemel Hempstead

Foster, S. (1994) *American Women Travellers to Europe*, Keele University Press, Keele

Foucault, M. ([1969] 1972) *Archaeology of Knowledge*, Tavistock, London

Foucault, M. ([1972] 1978) *History of Sexuality*, Vol. 1, Penguin, Harmondsworth

Fussell, P. (1980) *Abroad: British Literary Travelling Between the Wars*, Oxford University Press, Oxford

Ghose, I. (1997) *The Female Gaze: Nineteenth Century Women Travellers in India*, Cambridge University Press, Delhi

Ghose, I. ed. (1998) *Memsahibs Abroad: Writings by Women Travellers in Nineteenth-Century India*, Oxford University Press, New Delhi

Grewal, I. (1996) *Home and Harem: Nation, Gender and Empire and the Cultures of Travel*, Leicester University Press, Leicester

Harraway, D. (1997/1988) "Situated knowledges: the science question in feminism and the privilege of partial perspective", pp. 44–53, in McDowell, L. and Sharp, J. eds. *Space Gender and Knowledge: Feminist Readings*, London, Arnold

Hibbert, C. (1969) *The Grand Tour*, Thames Methuen, London

Hulme, P. (1986) *Colonial Encounters: Europe and the Native Caribbean 1492–1797*, Methuen, London

Hulme, P. and Ireson, N. (1998) *Cannibalism and the Colonial World*, Cambridge University Press, Cambridge

Jayawardena, K. (1995) *The White Woman's Other Burden: Western Women and South Asia During British Rule*, Routledge, London

Joyce, E. (1984) "White man's burden: white woman's lark—Mary Kingsley and the myth of the explorer hero", pp. 99–117, Trent Papers in Communication 2, Power and Communication—feminist perspectives, Nottingham

Kolodny, A. (1984) *The Land Before Her: Fantasy and Experience of the American Frontiers, 1630–1860*, University of North Carolina Press, Chapel Hill and London

Lewis, R. (1996) *Gendering Orientalism: Race, Femininity and Representation*, Routledge, London

Longden, K. (forthcoming) *Knitting the Classes Together*, unpublished PhD thesis, Sheffield Hallam University, Sheffield

Low, G.C. (1993) "His stories: narratives and images of imperialism," pp. 187–220, in Carter, E., Donald, J. and Squires, J. eds. *Space and Place: Theories of Identity and Location*, Lawrence and Wishart, London

Low, G.C. (1996) *White Skins Black Masks: Representation and Colonialism*, Routledge, London

Massey, D. (1994) *Space, Place and Gender*, Polity Press, Cambridge

McClintock, A. (1995) *Imperial Leather: Race, Gender and Sexuality in the Colonial Contest*, Routledge, London

McDowell, L. and Sharp, J. eds. (1997) *Space, Gender, Knowledge: Feminist Readings*, Arnold, London

McEwan, C. (1994) "Encounters with West African women: textual representations of difference by white women abroad", pp. 73–100, in Blunt, A. and Rose, G. eds. *Writing Women and Space: Colonial and Postcolonial Geographies*, Guilford, New York

McGreevy, P. (1992) "Reading the texts of Niagara Falls: the metaphor of death", pp. 50–72, in Barnes, T. and Duncan, J. eds. *Writing Worlds: Discourse, Text and Metaphor in the Representation of Landscape*, Routledge, London

Melman, B. (1995) *Women's Orients: English Women and the Middle East, 1718–1918*, Macmillan, Basingstoke

Middleton, D. ([1965] 1982) *Victorian Women Travellers*, Dutton, New York

Midgley, Clare ed. (1998) *Gender and Imperialism*, Manchester University Press, Manchester

Miller, L. (1976) *On Top of the World: Five Women Explorers in Tibet*, Paddington Press, London

Mills, S. (1991) *Discourses of Difference: Women's Travel Writing and Colonialism*, Routledge, London

Mills, S. (1994) "Knowledge, gender, empire", pp. 29–50, in A. Blunt and G. Rose eds. *Writing Women and Space: Colonial and Postcolonial Geographies*, Guilford, New York

Mills, S. (1995) "Discontinuity and postcolonial discourse", pp. 73–88, *Ariel*, 26/3, July

Mills, S. (1996a) "Gender and colonial space", pp. 125–147, in *Gender Place and Culture*, Vol. 2

Mills, S. (1996b) "Colonial domestic space", pp. 46–61, in *Renaissance and Modern Studies*, Vol. 39

Mills, S. (1997) *Discourse*, Routledge, London

Mills, S. (2000) "Written on the landscape: Mary Wollstonecraft's *Letters Written During a Short Residence in Sweden, Norway and Denmark*", in Gilroy, A. ed. *Romantic Geographies*, Manchester University Press, Manchester

Morgan, S. (1996) *Place Matters: Gendered Geography in Victorian Women's Travel Books about Southeast Asia*, Rutgers University Press, New Jersey

Morris, M. ed. (1994) *The Virago Book of Women Travellers*, Virago, London

Norwood, V. and Monk, J. eds. (1987) *The Desert is No Lady: South West Landscapes in Women's Writing and Art*, Yale University Press, New Haven

Oliver, C. (1982) *Western Women in Colonial Africa*, Greenwood Press, Westport, Connecticut

Phillips, R. (1997) *Mapping Men and Empire: A Geography of Adventure*, Routledge, London

Pratt, M.L. (1992) *Imperial Eyes: Travel Writing and Transculturation*, Routledge, London

Rennie, N. (1998) *Far-Fetched Facts: The Literature of Travel and the Idea of the South Seas*, Oxford University Press, Oxford

Richards, T. (1993) *The Imperial Archive: Knowledge and the Fantasy of* Empire, Verso, London

Rigby E. (1845) "Lady Travellers", *Quarterly Review*, LXXVI, No. CLI

Robinson, J. (1990) *Wayward Women: A Guide to Women Travellers*, Oxford University Press, Oxford

Robinson, J. ed. (1995) *Unsuitable for Ladies: An Anthology of Women Travellers*, Oxford University Press

Rose, G. (1993) *Feminism and Geography: The Limits of Geographical Knowledge*, Routledge, London

Said, E. ([1978] 1991) *Orientalism*, Penguin, Harmondsworth

Said, E. (1993) *Culture and Imperialism*, Chatto and Windus, London

Schriber, M.S. (1995) *Telling Travels: Selected Writings by Nineteenth-Century American Women Abroad*, Northern Illinois University Press, DeKalb

Scott, P. (1966) *The Raj Quartet*, Mandarin, London

Sharpe, J. (1993) *Allegories of Empire: The Figure of Woman in the Colonial Text*, University of Minnesota Press, Minneapolis

Sinha, M. (1992) "Chathams, Pitts and Gladstones in petticoats: the politics of gender and race in the Ilbert Bill controversy", pp. 98–118, in Chaudhuri, N. and Strobel, M. eds. *Western Women and Imperialism: Complicity and Resistance*, Indiana University Press, Bloomington

Sinha, M. (1995) *Colonial Masculinity*, Manchester University Press, Manchester

Skeggs, B. (1997) *Formations of Class and Gender*, Sage, London

Spain, D. (1992) *Gendered Spaces*, University of North Carolina Press, Chapel Hill

Stevenson, C.B. (1982) *Victorian Women Travel Writers in Africa*, Twayne, Boston

Stoler, A. (1997) "Making empire respectable: the politics of race and sexual morality in twentieth century colonial cultures", pp. 373–399, in Lamphere, L., Ragone, H. and Zavella, P. eds. *Situated Lives: Gender and Culture in Everyday Life*, Routledge, London

Stoler, A. and Cooper, F. eds. (1997) *Tensions of Empire: Colonial Cultures in a Bourgeois World*, University of California Press, Berkeley

Ware, V. (1992) *Beyond the Pale: White Women, Racism and History*, Verso, London

Bibliography

Wetherill, M. and Potter, J. (1992) *Mapping the Language of Racism: Discourse and the Legitimisation of Exploitation*, Hemel Hempstead, Harvester Wheatsheaf

Wex, M. (1979) *Let's Take Back our Space: Female and Male Body-Language as a Result of Patriarchal Structures*, Frauenliteraturverlag Hermine Fees, Berlin

Whitehead, N. (1996) "Introduction", *The Discoverie of the Large, Rich and Bewtiful Empyre of Guiana by Sir Walter Raleigh*, Manchester University Press, Manchester

Wilson, E. (1991) *The Sphinx in the City: Urban Life, Control of Disorder and Women*, Virago, London

Yaeger, P. (1989) "Toward a female sublime", pp. 191–212, in Kauffman, L. ed. *Gender and Theory: Dialogues on Feminist Criticism*, Blackwell, Oxford

Yonge, C. ([1887] 1889) *Womankind*, Walter Smith and Innes, London

Young, I.M. (1989) "Throwing like a girl: a phenomenology of female bodily comportment, motility and spatiality", pp. 51–70, in Allen, J. and Young, I.M. eds. *The Thinking Muse: Feminism and Modern French Philosophy*, Indiana University Press, Bloomington

Young, R. (1993) *Colonial Desire: Hybridity in Theory, Culture and Race*, Routledge, London

Youngs, T. (1994) *Travellers in Africa: British Travelogues 1850–1900*, Manchester University Press, Manchester

Youngs, T. (1997) "Buttons and souls: some thoughts on commodities and identity in women's travel writing", pp. 117–141, *Studies in Travel Writing*, No. 1, Spring

Index